Frommer's®

Belize

4th Edition

by Eliot Greenspan

WILEY

Wiley Publishing, Inc.

Published by:
WILEY PUBLISHING, INC.
111 River St.
Hoboken, NJ 07030-5774

ISBN 978-0-470-88770-7 (paper); 978-1-118-00368-8 (ebk); 978-1-118-00369-5 (ebk); 978-1-118-00370-1 (ebk)

Editor: Anuja Madar
Production Editor: Jonathan Scott
Cartographer: Nick Trotter
Photo Editor: Richard Fox
Production by Wiley Indianapolis Composition Services
Front Cover Photo: Jaguar in tree, Panthera onca, Belize ©William Ervin / PhotoLibrary
Back Cover Photo: Little Water Caye, in the Stann Creek District, off the town of Placencia: Man kayaking, Belize Central America Caribbean ©24BY36 / Alamy Images

For information on our other products and services or to obtain technical support, please contact our Customer Care Department within the U.S. at 877/762-2974, outside the U.S. at 317/572-3993 or fax 317/572-4002.

Wiley also publishes its books in a variety of electronic formats. Some content that appears in print may not be available in electronic formats.

Manufactured in the United States of America

5   4   3   2   1

CONTENTS

LIST OF MAPS

ABOUT THE AUTHOR

Eliot Greenspan is a poet, journalist, musician, and travel writer who took his backpack and typewriter the length of Mesoamerica before settling in Costa Rica in 1992. Since then, he has worked steadily as a travel writer, freelance journalist, and translator, and has continued his travels in the region. In addition to this book, he is the author of *Frommer's Guatemala, Frommer's Costa Rica, Frommer's Ecuador, Frommer's Costa Rica Day By Day* and *Costa Rica For Dummies,* as well as the chapter on Venezuela in *Frommer's South America.* He is also the author of the poetry collection *Map of You, Map of Me.*

ACKNOWLEDGMENTS

Thanks are due to Chrissie Long and Derek Marin, who did excellent phone, fax, and fact-checking work on this edition. The wonderful folks at the Belize Tourism Board and Patty Tazalla of BVK were invaluable in helping me organize my travels. Too many friends, industry contacts, and fellow travelers have shared their knowledge, hospitality, and experiences in Belize to mention here, but their insights, comments, recommendations, and offhand reviews have contributed immensely to this book, and I thank them. And finally, a big tip of my hat to my editor, Anuja Madar.

—Eliot Greenspan

HOW TO CONTACT US

In researching this book, we discovered many wonderful places—hotels, restaurants, shops, and more. We're sure you'll find others. Please tell us about them, so we can share the information with your fellow travelers in upcoming editions. If you were disappointed with a recommendation, we'd love to know that, too. Please write to:

Frommer's Belize, 4th Edition
Wiley Publishing, Inc. • 111 River St. • Hoboken, NJ 07030-5774
frommersfeedback@wiley.com

AN ADDITIONAL NOTE

Please be advised that travel information is subject to change at any time—and this is especially true of prices. We therefore suggest that you write or call ahead for confirmation when making your travel plans. The authors, editors, and publisher cannot be held responsible for the experiences of readers while traveling. Your safety is important to us, however, so we encourage you to stay alert and be aware of your surroundings. Keep a close eye on cameras, purses, and wallets, all favorite targets of thieves and pickpockets.

FROMMER'S STAR RATINGS, ICONS & ABBREVIATIONS

Every hotel, restaurant, and attraction listing in this guide has been ranked for quality, value, service, amenities, and special features using a **star-rating system.** In country, state, and regional guides, we also rate towns and regions to help you narrow down your choices and budget your time accordingly. Hotels and restaurants are rated on a scale of zero (recommended) to three stars (exceptional). Attractions, shopping, nightlife, towns, and regions are rated according to the following scale: zero stars (recommended), one star (highly recommended), two stars (very highly recommended), and three stars (must-see).

In addition to the star-rating system, we also use **seven feature icons** that point you to the great deals, in-the-know advice, and unique experiences that separate travelers from tourists. Throughout the book, look for:

special finds—those places only insiders know about

fun facts—details that make travelers more informed and their trips more fun

kids—best bets for kids and advice for the whole family

Special moments—those experiences that memories are made of

overrated—places or experiences not worth your time or money

insider tips—great ways to save time and money

great values—where to get the best deals

The following **abbreviations** are used for credit cards:

AE	American Express	**DISC**	Discover	**V**	Visa
DC	Diners Club	**MC**	MasterCard		

TRAVEL RESOURCES AT FROMMERS.COM

Frommer's travel resources don't end with this guide. Frommer's website, **www.frommers. com**, has travel information on more than 4,000 destinations. We update features regularly, giving you access to the most current trip-planning information and the best airfare, lodging, and car-rental bargains. You can also listen to podcasts, connect with other Frommers. com members through our active-reader forums, share your travel photos, read blogs from guidebook editors and fellow travelers, and much more.

THE BEST OF BELIZE

Belize proves the cliché that big things come in small packages. This tiny Central American country has the longest continuous barrier reef in the Western Hemisphere; the largest known Classic Mayan city, Caracol; and the highest concentration per square mile of the largest new-world cat, the jaguar. It also has one of the most extensive and easily accessible cave systems for amateur and experienced spelunkers alike, as well as a nearly endless supply of some of the world's best snorkeling and scuba-diving opportunities. Depending on your personal preferences, you can choose to stay in an intimate and luxurious hotel, an isolated nature lodge in the heart of the Mundo Maya, or a tent on your own desert island. Or you can sample all three. The best part about all these world-class places and experiences is that Belize's compact size makes it easy to sample a wide range of them in a short period of time. The lists below should help you zero in on a few personal bests of your own.

THE best PURELY BELIZEAN EXPERIENCES

- **Betting on a Chicken Drop:** A chicken drop is a sort of poor man's version of roulette, and much more fun. Numbers are painted on a grid and bets are placed. Then, a chicken is set loose on a wire mesh screen suspended over the grid. The winner is chosen by the chicken's first "drop." In addition to any monetary winnings, the "winner" often must clean the grid. You'll find a chicken drop held every Wednesday night at the Pier Lounge on Ambergris Caye. See "Ambergris Caye" in chapter 7.
- **Sitting on the Dock of a Caye:** One of the most distinctive features of most beachfront hotels in Belize is the private pier jutting out into the

The Best of Belize

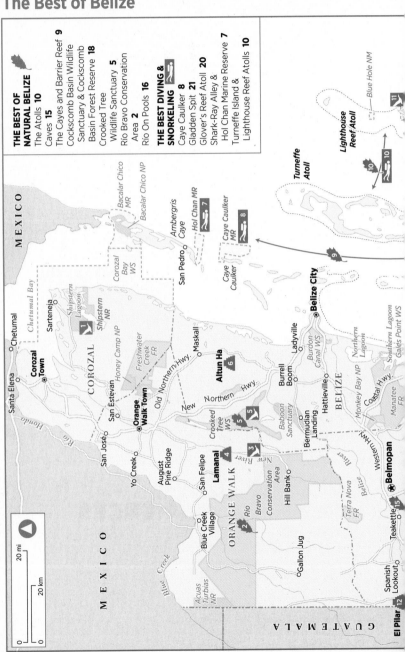

THE BEST OF NATURAL BELIZE
The Atolls **10**
Caves **15**
The Cayes and Barrier Reef **9**
Cockscomb Basin Wildlife Sanctuary & Cockscomb Basin Forest Reserve **18**
Crooked Tree Wildlife Sanctuary **5**
Rio Bravo Conservation Area **2**
Rio On Pools **16**

THE BEST DIVING & SNORKELING
Caye Caulker **8**
Gladden Spit **21**
Glover's Reef Atoll **20**
Shark-Ray Alley & Hol Chan Marine Reserve **7**
Turneffe Island & Lighthouse Reef Atolls **10**

THE BEST BIRD-WATCHING

Caracol **17**
Cockscomb Basin
  Forest Reserve **18**
Crooked Tree
  Wildlife Sanctuary **5**
Half Moon Caye
  National Monument **11**
Man-O-War Caye **19**
New River Lagoon **3**
Shipstern Nature Reserve **1**

THE BEST MAYAN RUINS

Altun Ha **6**
Caracol **17**
El Pilar **12**
Lamanai **4**
Tikal **14**
Xunantunich **13**

KEY TO ABBREVIATIONS

----- Reef
- - - Marine Reserve
        boundary

AR Archaeological Reserve
FR Forest Reserve
MR Marine Reserve
NP National Park
NM Natural Monument
NR Nature Reserve
PR Private Reserve
WS Wildlife Sanctuary

Half Moon Caye NM

*Glover's
Reef Atoll*

Glover's Reef MR

CARIBBEAN

SEA

*South Water
Caye MR*

*Sapodilla
Cayes MR*

Laughing Bird
Caye NP

Gales Point
Mullins River
Grants
Works
FR
Dangriga
Hopkins Village
Hopkins
Village
Mayflower
Bocawina
NP
STANN
CREEK
Maya
Beach
Placencia
Mango
Creek
FR
Monkey Caye FR
Monkey River
Payne's
Creek NP
Port
Honduras
MR

Hummingbird Hwy.
Middlesex
Blue Hole NP **15**
Sibun
FR
Sittee River
FR
Victoria Peak NM
Cockscomb Basin
WS **18**
Maya Mountain
FR **18**
Swasey
Bladen
FR
Monkey River
Deep
River
FR
Bladen NR

Tapir
Mountain
NR
CAYO
San Ignacio **15**
San Antonio
Mountain Pine Ridge **16**
Chiquibul
NP
Vaca
FR
Chiquibul
FR
MAYA
MOUNTAINS
Columbia River FR
Bladen NR

Kunantunich **14**
Kunantunich **13**
Caracol
AR **17**
Caracol **17**

Gulf of
Honduras

TOLEDO
Big Falls
Machaca Creek FR
Agua Caliente Luha WS
Punta
Gorda
Barranco
San Antonio
Blue
Creek
Temash-
Sarstoon
NP
Bahía de
Amatique
Sarstoon River
GUATEMALA

sea. Many of these have a thatch-roofed shade structure at the end, often strung with hammocks. This is a great place to read a book, take a siesta, or simply spend an hour or two marveling at the ocean's amazing shades of blue. See chapters 7 and 8.

○ **Staying with a Maya Family:** It certainly isn't going to be like a night at the Four Seasons, but if you're looking for a real cultural exchange, you should consider staying with a traditional Maya family. **The Maya Village Homestay Network** (𝄞 **722-2470;** demdatsdoin@btl.net) can organize this for you. See "Punta Gorda & the Toledo District" in chapter 8.

○ **Spending the Night in a Maya Ceremonial City:** An intimate and rather luxurious nature lodge, **Chan Chich Lodge** (𝄞 **800/343-8009** in the U.S., or 223-4419 in Belize; www.chanchich.com) is built right on the site of a minor Mayan ceremonial city. The hills just outside your private cabin are unexcavated residences and pyramids. Ruins and basic excavations dot the grounds, and the surrounding rainforests are rich in bird and animal life. See p. 211.

THE best OF NATURAL BELIZE

○ **The Cayes & Barrier Reef:** Running the entire length of the country's coastline, the Belize Barrier Reef is the second-longest continuous barrier reef in the world. Here you will find some of the best snorkeling opportunities and scuba-diving sites in the world. Moreover, the barrier reef is lined with hundreds and hundreds of small islands, or cayes. Most are uninhabited. These cayes range in size from tiny patches of sand or mangrove smaller than a football field to the larger and more developed vacation destination islands of Caye Caulker and Ambergris Caye. Whether you want the hustle and bustle of the latter, the deserted isle feel of a smaller or even private caye, or something in between, your choices are many and uniformly inviting. See chapters 7 and 8.

○ **The Atolls:** Belize's three mid-ocean atolls are arguably more spectacular than the barrier reef and its many cayes. Unique formations of small islands and reef surrounding a mid-ocean saltwater lagoon, atolls are an isolated and stunning phenomena. Belize has three of them: Turneffe Island, Lighthouse Reef, and Glover's Reef. These atolls are very sparsely developed, and any visit here will be imbued with a sense of adventure, isolation, and romance. See "The Outer Atolls" in chapter 7 and "Dangriga" in chapter 8.

○ **Cockscomb Basin Wildlife Sanctuary & Cockscomb Basin Forest Reserve** (Southern Belize): This is a huge protected area composed of rugged, forested mountains. The sanctuary was designed to protect and help researchers study the largest new-world cat, the jaguar. The park is also home to Belize's other four wildcat species, as well as Baird's tapirs, coati-mundi, tayra, kinkajous, deer, peccaries, anteaters, and armadillos, and some 300 species of birds. Inside the park you'll also find Victoria Peak, the country's highest mountain. See "Dangriga" in chapter 8.

○ **Crooked Tree Wildlife Sanctuary** (Northern Belize): This preserve is a swampy lowland that is home to more than 250 resident species of birds and serves as a resting spot for scores of migratory species. It is also the principal nesting site of the endangered jabiru stork, the largest bird in the Americas. The sanctuary is an excellent place to spot other wildlife as well, including crocodiles, iguanas, coati-mundi, and howler monkeys. The best way to explore Crooked Tree is by paddling around the network of lagoons in a dugout canoe. See "En Route North: Crooked Tree Wildlife Sanctuary" in chapter 9.

o **Río Bravo Conservation Area** (Northern Belize): This massive mixed tract of virgin forest, sustainable-yield managed forest, and recovering reforestation areas is home to nearly 400 bird species and more than 200 species of tropical trees. It also supports a healthy population of most of the new-world cat species, and is one of the best areas in the Americas to try your luck in spotting a jaguar. The Río Bravo Conservation Area is also home to La Milpa, an ongoing excavation of a major Mayan ceremonial city. See "Going West: Río Bravo Conservation Area, La Milpa & Chan Chich" in chapter 9.

o **Caves** (Cayo District and Western Belize): Belize has an extensive network of caves, which were considered by the ancient Maya to be a mystical portal between the world of the living and the underworld of spirits and the dead. They called this mystical realm Xibalba. In almost every explored cave in Belize, some evidence of use by the Mayans has been uncovered. Fire pits, campsites, burial mounds, and ritual altars have all been found. Numerous pieces of pottery and abundant skeletons, bones, and artifacts have also been encountered. These caves are relatively easily accessible and you should not leave Belize without at least one foray into Xibalba. There are lots of great caves to visit, but if you had to choose just one, I'd recommend **Actun Tunichil Muknal** (p. 226). See chapter 10.

o **Río on Pools** (Cayo District and Western Belize): This series of flowing falls and pools is somewhat reminiscent of Ocho Ríos in Jamaica. While the views and swimming are fine at the base of the falls, it's worth the hike upstream to even better views and numerous pools flowing between big rocks, which are perfect for sunbathing. This place can get crowded on weekends, when locals come for family picnics and getaways. See "Mountain Pine Ridge & Caracol" in chapter 10.

THE best DIVING & SNORKELING

Belize is rightly considered one of the top scuba diving and snorkeling destinations on the planet. The Belize Barrier Reef, second only to Australia's Great Barrier Reef, runs the length of its coastline, and the country has three open-ocean atolls. Diving and snorkeling are superb all along the barrier reef; the following are just a few of the truly standout sites and dives.

o **Shark-Ray Alley & Hol Chan Marine Reserve** (Northern Cayes and Atolls): These two very popular snorkeling sites are threatened with overcrowding but still live up to their billing. Shark-Ray Alley guarantees a very close encounter with schools of large stingrays and nurse sharks. The experience provides a substantial adrenaline rush for all but the most nonchalant and veteran divers. Hol Chan Marine Reserve is an excellent snorkeling destination composed of a narrow channel cutting through a rich and well-maintained shallow coral reef. See "Ambergris Caye" in chapter 7.

o **Caye Caulker** (Northern Cayes and Atolls): If you're looking for a relaxed vacation spot to serve as a base for some good snorkeling, you can't do much better than Caye Caulker, which has some excellent and easily accessible snorkeling sites. It's also much less developed and less crowded than its more popular neighbor,

Ambergris Caye. Many of the dive sites are a very short boat ride from shore. See "Caye Caulker" in chapter 7.

o **Turneffe Island & Lighthouse Reef Atolls** (Northern Cayes and Atolls): For many divers coming to Belize, these spots are the holy grail, and justifiably so. Both of these mid-ocean atoll formations feature nearly endless opportunities for world-class wall, drift, and coral-garden diving. As a cherry to top this cake, this is also where you'll find the Blue Hole. A host of dive operators all across Belize offer day trips to dive these sites, although these usually involve a 90-minute to 3-hour ride each way. Alternatively, you can stay at one of the very few lodges out here, or take a vacation on a live-aboard dive boat. See "The Outer Atolls" in chapter 7.

o **Glover's Reef Atoll** (Southern Belize): Glover's Reef is the third of Belize's mid-ocean atolls. The diving here is spectacular and underexploited. As compared to the Turneffe Island and Lighthouse Reef atolls, far fewer day-trippers visit the dive sites around Glover's Reef Atoll. The best way to really take advantage of the diving and snorkeling is to stay out here, and for this, **Isla Marisol Resort** (© 888/623-5403 in the U.S. and Canada; www.islamarisolresort.com) is your best option. See "Dangriga" in chapter 8.

o **Gladden Spit** (Southern Belize): More or less due east of Placencia, Gladden Spit is a world-renowned spot for diving with massive whale sharks. This mid-ocean site is the natural spawning ground for a variety of marine species. Whale sharks come regularly to feed on the energetically rich and very plentiful reproductive effluence. Whale shark sightings are fairly common here from late March to early July, and to a much lesser extent from August to October and in December and January. Since the sharks tend to feed and cruise close to the surface, snorkelers and divers alike can also enjoy the spectacle, although the waters here can be rough, and it's best to scuba dive. See "Placencia" in chapter 8.

THE best NONDIVING ADVENTURES

o **Chartering a Sailboat for Some Isolated Island Explorations:** The protected waters, steady gentle trade winds, and hundreds of isolated islands and anchorages make Belize an ideal place for bareboat charters. You can charter these as bareboats, or with a skipper and crew. Given the shallow draft, increased interior space, and reduced drag, a multihull is your best bet. **The Moorings** (© 888/952-8420 in the U.S. and Canada, or 523-3351; www.moorings.com) and **TMM** (© 800/633-0155 in the U.S., or 226-3026; www.sailtmm.com) are two large-scale charter companies with operations on Ambergris Caye and in Placencia. See "Ambergris Caye" in chapter 7 and "Placencia" in chapter 8.

o **Fly-Fishing for Bonefish, Permit & Tarpon on the Outer Atoll Flats:** Belize is a world-class fishing destination, and while offshore fishing for bigger game is possible, the real draw here is fly-fishing for feisty and world-record-size bonefish, permit, and tarpon (actually, the tarpon get as big as most deep-sea game). **Turneffe Flats** (© 888/512-8812 in the U.S. and Canada, or 220-4046 in Belize; www.tflats.com) is an excellent fishing operation located on Turneffe Island Atoll. See "The Outer Atolls" in chapter 7.

○ **Kayaking & Camping Around Glover's Reef Atoll:** The relatively calm protected waters of the atoll and manageable distances between islands make this a perfect place to explore under your own power, paddling a one- or two-person sea kayak. Both **Island Expeditions** (𝓒 **800/667-1630** or 604/452-3212 in the U.S., or 220-4046 in Belize; www.islandexpeditions.com) and **Slickrock Adventures** (𝓒 **800/390-5715** or 435/259-4225 in the U.S.; www.slickrock.com) run various adventurous multiday kayak tours to small camps and lodges on private isolated cayes of Glover's Reef Atoll. See "Dangriga" in chapter 8.

○ **Riding an Inner Tube Through the Caves Branch River Cave System** (Cayo District and Western Belize): This is certainly the most popular and probably the easiest way to explore Belize's vast network of caves. You strap on a battery-powered headlamp, climb into the center of an inflated car inner tube, and gently float through a series of limestone caves, your headlamp illuminating the stalactites and the occasional bat. The entire sensation is eerie and slightly claustrophobic, but fun nonetheless—especially if you go with a small group on a day when the caves are not crowded. See "Belmopan" in chapter 10.

○ **Canoeing, Kayaking, or Inner Tubing on the Macal or Mopan Rivers** (Western Belize): These two rivers converge around the city of San Ignacio, in the Cayo District. Upstream from town on either river are ample opportunities for paddling or floating. Depending on the water level and the section you choose, this can range from a lazy canoe or inner-tube paddle to a Class III kayak trip over rushing rapids. Any of the hotels in the Cayo District can help you organize one of these adventures. See "San Ignacio" in chapter 10.

○ **Horseback Riding Through the Cayo District** (Western Belize): The Cayo District is a perfect area to explore on horseback. Rides can be combined with visits to jungle waterfalls and swimming holes, as well as nearby Mayan ruins. **Mountain Equestrian Trails** (𝓒 **669-1124;** www.metbelize.com) has one of the better stables and horse-riding operations in the Cayo District. See "San Ignacio" and "Mountain Pine Ridge & Caracol" in chapter 10.

THE best DAY HIKES & NATURE WALKS

○ **Cockscomb Basin Forest Reserve** (Southern Belize): This large forest reserve has an excellent network of well-maintained trails. The Cockscomb Basin Forest Reserve—in addition to being the only dedicated reserve designed to protect the endangered jaguar—is also home to an amazing array of tropical flora and fauna. Truly adventurous hikers can arrange to climb Belize's tallest mountain, Victoria Peak, which is found inside this reserve. See "Dangriga" in chapter 8.

○ **Guanacaste National Park** (Cayo District and Western Belize): This small national park is located right on the side of the Western Highway, about 3.2km (2 miles) north of Belmopan. The gentle trails and easy accessibility here make this an excellent choice for an introduction to tropical forests. There are nearly 3.2km (2 miles) of well-marked and well-maintained trails in the park, with several benches for sitting and observing wildlife. The park is named after a giant Guanacaste tree, and is bordered on the west by Roaring Creek and on the north by the Belize River. See "Belmopan" in chapter 10.

- **Blue Hole National Park** (Cayo District and Western Belize): This hike combines a pleasant 2.4km (1.5-mile) hike through dense primary and secondary tropical forest with the chance to hike farther inside the large and long St. Herman's Cave, while also stopping for a refreshing dip in the park's beautiful namesake swimming hole, or cenote, here. If you hire a guide, you can actually hike for several miles more inside the stunning **Crystalline Cave.** See "Belmopan" in chapter 10.

- **Tikal National Park** (Tikal, Guatemala): In addition to being one of the best excavated and preserved ancient Mayan cities, Tikal offers an extensive trail network running through dense tropical rainforest. Howler and spider monkeys clamor overhead, and parrots squawk through the canopy. You can see a wealth of tropical fauna here, as you slowly wander from plaza to plaza and pyramid to pyramid. See "Tikal" in chapter 11.

THE best BIRD-WATCHING

Belize is home to some 618 species of resident and migratory birds. With varied ecosystems including coastal mangroves and swamps, isolated barrier-reef cayes, dense tropical rainforest, and clear, open savannahs, Belize is a wonderful destination for avid bird-watchers and amateurs alike.

- **Half Moon Caye National Monument** (Northern Cayes and Atolls): This isolated wildlife and marine reserve is a major nesting site for the red-footed booby. Thousands of these birds can be spotted on the island at any one time; it's an amazing sight. In addition, you can spot a wide range of resident and migratory seabirds here. See "The Outer Atolls" in chapter 7.

- **Man-O-War Caye** (Southern Belize): This small caye is a government-monitored bird sanctuary and major nesting site for the magnificent frigate, or man-o-war. Circling the island in a small boat, you'll see hundreds of these large seabirds roosting on and hovering above the tiny caye. In addition to the frigates, the island is home to a large community of brown boobies. See "Dangriga" in chapter 8.

- **Cockscomb Basin Forest Reserve** (Southern Belize): In addition to its jaguar reserve, the Cockscomb Basin Forest Reserve is home to a large number of tropical forest–dwelling bird species. This is one of the best sites in Belize to spot the large and loud scarlet macaw, as well as several toucan species and the imposing king vulture. See "Dangriga" in chapter 8.

- **Crooked Tree Wildlife Sanctuary** (Northern Belize): This rich wetland is perhaps the top bird-watching site in Belize. Home to hundreds of resident and migrant species, it is one of the best spots to see the giant and rare jabiru stork, especially during the dry season. You can spot various heron and kingfisher species here, as well as the yellow-lored parrot and Yucatán jay. See "En Route North: Crooked Tree Wildlife Sanctuary" in chapter 9.

- **New River Lagoon** (Northern Belize): This wide-open lagoon is reached via the winding and narrow New River, and it branches off into a network of narrow canals, streams, and marshlands, the perfect and preferred habitat for a wide range of bird species. Common species sighted include the black-collared hawk, northern jacana, and purple gallinule. You can combine a bird-watching trip here with a visit to the Lamanai Mayan ruin, which also has wonderful opportunities for bird-watching all along its trails and from the peaks of its pyramids. See "The Submerged Crocodile: Lamanai" in chapter 9.

- **Shipstern Nature Reserve** (Northern Belize): Covering some 8,903 hectares (22,000 acres), including several distinct ecosystems, Shipstern Nature Reserve is home to more than 250 bird species. You can explore the area on foot, as well as in little dugout canoes and flat-bottomed boats. See "Corozal Town" in chapter 9.
- **Caracol** (Cayo District and Western Belize): Also a major Mayan ruin, Caracol and its surrounding forest are prime bird-watching destinations. The area is replete with numerous tropical forest species, including such beauties as the keel-billed motmot, violaceous trogon, ocellated turkey, crested guan, and great curassow. Some visitors have even spotted the harpy eagle here. See "Mountain Pine Ridge & Caracol" in chapter 10.

THE best MAYAN RUINS

- **Altun Ha** (Northern Belize): One of the most easily accessible Mayan ruins from Belize City, Altun Ha is a small yet well-preserved site featuring two large central plazas surrounded by midsized pyramids and mounds. Only a few of the most imposing temples, tombs, and pyramids have been uncovered and rebuilt; hundreds more lie under the jungle foliage. Many jade, pearl, and obsidian artifacts have been discovered here, including the unique jade-head sculpture of **Kinich Ahau** (the Mayan sun god), the largest carved jade piece from the Mayan era. See "Along the Old Northern Highway: Altun Ha & Maruba Resort Jungle Spa" in chapter 9.
- **Lamanai** (Northern Belize): One of the more interesting and picturesque Mayan ruins in Belize, Lamanai features three large pyramids, a couple of residential areas, various restored stelae, and open plazas, as well as a small and unique ball court. Moreover, the ruins of two 16th-century Spanish churches are nearby. The site is set on the banks of the New River Lagoon. Since it was still occupied by the Maya when the Spanish arrived, Lamanai is one of the few sites in Belize to retain its traditional name. See "The Submerged Crocodile: Lamanai" in chapter 9.
- **Xunantunich** (Cayo District and Western Belize): Xunantunich is an impressive, well-excavated, and easily accessible Mayan site, close to San Ignacio. Xunantunich was a thriving Mayan city during the Classic Period, from about A.D. 600 to 900. You'll find carved stelae and one very tall main pyramid here. To reach the ruins, you must cross the Mopan River aboard a tiny hand-cranked car-ferry in the village of San José Succotz. See "San Ignacio" in chapter 10.
- **El Pilar** (Cayo District and Western Belize): El Pilar just may be the most under-appreciated major Mayan city in Mesoamerica. The site is huge, with more than 25 known plazas, covering some 40 hectares (100 acres) that straddle the Belize and Guatemala border. Excavation and exploration here are in their early stages, and I actually think that, in time, El Pilar will join the ranks of Caracol and Tikal as one of the major Classic Mayan sites of this region. See "San Ignacio" in chapter 10.
- **Caracol** (Cayo District and Western Belize): Caracol (www.caracol.org) is the largest known Mayan archaeological site in Belize, and one of the great Mayan

city-states of the Classic era. Located deep within the Chiquibil Forest Reserve, the ruins are not nearly as well excavated as those at Tikal, Xunantunich, or any number of other sites. However, this is part of Caracol's charm. The main pyramid here, **Caana** or "Sky Palace," stands some 41m (135 ft.) high; it is the tallest Mayan building in Belize and still the tallest man-made structure in the country. See "Mountain Pine Ridge & Caracol" in chapter 10.

o **Tikal:** Just over the Belizean border in neighboring Guatemala, **Tikal** is the grandest of the surviving Classic Mayan cities. Tikal is far more extensively excavated than any ruins in Belize. The pyramids here are some of the most perfect examples of ceremonial architecture in the Mayan world. The peaks of several temples poke through the dense rainforest canopy. Toucans and parrots fly about, and the loudest noise you'll hear is the guttural call of howler monkeys. In its heyday, the city probably covered as much as 65 sq. km (25 sq. miles) and supported a population of more than 100,000. See "Tikal" in chapter 11.

THE best VIEWS

o The **Blue Hole** is probably best experienced and viewed from above. A perfectly round sinkhole measuring some 305m (1,000 ft.) across in the middle of the Lighthouse Reef Atoll lagoon, the Blue Hole appears as a deep, dark blue circle in a sea of shimmering turquoise. The best way to get this bird's-eye view is with **Astrum Helicopters** (© **888/278-7864** in the U.S. and Canada, or 222-5100 in Belize; www.astrumhelicopters.com). See chapters 3 and 7 for more information.

o If you're lucky enough to grab a seat along the railing at the **Wet Lizard** (© **223-5973**; www.thewetlizard.com), you'll have a ringside seat to the hustle and bustle of Belize City's busy harbor. Traditional sailboats bob at anchor, speedboats come and go to and from the cayes, and cruise ship tenders provide a steady shuttle service for passengers between the offshore ships at anchor and the city's main pier. See chapter 6.

o Try watching the **sun rise over the New River Lagoon** from a hammock strung on the front porch of your veranda at the **Lamanai Outpost Lodge** (© **888/733-7864** in the U.S., or 672-2000 in Belize; www.lamanai.com). It is a view you'll always treasure. The view is lovely throughout the day, but it's worth waking up early for. See chapter 9.

o Although the **main temple at Cerros** is just a diminutive 21m (70 ft.) tall, it offers excellent views across Corozal Bay. Moreover, this is an easy climb for most, and far easier than the climbs to the tops of most other major Mayan ceremonial pyramids. See chapter 9.

o The main pyramid at Xunantunich, **El Castillo,** rises to 39m (127 ft.). It's a steep climb, but the view from the top is worth it. On a clear day, you'll be able to make out the twin border towns of Benque Viejo, Belize, and Melchor de Menchos, Guatemala. See chapter 10.

o Poking their heads over the dense rainforest canopy, the **pyramids of Tikal** offer some of the best views to be found in all of Central America. Temple IV is the tallest and the preferred platform for enjoying this view, but Temple II, just off the Great Plaza, is really just as good. Get here early, or stay late, to enjoy the views without the hustle and bustle of busloads of tourists. See chapter 11.

THE best DESTINATIONS FOR FAMILIES

- **Belize Zoo** (near Belize City): The Belize Zoo (② **220-8004;** www.belizezoo.org) houses more than 125 animals, all native Belizean species. It is considered a national treasure and a model for the possibilities of a conservation-based zoo. The zoo itself is wonderfully laid out, on meandering trails with large and well-maintained enclosures for the animals. For a real treat, you can stay in some cozy cabins here and take a private night tour of the zoo. See "What to See & Do" in chapter 6.

- **Old Belize** (Belize City): Old Belize (② **222-4129;** www.oldbelize.com) is part museum, part playground, part beach, and part adventure attraction. There's something here for everyone, and plenty for the kids, including a large water slide. It's easy to spend several hours, if not a whole day, here. See p. 98.

- **Ambergris Caye** (Northern Cayes and Atolls): Ambergris Caye is the most developed of Belize's beach and diving destinations. As such, it has the greatest selection of hotels and activities, many of them either geared toward or just plain great for kids. From snorkeling and paragliding to touring the island on golf carts and visiting the Butterfly Jungle, there's plenty to keep families and kids of all ages occupied here. **Xanadu Island Resort** (② **226-2814;** www. xanaduresort-belize.com) and **Captain Morgan's Retreat** (② **888/653-9090** or 307/587-8914 in the U.S., or 226-2207 in Belize; www.belizevacation.com) are two good choices for families. See "Ambergris Caye" in chapter 7.

- **Almond Beach Belize & Jaguar Reef Lodge** (Hopkins Village, Southern Belize; **866/824-1516** in the U.S. and Canada, or 520-7040 in Belize; www.jaguarreef. com): This mid-size beachfront resort has a range of amenities and activities that will make parents happy and keep kids occupied. In addition to a couple of pools and a long beach, this place has sea kayaks and mountain bikes, and an extensive menu of daily tours and activities. See p. 169.

- **The Inn at Robert's Grove** (Placencia, Southern Belize; ② **800/565-9757** in the U.S., or 523-3565 in Belize; www.robertsgrove.com): This is another small beach resort that is well-suited for families. As at Almond Beach Belize & Jaguar Reef Lodge, there's a wide enough range of activities available here to keep families active and interested for a full vacation. What makes this place trump Jaguar Reef are two private cayes, excellent restaurants, and outstanding service. See p. 180.

- **Cayo District** (Western Belize): The Cayo District is the heart of Belize's Mayan world, as well as its prime ecotourism destination. Between a full plate of active adventure activities and a steady diet of Mayan ruins and ancient burial caves, families will find this a great place to spend time in Belize. Not only is **Chaa Creek** (**877/709-8708** in the U.S. and Canada, or 824-2037 in Belize; www. chaacreek.com) extremely comfortable for families, but they also have their own butterfly breeding project and natural history museum on-site. And if parents need a little pampering, they also have an excellent spa. See chapter 10.

- **Caves Branch** (Cayo District and Western Belize): You'll be heroes in your kids' eyes after you take them inner-tubing through the dark and spooky network of limestone caves traversed by the slow-moving Caves Branch River. Families with a real hankering for adventure should head to **Ian Anderson's Caves Branch**

(📞 **822-2800;** www.cavesbranch.com), which offers a wide range of guided cave adventures and accommodations that run the gamut from quite plush to nearly camping. See "Belmopan" in chapter 10.

THE best LUXURY HOTELS & RESORTS

○ **The Great House** (Belize City; 📞 **223-3400;** www.greathousebelize.com): Housed in an old wooden mansion a half-block from the lighthouse, this place offers cozy, well-equipped rooms with an intimate and elegant vibe. Try for one of the top-floor rooms with great views over the harbor and city. See p. 92.

○ **Radisson Fort George Hotel & Marina** (Belize City; 📞 **800/333-3333** in the U.S., or 223-3333 in Belize; www.radisson.com): This is the top business-class and luxury hotel in Belize City. This oceanfront hotel is located in the quiet Fort George neighborhood, out by the lighthouse, just a block from the cruise ship tourist village. The hotel has two swimming pools, a well-equipped gym, several restaurants and bars, and easy access to the best Belize City has to offer. See p. 92.

○ **Victoria House** (Ambergris Caye; 📞 **800/247-5159** in the U.S., or 226-2067; www.victoria-house.com): Casual elegance and attentive service await you at this Ambergris Caye resort. A varied collection of rooms, suites, and villas is spread around an expansive piece of land planted with lush tropical gardens. The hotel also has one of the best restaurants in the country, as well as a wonderful patch of soft white-sand beach. See p. 125.

○ **Mata Chica** (Ambergris Caye; 📞 **223-0002;** www.matachica.com): This intimate beachfront hotel oozes a refined and relaxed air of style. The individual cabins are very inviting and artistically designed. The excellent restaurant, chic bar, large pool, and intuitive staff make this my top choice on northern Ambergris Caye. See p. 127.

○ **Cayo Espanto** (just off the coast of Ambergris Caye; 📞 **888/666-4282** in the U.S. and Canada; www.aprivateisland.com): What could be more decadent and luxurious than staying in a private villa with a private swimming pool, a private dock, and a personal butler, all on an almost private island? (There are seven villas here, and if you really want to go all out, you can rent out the whole island if you like.) This place pulls out all the stops, providing all the conveniences, perks, and pampering possible on a desert-island getaway. See p. 128.

○ **Turtle Inn** (Placencia; 📞 **800/746-3743** in the U.S. and Canada, or 824-4912 in Belize; www.turtleinn.com): Building on the experience gained from his Blancaneaux Lodge, and building upon the ruins of a hotel destroyed by Hurricane Iris, director Francis Ford Coppola has created one of the top high-end hotels in Belize. The individual villas here are some of the most beautiful and spacious in the country. The hotel is set right on an excellent stretch of beach, and the service and dining are top-notch. See p. 180.

○ **Machaca Hill Lodge** (Punta Gorda; 📞 **722-0050;** www.machacahill.com): This is by far the most luxurious option around Punta Gorda, and one of the top rainforest lodges in the country. This place features a series of large and plush individual cabins set on a thickly forested hillside. See p. 193.

○ **Maruba Resort Jungle Spa** (off the Old Northern Hwy.; 📞 **800/627-8227** in the U.S., or 225-5555; www.maruba-belize.com): This boutique resort and spa is set in a patch of lush forest and flowering gardens. The whole operation is an eclectic orgy designed to please the eyes and all other senses. The individual villas here are spectacular. A wide range of spa treatments is available, and excellently and professionally done. Don't miss out on their signature Mood Mud Massage, perhaps one of the few massage experiences for which you'll want to bring a camera. See p. 201.

- **Chaa Creek** (off the road to Benque Viejo, Cayo District; **877/709-8708** in the U.S. and Canada, or 824-2037 in Belize; www.chaacreek.com): A pioneer nature lodge in Belize, this collection of individual and duplex cottages was also a pioneer in the whole concept of rustic luxury. Cool terra-cotta tile floors, varnished wood, thatched roofs, and beautiful Guatemalan textiles and handicrafts are elegantly yet simply combined. The property is set on a steep hillside over the lovely Macal River. Service is very friendly and personable, and the lodge provides easy access to a wealth of natural adventures and ancient Mayan wonders. See p. 244.

- **Ka'ana** (on the outskirts of San Ignacio, Cayo District; ℂ **877/522-6221** in the U.S. and Canada, or 824-0430 reservations office in Belize, or 820-3350 hotel; www.kaanabelize.com): This boutique resort offers an enticing blend of creature comforts and easy access to the region's many adventures, Mayan ruins, and natural treasures. The individual bungalows and rooms are packed with amenities, and the restaurant here is the best in the region. See p. 239.

- **Blancaneaux Lodge** (Mountain Pine Ridge Reserve, Cayo District; ℂ **800/746-3743** in the U.S. and Canada, or 824-4912 in Belize; www.blancaneaux.com): Francis Ford Coppola's first Belizean mountain retreat remains one of the most elegant and luxurious nature lodges in the country. The hotel is set on a steep pine-forested hillside, overlooking the Privassion River and a series of gentle falls. The individual cabanas all are spacious, are beautifully decorated, and feature a private balcony or deck designed to take in the excellent views. The hotel also boasts a wonderful riverside spa facility. See p. 252.

- **La Lancha Resort** (Lago Petén Itzá, Petén; ℂ **800/746-3743** in the U.S. and Canada, or ℂ/fax 502/7928-8331 in Guatemala; www.lalanchavillage.com): Set on a steep, high hillside overlooking the lake, this is the most luxurious option close to the amazing ruins of Tikal. Another of Francis Ford Coppola's regional resorts, this place has rooms once again decorated with style, featuring furniture and artwork from around the world. The food is also excellent. See p. 272.

THE best MODERATELY PRICED HOTELS

- **San Pedro Holiday Hotel** (Ambergris Caye; ℂ **713/893-3825** in the U.S. and Canada, or 226-2014 in Belize; www.sanpedroholiday.com): This brilliantly white three-building complex with painted purple and pink trim sits in the center of San Pedro town. This was the first hotel on Ambergris Caye when Celi McCorkle opened it more than 40 years ago, and it's still one of the best. Grab a room with an oceanview balcony, and you'll be in tropical vacation heaven. See p. 123.

- **Tides Beach Resort** (Ambergris Caye; ℂ **226-2283;** www.ambergriscaye.com/tides): Every room comes with either a private or shared balcony or veranda overlooking the Caribbean Sea. The hotel and its in-house dive shop are run by the very friendly and highly respected local couple of Patojo and Sabrina Paz. See p. 123.

○ **Seaside Cabanas** (Caye Caulker; ✆ **226-0498;** www.seasidecabanas.com): This place offers up comfy rooms, a fabulous location, a complete range of amenities, and an oceanview pool, all at a great price. See p. 142.

○ **Ranguana** (Placencia; ✆ **523-3112;** www.ranguanabelize.com): These simple, comfortable, and cool individual cabins are located just off the "sidewalk" in the center of Placencia Village. Some of them are beachfront cabins, and the others are just a few steps farther away from the sea. See p. 182.

○ **Coral House Inn** (Punta Gorda; ✆ **722-2878;** www.coralhouseinn.net): By far the best option in the town of Punta Gorda itself, this little bed-and-breakfast is facing the sea across a well-tended lawn and garden. The hotel offers neat rooms, a refreshing pool, and a friendly, welcoming vibe. See p. 194.

○ **Almond Tree Hotel Resort** (Corozal Town; ✆ **628-9224;** www.almondtreeresort. com): This small, oceanfront hotel is the best option in Corozal. There's a friendly vibe to the operation, with guests quickly feeling part of the family. See p. 217.

○ **Cahal Pech Village Resort** (San Ignacio, Cayo District; ✆ **824-3740;** www. cahalpech.com): With a commanding hillside perch, this collection of individual cabins and hotel rooms is an excellent option in the San Ignacio area. The resort is located just beyond the entrance to the Cahal Pech Mayan ruins, and a whole host of tours and activities can be arranged here. See p. 240.

○ **Black Rock Jungle River Lodge** (Cayo District; ✆ **820-4049;** www.blackrock lodge.com): Located down a long dirt road on the edge of a cliff overlooking the Macal River, this place offers all the benefits and amenities of a top-notch ecolodge at very reasonable rates. See p. 246.

THE best BUDGET HOTELS

○ **Belcove Hotel** (Belize City; ✆ **227-3054;** www.belcove.com): This budget hotel is set on the banks of Haulover Creek, just a block from the Swing Bridge and the heart of downtown Belize City. The old wooden building is in funky shape, but the riverview balconies are one of my favorite spots in all of Belize to sit and read a book, or watch the sporadic action on the river and streets below. See p. 93.

○ **Ruby's** (Ambergris Caye; ✆ **226-2063;** www.ambergriscaye.com/rubys): Located right on the waterfront in the center of San Pedro, this hotel is situated such that most of the rooms overlook the ocean, and the best ones come with a balcony. This is one of the older and more historic hotels on the island, and you just can't do much better on Ambergris Caye for this price. See p. 124.

○ **De Real Macaw** (Caye Caulker; ✆ **226-0459;** www.derealmacaw.biz): This small compound on Front Street in Caye Caulker is a great bargain. The hotel is close to all the action, and the rooms are clean, cool, and comfortable. Plenty of trees strung with hammocks make this a great place for a well-deserved tropical siesta. See p. 142.

○ **Maxhapan Cabins** (Caye Caulker; ✆ **226-0118;** maxhapan04@hotmail.com): There are only three rooms here, but if you score one, you'll be treated to a clean, cozy wooden cabin in a tranquil little oasis just on the outskirts of Caye Caulker's hustle and bustle. See p. 143.

- **Tree Tops Guest House** (Caye Caulker; ✆ **226-0240;** www.treetopsbelize.com): While the best rooms here actually fall into the moderately priced category (and are some of the best rooms on Caye Caulker), the whole place offers such good value for your money that it's getting a listing in this category. The budget rooms here continue to set the standard on Caye Caulker, and the service is friendly, knowledgeable, and attentive. See p. 143.

- **Tipple Tree Beya** (Hopkins Village; ✆/fax **520-7006;** www.tippletree.net): There are just five simple rooms at this friendly hostel-like option at the southern end of Hopkins Village. However, if the rooms are full, you can also camp. The hotel sits on a lovely section of beach and is within easy walking distance of the small Garífuna village of Hopkins. See p. 170.

- **Jungle Jeanie's by the Sea** (Hopkins Village; ✆ **523-7047;** www.junglebythe sea.com): Located at the southern end of this small traditional Garífuna fishing village, the individual wooden cabins are just steps from the ocean on a beautiful patch of beach. See p. 170.

- **Tradewinds** (Placencia; ✆ **523-3122;** www.placencia.com): Set on a curving spit of sand at the southern edge of Placencia, the individual cabins here are so close to the water's edge that I worry it's only a matter of time before the ocean reclaims them. But if you get here soon enough and land one of them, you'll likely never want to leave. Each has a private front porch strung with a hammock, where you can swing and listen to the lapping waves. See p. 182.

- **Mirador Hotel** (Corozal Town; ✆ **442-0189;** www.mirador.bz): While the large concrete building is a bit imposing and lacking in warmth, you can't beat the view or location of this downtown hotel. And the price is pretty right as well. See p. 219.

- **Midas Tropical Resort** (San Ignacio, Cayo District; ✆ **824-3172;** www.midas belize.com): Sure, you can stay in San Ignacio for a little less, but this collection of cottages and cabins is just a half-mile or so from downtown, right on the banks of the Macal River. You can also camp here. The whole thing has the feel of an isolated nature lodge at a fraction of the cost. See p. 241.

- **The Trek Stop** (Benque Viejo, Cayo District; ✆ **823-2265;** www.thetrekstop. com): This little hotel is a great choice for active travelers, college kids, and anyone looking to commune with nature and have a little adventure. The hotel is located just across the road from a beautiful section of the Mopan River and near the ferry crossing for Xunantunich. See p. 247.

- **Hotel Santana** (Flores, Petén, Guatemala; ✆/fax **502/7867-5123** or 7867-5193; www.santanapeten.com): This lakefront hotel is the best budget choice on the island of Flores. In fact, it might just be the best hotel on the tiny island itself, regardless of price. See p. 282.

THE best RESTAURANTS

- **Wet Lizard** (Belize City; ✆ **223-5973**): This often-rowdy little restaurant and bar serves up excellent fresh seafood and burgers in an open-air setting overlooking the Swing Bridge and Belize Harbor. This is a great place to savor some late-afternoon conch fritters and a refreshing drink. See p. 95.

- **Elvi's Kitchen** (San Pedro, Ambergris Caye; ✆ **226-2176;** www.elviskitchen. com): Elvia Staines has come a long way since she began selling hamburgers out of a takeout window more than 36 years ago. Today her friendly and very popular restaurant oozes island charm. The restaurant is a thatched, screened-in building with picnic tables, with a large flamboyant tree growing up through the roof and a floor of crushed shells and sand. No visit to Ambergris Caye is complete without a meal here. See p. 130.

- **Palmilla** (Ambergris Caye; ℰ 226-2067): This is easily the most elegant and finest dining to be had on Ambergris Caye, if not in all of Belize. The atmosphere is island formal, meaning relaxed yet refined at the same time, and the chefs here prepare the freshest of local ingredients with a creative blend of techniques, spices, and cuisines from around the world. When the weather's nice, you can dine under the stars by candlelight. See p. 131.

- **Rojo Lounge** (Ambergris Caye; ℰ 226-4012): The folks at Azul Resort, an isolated little place on Northern Ambergris Caye, serve very creative and well-prepared fusion cuisine in a relaxed and inviting open-air ambience. The menu features some of the more creative fusion items to be had—no mean feat, given the competition— and there are also nightly specials. See p. 132.

- **Habaneros** (Caye Caulker; ℰ 226-0487): Featuring a creative menu with influences from various Caribbean and Asian cuisines, this is a perennial must-visit restaurant on Caye Caulker. Be sure to grab one of the outdoor tables on the wraparound porch. See p. 144.

- **Don Corleone** (Caye Caulker; ℰ 226-0025): This is my favorite Italian restaurant in Belize. Owner-chef Luca Luca Michelus has an impeccable pedigree, with successful restaurant runs in both Italy and New York. Here, his classical Italian cuisine is blended with local influences and immediate access to an amazing daily catch of fresh fish and seafood. See p. 144.

- **Maya Beach Hotel Bistro** (Placencia; ℰ 520-8040; www.mayabeachhotel.com): This unassuming hotel restaurant serves up my favorite food on the Placencia peninsula. The menu is peppered with creative concoctions and hearty favorites, and the open-air main dining room is set just a few steps from the sea. See p. 183.

- **Chef Rob's** (Hopkins Village; ℰ 670-0445): For decades, Chef Rob garnered fame in top kitchens around Belize before finally setting up shop in the sleepy Garífuna village of Hopkins. The creative and eclectic menu changes nightly, with Chef Rob working his magic in a tiny show kitchen just off the even tinier bar. See p. 171.

- **Marian's Bayview** (Punta Gorda; ℰ 722-0129): The ambience and decor here are basic—at best—but the mix of Indian and Belizean cuisine is some of the most spectacular in southern Belize. The small menu changes regularly but always includes some of Marian's expertly prepared spicy East Indian fare. See p. 196.

- **Patty's Bistro** (Corozal Town; ℰ 402-0174): Set in a simple room in the heart of downtown Corozal, this homey place has earned a well-deserved reputation as the best restaurant in northern Belize. Traditional Belizean and Mexican standards are done to perfection. See p. 220.

- **La Ceiba** (at Ka'ana, just outside San Ignacio; ℰ 820-3350): Young Belizean chef Sean Kuylen has set up shop at this beautiful boutique hotel. His cooking showcases traditional regional cuisine, updated with classical French and contemporary fusion touches. See p. 242.

- **La Luna** (Flores, Guatemala; ℰ 502/7867-5443): If you find yourself in Flores, Guatemala, be sure to seek out this hip little restaurant. The eclectic decor varies from room to room, but like the food, it is consistently creative and tasteful. See p. 283.

THE best AFTER-DARK FUN

Belize doesn't really have all that much in the way of nightlife. The capital city is small and relatively quiet by most international standards. In the capital and throughout the rest of the country, you'd be hard-pressed to find a truly notable bar or club. Still, some unique after-dark destinations and activities are out there and should not be missed.

○ **Stargazing:** This is one of my favorite nighttime activities, but it is especially rewarding when there is no (or little) ambient light. Given its sparse development and low population density, Belize offers a wealth of opportunities for some truly spectacular stargazing. Your best spots are the isolated beach getaways of Belize's three mid-ocean atolls, but you can also enjoy the astronomical splendor from any number of deserted beaches or rural mountain getaways.

○ **Night Diving:** If you've come to Belize to scuba dive, you should definitely try a night dive. Many creatures are nocturnal, and the reefs here come alive at night. Moreover, the brilliant colors of the coral and sea life really shine under the strong glare of an underwater light, and there's something truly eerie about the experience. All of the major dive destinations and resorts offer night diving. See chapter 5 and the destination chapters for more details.

○ **Riverside Tavern** (Belize City; ✆ **223-5640**): Featuring excellent steaks, fresh fish, and the country's best burgers and bar food, this place is a local favorite. There are TV screens for sporting events and there's always an interesting mix of locals, expatriates, and tourists alike. See p. 97.

○ **The Palapa Bar** (Ambergris Caye; **226-3111**; www.palapabarandgrill.com): Built out over the water, this place has a rambunctious and friendly bar scene. They also often have live music. See "Ambergris Caye" in chapter 7.

○ **Barefoot Beach Bar** (Placencia; ✆ **523-3515**): Located on the beachfront, just off the central sidewalk, this casual outdoor spot is the best place in Placencia to enjoy some live music or a simple drink with friends in a totally tropical setting, befitting the place. See "Placencia" in chapter 8.

○ **Moonrise at Tikal:** Watching the full moon rise from the top of Temple IV in Tikal is one of the highlights of my many travels to this region. You'll have to stay at one of the hotels on-site to do this, and you may even have to persuade or bribe a park guard. You'll also have to time your visit with the moon phase. But if all these things come together, you're in for a memorable and awe-inspiring evening. See "Tikal" in chapter 11.

THE best WEBSITES ABOUT BELIZE

○ **Latin American Network Information Center** (http://lanic.utexas.edu/la/ca/belize): Hosted by the University of Texas Latin American Studies Department, this site houses a vast collection of links to all sorts of information about Belize. This is hands down the best one-stop shop for Web browsing on the country, with helpful links to a wide range of tourism, government, local media, and general-information sites.

o **Belize by Naturalight** (www.belizenet.com): This is probably the single best collection of links to Belize's individual hotels, restaurants, and attractions. The site also boasts links to the various regions and destinations within Belize, as well as links to most other major and important websites on the country.

o **The Belize Forums** (www.belizeforum.com): These are active and informative forums on living in and traveling around Belize. Several regular posters are quite knowledgeable and are generous with that knowledge.

o **Belize News** (www.belizenews.com): This site provides access to all of Belize's major online news sources, including the online editions of all the major Belizean print newspapers.

o **The Toucan Trail** (www.toucantrail.com): This is an excellent site geared toward budget travelers, with extensive links and comprehensive information.

o **Belize Bus Blog** (http://belizebus.wordpress.com): This site offers the best and most up-to-date info on bus travel inside of Belize, as well as other tips, recommendations, and helpful links.

o **United States Embassy in Belize** (http://belize.usembassy.gov): This is the official site of the U.S. Embassy in Belmopan. In addition to handy contact information, you'll find a range of useful information, news reports, and links here.

o **Belize Tourist Board** (www.travelbelize.org): This is the official site of the Belize Tourist Board. It has its fair share of information and links, although you'll probably end up being directed to one of the other sites mentioned earlier.

BELIZE IN DEPTH

"You'd betta Belize it!" goes the common local exclamation. But before you can Belize it, you betta know a little bit about this little bitty country. Belize is the second-youngest nation in the Western Hemisphere, having been granted independence from Britain in 1981. It's also a decidedly sparsely populated country, with just more than 300,000 citizens and no large cities. Belize is the only country in Central America where English is the official and predominant language.

Originally a major part of the ancient Mayan empire, Belize was next settled by pirates and then colonized by the British, who used slave labor. The descendants of each of these groups are woven into the historical lore and cultural fabric of modern Belize. Add to the mix the independent Garífuna people, who settled along the remote southern shore in the early part of the 19th century, and the more recent waves of Mexican, Chinese, and East Indian immigrants, and you have an idea of the cultural meld that constitutes this unique Central American country. Surprisingly, Belizeans of all cultural stripes tend to get along a lot better and with far fewer outward and untoward shows of racism than citizens of most other nations. This is a small country. The sense of community is strong and, even in the big city, people tend to know their neighbors and almost everyone is somehow related.

Tourism is a major social, economic, and cultural force in Belize, and the country offers a wide range of attractions for visitors, from sun-'n'-fun beach vacations to active adventures and ecotourism explorations. This chapter will help you get acquainted with the history, people, culture, and natural environment of this small yet very diverse and exciting Central American nation.

BELIZE TODAY

Belize is a developing nation, limited by a small economy, a tiny industrial base, a huge trade deficit, widespread unemployment, and a historic dependence on foreign aid. These problems have only been compounded since independence. Sugar, bananas, and citrus are the principal cash crops, though seafood exports also help. A modest oil find in 2005 has allowed the country to produce and export as much as 3,500 barrels of crude oil per day. Tourism is also an important source of income and jobs, responsible for providing 25% of the nation's jobs and 18% of its GDP. Increasingly, Belizeans whose fathers and grandfathers were farmers or fishermen find themselves hotel owners, tour guides, waiters, and cleaning personnel.

Belize has a population of some 310,000, roughly half of whom live in one of the six major towns or cities, with the rest living in rural areas or small villages. About 45% of the population is considered mestizo, descendants of mixed Spanish, Mexican, and/or Mayan blood. Making up 30% of the population are the Kriols, predominantly black descendants of slaves and the early British colonists. Belize's three Mayan tribes—Yucatec, Mopan, and Kekchi—make up around 10% of the population. The Garifuna constitute approximately 6.5% of the population, while a mix of whites of British descent, Mennonites, Chinese, and East Indians fill out the rest.

In general, the pace of life and business is slow in Belize. You'll seldom find people rushing down the sidewalks or dirt streets. There are only four major highways in the country, and traffic is never heavy. In fact, all of these highways actually have speed bumps along their length, as they pass through the many roadside towns and villages.

Belize held its first parliamentary elections in 1984. Since then, power has ping-ponged back and forth between the United Democratic Party (UDP) and the People's United Party (PUP). The former is a more conservative, free market–oriented party, while the latter champions a more liberal, social-democratic agenda. In the August 1998 elections, PUP won 26 of the 29 parliamentary seats, while the UDP managed to win just 3. However, by 2005, discontent with the PUP over tax increases and widespread corruption had grown, and there were public demonstrations and disturbances. The UDP pummeled them in the 2006 municipal elections,

speaking OF TONGUES

English is the official language of Belize, but a traveler will most likely run across a wide range of languages. Three centuries of colonization have given the Queen's English some foothold here; however, a large percentage of the local population, particularly black Kriols, speak a Kriol English that is downright unintelligible to most English-speaking visitors. In recent years there have been attempts to standardize and record the Kriol dialect, and you may see it written out on billboards and in newspapers. *How Fi Rite Bileez Kriol (How to Write Belize Creole)* is a helpful pamphlet that can sometimes be found at local bookstores and gift shops, and an excellent

and entertaining reference if you want to take a stab at Kriol.

Moreover, this is still Central America, and Spanish is widely spoken in Belize, especially in the northern and western regions near the borders with Mexico and Guatemala. If that's not enough, Belize has three relatively homogenous ethnic groups, the Garífunas and the Kekchi and Mopan Mayas, each of whom has a distinct language. Finally, rounding out this polyglot pastiche, you may also hear some Chinese, Arabic, Hindi, or even the archaic German used by the country's small Mennonite community.

Check out chapter 13 for some useful terms and phrases in Kriol and Spanish.

and again in the 2008 national elections, electing Dean Barrow as the country's first black prime minister and maintaining a strong majority of parliamentary seats.

LOOKING BACK AT BELIZE

Early History

Before the arrival of the first Europeans, this was the land of the ancient Mayas. Although most people think of Mexico's Mayan cities in the Yucatán and Guatemala's Tikal when they think of *El Mundo Maya*, or the Maya World, ongoing archaeological discoveries show that what is today known as Belize was once a major part of the Mayan Empire. River and coastal trade routes connected dozens of cities and small towns throughout this region to each other and to the major ceremonial and trading cities of Mexico and Guatemala. Caracol, a Maya ruin in the Cayo District of western Belize, is a huge ceremonial city that defeated Tikal in battle in A.D. 562. Other sites, such as Lamanai, Altun Ha, and Xunantunich, were thriving ceremonial and trade centers, with impressive ruins and artifacts. Moreover, ongoing excavations at sites such as Pilar and La Milpa may eventually reveal other cities and ceremonial sites of equal or greater importance.

One of the earliest known Mayan cities in Mesoamerica, Cuello is located just outside of Orange Walk Town and has been dated to B.C. 2000 or earlier. Mayan history is often divided into several distinct periods: Archaic (10,000–2000 B.C.), Pre-Classic (2000 B.C.–A.D. 250), Classic (A.D. 250–900), and Post-Classic (900–1540). Within this timeline, the Classic Period itself is often divided into Early, Middle, Late, and Terminal stages. At the height of development, as many as two million Maya may have inhabited the region that is today known as Belize. No one knows for sure what led to the decline of the Classic Maya, but somewhere around A.D. 900 their society entered a severe and rapid decline. Famine, warfare, deforestation, and religious prophecy have all been cited as possible causes. Nevertheless, Belize is somewhat unique in that it had several major ceremonial or trading cities still occupied by Maya when the first Spanish conquistadors arrived.

Spanish Attempts at Conquest

Christopher Columbus sailed past the Belize coast in 1502, and even named the Bay of Honduras, but he never anchored or set foot ashore here, and the Spanish never had much success in colonizing Belize. In fact, they met with fierce resistance from the remaining Maya. Part of their problem may have come from Gonzalo Guerrero, a Spanish sailor who was shipwrecked off the coast of Belize and the Yucatán in the early years of the 16th century. Originally pressed into slavery, Guerrero eventually married the daughter of a Mayan ruler, and became an important warrior and military advisor in the Maya battles with the Spanish.

To be sure, the Spanish led various attacks and attempts at conquest and control of the territory that is present-day Belize. Many of these were brutal and deadly. They were also able to set up some missionary outposts, most notably those near Lamanai, where travelers today can still see the ruins of these early Spanish churches. Nevertheless, by the mid-1600s, the Spanish had been militarily forced to abandon all permanent settlements and attempts at colonialism in Belize, concentrating their efforts on more productive regions around Central and South America and the Caribbean Sea.

The British Are Coming

Belize likes to play up the fact that it was founded by pirates and buccaneers, and indeed, these unsavory characters were among the first to make this region their base of operations. Many of these pirates and buccaneers used the Belize coastline and its protected anchorages as hideouts and bases following their attacks on Spanish fleets transporting gold and silver treasures from their more productive colonies.

By the mid–17th century, British loggers were settling along the coast and making their way up the rivers and streams in search of mahogany for shipbuilding and other types of wood for making dyes. Proud and independent, these early settlers called themselves "Baymen" (after the Bay of Honduras). Politically, the Baymen trod a delicate balance between being faithful British subjects and being fiercely independent settlers.

Belize by Any Other Name

There's some debate as to the origin of the name "Belize." Some claim it is the timeworn corruption of the name Wallace, one of the early buccaneer captains to set anchor here. Others claim it comes from the Mayan word *beliz,* which translates as "muddy water."

Throughout this period and into the 18th century, the Spanish launched regular attacks on pirate bases and Baymen settlements in Belize. Spanish attacks devastated early settlements in Belize in 1679, 1717, 1730, and 1754, although after the dust cleared and the Spanish fleet moved on, the Baymen would always return. As the attacks increased in intensity, the Baymen sought more and more support from the British. In 1763, Spain and Britain signed the Treaty of Paris, which granted Britain official rights to log in Belize, but maintained Spanish sovereignty. Still, in 1779, Spain attacked the principal Belizean settlement on St. George's Caye, capturing 140 British and Baymen settlers and 250 slaves and shipping them off into custody on Cuba.

Diplomatic and military give and take between Spain and Britain ensued until 1798, when the Baymen won a decisive military victory over a larger Spanish fleet, again just off the shores of St. George's Caye. The Battle of St. George's Caye effectively ended all Spanish involvement and claim to Belize, and it solidified Belize's standing within the British Empire.

In 1862, with more or less the same borders it has today, Belize was formally declared the colony of British Honduras (after functioning as a colony for the previous century). This small colonial outpost became a major source of hardwood and dyewood for the still-expanding British Empire. The forests were exploited, and agriculture was never really encouraged. The British wanted their colony to remain dependent on the mother country, so virtually all the necessities of life were imported. Few roads were built, and the country remained unexplored and undeveloped, with a tiny population mostly clustered along the coast.

Throughout the 18th and 19th centuries, African slaves were brought to British Honduras. The slave period was marked by several revolts and uprisings. Black Caribs, today known as Garífuna, also migrated here from the Bay Islands of Honduras, although they originally hailed from the Caribbean island of St. Vincent. Beginning in the early 1800s, the Garífuna established their own villages and culture along the southern coast, predominantly in the towns of Dangriga and Punta Gorda.

Mayan Sites in Belize

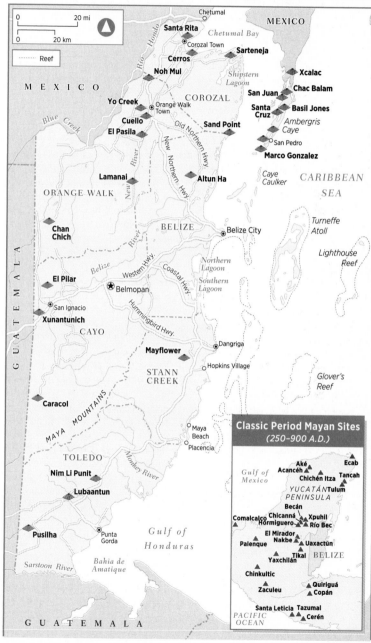

0   20 mi
0   20 km

------- Reef

Chetumal

MEXICO

Santa Rita
Corozal Town
Chetumal Bay

Sarteneja

Cerros

Noh Mul

Shipstern Lagoon

MEXICO

Yo Creek
Orange Town
Orange Walk

COROZAL

Xcalac

Chac Balam

San Juan

Santa Cruz

Basil Jones

Ambergris Caye

Cuello

El Pasila

Sand Point

San Pedro

Marco Gonzalez

Blue Creek

Old Northern Hwy.

Lamanai

Altun Ha

Caye Caulker

CARIBBEAN SEA

ORANGE WALK

New River

New Northern Hwy.

Chan Chich

BELIZE

Belize City

Turneffe Atoll

Northern Lagoon

Lighthouse Reef

El Pilar

Belize River

Western Hwy.

★ Belmopan

Coastal Hwy.

Southern Lagoon

San Ignacio

Xunantunich

CAYO

Hummingbird Hwy.

Dangriga

Mayflower

Hopkins Village

Glover's Reef

STANN CREEK

G U A T E M A L A

Caracol

MAYA MOUNTAINS

Maya Beach

Placencia

TOLEDO

Nim Li Punit

Monkey River

Lubaantun

Pusilha

Punta Gorda

Gulf of
Honduras

Sarstoon River

Bahia de
Amatique

G U A T E M A L A

Classic Period Mayan Sites
(250–900 A.D.)

*Gulf of
Mexico*

Aké
Acancéh
Chichén Itza

Ecab

Tancah

*YUCATÁN
PENINSULA*

Tulum

Becán

Comalcalco
Hormiguero
Chicanná

Xpuhil
Río Bec

El Mirador
Nakbe

Palenque

Uaxactún

BELIZE

Tikal
Yaxchilán

Chinkultic

Zaculeu

Quiriguá
Copán

Santa Leticia

Tazumal
Cerén

*PACIFIC
OCEAN*

Place Your Bet

Whether or not you're the gambling type, you'll want to wager a few bucks on a **chicken drop**. This very loose variation on roulette involves wagering on a number written on a wooden board. Above the board is a wire cage. Once all the bets are in, a chicken is placed in the cage, and the number where the chicken's poop lands wins the pot. The "lucky" winner, however, usually must clean up the board before collecting. There's a chicken drop every Wednesday night at 6pm at the **Pier Lounge** (p. 132) at the Spindrift Hotel.

The Abolition Act of 1833 abolished slavery throughout the British Empire, and former Belizean slaves and Garífuna villagers slowly began to integrate into the economic and cultural life of this budding colony.

During the mid–19th century, many Mexican and Guatemalan refugees of the bloody Caste Wars fled across the borders into British Honduras and founded such towns as Corozal Town and Benque Viejo. A century later, further waves of Guatemalan, Salvadoran, and Honduran refugees, who were fleeing civil wars and right-wing death squads, immigrated to Belize during the 1970s and 1980s.

From Independence to the Present

In the early 1960s, groundwork was laid by the People's United Party for granting British Honduras independence. In 1973, the country's name was officially changed to Belize. Although the 1964 constitution granted self-government to the British colony, it was not until September 21, 1981, that Belize finally gained its true independence, making it Central America's newest nation. The delay was primarily due to Guatemala's claim on the territory. Guatemala actually sent troops into the border Petén Province several times during the 1970s. Fearful of an invasion by Guatemalan forces, the British delayed granting full independence until an agreement could be reached with Guatemala. Although to this day no final agreement has actually been inked, tensions cooled enough to allow for the granting of full sovereignty in 1981. British troops officially pulled out of Belize in 1994. The British legacy in Belize is a relatively stable government with a parliamentary system and regular elections that are contested by two major parties and several smaller parties. The country is still a member of the Commonwealth.

It was big news when oil was discovered near the Mennonite community of Spanish Lookout in 2005. It has quickly become a major export and economic boon, with international crude prices helping substantially on that front. The country currently exports approximately 3,500 barrels of oil per day.

THE LAY OF THE LAND

Belize is a narrow strip of land on the Caribbean coast of Central America, located due south of Mexico's Yucatán Peninsula. It covers an area of just under 23,210 sq. km (9,000 sq. miles), about the same size as the state of Massachusetts, and is bordered on the west and south by Guatemala and on the east by the Caribbean Sea. Offshore from mainland Belize are hundreds of tiny islands, known as cayes (pronounced "keys"), which rise from the world's second-longest barrier reef, which extends for more than 298km (185 miles) along the Belizean coast. From the broad, flat coastal plains, Belize rises to form the **Maya Mountains,** mountain peaks of more than 914m (3,000 ft.) and the source of the many rivers that wind through the country. For centuries these rivers were the principal means of transportation within Belize. Moreover, most of these mountains are limestone karst formations, which has left them coursed with caves, caverns, and underground rivers.

Even though much of Belize's primary forest and tropical hardwoods were harvested throughout the past 3 centuries, population density has always been extremely low, and the forest reclaims ground quickly. Though Belize lacks much true primary tropical rainforest, it does possess large expanses of tropical moist and lowland secondary rainforest, as well as mangrove, swamp, and even highland pine forests. In fact, nearly 65% of Belize is uninhabited, while more than 20% of the country and its offshore reefs are considered protected land, private reserve, or marine reserve. The combination of a low level of human population and conscious conservation efforts has been a boon for a wide range of flora and fauna.

Flora & Fauna

At least 618 species of migratory and resident birds have been identified in Belize, including the massive jabiru stork, the scarlet macaw, and the keel-billed toucan. Belize is also home to the densest concentration of jaguars on the planet. Revered by the ancient Maya and feared by most jungle dwellers, the jaguar is the largest new-world cat, and can reach more than 1.8m (6 ft.) in length and weigh more than 113kg (250 lb.). The **Cockscomb Basin Wildlife Sanctuary** (p. 165) was created as the world's only jaguar preserve.

In addition to the jaguar, Belizean forests are home to four other wild cats, the puma, ocelot, margay, and jaguarundi, as well as such quintessential jungle dwellers as howler monkeys, green iguanas, and boa constrictors. The tapir is the country's national animal. Also called a mountain cow, the tapir is docile, curious, and entirely vegetarian. Still, these wild creatures stand nearly 1.5m (5 ft.) tall and can weigh more than 227kg (500 lb.).

Bird-watchers will want to visit several of Belize's lowland and offshore sanctuaries, including **Crooked Tree Wildlife Sanctuary** (p. 202), the **Shipstern Nature Reserve** (p. 216), **Río Bravo Conservation Area** (p. 210), and the **Half Moon Caye National Monument** (p. 148).

Off Belize's coast, the barrier reef is a world all its own. Though the cayes are little more than low, flat coral and limestone outcroppings, the myriad of underwater flora and fauna here is truly astounding. Colorful angelfish, parrotfish, and trigger-fish feed on the multicolored coral. Giant sponges provide homes and feeding grounds for hundreds of smaller fish and delicate coral shrimp. Under the rocks and caverns dwell lobsters, moray eels, and octopuses. Larger predators such as sharks and barracudas cruise the reefs for their plentiful prey, while manta and spotted eagle rays glide gracefully over the sand bottoms and conch thrive in the sea grass. The **Gladden Spit** area, off the coast from Placencia, is quickly being recognized as one of the world's top spots to snorkel and dive with giant whale sharks, while Belize's three mid-ocean atolls are wonderlands for a wide range of nature-loving adventurers and travelers.

Although it might seem strange to think of it, the cayes also support a unique and endangered forest environment, the **littoral forest,** as well as rich **mangroves.** These saltwater-tolerant environments are major breeding and life-support grounds for a broad range of fauna.

See "Tips on Health, Safety & Etiquette in the Wilderness" in chapter 5 for additional tips on enjoying Belize's natural wonders, and see chapter 14 for more information on the fauna and flora of Belize.

ART & ARCHITECTURE

With its tiny population and relative isolation from the outside world, Belize lacks the vibrant cultural scene found in larger, more cosmopolitan countries. Still, if you poke around, you'll find some respectable local music, literature, art, and architecture to enjoy. For current information about the arts and what might be happening while you're in Belize, contact the **Belize Arts Council** (© **227-2110**), which is housed in the Bliss Centre for the Performing Arts (p. 98) in Belize City.

Architecture

Only a few colonial buildings of any interest survive in Belize City. Most of the rest have succumbed to the ravages of time or were destroyed in the major hurricanes of 1931 and 1961. The most prominent survivors are the brick **St. John's Cathedral** and the downtown **Paslow Building,** which houses the city's main post office. **Clapboard houses** built on stilts are the most typical architectural feature, and quite a few of these buildings, often painted in the pastel colors that are so popular throughout the Caribbean, can be seen in Belize City and in small towns around the country, but most commonly along the coast and out on the cayes.

If you're looking for classic monumental architecture, however, you're in luck. Stone fares better than wood in these parts. The two tallest structures in Belize remain the Mayan pyramids at **Caracol** and **Xunantunich.** Moreover, the country is dotted with lesser sites, and one almost entirely unexcavated city, **Pilar,** which might prove to be the largest Classic-era Mayan city in the region. For those looking to see perhaps the finest example of Classic Mayan ceremonial architecture, a trip to neighboring Guatemala and the ruins at **Tikal** are a must.

Art

Belizean artists range from folk artists and artisans working in a variety of forms, materials, and traditions to modern painters, sculptors, and ceramicists producing beautiful representational and abstract works.

Out in the western Cayo district, the traditional Mayan arts are kept alive by several talented artisans working in carved slate bas-reliefs. Of these, the **García sisters,** who run a gallery and small museum in the Mountain Pine Ridge area, are the prime proponents.

Perhaps the most vibrant place to look for modern art is Dangriga, where Garífuna painters such as **Benjamín Nicholas** and **Pen Cayetano** have produced wonderful bodies of work depicting local life in a simple style. **Walter Castillo** is another excellent modern painter.

Several galleries in Belize City and San Pedro carry a wide range of locally produced art; see chapters 6 and 7, respectively, for more information.

BELIZE IN BOOKS, FILM & MUSIC
Literature

Belize doesn't have a strong literary tradition. However, most gift shops and bookstores around the country have a small collection of locally produced short stories, poetry, fiction, and nonfiction. In recent years, there has been a trend to resuscitate and transcribe the traditional Mayan and Garífuna tales and folklore, along with the publication of modern pieces of fiction and nonfiction either set in Belize or written by Belizeans.

RECOMMENDED BOOKS

For a good, comprehensive look at the country's history, check out *Understanding Belize: A Historical Guide* (Harbour Publishing, 2006), by Alan Twigg. For a more firsthand, somewhat opinionated and local take on the subject, you could turn to Assad Shoman's *Thirteen Chapters of a History of Belize* (Angelus Press, 2000).

If you're more interested in a mix of modern history and the environment, don't miss *The Last Flight of the Scarlet Macaw* ★★ (Random House, 2008), by Bruce Barcott, which tells the story of Sharon Matola's fight to stop the Chalillo dam on the Macal River. Matola is the founder and director of the Belize Zoo, and the dam destroyed important habitat of the fragile and endangered Belizean macaw population. The book is far more interesting and better written than the above description might lead you to believe.

To prepare your eyes for possible sensory overload when you arrive in Belize, you may want to get your hands on a copy of Thor Janson's coffee-table book of photography, *Belize: Land of the Free by the Carib Sea* ★★ (Bowen and Bowen Ltd., 2000). This book is chock-full of beautiful photos of Belizean countryside, wildlife, local festivities, and people.

If the wildlife and nature pictures in Janson's book move you and leave you anxious to see the real deal, there are a slew of books dedicated to observing the wonders of Belizean flora and fauna. Updated and reissued in 2004, Les Beletsky's *Belize and Northern Guatemala: The Ecotravellers' Wildlife Guide* ★★ (Natural World Academic Press, 2004), which features descriptions and color plates of most of the commonly spotted mammals, birds, amphibians, reptiles, fish, and corals, is probably the best all-around field guide for first-timers and armchair naturalists. Those with more specific interests in, say, birds, butterflies, or ocean species can find any number of more specific field guides.

Jaguar: One Man's Struggle to Establish the World's First Jaguar Preserve (Island Press, 2000), by Alan Rabinowitz, is an account of the author's time in Belize studying and working to protect jaguars. As you might have already guessed from the title, Rabinowitz was a major force in the establishment of the world's first jaguar preserve in the Cockscomb Basin Wildlife Sanctuary.

Maya-philes will want to have some reference material handy when visiting the many Belizean ruins. *The Maya* ★ (Thames and Hudson, 2005), by Michael D. Coe, is a good primer on the history of this advanced and enigmatic culture, as is *Chronicle of the Maya Kings and Queens* (Thames and Hudson, 2005), by Simon Martin and Nicolai Grube. However, I find *A Forest of Kings: The Untold Story of the Ancient Maya* ★★ (Harper Perennial, 1992), by David Freidel and Linda Schele, to be a better read, and one that gives a good feel for what life might have been like in the Mayan world. To delve into the intricacy and reasoning behind the Mayan aesthetic legacy, check out Mary Ellen Miller's book, **Maya Art and Architecture** (Thames and Hudson, 1999). Anabel Ford has published a helpful pamphlet/book titled **The Ancient Maya of Belize: Their Society and Sites** that is available at many bookstores and gift shops in Belize.

There is also a host of excellent books on the Maya and Tikal. **Tikal: An Illustrated History of the Ancient Maya Capital** ★, by John Montgomery (Hippocrene Books, 2001), is a good place to start. **The Lords of Tikal: Rulers of an Ancient Maya City** (Thames & Hudson, 2000), by Peter D. Harrison et al., is a similar option.

The history of Ix Chel Farm is chronicled in **Sastun: My Apprenticeship with a Maya Healer** ★ (HarperOne, 1995), by Rosita Arvigo, who spent years studying with Mayan bush doctor Don Elijio Panti. If this book on Belizean natural medicine doesn't satisfy your shamanistic tendencies, don't fret; there are several additional books on the subject. Check out **One Hundred Healing Herbs of Belize** (Lotus Press, 1993), by Arvigo and Michael Balick; or **Rainforest Home Remedies: The Maya Way to Heal Your Body and Replenish Your Soul** ★ (HarperOne, 2001), by Rosita Arvigo and Nadine Epstein.

Belize, A Novel ★ (BookSurge Publishing, 2008), by Carlos Ledson Miller, is a lively novel covering 4 decades of life in a family, beginning with the disastrous consequences and events of Hurricane Hattie. Meanwhile, **Belize Survivor: The Darker Side of Paradise** ★★ (NK Marketing, 2007), by Nancy Koerner, is a stark and well-written account of a woman's personal struggle with spousal abuse, set within the framework of an expatriation to Belize.

If you're bringing along the little ones, or even if you're leaving them behind but want to share a little bit of Mayan culture, look for Pat Mora's beautifully illustrated book **The Night the Moon Fell: A Maya Myth** ★ (Groundwood Books, 2000). Or, for a handy little picture book filled with photographs of Mayan daily life, check out **Hands of the Maya: Villagers at Work and Play** (Henry Holt & Company, 2002), by Rachel Crandell. Older children and adults alike should read **Beka Lamb** ★ (Heinemann, 1986), by Zee Edgell; it's a beautiful coming-of-age story by one of Belize's most prolific modern fiction writers.

Music

The most distinctive and popular form of Belizean music you will come across is **Punta** and **Punta Rock.** Punta is similar to many Afro-Caribbean and Afro-pop music forms, blending traditional rhythms and drumming patterns with modern electronic instruments (Punta is usually more rootsy and acoustic than Punta Rock, which features electric guitars and keyboards). Pen Cayetano is often credited as being the founder of Punta Rock; you will find his discs and cassettes for sale throughout Belize, as well as those by his successors Andy Palacio, the Garífuna Kids, Travesia Band, Peter Flores (aka Titiman), and Chico Ramos. Punta music is usually sung in the Garífuna dialect, although the latest incarnations feature lyrics in English and even Spanish. Dancing to Punta and Punta Rock is sensuous and close, often settling into a firm butt-to-groin grind.

Paranda is another modern yet more traditional offshoot of Garífuna music and culture. Featuring acoustic guitars and rhythm ensembles, paranda is a lively, syncopated musical form. Paul "Nabby" Nabor is a popular paranda artist. A similar

Perhaps the best known and most popular proponent of Punta music, Andy Palacio, died on January 19, 2008, at the age of 48. In addition to his musical fame, Palacio, who was born in the southern village of Barranco, was a tireless prominent proponent of all facets of Garífuna culture. His final album, *Wátina,* was released in 2007 to critical acclaim and was awarded the prestigious WOMEX award for World Music.

and rootsy form of contemporary folk music that comes from the Kriol tradition is known as **brukdown.**

In northern and western Belize, near the Mexican and Guatemalan borders, the local **mestizo** musical forms reflect their Spanish roots with marimba bands and Spanish-language folk songs influenced by the mariachi and ranchero traditions.

There is very little in the way of a club or live music scene in Belize. However, at the hotels in the southern Garífuna region, you are likely to be treated to a performance of traditional Garífuna drumming and dance, and at a few clubs around Belize City, San Pedro, and other popular tourist destinations, you should be able to find various rock, reggae, and Punta Rock bands playing.

The best online sources I've found for Belizean music are www.stonetreerecords.com and www.calabashmusic.com. I'd avoid the various vendors selling bootleg cassettes and CDs on the side of the road, since the quality can be sketchy, and the artists don't receive a dime.

Film

Although it wasn't a box-office hit, you might want to rent a copy of *The Mosquito Coast* (1986), which was filmed in Belize. Starring Harrison Ford and River Phoenix and directed by Peter Weir, the film is about an inventor who relocates his family to the Central American jungle. Other films shot in Belize include *Dogs of War* (1980), which features Christopher Walken, and *Heart of Darkness* (1994), with John Malkovich.

Perhaps the most relevant and readily available film for most tourists is *Three Kings of Belize* (Stonetree Records, 2007). Directed by Katia Paradis, this documentary provides an intimate look into the lives of Belizean musicians Paul Nabor, Florencio Mess, and Wilfred Peters. All three of these men are distinct. Nabor is a Garífuna singer, songwriter, and guitarist; Mess plays a traditional Mayan harp; and the recently deceased Kriol accordionist Mr. Peters was known across Belize as the "King of Brukdown." You will find *Three Kings of Belize* on DVD for sale at bookstores and gift shops all over Belize.

Another good DVD selection is *Sastun* (Create Space, 2009), Guido Verweyen's documentary look into the relationship between Rosita Arvigo and famed Mayan healer Don Elijio Panti. This provides an excellent compliment to Arvigo's book (see above).

BELIZEAN FOOD & DRINK

While it is hard to pin down any truly distinctive Belizean cuisine, what you will find in Belize is a mix of Caribbean, Mexican, African, Spanish, and Mayan culinary influences. You'll also find burgers, pizzas, Chinese food, and even Indian restaurants.

Belize's strongest suit is its **seafood.** Fresh fish, lobster, shrimp, and conch are widely available, especially in the beach and island destinations. Belize has historically been a major exporter of lobster, but overharvesting has caused the population to decline. It is still readily available and relatively inexpensive, but there is a lobster season, from June 15 to February 14.

Rice and beans is a major staple, often served as an accompaniment to almost any main dish. A slight difference is to be inferred between "rice and beans," which are usually cooked (sometimes in coconut milk) and served together, and "beans and rice," which are usually cooked and served separately. Belizeans tend to use a small red bean, but black beans are sometimes used.

Aside from rice and beans, if there were such a thing as a national dish it would be **stew chicken** and its close cousins stew beef and stew fish. These Kriol-based recipes are dark stews that get their color from a broad mix of spices, as well as red *recado,* which is made from annatto seed or achiote. A similar and related stew commonly found around Belize is **chimole,** which is sometimes called black gumbo.

Perhaps the most distinctive element of Belizean cuisine and dining is **Marie Sharp's Hot Sauce.** Almost no dining table is complete without a bottle of Marie Sharp's. The original Marie Sharp's is a very spicy sauce made from a base of habanero peppers, carrots, and onions. Currently, Marie Sharp's has a wide range of different hot sauces, jams, and chutneys. If you have a hankering for the hot stuff, you will find that your options aren't confined to Marie Sharp's. In many restaurants, you will often see a jar of habanero peppers and onions marinating in simple white vinegar. Marie Sharp's original sauce was named **Melinda's;** however, she no longer has anything to do with Melinda's (it's not even made in Belize anymore). One other local hot sauce you might see is **Lizette's,** which is also quite good.

A new local product to look out for is homemade organic chocolate, which you'll see in supermarkets and gift shops around the country under the label **Goss Chocolate** (www.gosschocolate.com).

Meals & Dining Customs

Belizeans tend to eat three meals a day, in similar fashion and hours to North Americans. Breakfast tends to be served between 6:30 and 9am; lunch, between noon and 2pm; and dinner, between 6 and 10pm. Most meals and dining experiences are quite informal. In fact, there are only a few restaurants in the entire country that could be considered semiformal, and none requires a jacket or tie, although you could certainly wear them.

I have separated restaurant listings throughout this book into three price categories based on the average cost per person of a meal, including tax and service charge. The categories are **Expensive,** more than BZ$50; **Moderate,** BZ$20 to BZ$50; and **Inexpensive,** less than BZ$20. Note, however, that individual items in the listings— entrees, for instance—do not include the sales or service taxes. Keep in mind that there is an additional 12.5% GST tax, and a 10% service charge is often added. Belizeans rarely tip, but that doesn't mean you shouldn't. If the service is particularly good and attentive, you should probably leave a little extra.

FOOD

BREAKFAST The typical breakfast in Belize is quite simple, usually anchored by some scrambled eggs and refried red or black beans. However, instead of toast, you will often have a choice of tortillas, **johnnycakes,** or **fry jacks** to accompany them. A johnnycake is a semidry, baked, round flour biscuit, served with butter or stuffed with ham and/or cheese. Fry jacks are a similar batter and shape, but deep-fried, and either served as is or dusted with confectioner's sugar. The most common tortillas served in Belize are corn tortillas.

APPETIZERS   **Conch fritters** are by far the country's most popular and tastiest appetizer. These deep-fried balls of flour batter and chopped conch meat are on most bar and restaurant menus in the country, particularly on the cayes and along the coast. Try some.

SANDWICHES & SNACKS   Belize's light menus show a heavy Mexican and American influence. Many simple eateries and roadside carts will feature simple tacos, tamales (also called *dukunu*), or **garnaches.** The latter, a fried corn tortilla topped with beans, cheese, or shredded meat or chicken, would probably be considered a tostada by many. Popular stuffed pastries include meat pies and *panades,* small, deep-fried empanadas.

You can also get traditional sandwiches, often served on sliced white bread, as well as American-style burgers. I personally recommend looking for fish, shrimp, or conch burgers, which are available at most beach and island destinations.

MEAT, POULTRY & WILD GAME   Belizeans also eat a fair amount of meat and poultry, as well as some more interesting game. Because Belize only recently began to raise its own beef, the country relied for a long time on wild game. Some of the more interesting game items you might see on a Belizean menu include **gibnut** (paca) and **iguana.** The gibnut is a large rodent, *Agouti paca,* which some say tastes like rabbit, although I find it a bit gamier. Iguana is frequently called "bamboo chicken," and it does actually taste a bit like chicken. Occasionally, you may also come across wild boar, armadillo, or some other forest-dwelling creature.

 The Queen's Rat

The gibnut is often called "The Queen's Rat" or "The Royal Rat" because Queen Elizabeth was served gibnut during a visit here. Headlines in London read "Queen Eats Rat."

Another popular wild animal found in restaurants is the **sea turtle,** endangered all over the world, including in Belize. It's not yet illegal to sell sea turtle within Belize, but international agreements prohibit its export. Please don't order turtle steak, turtle soup, or turtle eggs. In fact, I'm a little hesitant to recommend the eating of wild game at all. So far, there's no reliable data on the impact that the hunting of wild game has had or could have, but there is reason for concern. Belize is struggling to preserve its natural environment, and as long as people order wild game, it will continue to show up on menus. Exceptions would be any farm-raised wild animals, such as iguanas. When harvested from commercial "iguana farms," this wild game actually has the potential to mix sustainable yield with modern conservation.

SEAFOOD   Seafood is the basic staple of most of the country's coastal and island destinations. It is fresh and plentiful. Shrimp, conch, lobster (in season), and a variety of fish are almost always on the menu. You're best off sticking to simple preparations, either grilled or fried. My favorite fishes are grouper, snapper, and dorado (or mahimahi). You will also come across barracuda, shark, and marlin. You'll rarely find **snook** on the menu, and if so, you should definitely try this delicate white fish.

If you are in a Garífuna region, you should not miss the chance to try **hudut,** a fish stew or whole fish preparation served in a coconut-milk broth, often accompanied by mashed, fried green plantains. **Sere** is a very similar Kriol dish that seems more like a traditional fish or seafood stew, but again, based on a coconut-milk broth.

Ceviche, a cold marinade of fish, conch, and/or shrimp "cooked" in lime juice and seasoned, is a great treat for lunch or as an appetizer.

VEGETABLES On the whole, you'll find vegetables surprisingly lacking in Belizean meals. Fresh garden salads are rare and hard to come by. A lack of fresh ingredients makes other vegetable dishes and sides almost as uncommon. Most restaurant meals come accompanied by a simple slaw of grated cabbage, or a potato or beet salad.

FRUITS Belize has a wealth of delicious tropical fruits. The most common are mangoes (the season begins in May), papayas, pineapples, melons, and bananas. Other fruits you might find include the **fruit of the cashew tree,** which has orange or yellow glossy skin, and **carambola** (star fruit), a tart fruit whose cross sections form perfect stars.

DESSERTS Belize doesn't have a very extravagant or refined dessert culture. After all, the country was colonized by the British, not the French. However, you can find homemade coconut pie, chocolate pie, or bread pudding on most menus. Flan, an egg-and-condensed-milk custard imported from Mexico, is also popular.

DRINKS

BEVERAGES Most major brands of soft drinks are available, as are fresh lime juice (limeade) and orange juice. You're in the tropics, so expect to find fresh shakes made with papaya, pineapple, or mango.

One of the most unique drinks you're likely to sample anywhere is a **seaweed shake,** a cooling concoction made of dried seaweed, evaporated and condensed milk, cinnamon, and nutmeg, and blended with ice. Seaweed shakes are sometimes kicked up with a shot of rum or brandy.

WATER Much of the drinking water in Belize is **rainwater.** People use the roofs of their houses to collect water in a cistern, which supplies them for the year. Tap water isn't generally considered safe to drink, even in most cities and popular tourist towns. The water in Belize City and San Ignacio is relatively safe to drink, but travelers often get a touch of diarrhea whenever they hit a foreign country, so always play it safe. Ask for bottled drinking water at your hotel, and whenever you can, pick up a bottle of spring or purified water (available in most markets) to have handy.

BEER, WINE & LIQUOR The Belize Brewing Company's **Belikin** beer is the national beer of Belize. It comes in several varieties, including Belikin Lager, Belikin Premium, and Belikin Stout. The recipes and original brew masters all came from Germany. Both the lager and the premium are full-bodied, hearty beers. The Belikin brewery also bottles a **locally produced Guinness Stout,** as thick and rich as its brand name demands.

As you'll find throughout the Caribbean, rum is the liquor of choice in Belize. There are several brands and distilleries producing rum in Belize. Probably the finest Belizean rum is the 5-year-aged **Prestige.** One of the most popular brands you'll come across is **1 Barrel,** which has a hint of vanilla, and is slightly sweet for my taste.

Belize doesn't produce any traditional wines of note. The climate and soil are not very well suited for growing the right kinds of grapes. On Ambergris Caye, the **Rendezvous Restaurant & Winery** (p. 132) does in fact import grape juice for the purpose of producing and bottling their own wines, although they are really more of a novelty than a delicacy.

Several different **fruit wines** are produced in Belize using native fruits, including pineapple and even banana. These wines are very sweet and are more a novelty than anything else. In remote parts of the country, you'll find homemade fruit wines that are a bit like hard cider.

PLANNING YOUR TRIP TO BELIZE

3

Belize offers a wealth of vacation options, including sun-and-fun beach time, dedicated scuba diving or fishing trips, and themed vacations exploring the ancient Mayan culture and archaeology. Moreover, given the compact size of the country, it's very possible to cover a lot of ground in a short time, and to mix and match these options. Whatever your interests, this chapter (as well as chapter 5) will provide you with all the tools and information necessary to plan and book your trip.

WHEN TO GO

Belize's high season for tourism runs from late November to late April, which coincides almost perfectly with the chill of winter in the United States, Canada, and Great Britain. The high season is also the dry season. If you want some unadulterated time on a tropical beach and a little less rain during your rainforest experience, this is the time to visit. During this period (and especially around the Christmas and Easter holidays), the tourism industry operates at full tilt—prices are higher, attractions are more crowded, and reservations need to be made in advance.

The weather in Belize is subtropical and generally similar to that of southern Florida. The average daytime temperature on the coast and cayes is around 80°F (27°C), although it can get considerably warmer during the day during the summer months. During the winter months, when northern cold fronts extend their grip south, it can get downright nippy. In fact, from late December to February, "northers" can hit the coastal and caye areas hard, and hang around for between 3 and 5 days, putting a severe crimp in any beach vacation. The best months for guaranteed sun and fun are March through May.

The rainy season runs from June to mid-November, while the hurricane season runs from July to October, with the most active months being August, September, and October. For the most part, the rainy season is characterized by a dependable and short-lived afternoon shower. However, the amount of rainfall varies considerably with the regions. In the south, there may be more than 150 inches of rain per year, while in the north, it rarely rains more than 50 inches per year. Usually there is also a brief dry period in mid-August, known as the *mauger*. If you're skittish about rain and hurricanes, don't come to Belize between late August and mid-October, the height of both the rainy and hurricane seasons. However, if you do come, you should be able to land some good bargains.

The Cayo District and other inland destinations tend to be slightly cooler than the coastal and caye destinations, although since there is generally little elevation gain, the differences tend to be slight.

Average Monthly Temperatures & Rainfall in Belize

	JAN	FEB	MAR	APR	MAY	JUNE	JULY	AUG	SEP	OCT	NOV	DEC
Temp (°F)	73	76	78	80	82	82	82	82	81	79	75	74
Temp (°C)	23	24	26	27	28	28	28	28	27	26	24	23
Days of Rain	12	6	4	5	7	13	15	14	15	16	12	14

Public Holidays

Official holidays in Belize include **January 1** (New Year's Day), **March 9** (Baron Bliss Day), Good Friday, Holy Saturday, Easter Sunday, Easter Monday, **May 1** (Labour Day), **May 24** (Commonwealth Day), **September 10** (St. George's Caye Day), **September 21** (Independence Day), **October 12** (Pan American Day), **November 19** (Garífuna Settlement Day), **December 25** (Christmas Day), **December 26** (Boxing Day), and **December 31** (New Year's Eve).

Government offices and banks are closed on official holidays, transportation services are reduced, and stores and markets may also close.

Belize Calendar of Events

Some of the events listed here might be considered more of a community celebration or tradition than an event—there's not, for instance, a Deer Dance Festival PR Committee that readily dispenses information. If I haven't listed a contact number, your best bet is to call the **Belize Tourism Board** at © **800/624-0286** in the U.S. and Canada, or 227-2420 in Belize, or visit www.travelbelize.org for additional information.

For an exhaustive list of events beyond those listed here, check http://events.frommers.com, where you'll find a searchable, up-to-the-minute roster of what's happening in cities all over the world.

JANUARY

Krem New Year's Cycling Classic. This New Year's Day road race starts in Corozal Town and ends in Belize City. The competitors are mostly Belizean, although Guatemalan and Mexican teams occasionally enter. The winners usually take around 3½ to 4 hours to cross the finish line; crowds usually form at the start and finish points. January 1.

FEBRUARY

International Billfish Tournament. Hosted by the Radisson Fort George Hotel and Marina (© **800/333-3333** in the U.S., or 223-3333; www.radisson.com), this multiday event features cash prizes. Early February.

Valentine's Day Cycle Race. This is Belize's premier road race. Starting in San Ignacio, cyclists pedal to Benque Viejo, turn around, and race all the way back to Belize City. For more information, check out **www.belizecycling.com**. February 14.

Carnival. Nationwide celebrations during the week before Lent. Larger towns have parades and dance competitions. In San Pedro, watch out for getting "painted."

MARCH

La Ruta Maya Belize River Challenge. This 4-day canoe race begins in San Ignacio in the Cayo District and ends at the Swing Bridge in Belize City. For more details, visit www.larutamayabelize.com. March 6 to 9.

Baron Bliss Day. The day is marked with nationwide celebrations of Belize's benefactor. The greatest festivities are held in Belize City, which hosts a regatta, as well as horse- and footraces. March 9.

MAY

Labour Day. After a national address by the prime minister or minister of labor (carried on all local radio and television stations), the rest of Labour Day is filled with street celebrations, regattas, and horse races. May 1.

Cashew Festival, Crooked Tree Village. Celebrating the cashew harvest, this weekend celebration features local booths selling everything possible under the sun made with this coveted nut, including cashew wine and cashew jelly. Live music and general revelry accompany the celebrations. First weekend in May.

National Agriculture & Trade Show, Belmopan. This national fair is geared toward farmers, cattle ranchers, large-scale agribusiness, and buyers, but it's still an interesting event to tour or visit if you're in the country at the time. Mid-May.

Toledo Cacao Fest, Punta Gorda. Chocolate lovers should head to southern Belize in late May for this festival. In addition to food and desserts, there are concerts, games, parades, and tour activities planned. For exact dates, see www.toledochocolate.com.

JUNE

Día de San Pedro, San Pedro, Ambergris Caye. This is a 3-day celebration of the island's patron saint, Saint Peter, or San Pedro. Boats are blessed, and there are parades and processions. June 27 to 29.

Lobster Festival, Placencia. During this extended weekend celebration of the opening of lobster season, this beach town pulls out all the stops. There's plenty of lobster to be had in a variety of preparations, at temporary outdoor stalls and restaurants around town. There are also concerts and dancing and an arts fair. Check www.placencia.com for the latest details. Late June.

JULY

Lobster Festival, Caye Caulker. Not to be outdone by Placencia, Caye Caulker also puts on a long weekend celebration of the start of lobster season. Food, music, and dancing are all served up in hearty portions around town. Early July.

AUGUST

Costa Maya Festival, San Pedro, Ambergris Caye. This is perhaps the largest festival in the country. Drawing participants from the neighboring countries of El Salvador, Mexico, Guatemala, and Honduras, this celebration features a steady stream of live concert performances, street parades, beauty pageants, and water shows and activities. Early August.

Deer Dance Festival, San Antonio, Toledo District. This 9-day Mayan festival is celebrated in the small Mayan village of San Antonio. Highlights include costumed and dance performances. Late August to early September.

SEPTEMBER

Independence Day. Patriotic parades and official celebrations are mixed with street parties, beauty pageants, and open-air concerts. September 21.

OCTOBER

Pan American Day. Formerly known as Columbus Day, this day now celebrates mestizo and Mayan culture with parades, street fairs, and concerts. October 12.

NOVEMBER

Garífuna Settlement Day. The greatest Garífuna celebration occurs in Dangriga, where Garífunas from across Belize and throughout the region gather to commemorate their arrival from St. Vincent in 1832. Street parades, religious ceremonies, and dance and drumming performances are all part of the celebrations throughout the southern coastal zone. November 19.

DECEMBER

Boxing Day. While Christmas Day is predominantly for family in Belize, Boxing Day is a chance to continue the celebration with friends, neighbors, and strangers. Dances, concerts, horse races, and general festivities are put on around the country. December 26.

ENTRY REQUIREMENTS
Passports

A current passport, valid through your departure date, is required for entry into Belize. Driver's licenses and birth certificates are not valid travel documents. In some cases you may be asked to show an onward or return plane ticket.

VISAS

No visas are required for citizens of the United States, the European community (including Ireland), Great Britain, South Africa, Australia, or New Zealand. Nationals of certain other countries do need a visa or consular permission to enter Belize. For a current list, see the Belize Tourism Board website (www.travelbelize.org), or call the nearest Belizean consulate or embassy.

Tourists are permitted a maximum stay of 30 days. The **Belize Department of Immigration and Nationality** in Belmopan (© **822-2423**) will sometimes grant an extension of up to 3 months. These extensions are handled on a case-by-case basis and cost BZ$25 for a maximum extension of 3 months.

If you have additional travel or visa questions about Belize, you can contact any of the following Belizean embassies or consulates: in the **United States** or **Canada,** 2535 Massachusetts Ave. NW, Washington, DC 20008 (© **202/332-9636;** www.embassyofbelize.org); in **Great Britain,** Belize High Commission, 22 Harcourt House, 45 Crawford Place, London, W1H 4LP (© **020/7723-3603;** www.belizehighcommission.com); and in **Australia,** 5/1 Oliver Rd., Roseville NSW (© **02/9905-8144**). There is no Belizean embassy or consulate in New Zealand.

For information on how to get a passport, go to "Passports" in the "Fast Facts" section of chapter 12—the websites listed provide downloadable passport applications as well as the current fees for processing passport applications. For an up-to-date, country-by-country listing of passport requirements around the world, go to the "Foreign Entry Requirement" Web page of the U.S. State Department at **http://travel.state.gov**.

Customs

WHAT YOU CAN BRING INTO BELIZE

Visitors to Belize may bring with them any and all reasonable goods and belongings for personal use during their stay. Cameras, computers, and electronic equipment, as well as fishing and diving gear for personal use, are permitted duty-free. Customs officials in Belize seldom check arriving tourists' luggage.

WHAT YOU CAN TAKE HOME FROM BELIZE

It is expressly illegal to take out any pre-Columbian artifact from Belize, whether you bought it, you discovered it, or it was given to you. Do not traffic in Maya artifacts.

For information on what you're allowed to bring home, contact one of the following agencies:

U.S. Citizens: U.S. Customs & Border Protection (CBP), 1300 Pennsylvania Ave. NW, Washington, DC 20229 (✆ **877/287-8667;** www.cbp.gov).

Canadian Citizens: Canada Border Services Agency, Ottawa, Ontario, K1A 0L8 (✆ **800/461-9999** in Canada, or 204/983-3500; www.cbsa-asfc.gc.ca).

U.K. Citizens: HM Customs & Excise, Crownhill Court, Tailyour Road, Plymouth, PL6 5BZ (✆ **0845/010-9000,** or 020/8929-0152 from outside the U.K.; www.hmce.gov.uk).

Australian Citizens: Australian Customs Service, Customs House, 5 Constitution Ave., Canberra City, ACT 2601 (✆ **1300/363-263,** or 612/6275-6666 from outside Australia; www.customs.gov.au).

New Zealand Citizens: New Zealand Customs, The Customhouse, 17–21 Whitmore St., Box 2218, Wellington, 6140 (✆ **04/473-6099** or 0800/428-786; www.customs.govt.nz).

Medical Requirements

No shots or inoculations are required to enter Belize. For more on medical concerns and recommendations, see "Health," p. 44.

GETTING THERE & GETTING AROUND

Getting There

BY PLANE

Belize City's **Philip S. W. Goldson International Airport** (✆ **225-2045;** www. pgiabelize.com; airport code BZE) is serviced by several airlines out of major U.S. hubs. **American Airlines, Continental, Delta, Grupo Taca,** and **US Airways** all have regular direct service to Belize. Flying time from Miami is just more than 2 hours.

There are no direct flights to Belize from Europe, Australia, New Zealand, mainland Asia, or Africa. From Canada, the only direct flights are seasonal winter charters. To get to Belize from any of these points of origin, you will have to connect through one of the U.S. hubs.

For additional help in booking your air travel to Belize, see chapter 12.

GETTING INTO TOWN FROM THE AIRPORT

The **Philip S. W. Goldson International Airport** is located 16km (10 miles) northwest of the city on the Northern Highway. There is no public bus service or shuttle van service. However, taxis are there to meet every flight. A taxi into town will cost BZ$50 to BZ$60.

By Cruise Ship

As many as one million tourists stop in Belize as part of a cruise itinerary per year. All ships call at Belize City and offer a wide range of day-tour options around the country. Cruise lines that offer stops in Belize as part of their Caribbean and Panama Canal routes include **Celebrity Cruises** (✆ 800/760-0654; www.celebritycruises.com), **Crystal Cruises** (✆ 888/722-0021; www.crystalcruises.com), **Holland America**

(© 877/932-4259; www.hollandamerica.com), **Norwegian Cruise Lines** (© 866/234-7650; www.ncl.com), **Princess** (© 800/774-6237; www.princess.com), **Radisson Seven Seas Cruises** (© 877/505-5370; www.rssc.com), **Royal Caribbean** (© 866/562-7625; www.rccl.com), and **Silver Sea Cruises** (© 800/722-9955; www.silversea.com).

It might pay off to book through a travel agency that specializes in cruises; these companies buy in bulk and stay on top of the latest specials and promotions. Try the **Cruise Company** (© 800/289-5505; www.thecruisecompany.com) or **World Wide Cruises** (© 800/882-9000; www.worldwidecruises.com).

Getting Around

BY PLANE

Traveling around Belize by commuter airline is common, easy, and relatively economical. Two local commuter airlines serve all the major tourist destinations around Belize. The carriers are **Maya Island Air** (© 223-1140; www.mayaairways.com) and **Tropic Air** (© 800/422-3435 in the U.S. or Canada, or 226-2012 in Belize; www.tropicair.com). They operate out of both the **Philip S. W. Goldson International Airport** and the Belize City **Municipal Airport.** In both cases, flights are considerably less expensive into and out of the Municipal Airport. See the destination chapters for specific details on schedules and costs.

BY CAR

There are only four major roads in Belize: the Northern, Western, Southern, and Hummingbird highways. All are just two-lane affairs, and all actually have speed bumps as they pass through various towns and villages along their way. Belize is only 113km or so (70 miles) wide, and around 402km (250 miles) long. Renting a car is an excellent way to see the country. If you are going to the Mountain Pine Ridge area of the Cayo District, or to the Gallon Jug or Lamanai areas, you will certainly need a four-wheel-drive vehicle. However, if you're just visiting the major towns and cities of San Ignacio, Placencia, Corozal, or Punta Gorda, you'll probably be fine in a standard sedan. That said, it's always nice to have the extra clearance and off-road ability of a four-wheel-drive vehicle, particularly during the rainy season (June through mid-Nov).

> ### Hit The Spot
>
> As you drive around Belize, keep an eye out for "cool spots." These roadside stands serve up cold drinks, a bit of shade, and sometimes food. Most are little more than simple shacks or a shady thatch-roof over a few rustic wooden tables and chairs or plastic lawn furniture. Many have colorful names such as Bamboo Cool Spot, Yam Wit Cool Spot, or Last Chance Cool Spot.

Among the major international agencies operating in Belize are **Avis** (© 225-2629; www.avis.com), **Budget** (© 223-2435; www.budget-belize.com), **Hertz** (© 223-5395; www.hertz.com), and **Thrifty** (© 207-1271; www.thrifty.com). **Crystal Auto Rental** ★ (© 0800/777-7777 toll-free in Belize, or 223-1600; www.crystal-belize.com) is a local company, with an excellent fleet and good prices. For a complete list of car-rental agencies and their contact information, see chapter 12, as well as the "Getting Around" sections of other major tourist-destination chapters.

Prices run between BZ$100 and BZ$220 per day for a late-model compact to a compact SUV, including insurance. Most of the rental companies above have a 25-year-old minimum age requirement for renting, although Crystal Auto Rental will rent to 21- to 24-year-olds, but with twice the deductible.

Often included in the price, car-rental insurance runs about BZ$24 to BZ$40 per day with an average deductible of around BZ$1,500, although sometimes for a few extra dollars per day you can get no-fault, no-deductible coverage.

Before driving off with a rental car, be sure that you inspect the exterior and point out to the rental-company representative every tiny scratch, dent, tear, or any other damage.

Note: It's sometimes cheaper to reserve a car in your home country than to book when you arrive in Belize. If you know you'll be renting a car, it's always wise to reserve it well in advance for the high season, as the rental fleet can't match demand.

MAPS   There are so few roads in Belize that you will probably be fine using the maps in this book, or the free maps given out at the airport or by your car-rental agency. If you really want a more detailed map, the Belize map produced by the **International Travel Maps and Books** (www.itmb.com) is a good option. You can get this and other maps at many bookstores and gift shops in Belize if you are unable to buy it in advance either online or at a bookstore near you. Alternatively, you can pick up a copy of Emory King's *Driver's Guide to Beautiful Belize* (Tropical Books, 2003).

GASOLINE   Gas stations can be found in all the major towns and tourist destinations. Gasoline is sold as "unleaded" and "super." Both are unleaded; super is just higher octane. Diesel is available at most gas stations as well. At press time, a gallon of super cost around BZ$10.

DRIVING RULES   A current foreign driver's license is valid for the time you are in Belize. Despite having been a British colony and current member of the Commonwealth, cars drive on the right-hand side of the road, just as in the United States. Seatbelt use is mandatory in Belize, and failure to comply carries a fine. One odd driving law in Belize is that drivers wishing to make a left-hand turn while traveling along any of the country's "highways" must first pull over to the right-hand shoulder until all oncoming and following traffic has cleared.

RENTER'S INSURANCE   Even if you hold **your own car-insurance policy** at home, coverage doesn't always extend abroad. Be sure to find out whether you'll be covered in Belize, whether your policy extends to all persons who will be driving the rental car, how much liability is covered in case an outside party is injured in an accident, and whether the *type* of vehicle you are renting is included under your contract.

Road Distances from Belize City			
Belmopan	84km (52 miles)	Orange Walk Town	89km (55 miles)
Benque Viejo	130km (81 miles)	Placencia	241km (150 miles)
Corozal Town	138km (86 miles)	Punta Gorda	330km (205 miles)
Dangriga	116km (72 miles)	San Ignacio	116km (72 miles)

car-rental TIPS

Most **major credit cards** provide some degree of coverage as well—provided that they were used to pay for the rental. Again, terms vary widely, so be sure to call your credit card company directly before you rent. Usually, if you are **uninsured** or are **driving abroad,** your credit card provides primary coverage as long as you decline the rental agency's insurance. This means that the credit card will cover damage or theft of a rental car for the full cost of the vehicle. If you already have insurance, your credit card will provide secondary coverage, which basically covers your deductible. *Credit cards will not cover liability* or the cost of injury to an outside party and/or damage to an outside party's vehicle.

BREAKDOWNS   Be warned that emergency services, both vehicular and medical, are extremely limited in Belize, and their availability is directly related to the remoteness of your location at the time of breakdown. You'll find service stations spread over the entire length of the major highways, and a fair number of these have tow trucks and mechanics. The major towns of Belize City, Belmopan, Orange Walk, Corozal, Dangriga, Punta Gorda, and San Ignacio all have hospitals, and most other moderately sized cities and tourist destinations have some sort of clinic or health-services provider.

Note: It should go without saying, but you cannot rent a car on or drive to any of the cayes or outer atolls.

BY BUS

Belize has an extensive network of commuter buses serving all of the major villages and towns and tourist destinations in the country. However, this system is used primarily by Belizeans. The buses tend to be a bit antiquated, and buyouts and bankruptcies within the industry have left the status of the local bus network in a state of confusion and limbo. See the destination chapters for specific details on schedules and costs, and be sure to check in advance, or as soon as you arrive, as schedules (and costs) do change regularly.

BY BOAT

While it's possible to fly to a few of the outer cayes, most travel between mainland Belize and the cayes and atolls is done by high-speed launch. There are regular water taxis between Belize City and Ambergris Caye, Caye Caulker, Caye Chapel, and St. George's Caye. Hotels and resorts on the other islands all either have their own boats or can arrange transport for you. See the destination chapters for specific details on how to get to the cayes and atolls by boat.

BY HELICOPTER

Astrum Helicopters ★ (*©* **888/278-7864** in the U.S. and Canada, or 222-5100 in Belize; www.astrumhelicopters.com) has a small fleet of sleek and modern helicopters. They will take you to just about any destination in Belize, including remote lodges, islands, and atolls. They will also take you out on sightseeing tours. Rates run between BZ$2,400 and BZ$7,200, depending upon the distance and number of passengers.

MONEY & COSTS

It's always advisable to bring money in a variety of forms on a vacation: a mix of cash, credit cards, debit cards, and, occasionally, traveler's checks.

Currency

The Belize dollar, abbreviated BZ$, is the official currency of Belize. It is pegged to the U.S. dollar at a ratio of 2 Belize dollars to 1 U.S. dollar. Both currencies are acceptable at almost any business or establishment around the country. As long as you have U.S. dollars or U.S. dollar-based traveler's checks, it is entirely unnecessary to change for Belize dollars in advance of your trip. However, travelers from Canada, Europe, Australia, and New Zealand will want to change a sufficient amount of their home currency to U.S. dollars before traveling. To check the very latest exchange rates before you leave home, point your browser to **www.oanda.com/convert/classic**.

Once you are in Belize, the change you receive will most likely be in Belize dollars, although it is not uncommon for it to be a mix of both currencies. However, do try to have some small-denomination bills for paying taxis, modest meal tabs, and tips.

The branch of the **Belize Bank** (*©* **225-2107**) at the international airport is open only Monday through Friday from 8:30am to 4pm. If you are flying out on a weekend, or outside of these hours, be sure to spend or exchange any Belize dollars beforehand.

Tip: Be careful to note whether the price you are being quoted is in Belize or U.S. dollars. Many hotels, restaurants, and tour operators actually quote in U.S. dollars. If in doubt, ask. At a two-to-one ratio, the difference can be substantial.

US$	Can$	UK£	Euro (€)	Aus$	NZ$
50¢	C$0.51	£0.34	0.41€	A$0.58	NZ$0.72

ATMs

The easiest and best way to get cash away from home is from an ATM (automated teller machine). The **Cirrus** (*©* **800/424-7787;** www.mastercard.com) and **PLUS** (*©* **800/843-7587;** www.visa.com) networks span the globe; look at the back of your bank card to see which network you're on, then call or check online for ATM locations at your destination. Be sure you know your personal identification number (PIN) and daily withdrawal limit before you depart.

Currently, in Belize, you will find internationally accessible ATMs only in major cities or towns and tourist destinations, including Belize City, San Pedro, Caye Caulker, Placencia, Punta Gorda, San Ignacio, Belmopan, Dangriga, and Corozal Town. It's wise to bring some spending cash and charge the rest of your bills. Try not to rely on your ATM card for an emergency cash bailout.

Note: It's probably a good idea to change your PIN to a four-digit PIN. While many ATMs in Belize will accept five- and six-digit PINs, some will accept only four-digit PINs.

WHAT THINGS COST IN BELIZE	BZ$	US$
Taxi from the airport to Belize City	50.00–60.00	25.00–30.00
Local taxi ride	6.00–16.00	3.00–8.00
Water taxi ride to Ambergris Caye	30.00	15.00
One-way flight to San Pedro from Municipal Airport	70.00	35.00
One-way flight to San Pedro from International Airport	126.00	63.00
Double room, expensive	250.00–400.00	125.00–200.00
Double room, moderate	120.00–250.00	60.00–125.00
Double room, inexpensive	50.00–120.00	25.00–60.00
Dinner for one without wine, expensive	80.00	40.00
Dinner for one without wine, moderate	40.00	20.00
Dinner for one, inexpensive	16.00	8.00
Bottle of Belikin beer	3.00–5.00	1.50–2.50
Bottle of Coca-Cola	2.00	1.00
Cup of coffee	1.50	0.75
Gallon of premium gas	10.00	5.00
Admission to most national parks	10.00	5.00
Admission to Belize Zoo	16.00	8.00
Two-tank dive with equipment	150.00–240.00	75.00–120.00
Exit tax	78.50	39.25

Credit Cards

Most major credit cards are accepted in Belize, although MasterCard and Visa are much more widely accepted than American Express, especially by smaller hotels, restaurants, and tour operators. While there are some exceptions, Diners Club and Discover are rarely accepted around Belize.

You can withdraw cash advances from your credit cards at banks or ATMs, but high fees make credit card cash advances a pricey way to get cash. Keep in mind that you'll pay interest from the moment of your withdrawal, even if you pay your monthly bills on time. Also, note that many banks now assess a 1% to 3% "foreign transaction fee" on **all** charges you incur abroad (whether you're using the local currency or your native currency).

Beware of hidden credit-card fees while traveling. Check with your credit or debit card issuer to see what fees, if any, will be charged for overseas transactions. Recent reform legislation in the U.S., for example, has curbed some exploitative lending practices. But many banks have responded by increasing fees in other areas, including fees for customers who use credit and debit cards while out of the country— even if those charges were made in U.S. dollars. Fees can amount to 3% or more of the purchase price. Check with your bank before departing to avoid any surprise charges on your statement.

Some credit card companies recommend that you notify them of any impending trip abroad so that they don't become suspicious when the card is used numerous times in a foreign destination and block your charges. Even if you don't call your credit card company in advance, you can always call the card's toll-free emergency number if a charge is refused—a good reason to carry the phone number with you. But perhaps the most important lesson here is to carry more than one card with you on your trip; a card might not work for any number of reasons, so having a backup is the smart way to go.

If Your Wallet Is Lost or Stolen

For tips and telephone numbers to call if your wallet is stolen or lost, go to "Lost & Found" in the "Fast Facts" of chapter 12.

HEALTH
Staying Healthy

The only major modern hospitals in Belize are located in Belize City, although there are smaller hospitals or clinics in every major town or city. In general, you should bring any prescription drugs you will need with you, although there are reasonably well-stocked pharmacies in most major towns and tourist destinations.

GENERAL AVAILABILITY OF HEALTHCARE

There are two major hospitals in Belize City: **Belize Medical Associates,** 5791 St. Thomas Kings Park (© **223-0303;** www.belizemedical.com), a modern, 24-hour private hospital, with emergency care and numerous private-practice physicians; and the city's main public hospital, the **Karl Heusner Memorial Hospital** on Princess Margaret Drive (© **223-1548**), which is also open 24 hours and has a wide range of facilities and services.

Most of the other towns and major tourist destinations have either a small hospital or a local health clinic, in addition to private-practice doctors. Any foreign consulate can provide a list of area doctors. If you get sick, consider asking your hotel concierge or front desk staff to recommend a local doctor—even his or her own. We list **additional emergency numbers** in the "Fast Facts" section of chapter 12, and I've listed hospitals and emergency numbers under "Fast Facts" in the regional destination chapters.

BEFORE YOU GO

If you suffer from a chronic illness, consult your doctor before your departure. For conditions such as epilepsy, diabetes, or heart problems, wear a **MedicAlert identification tag** (© **888/633-4298;** www.medicalert.org), which will immediately alert doctors to your condition and give them access to your records through MedicAlert's 24-hour hot line.

Pack **prescription medications** in your carry-on luggage, and carry prescription medications in their original containers, with pharmacy labels—otherwise they won't make it through airport security. Also bring along copies of your prescriptions in case you lose your pills or run out. Carry the generic name of prescription medicines, in case a local pharmacist is unfamiliar with the brand name. Don't forget an extra pair of contact lenses or prescription glasses.

If you worry about getting sick away from home, consider purchasing **medical travel insurance** and carry your ID card in your purse or wallet. In most cases, your existing health plan will provide the coverage you need.

COMMON AILMENTS

TROPICAL ILLNESSES   None of the major tropical illnesses is epidemic in Belize, and your chance of contracting any serious tropical disease in the country is slim. However, several mosquito-borne illnesses are present, particularly malaria and dengue.

Although **malaria** is found in Belize, it's far from epidemic. It is most common along the coastal lowlands, as well as in some of the more remote southern inland communities. Malaria prophylaxes are available, but several have side effects, and others are of questionable effectiveness. Consult your doctor as to what is currently considered the best preventive treatment for malaria. Be sure to ask whether a recommended drug will cause you to be hypersensitive to the sun—it would be a shame to come down here for the beaches and then have to hide under an umbrella the whole time. Because malaria-carrying mosquitoes usually come out at night, you should do as much as possible to avoid being bitten after dark. If you are in a malarial area, wear long pants and long sleeves, use insect repellent, and either sleep under a mosquito net or burn mosquito coils (similar to incense but with a pesticide).

Of greater concern may be **dengue fever,** which has had periodic outbreaks in Latin America since the mid-1990s. Dengue fever is somewhat similar to malaria and is spread by an aggressive daytime mosquito. This mosquito seems to be most common in lowland urban areas, and Belize City and Dangriga have been the hardest-hit cities in Belize. Dengue is also known as "bone-break fever" because it is usually accompanied by severe body aches. The first infection with dengue fever will make you very sick but should cause no serious damage. However, a second infection with a different strain of the dengue virus can lead to internal hemorrhaging and may be life-threatening. As with malaria, your best protection is to not get bitten. Use plenty of repellent, and wear light long-sleeved shirts and long pants, especially on bird-watching tours or nature hikes.

Many people are convinced that taking B-complex vitamins daily will help prevent mosquitoes from biting you. I don't think the American Medical Association has endorsed this idea yet, but I've run across it in enough places to think there may be something to it.

DIETARY RED FLAGS   Even though the water around Belize is generally safe, particularly in most of the popular tourist destinations, and even if you're careful to buy and drink only bottled water, you still may encounter some intestinal difficulties. Most of this is just due to tender northern stomachs coming into contact with slightly more aggressive Latin American intestinal flora. In extreme cases of diarrhea or intestinal discomfort, it's worth taking a stool sample to a lab for analysis. The results will usually pinpoint the amoebic or parasitic culprit, which can then be readily treated with available over-the-counter medicines.

If you have any strict dietary restrictions, be it for health, religious, or ethical reasons, be sure to check with your hotel in advance to ensure that you don't starve while on vacation.

BUGS, BITES & OTHER WILDLIFE CONCERNS   Although Belize has Africanized bees (the notorious "killer bees" of fact and fable) and several species of venomous snakes, your chances of being bitten are minimal, especially if you refrain from sticking your hands into hives or under rocks in the forest. If you know that you're allergic to bee stings, consult your doctor before traveling.

Snake sightings, much less snakebites, are very rare. Moreover, the majority of snakes in Belize are nonpoisonous. If you do encounter a snake, stay calm, don't make any sudden movements, and do not try to handle it. If you're bitten, seek medical attention immediately—don't try to bleed the area of the wound or suck the poison out.

Scorpions, black widow spiders, tarantulas, bullet ants, and other biting insects can all be found in Belize. In general, they are not nearly the danger or nuisance most visitors fear. (If you're a serious arachnophobe, stick to the beach resorts.) You should be fine if you watch where you stick your hands; in addition, you might want to shake out your clothes and shoes before putting them on to avoid any painful surprises.

The most prevalent and annoying biting insect you are likely to encounter, especially on the cayes and along the coast, are sand flies or "no-see-ums." These tiny biting bugs leave a raised and itchy welt, but otherwise are of no significant danger. Sand flies and no-see-ums tend to be most active around sunrise and sunset, or on overcast days. Your best protection is to wear light long-sleeved shirts and long pants when these bugs are biting.

TROPICAL SUN   Limit your exposure to the sun, especially during the first few days of your trip and, thereafter, from 11am to 2pm. Use a sunscreen with a high protection factor and apply it liberally. Remember that children need more protection than adults do.

Also, drink plenty of water and other fluids to avoid dehydration.

WHAT TO DO IF YOU GET SICK AWAY FROM HOME

Your hotel will be your best resource if you fall ill while traveling in Belize. Most hotels will be able to refer you to a local doctor, clinic, or hospital.

For travel abroad, you may have to pay all medical costs upfront and be reimbursed later. Medicare and Medicaid do not provide coverage for medical costs outside the U.S. Before leaving home, find out what medical services your health insurance covers. To protect yourself, consider buying medical travel insurance (see "Insurance" in the "Fast Facts" section of chapter 12).

Very few health insurance plans pay for medical evacuation back to the U.S. (which can cost US$10,000 and up). A number of companies offer medical evacuation services anywhere in the world. If you're ever hospitalized more than 150 miles from home, **MedjetAssist** (© **800/527-7478;** www.medjetassistance. com) will pick you up and fly you to the hospital of your choice virtually anywhere in the world in a medically equipped and staffed aircraft 24 hours a day, 7 days a week. Annual memberships are US$225 individual, US$350 family; you can also purchase short-term memberships.

We list **additional emergency numbers** in the "Fast Facts" section of chapter 12 as well as in the "Fast Facts" sections of the chapters on major towns and tourist destinations.

SAFETY

Belize City itself has a somewhat deserved reputation for being a dangerous city for travelers, especially after dark, and especially in neighborhoods off the beaten path.

See "Safety" in "Fast Facts: Belize City" in chapter 6 for more details. That said, if you use basic common sense and take standard precautions, you should have no problems staying safe in Belize.

Despite a seemingly relaxed and open drug culture at some of the popular beach and caye destinations, visitors should be very careful. Drugs, including marijuana, are strictly illegal, even in small quantities, and the laws are applied firmly to foreigners.

SPECIALIZED TRAVEL RESOURCES

In addition to the destination-specific resources listed below, please visit Frommers. com for specialized travel resources.

LGBT Travelers

Belize is a small, socially conservative, provincial country where public displays of same-sex affection are rare and considered somewhat shocking. In fact, homosexual sodomy is still illegal and even occasionally prosecuted here. There is virtually no open gay or lesbian bar or club scene in Belize City or any of the major tourist destinations. Gay and lesbian travelers should choose their hotels with care and be discreet in most public areas and situations.

The **International Gay and Lesbian Travel Association (IGLTA;** © **954/ 630-1637;** www.iglta.org), the trade association for the gay and lesbian travel industry, offers an online directory of gay- and lesbian-friendly travel businesses and tour operators.

Travelers with Disabilities

Most disabilities shouldn't stop anyone from traveling. There are more options and resources out there than ever before. However, in general, there are relatively few handicapped-accessible buildings or transport vehicles in Belize. A very few hotels offer wheelchair-accessible accommodations, and there are no public buses, commuter airlines, or water taxis thus equipped. In short, it's relatively difficult for a person with disabilities to get around in Belize.

Family Travelers

To locate accommodations, restaurants, and attractions that are particularly kid-friendly, refer to the "Kids" icons throughout this guide.

Hotels in Belize often give discounts for children 11 and under, and children under 3 or 4 years old are usually allowed to stay for free. Discounts for children and the cutoff ages vary according to the hotel, but in general, don't assume that your kids can stay in your room for free.

Many hotels, particularly on the cayes, offer rooms equipped with kitchenettes or full kitchen facilities. These can be a real money saver for those traveling with children, and I've listed many of these accommodations in the destination chapters that follow.

Hotels offering regular, dependable babysitting service are few and far between. If you will need babysitting, make sure your hotel offers it before you make your reservation.

Senior Travelers

Be sure to mention that you're a senior when you make your travel reservations. Although it's not common policy in Belize to offer senior discounts, don't be shy about asking for one anyway. You never know. Always carry some kind of identification, such as a driver's license, that shows your date of birth, especially if you've kept your youthful glow.

Many reliable agencies and organizations target the 50-plus market. **Road Scholar** (© 800/454-5768; www.roadscholar.org) arranges worldwide study programs for those ages 55 and older. **ElderTreks** (© 800/741-7956 or 416/558-5000 outside North America; www.eldertreks.com) offers small-group tours to off-the-beaten-path or adventure-travel locations, restricted to travelers 50 and older. Both of the above-mentioned companies have periodic trips Belize.

Due to its temperate climate, stable government, low cost of living, and friendly retiree incentive program, Belize is popular with retirees from North America. The country's retirement and incentive program is run by the **Belize Tourism Board** (© 800/624-0286 in the U.S. and Canada, or 227-2430 in Belize). They have a website dedicated to the subject at www.belizeretirement.org.

Student Travel

Check out the **International Student Travel Confederation** (**ISTC;** www.istc.org) website for comprehensive travel services information and details on how to get an **International Student Identity Card** (**ISIC),** which qualifies students for substantial savings on rail passes, plane tickets, entrance fees, and more. It also provides students with basic health and life insurance and a 24-hour help line. The card is valid for a maximum of 18 months. You can apply for the card online or in person at **STA Travel** (© 800/781-4040 in North America; © 132-782 in Australia; © 0871/230-0040 in the U.K.; www.statravel.com), the biggest student travel agency in the world; check out the website to locate STA Travel offices worldwide.

Although you won't find any discounts at the national parks, most museums and other attractions around Belize do offer discounts for students. It always pays to ask.

SUSTAINABLE TOURISM

Belize is a popular ecotourism destination. Some of the small hotels, isolated nature lodges, and tour operators around the country are pioneers and dedicated professionals in the sustainable tourism field. Other hotels, lodges, and tour operators are honestly and earnestly jumping on the bandwagon and improving their practices, while still others are simply "green-washing," using the terms "eco," "green," and "sustainable" in their promo materials, but doing little real good in their daily operations.

In 2010, Belize was ranked near the top for countries in the Americas in the Environmental Performance Index (EPI; http://epi.yale.edu). Despite this, and the substantial amounts of good work being done, and ongoing advances being made in the field, Belize faces severe environmental threats. Given the fact that the cayes are virtually flat islands, at sea level, protected by a fragile barrier reef, the dangers of ocean pollution and rising sea levels due to climate change pose a real and present danger to Belize.

sustainable PROPERTIES IN BELIZE

Following is a selection of hotels that I feel are making real efforts to implement sustainable practices. Throughout the book, I've tried to highlight hotels, as well as restaurants and other attractions, that pay more than mere lip service to sustainability.

Belize City:
Radisson Fort George Hotel & Marina (p. 92)
The Great House (p. 92)

The Northern Cayes & Atolls:
Xanadu Island Resort (p. 125)
Caye Reef (p. 141)
Island Expeditions's Half-Moon Caye adventure camp (p. 148)

South:
Manatee Lodge (p. 158)
Thatch Caye (p. 164)
Hamanasi (p. 169)
Machaca Hill Lodge (p. 193)
The Lodge at Big Falls (p. 194)
Coral House Inn (p. 194)
Hickatee Cottages (p. 195)
Nature's Way Guest House (p. 195)

The Maya Village Homestay Network (p. 193)

Northern Belize:
Lamanai Outpost Lodge (p. 210)
La Milpa Field Station (p. 211)
Chan Chich Lodge (p. 211)

The Cayo District & Western Belize:
Monkey Bay Wildlife Sanctuary (p. 228)
Ian Anderson's Caves Branch (p. 230)
Pook's Hill (p. 231)
Ka'ana (p. 239)
Chaa Creek (p.244)
Black Rock Jungle River Lodge (p. 246)
The Trek Stop (p. 247)
Blancaneaux Lodge (p. 252)
Hidden Valley Inn (p. 253)
Table Rock Camp & Cabañas (p. 254)
Crystal Paradise Resort (p. 255)

Tikal & Guatemala's Petén:
La Lancha Resort (p. 272)
Hotel Gringo Perdido (p. 273)
La Casa de Don David (p. 273)

To date there is no overall organizational structure or classification system to rate, train, and assist local hotels, restaurants, and tourism operators in sustainable tourism practices. The nascent **Sustainable Tourism Program** (© **227-2687;** www.sustainabletourismbz.org) is hoping to change all that. A National Sustainable Tourism Plan is expected to be adopted by early 2011.

Recycling is just beginning to gather momentum in Belize. You can now occasionally find separate bins for plastics, glass, and paper on town and city streets, at national parks, and at the country's more sustainable hotels and restaurants. This is a nascent phenomenon, but I expect it to continue to grow and spread. Your hotel will be your best bet for finding a place to deposit recyclable waste, especially if you choose a hotel that has instituted sustainable practices.

While sustainable tourism options are expanding in Belize, organic and sustainably grown fruits and vegetables (as well as coffee) are just beginning to become available. Very few restaurants feature organic produce, although hopefully that will change in the near future.

Several of the tour operators listed in the "Organized Adventure Trips" in chapter 5 (p. 65) have trips specifically geared toward ecotourists. You might also focus on

GENERAL RESOURCES FOR green TRAVEL

In addition to the recommendations and resources for Belize listed above, the following websites provide valuable wide-ranging information on sustainable travel. For a list of even more sustainable resources, as well as tips and explanations on how to travel greener, visit www.frommers.com/planning.

○ **Responsible Travel** (www.responsibletravel.com) is a great source of sustainable travel ideas; the site is run by a spokesperson for ethical tourism in the travel industry. **Sustainable Travel International** (www.sustainabletravelinternational.org) promotes ethical tourism practices and manages an extensive directory of sustainable properties and tour operators around the world.

○ **Carbonfund** (www.carbonfund.org), **TerraPass** (www.terrapass.

org), and **Cool Climate** (http://coolclimate.berkeley.edu) provide info on "carbon offsetting," or offsetting the greenhouse gas emitted during flights.

○ **Greenhotels** (www.greenhotels.com) recommends green-rated member hotels around the world that fulfill the company's stringent environmental requirements. **Environmentally Friendly Hotels** (www.environmentallyfriendlyhotels.com) offers more green accommodation ratings.

○ **Volunteer International** (www.volunteerinternational.org) has a list of questions to help you determine the intentions and the nature of a volunteer program. For general info on volunteer travel, visit **www.volunteerabroad.org** and **www.idealist.org**.

specific hotels and lodges that have an ecotourism bent or have implemented sustainable practices, such as those I recommend in the box below.

Finally, another great way to make your tourism experience more sustainable is to volunteer. For specific information on volunteer options in Belize, see "Ecologically Oriented Volunteer & Study Programs" in chapter 5.

See "The Lay of the Land" in chapter 2 for additional information on the various ecosystems and geographical highlights you'll find around the country. For information on Belize's national parks and info about what to expect and how to take care of yourself in the Belizean forests, caves, rivers, and seas, turn to chapter 5.

ANIMAL-RIGHTS ISSUES

Although there are currently no swim-with-the-dolphin attractions or tours in Belize, I wouldn't be surprised if someone opened one in the future. For information about the ethics of swimming with dolphins, visit the **Whale and Dolphin Conservation Society** (www.wdcs.org). For information on animal-friendly issues throughout the world, visit **Tread Lightly** (www.treadlightly.org).

STAYING CONNECTED

Telephones

Belize has a standardized seven-digit phone numbering system. There are no city or area codes to dial from within Belize.

To call Belize:
1. Dial the international access code: 011 from the U.S.; 00 from the U.K., Ireland, or New Zealand; or 0011 from Australia.
2. Dial the country code: 501.
3. Dial the seven-digit number.

To make international calls: To make international calls from Belize, first dial 00 and then the country code (U.S. or Canada 1, U.K. 44, Ireland 353, Australia 61, New Zealand 64). Next dial the area code and number. For example, if you wanted to call the British Embassy in Washington, D.C., you would dial ✆ 00-1-202-588-7800.

For directory assistance: Dial ✆ 113 if you're looking for a number inside Belize, and for numbers to all other countries dial ✆ 115 and (for a charge) an operator will connect you to an international directory-assistance operator.

For operator assistance: If you need operator assistance in making a call, dial ✆ 115, whether you're trying to make a local or an international call.

Toll-free numbers: Numbers beginning with 0800 and 800 within Belize country are toll-free, but calling a 1-800 number in the States from Belize is not toll-free. In fact, it costs the same as an overseas call.

Mobile Phones

Belize uses both **GSM** (Global System for Mobile Communications) and **CDMA** (Code Division Multiple Access) networks. If your cellphone is on a GSM or CDMA system, and you have a world-capable multiband phone such as many Sony Ericsson, LG, Motorola, or Samsung models, you can make and receive calls across civilized areas around much of the globe. Just call your wireless operator and ask for "international roaming" to be activated on your account. Per-minute charges can be high, though—up to $5 in Belize, depending on your plan.

Belize Telecommunications Limited (BTL) and their cellular division **DigiCell** (✆ **227-2017;** www.digicell.bz) have a virtual monopoly on GSM cellular service in Belize. Luckily, DigiCell offers affordable packages for SIM card activation. If you have an unlocked 850/1900MHz GSM phone, they sell local prepaid phone cards in various denominations, although the initial SIM card and activation costs BZ$50, including BZ$10 of calls. You can buy subsequent minutes in the form of scratch-off cards in a variety of denominations. Calls anywhere within Belize are BZ60¢, and you are not charged for incoming calls. The SIM chips and calling cards are sold at their desk at the airport or at one of their many outlets around Belize. Their website also has information on setting up your home phone for roaming in Belize. But be careful, the rates are quite high.

PLANNING A BELIZE wedding

Getting married in Belize is simple and straightforward. In most cases, all you need are current passports and a copy of the bride and groom's birth certificate. You'll also need a Belizean marriage license, which can be acquired with as little as 24-hour notice for BZ$510, although, if you do so in advance, and spend at least 3 days in the country, the cost is just BZ$200. For marriage license info, contact the **Registrar General's Office** ✆ **501/227-7377;** copies of the marriage license form can be downloaded from www.belizelaw.org. The marriage license must be signed by both participants in the presence of a justice of the peace and two witnesses. The justice of the peace also must notarize the license.

Things are only slightly more complicated if one or more of the partners was previously married or widowed. In such a case, the previously married partner must provide an official copy of the divorce decree. In the case of widows and widowers, an official copy of the deceased's death certificate is also required. Presently, Belize performs and recognizes same-sex marriages or civil unions.

Most travelers who get married in Belize do so in a civil ceremony officiated by the aforementioned local justice of the peace, although priests and ministers from most major Christian religious denominations can be found to perform the ceremony. If you're Jewish, Muslim, Buddhist, or a follower of some other religion, bringing your own officiant is a good idea.

For something different, you might try an extreme or adventurous wedding in Belize. Options include tying the knot at a Mayan ceremonial site or surrounded by coral reefs and sea creatures, while the bride, groom, witnesses, and officiate breathe through scuba gear. There are many beautiful natural wedding sites around the country, and your choices range from pristine beaches to lush tropical forests to candle-lit caves.

Most of the higher-end and romantic hotels in Belize have ample experience in hosting weddings. Many have an in-house wedding planner. Top choices include **Victoria House** (p. 125), **Mata Chica** (p. 127), **Cayo Espanto** (p. 128), **Turtle Inn** (p. 180), and **The Inn at Robert's Grove** (p. 180). If you want a remote, yet plush, rainforest lodge to serve as host and backdrop, try **Chaa Creek** (p. 244), **Blancaneaux Lodge** (p. 252), **Machaca Hill Lodge** (p. 193), or **Maruba Resort Jungle Spa** (p. 201).

If you're looking for service beyond what your hotel can offer, or if you want to do it yourself, check out www.belizeweddings.com, www.belizeweddingplanners.com, or www.idobelizeweddings.com.

Voice over Internet Protocol (VoIP)

Many travelers are accustomed to using a broadband-based telephone service (in technical terms, **Voice over Internet Protocol,** or **VoIP**) such as Skype (www.skype.com) or Vonage (www.vonage.com) to make free or inexpensive international calls from their laptop or a cybercafe. However, Belize's monopoly Internet service provider has blocked these services. Some hotels and businesses get their Internet connection via satellite, which bypasses this problem, but don't expect to have ready and easy access to VoIP connections while in Belize.

Internet & E-Mail

WITHOUT YOUR OWN COMPUTER

In Belize, you'll readily find cybercafes in most major destinations. Many of the more upscale, isolated nature lodges also provide guest connectivity in one form or another.

WITH YOUR OWN COMPUTER

More and more hotels, resorts, cafes, and retailers around Belize are offering high-speed Wi-Fi access, either free or for a small fee. Throughout the book, I list which hotels provide free, or for a fee, Wi-Fi and high-speed Ethernet access.

Belize uses standard U.S.-style two- and three-prong electric outlets with 110-volt AC current, and standard U.S.-style phone jacks. Still, wherever you go, it's a good idea to bring a **connection kit** with power and phone adapters, a spare phone cord, and a spare Ethernet network cable—or find out whether your hotel supplies them to guests.

TIPS ON ACCOMMODATIONS

Belize has no truly large-scale resorts or hotels. While the Radisson and Best Western chains have one property each in Belize City, there are no other chain hotels in Belize. Upscale travelers looking for over-the-top luxury have very few options here. True budget hounds will also find slim pickings, especially in the beach and caye destinations. What the country does have is a host of intimate and interesting **small to midsize hotels** and **small resorts.** Most of these are quite comfortable and reasonably priced by most international standards, although nowhere near as inexpensive as neighboring Mexico.

Belize is a noted ecotourism and bird-watching destination, and there are small nature-oriented **ecolodges** across the inland portion of the country. These lodges offer opportunities to see wildlife (including sloths, monkeys, and hundreds of species of birds) and learn about tropical forests. They range from Spartan facilities catering primarily to scientific researchers to luxury accommodations that are among the finest in the country.

At the more popular beach and resort destinations, specifically Ambergris Caye, Caye Caulker, and Placencia, you might want to look into renting a **condo** or efficiency unit, especially for longer stays.

Throughout this book, I've separated hotel listings into several broad categories: **Very Expensive,** BZ$400 and up; **Expensive,** BZ$252 to BZ$398; **Moderate,** BZ$122 to BZ$250; and **Inexpensive,** under BZ$120 for a double. *Rates given in this book do not include the 9% hotel tax.* This tax will add to the cost of your room, so do factor it in.

One item you're likely to want to bring with you is a beach towel. Your hotel might not provide one at all, and even if it does, it might be awfully thin.

For tips on surfing for hotel deals online, visit Frommers.com.

 Speak Up

If you are booking directly with your hotel (by phone, fax, or e-mail), remember that most hotels are accustomed to paying as much as 20% in commission to agents and wholesalers. It never hurts to ask if they will pass some of that on to you. Don't be afraid to bargain.

SUGGESTED BELIZE ITINERARIES

Don't be fooled by its size—there's a lot to see and do in Belize. And the fact that the country is so compact makes it easy to see and do a lot in a short time. Still, many visitors simply come for a solid week of rest and relaxation, fishing and/or scuba diving at a beach or island resort, without ever getting to know the rest of the country. The following itineraries are meant to serve as rough outlines to help you structure your time and get a taste of some of the country's must-see destinations. Other options include specialized itineraries focused on a particular interest or activity. Bird-watchers could design an itinerary that visits a series of prime bird-watching sites. Cave enthusiasts and spelunkers could design a trip to take in several of Belize's caves, including both wet and dry cave explorations.

THE REGIONS IN BRIEF

BELIZE CITY Belize City is a modest-size coastal port city located at the mouth of the **Belize River.** Although it's no longer the official governmental seat, Belize City remains the most important city—culturally, economically, and historically—in the country. It is also Belize's transportation hub, with the only international airport, an active municipal airport, a cruise-ship dock, and all the major bus-line and water-taxi terminals. Still, Belize City is of limited interest to most visitors, who quickly seek the more provincial and pastoral charms of the country's various tourist destinations and resorts. Belize City has a reputation as a rough and violent urban center, and visitors should exercise caution and stick to the most popular tourist areas of this small city.

THE NORTHERN CAYES & ATOLLS This is Belize's primary tourist zone and attraction. Hundreds of palm-swept offshore islands lie

between the coast of the mainland and the protection of the 298km (185-mile) **Belize Barrier Reef.** The reef, easily visible from many of the cayes, offers some of the world's most exciting snorkeling, scuba diving, and fishing. The most developed cayes here, **Ambergris Caye** and **Caye Caulker,** have numerous hotels and small resorts, while some of the less developed cayes maintain the feel of fairy-tale desert isles. In addition to the many cayes, there are two open-ocean atolls here, **Turneffe Island Atoll** and **Lighthouse Reef Atoll.** Each of these unique rings of coral, limestone, and mangrove cayes surrounds a central, protected saltwater lagoon.

For those whose main sport is catching rays, not fish, it should be mentioned that the cayes, and Belize in general, lack wide, sandy beaches. Although the water is as warm and clear blue as it's touted to be, most of your sunbathing will be on docks, deck chairs, or imported patches of sand fronting a sea wall or sea-grass patch of shallow ocean. Also, note that there are still no large-scale all-inclusive resorts like those found throughout much of the rest of the Caribbean.

SOUTHERN BELIZE Southern Belize encompasses two major districts, Stann Creek and Toledo. The former includes the **Cockscomb Basin Wildlife Sanctuary** and the coastal towns of **Dangriga, Hopkins Village,** and **Placencia.** Dangriga is the country's major center of **Garífuna culture,** while Hopkins Village is a quaint, oceanfront Garífuna village, and Placencia boasts what is arguably the country's best beach. Farther south, the Toledo District is Belize's final frontier. The inland hills and jungles are home to numerous Kekchi and Mopan Mayan villages. Hidden in these hills are some lesser known and less visited Mayan ruins, including **Lubaantun** and **Nim Li Punit.** The Toledo District is also emerging as an **ecotourism destination,** with the country's richest, wettest, and most undisturbed rainforests. Off the shores of southern Belize lie more cayes and yet another mid-ocean atoll, **Glover's Reef Atoll.** The cayes down here get far less traffic and attention than those to the north, and they are perfect for anyone looking for all of the same attractions, but fewer crowds.

NORTHERN BELIZE Anchored on the south by Belize City, this is the country's business and agricultural heartland. Toward the north lie **Orange Walk Town** and **Corozal Town.** Both of these small cities have a strong Spanish feel and influence, having been settled largely by refugees from Mexico's Caste War. The Maya also lived here, and their memories live on at the ruins of **Altun Ha, Lamanai, Cerros,** and **Santa Rita,** all in this zone. This is a land that was once submerged and is still primarily swamp and mangrove. Where the land is cleared and settled, sugar cane is the main cash crop, although bananas, citrus fruits, and pineapples are also grown. Toward the western section of this region lies the **Río Bravo Conservation Area,** a massive tract of virgin forest, sustainable-yield managed forest, and recovering reforestation areas. Northern Belize has some of the country's premier isolated nature lodges, as well as some of the prime destinations for bird-watchers, including the **Shipstern Nature Reserve** and **Crooked Tree Wildlife Sanctuary.**

THE CAYO DISTRICT & WESTERN BELIZE This mountainous district near the Guatemalan border has become Belize's second-most-popular destination. Here you'll find some of Belize's most beautiful countryside and most fascinating natural and man-made sights. The limestone mountains of this region are dotted with numerous caves, sinkholes, jagged peaks, underground rivers, and waterfalls. There are clear-flowing aboveground rivers that are excellent for swimming and canoeing, as well as mile after mile of unexplored forest full of wild animals and hundreds of bird species. Adventurers, nature lovers, and bird-watchers will definitely want to spend some time in the Cayo District. This is also where you'll find Belize's largest and most impressive Mayan ruins. In the remote **Mountain Pine Ridge** section of the Cayo District lies **Caracol,** one of the largest known Classic Maya cities ever uncovered. Closer to the main town of San Ignacio, you'll find **Xunantunich, Pilar** and the smaller **Cahal Pech.**

TIKAL & GUATEMALA'S PETEN   Just over Belize's western border lies Guatemala's **Petén province,** a massive and remote area of primary forest and perhaps Mesoamerica's most spectacular Maya ruin, **Tikal.** The level of preservation, restoration, and rich rainforest setting make Tikal one of the true wonders of the world, and an enchanting stop for anyone even remotely interested in the ancient Maya or archaeology. The surrounding jungles and small Guatemalan villages are easily accessible from Belize and allow travelers the chance to add yet another unique adventure to any itinerary.

BELIZE IN 1 WEEK

The timing is tight, but this itinerary packs a trio of Belize's best destinations into 1 week. It allows for a chance to visit a major Maya ruin, snorkel on the barrier reef, ride an inner tube on an underground river, and relax a bit on the beach.

Day 1: Arrive & Head to Placencia

Arrive in **Belize City** and grab a quick connecting flight to **Placencia ★★**. Spend the afternoon strolling along the beach and the town's famous sidewalk. For dinner, try the tapas and fusion fare served up at **Rumfish y Vino ★★** (p. 184). Then head back to the sidewalk after dinner, and enjoy some time mingling with locals and tourists alike at the **Barefoot Beach Bar ★** (p. 186).

Day 2: Way Down upon the Monkey River

In the morning, take a tour on the **Monkey River ★** (p. 178), where you're sure to see a rich array of wildlife. In the afternoon you can treat yourself to a spa treatment or get some snorkeling in. For dinner, head to the **Maya Beach Hotel Bistro ★★★** (p. 183).

Day 3: Cayo Calling

Fly back to Belize City and pick up a rental car for the drive to the **Cayo District ★★**. Stop at the **Belize Zoo ★★** (p. 101) or for a **cave tubing adventure** (p. 1047) near Jaguar Paw en route. Settle into one of the hotels in San Ignacio or one of the lodges located out on the way to Benque Viejo. If there's time, take an afternoon tour to the ruins at **Xunantunich ★★** (p. 235). For dinner, be sure to treat yourself to the creative cuisine offered up by chef Sean Kuylen at **La Ceiba ★★★** (p. 242).

Day 4: Climbing Caana

Wake up very early and head to the Mayan ruins at **Caracol** ★★ (p. 251), stopping at the **Río on Pools** ★★ and **Río Frío Cave** (p. 251) on your way back to San Ignacio.

Days 5 & 6: Fly to the Cayes

Head for the cayes. Choose between **Caye Caulker** ★★★, with its intimate funky charm, and **Ambergris Caye** ★★, with its wide choice of hotels, resorts, and restaurants. A whole range of activities and adventures awaits you here. Be sure to try the snorkel trip to **Hol Chan Marine Reserve** ★★ and **Shark-Ray Alley** ★★ (p. 117). You can also just chill in the sun and sand.

Day 7: Going Home

Return to **Belize City** in time for your international connection. If you have time, stop off at the **Belize Tourism Village** (p. 99) to do some last-minute shopping before you go.

BELIZE IN 2 WEEKS

If you have 2 weeks, you'll be able to hit all the highlights mentioned above, as well as some others, including a side trip to the ruins of Tikal, in neighboring Guatemala. And you can do all this at a slightly more relaxed pace to boot.

Day 1: Arrive & Head to Placencia

Arrive into **Belize City** and grab a quick connecting flight to **Placencia** ★★. Spend the afternoon strolling along the beach and the town's famous sidewalk. For dinner, try the tapas and fusion fare served up at **Rumfish y Vino** ★★ (p. 184). Then head back to the sidewalk after dinner, and enjoy some time mingling with locals and tourists alike at the **Barefoot Beach Bar** ★ (p. 186).

Day 2: Way Down upon the Monkey River

Take a tour on the **Monkey River** ★ (p. 178), where you're sure to see a rich array of wildlife. In the afternoon, treat yourself to a spa treatment, followed by dinner at the **Maya Beach Hotel Bistro** ★★★ (p. 183).

Day 3: Get Wet & Wild

Take a snorkel trip to **Laughing Bird Caye** ★★ (p. 176) and enjoy a picnic lunch on this tiny little gem of an island. If you happen to be here during **whale-shark season** (p. 176), swap out the Laughing Bird Caye trip for a chance to snorkel or scuba dive with the world's largest fish. In the afternoon, visit the small Garífuna village of **Seine Bight.**

Day 4: Punta Gorda

Fly down to the remote town of **Punta Gorda** in the far southern reaches of Belize. Get there in time to head out into the nearby mountains, where you'll find several small Mayan villages. Visit the village of San Antonio, and then head on to **Blue Creek** ★★ (p. 191), where you'll find a beautiful swimming hole in a forested river

BELIZE IN 1 WEEK

1 Belize City	**6** Caracol
2 Placencia	**7** Río Frío Cave
3 Monkey River	**8** Caye Caulker
4 Cayo District	**9** Ambregris Caye
5 Xunantunich	**10** Belize City

BELIZE IN 2 WEEKS

1 Belize City	**9** Mountain Pine
2 Placencia	Ridge
3 Monkey River	**10** Caracol
4 Laughingbird Caye	**11** Caye Caulker
5 Punta Gorda	**12** Lamanai
6 Cayo District	**13** Maruba Resort
7 Xunantunich	Jungle Spa
8 Tikal	**14** Belize City

4

SUGGESTED BELIZE ITINERARIES | Belize in 2 Weeks

that flows out from a jungle cave. **Earth Runnins' Café ★** is a great place for dinner and drinks. If you're lucky, there might just be a live band playing.

Days 5 & 6: Cayo Calling

Fly back to Belize City and pick up a rental car for the drive to the **Cayo District ★★**. Stop at the **Belize Zoo ★★** (p. 101) or for a **cave tubing adventure** (p. 107) near Jaguar Paw en route. Settle into one of the hotels in San Ignacio or one of the lodges located out on the way to Benque Viejo. If you have time, take an afternoon tour to the ruins at **Xunantunich ★★** (p. 235) or a gentle canoe trip on the **Macal**

River (p. 236). If you didn't visit Xunantunich the previous afternoon, you'll want to stop in on Day 6. You'll also want to check out the **Belize Botanic Gardens ★★** (p. 237) or the nearby **Chaa Creek Natural History Museum** and **Rainforest Medicine Trail ★** (p. 238). If you're hardy, you can visit both. At least 1 night you should splurge on a dinner at **La Ceiba ★★★** (p. 242) at the Ka'ana Resort (p. 239). The other night, I recommend hanging around downtown San Ignacio and trying the bar food and wood-oven pizzas at **Mr. Greedy's Pizzeria ★★** (p. 243), or the eclectic mix of Belizean, Indian, and Pan Asian cuisine served up at **Ko-Ox Han-Nah ★** (p. 243).

Days 7 & 8: Tikal Time

Take a 2-day/1-night trip to **Tikal ★★★** (p. 256). Stay at one of the lodges right at the ruins. Get an early start in order to beat the crowds and because the ruins here are so extensive. Make sure you set aside plenty of time to explore the amazing ruins here, but also schedule some time to enjoy the quaint little island city of **Flores** (p. 274). Return to Belize in the afternoon, and head to the **Mountain Pine Ridge ★★** area, staying either at **Blancaneaux Lodge ★★★** (p. 252) or **Five Sisters Lodge ★** (p. 255).

Day 9: Climb Caana

Visit the ruins at **Caracol ★★** (p. 251) and climb to the top of the tallest man-made structure in Belize. Stop at the **Rio Frio Cave** (p. 251) and **Río on Pools ★★** (p. 251) on your way back from the ruins.

Days 10, 11 & 12: Go Slow on Caye Caulker

It's time to head to funky **Caye Caulker ★★★**. Be sure to try the snorkel trip to **Hol Chan Marine Reserve ★★** and **Shark-Ray Alley ★★** (p. 117) while you're in the area. If you haven't gotten your fill of Mayan ruins, you can do a day trip to **Lamanai ★★** (p. 208). Any extra time you have you can use to chill in the sun and sand.

Days 13 & 14: Massage Your Muscles with Mud

Finish your trip off with some decadent pampering at the **Maruba Resort Jungle Spa ★★** (p. 201) before heading home from **Belize City.**

BELIZE FOR FAMILIES

Belize doesn't have any large resorts with well-staffed children's programs, nor will you find many activities or attractions specifically geared for the very young. Still, this English-speaking country is a great destination for families, especially if your children have an adventurous streak.

Day 1: Head for Hopkins

Arrive into **Belize City** and head straight to **Hopkins Village ★★★** (p. 166). Settle into a comfortable suite at **Almond Beach Belize & Jaguar Reef Lodge ★★** (p. 169).

Belize for Families & Mayan Ruins Highlight Tour

MAYAN RUINS HIGHLIGHT TOUR

1 Belize City	**8** Mountain Pine Ridge
2 Lamanai	**9** Caracol
3 Cayo District	**10** Ambergris Caye
4 Xunantunich	**11** Altun Ha
5 El Pilar	**12** Bacalar Chico N.P.
6 Cahal Pech	and Marine Reserve
7 Tikal	**13** Belize City

BELIZE FOR FAMILIES

1 Belize City	**5** Ambergris Caye
2 Hopkins Village	**6** Hol Chan
3 South Water Caye	Marine Reserve
4 Ian Anderson's	**7** Lamanai
Caves Branch	**8** Belize City

Day 2: Go Garífuna

Sign up for a class in traditional Garífuna drumming and dancing at the **Lebeha Drumming Center ★** (p. 168). When you and yours aren't banging a drum, take advantage of the resort's ample facilities and activity options, which include free use of the sea kayaks, Hobie Cats, and snorkel gear.

Days 3 & 4: A Nearly Deserted Island

Head out to **South Water Caye ★★★**. The island here is tiny, and the kids will no doubt fantasize about being stranded on a deserted island. The waters here are extremely calm and protected by the barrier reef, which lies just offshore. This is a great place to introduce the family to snorkeling, and to head out in individual or tandem kayaks.

Days 5 & 6: Into the Dark

On your way back north, stop off at **Ian Anderson's Caves Branch ★★** (p. 102). Accommodations here range from quite rustic to borderline luxurious. The folks here also offer adventure options that range from cushy to hard core. Most revolve around the surrounding forest and the area's namesake river, which runs through a series of underground caves. You can do a cave tubing adventure, but I recommend their "waterfall cave" excursion.

Days 7, 8 & 9: Sun & Fun in San Pedro

Head for **Ambergris Caye ★★**, with its wide choice of hotels, resorts, and restaurants. A whole range of activities and adventures available for the family are here. Be sure to schedule in a snorkel trip to **Hol Chan Marine Reserve ★★** (p. 117) and **Shark-Ray Alley ★★** (p. 117). More adventurous members of the family can try parasailing or windsurfing. Reserve 1 day for a visit to the Mayan ruins at **Lamanai ★★** (p. 208). You'll also want to visit the **Butterfly Jungle ★** (p. 119). Fly right from San Pedro to the international airport in **Belize City** in time for your return flight home.

MAYAN RUINS HIGHLIGHTS

Belize boasts dozens of known Mayan ruins of varying sizes and in varying states of excavation and exploration. The following itinerary hits most of the major ruins, and even allows you some time to visit the cayes. You could easily add on a side trip to the northern or southern zones, where there are several lesser-known ruins.

Day 1: The Sleeping Crocodile

Arrive in **Belize City** and head straight to **Lamanai,** staying right next door to the ancient Mayan city at the **Lamanai Outpost Lodge ★★** (p. 210). You'll probably arrive in the afternoon. Save the ruins for the next day, but take a boat tour on the New River Lagoon around sunset, and you'll see a host of bird species, and, most likely, a real crocodile or two.

Days 2 & 3: Life in Ruins

Spend the morning exploring the **Lamanai ruins ★★** (p. 208). Get there early before the tour groups arrive, and enjoy the peace and quiet of the site. Have lunch at the hotel and then head over to **Chan Chich Lodge ★★** (p. 211). Settle into your room here, which is set on the central plaza of a Mayan ruin. Spend the following day exploring the ruins at and around Chan Chich. If you have time, head over to nearby **La Milpa ★** (p. 211), a large site with an active and ongoing excavation.

Days 4, 5 & 6: Cayo Calling

Head to the **Cayo District ★★** and stay at one of the lodges in San Ignacio or on the way to Benque Viejo. Be sure to take a trip to **Actun Tunichil Muknal ★★★**

(p. 226). This tour takes almost a full day. Still, in the afternoon, you can squeeze in a visit to **Cahal Pech** (p. 247), which is right in the town of San Ignacio. Over the next 2 days, you can visit the ruins of **Xunantunich** ★★ (p. 235), **El Pilar** ★★ (p. 247), and the Mayan ceremonial burial cave at **Chechem Ha** ★ (p. 235). Caving is hard work, so be sure to treat yourself, at least 1 night, to the creative cuisine offered up by chef Sean Kuylen at **La Ceiba** ★★★ (p. 242).

Day 7 & 8: Tikal Time

Take a 2-day/1-night trip to **Tikal** ★★★ (p. 256). Stay at one of the lodges right at the ruins. Get an early start in order to beat the crowds and because the ruins here are so extensive. Make sure you set aside plenty of time to explore the amazing ruins here, but also schedule some time to enjoy the quaint little island city of Flores. Return to Belize in the afternoon of Day 8, and head to the **Mountain Pine Ridge** ★★ area (p. 248), staying at either **Blancaneaux Lodge** ★★★ (p. 252) or **Five Sisters Lodge** ★ (p. 255).

Day 9: Caracol

Get an early start for your visit of the ruins at **Caracol** ★★ (p. 251). And remember, at one point, Caracol defeated Tikal in battle. Stop at the **Río Frío Cave** and **Río on Pools** ★★ (p. 251) on your way back from the ruins.

Days 10 & 11: Enjoying the Cayes

Unwind for a couple of days on **Ambergris Caye** ★★. If you didn't get to visit **Altun Ha** ★ (p. 200) during your inland stint, you can easily visit as a day tour by boat and take a minivan from here. You can also arrange boat trips to the tiny ruins of Chac Balam in the **Bacalar Chico National Park & Marine Reserve** ★ (p. 120) or to **Cerros** (p. 215) outside Corozal.

Day 12: Heading Home

Return to **Belize City** in time for your international connection.

BELIZE CITY IN 1 DAY

While most tourists seek to avoid Belize City entirely—and I pretty much advise as much in this book—if you plan properly, Belize City can actually serve well as a good base if you have only a few days in the country.

Day 1: Getting to Know the City

Begin your day early at the **Fort George Lighthouse** and **Baron Bliss Memorial,** and follow the walking tour outlined on p. 99. When you reach the **Commercial Center,** be sure to stop in for a coffee and some fry jacks at **Big Daddy's Diner** (p. 96). After you finish the walking tour, head to the **Museum of Belize** ★★ (p. 98), the country's premier historical museum. For lunch, take a taxi out to **Old Belize** ★ (p. 98), and sit down at their oceanside open-air **Old Belize Bar & Grill** (p. 97). When you finish lunch, tour the small museum here in Old Belize, which offers a peek into various facets of the natural, cultural, and political history of the

Fort George Lighthouse **1**
Baron Bliss Memorial **2**
Commercial Center **3**
Big Daddy's Diner **4**
Museum of Belize **5**
Old Belize **6**
Wet Lizard **7**
Bird Isle's Restaurant **8**

country, or take a swim and enjoy some beach time at their **Cucumber Beach ★** area, which features a large saltwater swimming area and towering water slide.

At sunset, have a drink and some conch fritters at the **Wet Lizard ★**, 1 Fort St. (**© 223-5973;** p. 95). This might just hold you over for the night.

After night falls, head to the **Bird's Isle Restaurant & Bar ★** (p. 96), a delightful open-air spot right next to the ocean. Most nights you'll find either a live band or some lively karaoke. Another good option is the aptly named **Riverside Tavern ★★** (p. 97). This place has a more pub feel to it. At both of these restaurants, the best seats are outdoors on a waterfront deck area.

THE ACTIVE VACATION PLANNER

Belize is a fantastic destination for the active and adventurous traveler. The range of available sport and tour options is wide; the quality of the adventures and local tour operators is high; and the fact that the country is so compact allows you to mix and match. Whether your interests are scuba diving, snorkeling, fishing, sailing, spelunking, mountain biking, horseback riding, or bird-watching, Belize has some fabulous terrain and opportunities that are perfect for you. I hope that the following chapter, combined with the regional and destination chapters that follow it, will help you design and enjoy your dream vacation.

ORGANIZED ADVENTURE TRIPS

Because many travelers have limited time and resources, organized ecotourism or adventure-travel packages are a popular and efficient way of combining several activities. Bird-watching, cave exploring, and hiking can be teamed with, say, visits to classical Mayan ruins and a few days on an outlying caye for snorkeling and diving, sea kayaking, and more bird-watching.

Traveling with a group on an organized trip has several advantages over traveling independently. Your accommodations and transportation are arranged, and most (if not all) of your meals are included in the cost of a package. If your tour operator has a reasonable amount of experience and a decent track record, you should proceed to each of your destinations quickly without the snags and long delays that those traveling on their own can occasionally face. You'll also have the opportunity to meet like-minded souls who are interested in nature and active sports. Of course, you'll pay more for the convenience of having all your arrangements handled in advance.

In the best cases, group size is kept small (10–20 people), and the tours are conducted by knowledgeable guides who are either naturalists or biologists. Be sure to ask about difficulty levels when you're choosing a tour. While most companies offer "soft adventure" packages that those in moderately good (but not phenomenal) shape can handle, others focus on more hard-core activities geared toward only seasoned athletes or adventure travelers.

North America–Based Tour Operators

These agencies and operators specialize in well-organized and coordinated tours that cover your entire stay. Many travelers prefer to have everything arranged and confirmed before arriving in Belize, and this is a good idea for first timers and during the high season. *Note:* Most of these operators are not cheap, with 10-day tours generally costing in the neighborhood of US$2,000 to US$3,500 per person, not including airfare to Belize.

Bike Hike Adventures (✆ **888/805-0061** in the U.S. and Canada, or 604/731-2442 in Canada; www.bikehike.com) is a Canada-based company specializing in multiday, multiadventure tours for small groups. They have several different offerings in Belize. Their 9-day tour will have you horseback riding, mountain biking, cave tubing, and either snorkeling or diving. The cost is around US$2,500 per person, not including airfare to Belize.

International Expeditions ★ (✆ **800/234-9620** in the U.S. and Canada, or 205/428-1700 in the U.S.; www.ietravel.com) specializes in independent programs and natural history group tours. They run a regular 9-day tour to Belize and Tikal that takes in several of the major Mayan sites and tropical ecosystems, while staying in top-end lodges. The cost is US$3,700 per person, not including airfare to Belize.

Island Expeditions ★★ (✆ **800/667-1630** in the U.S. and Canada, or 522-3328 in Belize; www.islandexpeditions.com) runs various adventurous multiday land and sea tours around Belize. Kayaking the atolls is one of their strong suits, but they also combine this with inland adventures. These trips usually involve some island camping. Prices run around US$1,850 for a 7-day trip, not including airfare to Belize.

Journeys International (✆ **800/255-8735** in the U.S. and Canada, or 734/665-4407 in the U.S.; www.journeys-intl.com) offers small-group natural history and adventure packages around Belize, including trips especially geared toward families. Their 8-day family trip costs US$2,795 per adult, US$2,595 ages 12 to 15, and US$1,995 ages 11 and under. Airfare to Belize is extra.

Magnum Belize ★ (✆ **800/447-2931** in the U.S. and Canada; www.magnumbelize.com) is one of the largest wholesalers specializing in Belize. With years of experience and excellent staff on the ground, these folks offer a wide range of tour and adventure options, and good deals.

Sea & Explore Belize (✆ **800/345-8796** in the U.S. and Canada; www.seaexplore.com) has more than 20 years' experience booking travel to Belize, and offers both custom tours and well-priced packages for both adventure travelers and more traditional vacationers.

Slickrock Adventures ★★ (© 800/390-5715 toll free in the U.S. and Canada, or 435/259-4225 in the U.S.; www.slickrock.com) offers a variety of multiday land and sea tours around Belize. They specialize in sea-kayak and dive extravaganzas based out of their camp and lodge on the private Long Caye in Glover's Reef atoll. A full week with these folks, not including international airfare, costs around US$2,075.

U.K.-Based Tour Operators

Imaginative Traveller (© 44/1473-667-337 in the U.K.; www.imaginative-traveller.com) is a good-value operator specializing in budget student, group, and family travel. Their offerings in Belize focus on the entire Mundo Maya, and usually also take in parts of southern Mexico and Guatemala. These trips range in duration from 9 to 31 days.

Journey Latin America ★ (© 020/8747-8315 in the U.K.; www.journeylatin america.co.uk) is a large British operator specializing in Latin American travel. They offer a range of escorted tours around Latin America, including a few that touch down in Belize. They also design custom itineraries and often have excellent deals on airfare.

Belize-Based Tour Operators

Because many U.S.-based companies subcontract portions of their tours to established Belizean companies, some travelers like to set up their tours directly with these companies, thereby cutting out the middleman. While that means these packages are often less expensive than those offered by U.S. companies, it doesn't mean they are cheap. You're still paying for the convenience of having all your arrangements handled for you.

There are scores of tour agencies in Belize City and at all of the major tourist destinations around the country that offer a plethora of adventure options. These agencies, and the tour desks at most hotels, can arrange everything from cave tubing and Mayan-ruins tours to scuba diving and snorkeling. While it's generally quite easy to arrange most of these popular tours and adventures on the spur of the moment during your vacation, some are offered only when there are enough interested people or on set dates. If you have a very specialized tour or activity in mind, it pays to contact the hotel you will be staying at or a few of the companies listed here before you leave home, to find out what they might be doing when you arrive.

Belize Trips ★★★ (© 610-1923 or 223-0376; www.belize-trips.com) is the place to come to set up a custom tour. Owner and longtime resident Katie Valk is extremely knowledgeable, friendly, and responsive. She knows the country inside and out, and is adept at designing one-off itineraries, perfectly matched to her clients' needs and desires.

Destination Belize ★★ (© 523-4018 or 610-4718; www.destinationsbelize.com) is an excellent Belize-based company specializing in creating custom itineraries and tours.

Discovery Expeditions (© 223-0748; www.discoverybelize.com) is a longstanding and well-respected Belizean company with a broad offering of soft adventure and natural history tours.

S & L Travel & Tours ★ (℃ 227-7593; www.sltravelbelize.com) is one of the original tour operators in Belize, with some 30 years of experience in both adventure and regular tours. It's still one of the best, with excellent on-staff guides and a good working relationship with all the hotels.

ACTIVITIES A TO Z

Each listing in this section describes the best places to practice a particular sport or activity and lists tour operators and outfitters. If you want to focus on only one active sport during your time in Belize, these companies are your best bets for quality equipment and knowledgeable service.

Adventure activities by their very nature carry certain risks. In the past couple of years there have been several deaths and dozens of relatively minor injuries in activities ranging from mountain biking to white-water rafting to canopy tours. I try to list only the most reputable and safest of companies. However, if you ever have any doubt as to the safety of the guide, equipment, or activity, it's better to be safe than sorry. Moreover, know your limits and abilities and don't try to exceed them.

Biking

Belize is not a major biking destination. In fact, there are only four or so major paved roads in the entire country—the Northern, Western, Southern, and Hummingbird highways. Except for the wild Maya Mountains and Mountain Pine Ridge areas, the country is almost entirely flat. It would be possible to tour Belize's major mainland destinations on a touring bike, but the heat and humidity are often oppressive, and those few highways get plenty of traffic and generally don't have very wide shoulders.

The options are slightly more appealing for mountain bikers and off-track riders, however. Fat-tire explorations are relatively new and underexploited in Belize. Just about every major hotel in the Cayo District and the southern zone has mountain bikes for guest use or rental, or can hook you up with a local rental company. These bikes are fine for day trips and nontechnical riding. However, if you plan to do any serious biking, you might consider bringing your own rig, as quality mountain bike rentals are still a rarity in Belize. The **Mountain Pine Ridge Forest Reserve** and the area around it win my vote as the best place for mountain biking in Belize. The scenery's great, with primary and secondary forests, waterfalls, and plenty of trails. Truly hearty bikers can make it all the way to Caracol. See "Mountain Pine Ridge & Caracol" in chapter 10 for details.

Bird-Watching

With some 618 recorded species of resident and migrant birds identified throughout the country, and a wide variety of ecosystems and habitats, Belize abounds with great bird-watching sites. Even amateur bird-watchers should have little trouble checking off upwards of 100 species in a week's worth of watching.

Lodges with the best bird-watching include **Chan Chich Lodge** (p. 211) near Gallon Jug; **Lamanai Outpost Lodge** (p. 210) on the New River Lagoon; **Chaa Creek** (p. 244); **duPlooy's** (p. 245) or any of the nature lodges outside of San Ignacio; **Blancaneaux Lodge** (p. 252) or any of the lodges in the Mountain Pine Ridge

A Bird-Watcher's Bible

Any serious bird-watcher will want to pick up a copy of *Birds of Belize* (University of Texas Press), by H. Lee Jones. Published in January 2004, this dedicated guide to the birds of Belize was long overdue. The book is wonderfully illustrated by Dana Gardener, and includes 574 species of birds.

area; **Pook's Hill** (p. 231) outside of Belmopan; and **Machaca Hill Lodge** (p. 193), **Hickatee Cottages** (p. 195), and **The Lodge at Big Falls** (p. 194), all in the Toledo District.

Some of the best parks and reserves for serious birders are **Cockscomb Basin Forest Reserve** ★, for scarlet macaws and a host of primary forest dwellers; **Shipstern Nature Reserve** ★★, for scores of different sea- and shorebirds; **Crooked Tree Wildlife Sanctuary** ★★★, for large varieties of wading birds, including the jabiru stork; **Man-O-War Caye** ★★, a major nesting site for the magnificent frigate; **Caracol** Mayan ruins and the **Chiquibil National Park** ★★, for many different resident and migratory forest species; **Half Moon Caye,** for the vast nesting flocks of red-footed boobies; and the **Río Bravo Conservation Area** ★★, for ocellated turkeys and trogons. You'll also find excellent bird-watching in neighboring Guatemala's **Petén** ★★ province and around the **Tikal** ★★ area.

Bird-watchers staying on Ambergris Caye should certainly head to the **Bacalar Chico National Park & Marine Preserve.**

TOUR OPERATORS

Sierra Club ★ (© 415/977-5588 in the U.S.; www.sierraclub.org) leads at least one 10-day trip each year to Belize, often with a side trip to Guatemala. The focus is on bird-watching and natural history, but you'll also visit several Mayan ruins and spend some time on Caye Caulker. The cost is between US$2,500 and US$3,800 per person, not including airfare to Belize.

Victor Emanuel Nature Tours ★★ (© 800/328-8368 or 512/328-5221 in the U.S. and Canada; www.ventbird.com) is a very well-respected small-group tour operator specializing in bird-watching trips, and a pioneer of the genre in Belize. These tours focus primarily on the area around Chan Chich Lodge and Crooked Tree Wildlife Sanctuary, two of the country's prime bird-watching destinations, though some of their other tour options touch down around Lamanai and the Mountain Pine Ridge region.

Wings ★ (© 888/293-6443 or 520/320-9868 in the U.S. and Canada; www.wingsbirds.com) is also a specialty bird-watching travel operator with more than 30 years of experience in the field. Its 7-day Belize trip is based at the remote and luxurious Chan Chich Lodge and costs around US$3,900, not including airfare. Trip size is limited to eight people.

A BELIZEAN BIRDING COMPANY

In addition to the operator listed below, the **Belize Audubon Society** (© 223-4985; www.belizeaudubon.org) is an active and informative organization worth contacting.

5

THE ACTIVE VACATION PLANNER

Activities A to Z

Paradise Expeditions ★ (📞 824-2772; www.birdinginbelize.com) specializes in bird-watching trips and adventures. Based in San Ignacio in the Cayo District, these folks offer small-group package tours and personalized guided and unguided itineraries to a selection of the top birding spots and lodges in Belize and western Tikal. A 7-day/6-night tour costs around US$1,500 per person.

Caving

Belize is an excellent destination for spelunking. Whether you're passionate about cave exploration or you've never been underground in the dark, you should not leave Belize without venturing into one or more of its vast cave systems. The ancient Mayans believed caves to be a mystical portal between the world of the living and the underworld of spirits and the dead. They called this mystical realm Xibalba. In almost every explored cave in Belize, some evidence of use by the Mayans has been uncovered. Fire pits, campsites, burial mounds, and ritual altars have all been found. Numerous pieces of pottery, as well as skeletons, bones, and religious artifacts, have also been encountered.

The aptly named **Caves Branch region ★★**, just outside of Belmopan, is a prime (and certainly the most popular) place to go caving. The cave tube trips here, including the spectacular **Crystal Cave ★★**, are excellent introductions to the underworld. There are also several great caves for exploring in the Cayo District, including the **Barton Creek Cave ★** and **Chechem Ha ★**. Perhaps the most adventurous and rewarding cave to explore is **Actun Tunichil Muknal ★★★**. For more information, see chapter 10.

A SPECIALIZED CAVE TOUR OPERATOR

The premier cave adventure operator in Belize is **Ian Anderson's Caves Branch ★★**, Hummingbird Highway, Mile Marker 41½ (📞 822-2800; www.cavesbranch.com). The company has a lovely forested setting at a far upstream entrance to the Caves Branch River, and a wide variety of cave tours and explorations are offered; most full-day trips run from US$75 to US$105.

Cruising

Belize is blessed with some wonderful cruising grounds. Steady yet gentle trade winds, combined with protected internal passages and innumerable isolated islands and anchorages, make this a perfect place to explore by boat. Cruising options in Belize range from bareboat charters of modern catamarans and monohulls to funky converted Belizean fishing sloops pressed into the snorkel-and-sunset cruise market. Belize is also a major port of call for many Caribbean cruise lines. For information on the major cruise lines that ply the waters of Belize, see "By Cruise Ship" under "Getting There & Getting Around" in chapter 3.

Virtually any section of Belize's coast and its outlying cayes and barrier reef are perfect for sailing. At nearly every beach or dive destination, it is possible to get out on the water for a cruise. Given the choice, I'd say the more remote and isolated cayes of southern Belize are the best places to venture out to sea. The two operations listed below are by far your best bets for bareboat cruising.

YACHT OUTFITTERS

With their operations based in Ambergris Caye, **TMM ★** (📞 800/633-0155 in the U.S. and Canada, or 226-3026 in Belize; www.sailtmm.com) offers mostly catamarans, with the option for either bareboat or crewed chartering. See p. 119 for more information.

The Moorings ★ (① 888/952-8420 in the U.S. and Canada, or 523-3351 in Belize; www.moorings.com) has its main base in Placencia. They offer bareboat and crewed charters on both monohull and catamaran yachts.

Depending on the season and boat size, rates for a bareboat run between US$2,000 and US$7,000 per week, and crewed charters cost from US$3,000 to US$9,000 per week.

Fishing

Any angler worth his or her saltwater fly rod already knows that Belize is a world-class fishing destination. Fly-fishing on the flats for permit, tarpon, and bonefish is the main draw, and the fish are excellent all up and down the coast and on the saltwater flats the length of the barrier reef. Bonefish- and permit-fishing are good year-round, while tarpon are best sought from April to November, with July and August being the best months. The southern zone around Punta Gorda and Placencia is prime fishing grounds for permit, while the coastal mangroves and rivers are excellent spots to land lively snook.

Just beyond the barrier reef, anglers can land snapper, barracuda, jack, and grouper, while those who head farther out can stalk sailfish and marlin.

Action Belize (① 888/383-6319 in the U.S. and Canada, or 223-2987 in Belize; www.actionbelize.com) is a Belize City–based operation offering a vast array of package and custom tour options. They are especially good with fishing itineraries, and even have their own boats and captains. A 7-day/6-night trip with 4 full days of fishing costs US$1,359 per person, double occupancy. A full day of fishing starts at US$110 per person for cruise-ship passengers and independent travelers.

In late 2009, Belize enacted a law requiring all sport-fishing enthusiasts to have a fishing license. The cost of the license is BZ$20 per day and BZ$50 per week. Since its passage the law has been controversial, with locals and visitors alike confused as to where to obtain the license, who it pertains to, and whether certain fish are game fish. Officially, the licenses must be obtained from the **Ministry of Agriculture's Fisheries Department** (① 223-2623; species@btl.net). However, most licensed fishing guides and tour operators around the country can help you get a license.

FISHING LODGES

El Pescador ★ (Ambergris Caye; ① 800/242-2017 in the U.S. and Canada, or 226-2398 in Belize; www.elpescador.com) is a luxury lodge on the northern end of Ambergris Caye, specializing in fishing packages. They have excellent guides and boats.

Turneffe Flats ★★ (① 888/512-8812 in the U.S., or 220-4046; www.tflats.com) is a beautiful fishing lodge with a privileged position right on the ring of the Turneffe Island Atoll and its extensive mid-ocean lagoon and open-water flats. See p. 148 for a complete review.

Machaca Hill Lodge ★★★ (① 722-0050; www.machacahill.com) is by far the most luxurious lodge geared largely toward fisherman. Permit is the prime game sought here, and the hotel's guides are some of the best in the area. See p. 193 for a complete review.

Golf

Belize is not one of the world's great golfing destinations; in fact, it's not a golf destination at all. The country's only regulation course, the par-72 oceanfront **Caye Chapel Island Resort,** was shuttered in 2010, and there's no clear idea if or when it will open again.

Belize's only operational golf course is located on the outskirts of Belmopan. The **Roaring River Golf Course** (✆ 820-2031; www.belizegolf.net) is a par-64, 18-hole executive course. Greens fees run BZ$50 for 18 holes, and there's no charge for a set of clubs. A 9-hole round will run you BZ$35. The course is open every day of the year from dawn to dusk.

Horseback Riding

Although Belize is very sparsely populated, and much of it is ideal for exploring on the back of a horse, horseback riding is still a relatively undeveloped sport. The best place to grab a mount and explore is the Mountain Pine Ridge Forest Reserve, and the best outfitter to tour with here is **Mountain Equestrian Trails** (✆ 669-1124; www.metbelize.com). A half-day trip including lunch costs BZ$122 per person; a full-day trip costs BZ$166. Even if you're not staying here, most of the lodges in this area also offer horseback riding. For more information on riding in this region, see chapter 10.

A MONTANA COWBOY IN CENTRAL BELIZE

Banana Bank Lodge ★, Western Highway, Mile Marker 47½ (✆ 820-2020; www.bananabank.com), is a rustic riverside lodge owned by a former cowboy from Montana. Horseback riding is a major attraction here, so avid riders will feel right at home. For more information on this hotel, see p. 230.

Kayaking & Canoeing

Belize lacks the major white water necessary for serious rapid enthusiasts. Most of the rivers here are rated Class I, II, or III. Still, many of these rivers are quite well suited for gentle canoe explorations and less technical kayaking adventures. The Macal and Mopan rivers in the Cayo District are perfect for these types of adventures, and most of the hotels and tour operators in the area offer a range of these types of tours. See chapter 10 for more information.

However, sea kayaking in Belize is excellent. The relatively calm waters and protection provided by the barrier reef and mid-ocean atoll lagoons, combined with a string of small, relatively closely spread cayes, makes this a perfect place to tour and explore by sea kayak. **Glover's Reef Atoll** is probably the most popular and best place for a sea kayak adventure; see "Dangriga" in chapter 8 for more information.

OUTFITTERS

Island Expeditions ★★ (✆ 800/667-1630 in the U.S. and Canada, or 522-3328 in Belize; www.islandexpeditions.com) runs various multiday kayaking tours to the outer atolls, Glover's Reef Atoll, and the coral islands along the southern stretch of Belize's barrier reef. These folks offer up quite a bit of flexibility, allowing you to design a trip that is part guided, part independent exploration, and part inland adventure. An 8-day/7-night excursion runs US$1,500 to US$2,000.

Slickrock Adventures ★★ (© 800/390-5715 toll free in the U.S. and Canada, or 435/259-4225 in the U.S.; www.slickrock.com) specializes in multiday kayak tours around Glover's Reef Atoll, and they even have their own rustically comfortable base camp and lodge on a private caye here. An 8-day/7-night trip costs US$2,075 per person.

Scuba Diving & Snorkeling

Belize is one of the world's top spots for scuba diving and snorkeling. I've said it before, and I'll probably say it again, but Belize has the second-longest barrier reef in the world, as well as three spectacular mid-ocean atolls. The diving and snorkeling all along this reef and at the atolls are world-class. In general, the reef is in very healthy shape and the water quality and visibility are consistently excellent.

Amateur or casual divers and snorkelers should really be happy almost anywhere in Belize, and every major beach and island destination has easy access to some fabulous dive and snorkel sites. Truly dedicated divers will probably want to head to one of the outer atolls. **Glover's Reef ★★**, **Turneffe Island ★★**, and **Lighthouse Reef atolls ★★** all offer outstanding diving opportunities. The Blue Hole and several other sites on Lighthouse Reef Atoll make it the top choice for scuba divers, among a crowded field. **Shark-Ray Alley ★★** and **Hol Chan Marine Reserve ★★** are two deservedly popular snorkel spots just off of Ambergris Caye, although overpopularity and overcrowding are threatening the experience there. And finally, only just becoming known to cognoscenti, the **Gladden Spit ★★** area, off the coast from Placencia, is one of the top spots on the planet to snorkel or dive with giant whale sharks.

There are several dedicated dive resorts around Belize. Another option for hardcore divers is to stay on a live-aboard dive boat. These midsize vessels usually carry from 10 to 20 divers in private staterooms. The boats feature fully equipped dive operations and a host of amenities. One of the advantages here is that you get to hit several of the top reef and atoll sites in a weeklong vacation.

Information on snorkeling, scuba diving, and local operators is in each of the destination chapters that follow. Almost every beach resort in Belize, as well as most hotels in Belize City, either has its own dive shop and operation or can hook you up with a local crew. Below are listed a couple of live-aboard operations, and a couple of the best dedicated dive resorts in Belize.

Note: While many of the beach and island hotels and all of the dive shops in Belize have snorkeling and diving gear for rent, you might consider bringing your own. If nothing else, bring your own mask. A good, properly fitting mask is the single-most-important factor in predicting the success of a dive outing. Faces come in all sizes and shapes, and I really recommend finding a mask that gives you a perfect fit. Fins are a lesser concern, as most operators should have fins to fit your feet. As for your own snorkel, well, in this day and age, I think you should want your own. If you plan on going out snorkeling or diving more than a few times, the investment will more than pay for itself.

LIVE-ABOARD DIVE BOATS

Aggressor Fleet ★★ (© 800/348-2628 or 706/992-2531 in the U.S. and Canada; www.aggressor.com) has the 34m (112-ft.) *Aggressor III,* a comfortable dive boat with deluxe staterooms. Rates are around US$2,500 to US$2,900 per week.

Peter Hughes Diving ★★ (☏ **800/932-6237** or 305/669-9391 in the U.S. and Canada; www.peterhughes.com) runs the *Sundancer II,* a 42m (138-ft.) yacht with 10 staterooms. Rates range from US$1,895 to US$2,095 per week.

Tip: Both boats are very comfortable and well-equipped, with full dive and photo-lab operations, rental equipment, attentive service, and plenty of deck and lounge areas. Each boat has one or two master staterooms with a queen-size bed for couples. The *Aggressor III* features TVs and VCRs in every stateroom, and even has a hot tub on the upper deck. Couples will probably prefer the *Aggressor III*'s wider lower bunk of their staggered quasi–bunk bed arrangement, while buddies traveling together may be more comfortable with the two separate single beds in the standard staterooms on the *Sundancer II.*

DIVING RESORTS & OUTFITTERS

In addition to the folks listed below, check the listings at specific beach and island destinations in the regional chapters, particularly those in Placencia, Ambergris Caye, Caye Caulker, and the outer cayes and atolls.

Hamanasi ★★★ (☏ **877/552-3483** in the U.S., or 520-7073 in Belize; www.hamanasi.com) is an excellent dive resort located on a beautiful patch of beach south of Hopkins Village. The location grants good access to a wide range of dive sites, including the outer atolls. See p. 169 for a complete review.

Isla Marisol Resort ★★ (☏ **888/623-5403** in the U.S. and Canada; www.islamarisolresort.com) has the distinct advantage of being located on Glover's Reef Atoll, an isolated spot loaded with world-class dive sites. See p. 163 for a complete review.

> **When a Package Isn't a Deal**
>
> While it's often tempting to purchase all-inclusive dive packages before coming to Belize, this limits your flexibility. For example, if the weather and water are really rough, you're already committed, even though you might prefer taking an inland tour to a Mayan ruin instead of a rough dive.

St. George's Caye Resort ★★ (☏ **800/813-8498** in the U.S. and Canada; www.gooddiving.com) is a boutique resort located close to Belize City and well located for trips to most major dive destinations in the country. See p. 146 for a complete review.

The Inn at Robert's Grove ★★ (☏ **800/565-9757** in the U.S., or 523-3565 in Belize; www.robertsgrove.com) is an excellent luxury resort in Placencia, with a top-notch dive operation. See p. 180 for a complete review.

Spas & Retreats

So far the trend toward destination spas and yoga or tai chi retreats hasn't caught on in Belize. In fact, there are no true dedicated destination spas or retreats in the country yet. However, the two places listed below do a pretty good job at what they do.

Primarily a nature lodge and ecotourism resort, **Chaa Creek** ★★, off the road to Benque Viejo in the Cayo District (☏ **824-2037;** www.chaacreek.com), has a very nice full-service day spa offering a wide range of body and skin treatments. Multiday packages are available and can be designed to give the feel of a full-destination spa experience. See p. 244. for a complete review of the resort.

No longer is underwater photography and video the exclusive realm of professionals with very expensive equipment. Generic and custom waterproof housings can be purchased for most modern digital still and video cameras. However, if you don't own your own underwater camera or casing, you might want to bring one or more cheap, disposable waterproof or underwater cameras. Alternatively, many dive shops will rent professional or semiprofessional underwater still and video cameras for about US$20 to US$40 per day.

Maruba Resort Jungle Spa ★★ (✆ 800/627-8227 in the U.S. and Canada, or 225-5555 in Belize; www.maruba-spa.com) is a true spa, offering a wide range of treatments and packages. Their various massages, their mud and exfoliating treatments, and the general sense of sensual overload and pampering are all top-notch. But aside from horseback riding options, they don't really offer any of the classes or active exercise programs that you would expect at a destination spa. For more information, see "Along the Old Northern Highway: Altun Ha & Maruba Resort Jungle Spa" in chapter 9.

Windsurfing & Kitesurfing

Its steady trade winds and calm waters make Belize a great place for beginning and intermediate windsurfers, and a good place to learn how to kiteboard. More advanced boardsailors would probably want more extreme conditions, but this is a great place to learn and perfect your skills. That said, this is still a relatively minor activity in Belize. Your best bet for either of these activities is to check in with the folks at **Sail Sports Belize** (✆ 226-4488; www.sailsportsbelize.com) on Ambergris Caye, or **Kitexplorer** (✆ 623-4613; www.kitexplorer.com) on Caye Caulker. Both offer top-notch equipment rentals and lessons in both sports.

BELIZE'S TOP PARKS & BIORESERVES

Belize has a broad mix of national parks, forest reserves, marine reserves, natural monuments, wildlife sanctuaries, archaeological reserves, and private reserves. All told, more than one-fifth of the country's landmass and much of its offshore waters are, to some extent, protected areas. In fact, the entire Belize Barrier Reef was declared a World Heritage Site by UNESCO in 1996.

Most of the national parks charge a BZ$10 per-person per-day fee for any foreigner, although some have begun charging slightly more and a few slightly less. Belizeans and foreign residents often pay less. At parks where camping is allowed, an additional charge of around BZ$4 per person per day is usually charged. Fees at private reserves vary, but are similar to those listed above.

The following section is not a complete listing of all of Belize's national parks, protected areas, and private reserves, but rather a selective list of those parks that are of greatest interest and accessibility. They're the most popular, but they're also among the best. You'll find detailed information about food and lodging options near each of the individual parks in the regional chapters that follow.

Northern Cayes & Atolls

BACALAR CHICO NATIONAL PARK & MARINE RESERVE This is one of the newer additions to Belize's national park system. In addition to being home to scores of bird, animal, and plant species (many of which are endemic), the park also features several ancient Mayan ceremonial and trading sites. Nearly 200 species of birds have been spotted here, and the park allegedly contains all five wildcat species found in Belize, including the jaguar. The park is accessible only by boat, but once you get here, there are several trails. **Location:** On the far northern end of Ambergris Caye. For more details, see "Ambergris Caye" in chapter 7.

HALF MOON CAYE NATIONAL MONUMENT This is a combined land and marine reserve. Half Moon Caye itself is the principal nesting ground for the red-footed booby, as well as for both hawksbill and loggerhead turtles. There is a visitor center here, and overnight camping is permitted with prior arrangement. **Location:** On the southern tip of the Lighthouse Reef Atoll. For more information, see "The Outer Atolls" in chapter 7.

HOL CHAN MARINE RESERVE *Hol chan* is a Mayan term meaning "little channel," which is exactly what you'll find here—a narrow channel cutting through the shallow coral reef. The reserve covers 7.8 sq. km (3 sq. miles) and is divided into three zones: the reef, the sea-grass beds, and the mangroves. The walls of the channel are popular with divers, and the shallower areas are frequented by snorkelers. Some of the exciting residents of the area are large green moray eels, stingrays, and nurse sharks (harmless). **Location:** 6.4km (4 miles) southeast of San Pedro on Ambergris Caye. For more details, see "Ambergris Caye" in chapter 7.

Southern Belize

COCKSCOMB BASIN WILDLIFE SANCTUARY The world's first jaguar reserve, this place covers nearly 389 sq. km (150 sq. miles) of rugged, forested mountains and has the greatest density of jaguars on the planet. Other resident mammals include tapirs, otters, coati-mundi, tayra, kinkajous, deer, peccaries, anteaters, armadillos, and four other species of wildcats, as well as nearly 300 species of birds. The sanctuary is part of the even larger Cockscomb Basin Forest Reserve. Trails inside the park range from gentle and short to quite arduous and long. During the dry season, you can even climb Victoria Peak here, which, at 1,122m (3,681 ft.), is the country's highest mountain. **Location:** 10km (6¼ miles) west of the Southern Highway, at a turnoff 32km (20 miles) south of Dangriga. For more information, see "Dangriga" in chapter 8.

FIVE BLUES LAKE NATIONAL PARK The main attraction here is a stunning cenote, whose various hues of blue give the park its name. All around the park lie forested lands and beautiful karst hill formations. **Location:** Mile Marker 32 on the Hummingbird Highway. For more information, see "Dangriga" in chapter 8.

GLOVER'S REEF ATOLL MARINE RESERVE This stunning and isolated mid-ocean coral formation features an oval-shaped central lagoon nearly 35km (22 miles) long. The steep-walled reefs here offer some of the best wall diving anywhere

Belize's National Parks & Nature Reserves

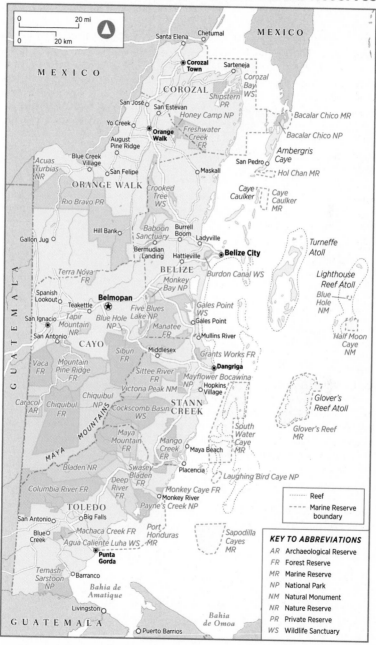

MEXICO

Santa Elena Chetumal

Corozal Town

Sarteneja

Corozal Bay WS

COROZAL

Shipstern PR

San José San Estevan

Honey Camp NP

Yo Creek

Orange Walk

Freshwater Creek FR

Bacalar Chico MR

Bacalar Chico NP

August Pine Ridge

Acuas Turbias NR

Blue Creek Village

San Felipe

Maskall

San Pedro

Ambergris Caye

Hol Chan MR

ORANGE WALK

Crooked Tree WS

Rio Bravo PR

Caye Caulker

Caye Caulker MR

Hill Bank

Gallon Jug

Baboon Sanctuary

Burrell Boom

Ladyville

Bermudian Landing

Hattieville

Belize City

Turneffe Atoll

Terra Nova FR

BELIZE

Burdon Canal WS

Lighthouse Reef Atoll

Spanish Lookout

Monkey Bay NP

Blue Hole NM

San Ignacio

Teakettle

Belmopan

Five Blues Lake NP

Gales Point WS

Gales Point

Tapir Mountain NR

Blue Hole NP

Manatee FR

Mullins River

Half Moon Caye NM

San Antonio

CAYO

Sibun FR

Middlesex

Grants Works FR

Vaca FR

Mountain Pine Ridge FR

Sittee River FR

Dangriga

Mayflower Bocawina NP

Hopkins Village

Glover's Reef Atoll

Caracol AR

Chiquibul FR

Chiquibul NP

Victoria Peak NM

Cockscomb Basin WS

STANN CREEK

Glover's Reef MR

Maya Mountain FR

Mango Creek FR

Maya Beach

South Water Caye MR

MAYA MOUNTAINS

Bladen NR

Swasey Bladen FR

Placencia

Laughing Bird Caye NP

Columbia River FR

Deep River FR

Monkey Caye FR

Monkey River

Payne's Creek NP

TOLEDO

San Antonio

Big Falls

Port Honduras

Sapodilla Cayes MR

Blue Creek

Machaca Creek FR

Agua Caliente Luha WS

MR

Punta Gorda

Temash-Sarstoon NP

Barranco

Bahia de Amatique

Livingston

GUATEMALA

Bahia de Omoa

Puerto Barrios

MEXICO

GUATEMALA

	Reef
- - -	Marine Reserve boundary

KEY TO ABBREVIATIONS

AR Archaeological Reserve
FR Forest Reserve
MR Marine Reserve
NP National Park
NM Natural Monument
NR Nature Reserve
PR Private Reserve
WS Wildlife Sanctuary

0 20 mi
0 20 km

in the Caribbean. The entire atoll was declared a World Heritage Site by the United Nations. **Location:** 121km (75 miles) southeast of Belize City; 45km (28 miles) east of Dangriga. For more information, see "Dangriga" in chapter 8.

Northern Belize

CROOKED TREE WILDLIFE SANCTUARY This swampy lowland is home to more than 250 resident species of birds and serves as a resting spot for scores of migratory species. During a visit here, you are sure to spot any number of interesting water birds. However, the sanctuary was established primarily to protect Belize's main nesting site of the endangered jabiru stork, the largest bird in the Western Hemisphere. Crocodiles, iguanas, coati-mundi, and howler monkeys are all frequently sighted. There are six major lagoons here connected by a series of creeks, rivers, and wetlands. The best way to explore the preserve is by dugout canoe. **Location:** 53km (33 miles) northwest of Belize City. For more information, see "En Route North: Crooked Tree Wildlife Sanctuary" in chapter 9.

RIO BRAVO CONSERVATION AREA This 105,218-hectare (260,000-acre) tract is a mix of virgin forest, sustainable-yield managed forest, and recovering reforestation areas. The land is home to nearly 400 bird species and more than 200 species of tropical trees. It also supports a healthy population of most of the new-world cat species, and is one of the best areas in the Americas for spotting a jaguar, even better than Cockscomb Basin. La Milpa, one of Belize's largest known Mayan sites, is located within this reserve, and Río Bravo is bordered by some 101,171 hectares (250,000 acres) of private reserve at Chan Chich, as well as the Kalakmul Reserve in Mexico and the Maya Biosphere Reserve in Guatemala, making it part of a massive regional biological and archaeological protected area. **Location:** 89km (55 miles) southwest of Orange Walk Town. For more information, see "Going West: Río Bravo Conservation Area, La Milpa & Chan Chich" in chapter 9.

SHIPSTERN NATURE RESERVE The 8,903 hectares (22,000 acres) of this reserve protect a variety of distinct ecosystems and a wealth of flora and fauna. Shipstern Nature Reserve is home to more than 250 bird species, and its mangroves, lagoons, and flat wetlands offer some of the best bird-watching sites in Belize. The lagoons and wetlands here are home to manatees and Morelet's crocodiles. The reserve also has lowland tropical dry forest unique to Belize, as well as a butterfly-breeding project. **Location:** 60km (37 miles) north of Orange Walk Town. For more information, see "Corozal Town" in chapter 9.

The Cayo District & Western Belize

BLUE HOLE NATIONAL PARK This park gets its name from a crystal-clear pool, or cenote, formed in a collapsed cavern. A short, well-marked trail leads to the main attraction here. Dense jungle surrounds a small natural pool of deep turquoise. This park also features **St. Herman's Cave,** one of the largest and—at one time—most easily accessible caves in Belize. The trail that connects the cenote and the cave passes through lush and beautiful primary and secondary tropical forests that are rich in flora and fauna. **Location:** 19km (12 miles) south of Belmopan on the Hummingbird Highway. For more information, see "Belmopan" in chapter 10.

CARACOL ARCHAEOLOGICAL RESERVE Caracol is the largest known Mayan archaeological site in Belize, and one of the great Mayan city-states of the

Classic era. So far three main plazas with numerous structures and two ball courts have been excavated. Caracol is located deep within the **Chiquibil Forest Reserve,** which is a largely undeveloped tract of primary and secondary tropical rain and pine forests. The bird-watching here is excellent. **Location:** 80km (50 miles) from the Western Highway at a turnoff just south of San Ignacio. For more information, see "Mountain Pine Ridge & Caracol" in chapter 10.

GUANACASTE NATIONAL PARK This 20-hectare (50-acre) park is named for a huge old guanacaste, or tubroos, tree that is found within the park. There are nearly 3.2km (2 miles) of well-marked and well-maintained trails in the park. The park is bordered on the west by Roaring Creek and on the north by the Belize River. Among the animals you might see are more than 120 species of birds, large iguanas, armadillos, kinkajous, deer, agoutis (large rodents that are a favorite game meat in Belize), and jaguarundis (small jungle cats). **Location:** 3.2km (2 miles) north of Belmopan, where the Hummingbird Highway turns off the Western Highway. For more information, see "Belmopan" in chapter 10.

MONKEY BAY The combined Monkey Bay Wildlife Sanctuary and Monkey Bay Nature Reserve represent more than 1,344 hectares (3,320 acres) of private, protected reserve of forest and wetlands. More than 250 species of birds have been recorded here so far, and the number is growing. There are hiking trails, as well as canoe tours on the Sibun River. **Location:** 50km (31 miles) west of Belize City, just off the Western Highway. For more information, see "Belmopan" in chapter 10.

Tikal, Guatemala

TIKAL NATIONAL PARK While it's obviously not in Belize, the close proximity and convenient access have earned this spectacular Guatemalan national park and ancient Mayan ceremonial city a place on this list and in this book. Surrounded by dense, virgin tropical rainforest, the Tikal ruins are perhaps the most spectacularly preserved and restored Mayan ruins yet uncovered. **Location:** 100km (62 miles) northwest of the Belize border; 64km (40 miles) north of Flores. For more information, see "Tikal" in chapter 11.

TIPS ON HEALTH, SAFETY & ETIQUETTE IN THE WILDERNESS

Much of what is discussed below is common sense. For more detailed information, see "Health" and "Safety" in chapter 3.

Taking Care

While most tours are safe, there are risks involved in any adventurous activity. Know and respect your own physical limits before undertaking any strenuous activity. Be prepared for extremes in temperature and rainfall and for wide fluctuations in weather. A sunny morning hike can quickly become a cold and wet ordeal, so it's usually a good idea to carry along some form of rain gear when hiking in the rainforest, or to have a dry change of clothing waiting at the end of the trail. Make sure to bring along plenty of sunscreen when you're not going to be covered by the forest canopy.

If you do any backcountry packing or camping, remember that it really *is* a jungle out there. Don't go poking under rocks or fallen branches. Snakebites are very rare, but don't do anything to increase the odds. If you do encounter a snake, stay calm, don't make any sudden movements, and *do not* try to handle it. Also, avoid swimming in major rivers unless a guide or local operator can vouch for their safety. Though white-water sections and stretches in mountainous areas are generally pretty safe, most mangrove canals and river mouths in Belize support healthy crocodile and caiman populations.

Bugs and bug bites will probably be your greatest health concern in Belize, and even they aren't as big a problem as you might expect. Mostly bugs are an inconvenience, although mosquitoes can carry malaria or dengue (see "Health," in chapter 3, for more information). A strong repellent and proper clothing will minimize both the danger and the inconvenience; you may also want to bring along some cortisone or Benadryl cream to soothe itching. At the beaches, you'll probably be bitten by sand fleas, or "no-see-ums." These nearly invisible insects leave an irritating welt. Try not to scratch, as this can lead to open sores and infections. No-see-ums are most active at sunrise and sunset, so you might want to cover up or avoid the beaches at these times.

And remember: Whenever you enter and enjoy nature, you should tread lightly and try not to disturb the natural environment. There's a popular slogan well known to most campers that certainly applies here: "Leave nothing but footprints, take nothing but memories." If you must take home a souvenir, take photos. Do not cut or uproot plants or flowers. Pack out everything you pack in, and *please* do not litter.

Searching for Wildlife

Animals in the forests are predominantly nocturnal. When they are active in the daytime, they are usually elusive and on the watch for predators. Birds are easier to spot in clearings or secondary forests than they are in primary forests. Unless you have lots of experience in the tropics, your best hope for enjoying a walk through the jungle lies in employing a trained and knowledgeable guide. (By the way, if it's been raining a lot and the trails are muddy, a good pair of rubber boots comes in handy. These are usually provided by the lodges or at the sites, where necessary.)

Here are a few helpful hints:

o **Listen.** Pay attention to rustling in the leaves; whether it's monkeys up above or pizotes on the ground, you're most likely to hear an animal before seeing one.

o **Keep quiet.** Noise will scare off animals and prevent you from hearing their movements and calls.

o **Don't try too hard.** Soften your focus and allow your peripheral vision to take over. This way you can catch glimpses of motion and then focus in on the prey.

o **Bring your own binoculars.** It's also a good idea to practice a little first to get the hang of them. It would be a shame to be fiddling around and staring into space while everyone else in your group oohs and aahs over a trogon or honeycreeper.

o **Dress appropriately.** You'll have a hard time focusing your binoculars if you're busy swatting mosquitoes. Light, long pants and long-sleeved shirts are your best bet. Comfortable hiking boots are a real boon, except where heavy rubber boots are necessary. Avoid loud colors; the better you blend in with your surroundings, the better your chances are of spotting wildlife.

- **Be patient.** The jungle isn't on a schedule. However, your best shots at seeing forest fauna are in the very early-morning and late-afternoon hours.
- **Read up.** Familiarize yourself with what you're most likely to see. Most lodges and hotels have a copy of ***Birds of Belize*** (University of Texas Press, 2004), by H. Lee Jones, and other wildlife field guides, although it's always best to have your own. A good all-around book to have is Les Beletsky's ***Belize and Northern Guatemala: The Ecotravellers' Wildlife Guide*** ★★ (Natural World Academic Press, 2004).

ECOLOGICALLY ORIENTED VOLUNTEER & STUDY PROGRAMS

Below are some institutions and organizations that are working on ecology and sustainable development projects.

Cornerstone Foundation ★★ (*©* 678-9909; www.cornerstonefoundation belize.org), based in San Ignacio in the Cayo District, is an excellent and effective nonreligious, nongovernmental peace organization with a variety of volunteer and cultural exchange program opportunities. Programs range from AIDS education to literacy campaigns to renewable resource development and use. Overall, costs are pretty low and reflect the costs of basic food, lodging, and travel in country, with some extra going to support the organization and its work.

Earthwatch Institute ★ (*©* 800/776-0188 in the U.S. and Canada; www.earthwatch.org) organizes volunteers to go on research trips to help scientists collect data and conduct field experiments in a number of scientific fields and a wide range of settings. Current expeditions to Belize focus on the study and field research on manatees. Fees for food and lodging average around US$2,500 for a 9-day expedition, excluding airfare.

Habitat for Humanity International ★ (*©* 800/422-4828 in the U.S. and Canada, or 227-6818 in Belize; www.habitat.org) is a nonprofit, nondenominational Christian volunteer organization, specializing in building individual housing for needy folks around the world. Habitat has an independent chapter in Belize and sometimes runs organized Global Village programs here. It usually costs between US$1,400 and US$1,800 per person for a 2-week program, including room, board, and in-country transportation (but not airfare to Belize).

International Zoological Expeditions ★★ (*©* 800/548-5843 in the U.S. and Canada; www.ize2belize.com) has two research and educational facilities in Belize, on South Water Caye and in Blue Creek Village. IZE organizes and administers a variety of educational and vacation trips to these two stations, for both school groups and individuals. A 10-day program usually costs about US$1,300 to US$1,800 per student.

Maya Research Program at Blue Creek ★ (*©* 817/831-9011 in the U.S.; www.mayaresearchprogram.org) runs volunteer and educational programs at an ongoing Mayan archaeological dig. Two-week sessions allow participants to literally dig in and take part in the excavation of a Mayan ruin. The cost is US$1,750 for the 2-week program; discounts are available for students and longer stays.

Monkey Bay Wildlife Sanctuary (© 820-3032; www.monkeybaybelize.org) is a private reserve and environmental education center that specializes in hosting study-abroad student groups. They also run their own in-house educational programs and can arrange a variety of volunteer stays and programs, including homestays with local Belizean families. See "Belmopan" in chapter 10 for complete details.

Sustainable Harvest International ★★ (© 800/548-5843 in the U.S. and Canada; www.sustainableharvest.org) offers unique programs based on sustainable farming techniques and practices. Their Belize program focuses on organic cacao production in the southern Stann Creek and Toledo districts. The 8-day program usually costs about US$2,000 per person, with discounts available for students and children.

Toledo Institute for Development and Environment ★ (© 722-2274; www.tidebelize.org) is a small, grassroots environmental and ecotourism organization working on sustainable development and ecological protection issues in the Toledo District. Contact them directly if you are interested in volunteering.

BELIZE CITY

L ong ago stripped of its status as the country's capital, Belize City remains Belize's business, transportation, and cultural hub. Sooner or later you'll spend at least some time here, unless you do all your in-country traveling by air or have a very precisely planned itinerary. For some, since the country itself is so small, Belize City makes a convenient base for a host of interesting day trips to most of the country's major destinations and attractions.

With a population of some 71,000, Belize City is surrounded on three sides by water, and at high tide it is nearly swamped. It's a strange, dense warren of narrow streets and canals (the latter being little more than open sewers, and pretty pungent in hot weather), modern stores, dilapidated shacks, and quaint wooden mansions, coexisting in a seemingly chaotic jumble.

The city was originally settled by the ancient Mayans, who lived up and down the coast here. By the mid-1600s, pirates were using the current site of Belize City as a hideout and provisioning spot. Soon after, the British arrived and set up a logging base here, fueled by slave labor. Logs were harvested inland and floated down the Belize River for milling and shipping. This logging base soon became a colonial settlement and the seat of Britain's colonial empire on the Central American isthmus. Belize City itself is said to sit on a foundation of wood chips, discarded ships' ballast, and empty rum bottles.

Belize City has historically been beset by tragedy. The entire population abandoned the city and moved to St. George's Caye in 1779 following a Spanish attack. The Baymen, as the British settlers called themselves, returned and resettled the city in 1784. Massive fires razed much of the city in 1804, 1806, and 1856. Deadly hurricanes inflicted heavy damage in 1931 and 1961. Between these events, the residents endured smallpox, yellow fever, and cholera epidemics. Belize City had been declared the capital of British Honduras in 1892, but after Hurricane Hattie struck in 1961, the country's capital was relocated inland to Belmopan.

Despite a reputation for crime and violence, periodic devastation from passing hurricanes, and the loss of its capital status, Belize City remains the urban heart and soul of Belize. Most visitors treat Belize City merely as a transition point and transportation hub. This is probably what you'll want to do, too. But if you've got a day or two to burn on a layover here,

Belize City

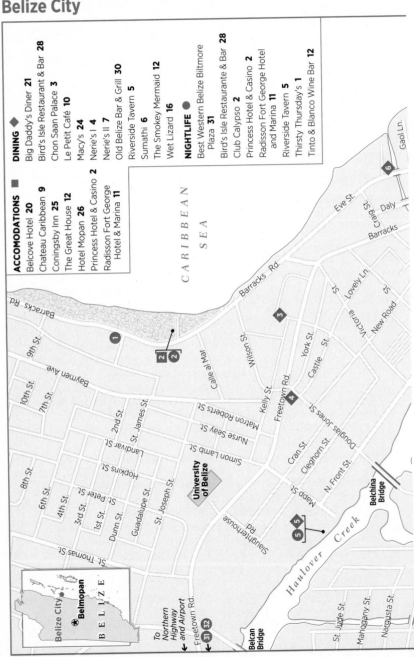

ACCOMODATIONS ■

Belcove Hotel **20**
Chateau Caribbean **9**
Coningsby Inn **25**
The Great House **12**
Hotel Mopan **26**
Princess Hotel & Casino **2**
Radisson Fort George
Hotel & Marina **11**

DINING ◆

Big Daddy's Diner **21**
Bird's Isle Restaurant & Bar **28**
Chon Saan Palace **3**
Le Petit Café **10**
Macy's **24**
Nerie's I **4**
Nerie's II **7**
Old Belize Bar & Grill **30**
Riverside Tavern **5**
Sumathi **6**
The Smokey Mermaid **12**
Wet Lizard **16**

NIGHTLIFE ●

Best Western Belize Biltmore
Plaza **31**
Bird's Isle Restaurante & Bar **28**
Club Calypso **2**
Princess Hotel & Casino **2**
Radisson Fort George Hotel
and Marina **11**
Riverside Tavern **5**
Thirsty Thursday's **1**
Tinto & Blanco Wine Bar **12**

Marine   Parade

Cork St.

Dredge St.

Fort   St.

Belize Harbour

Handyside   St.

N. Front   St.

Swing Bridge

Battlefield Park

Foreshore   Southern

Regent St.

Church   St.

Bishop St.

Albert St.

King St.

Prince St.

Dean St.

South St.

Wagner Ln.

Berkley St.

Albert St.

Queen Charlotte St.

Rectory Ln.

Palm Ln.

Racecourse   St.

W.

West   West

Water Ln.

Regent   St.

Bagdad St.

Orange St.

Glyn   St.

George St.

Plues St.

West Canal St.

East Canal St.

Far West St.

West St.

King St.

Tigris St.

Dean St.

Basra St.

Euphrates Ave.

Allenby St.

Tanoomah St.

Amara Ave.

East Collet Canal St.

Mosul St.

ut Ave.

ax Ave.

Magazine Rd.

Bus Terminal

Vernon St.

Johnson St.

Woods St.

Logwood St.

Banak St.

Hiccatee St.

Cemetery   Rd.

Sarstoon St.

Lake View St.

Cura

To Western Highway

Hutson St.

Keyhole Alley

Eyre St.

Gabourel Lane

Cabourel Lane

N. Park St.

Memorial Park

S. Park St.

Rd.

Queen St.

Pickstock   St.

N. Front St.

Hydes Lane

Hyde's Lane

To Western Highway

$ Bank/ATM
✚ Church
✚ Hospital
ℹ Information
Lighthouse
P Police
⊠ Post office

0   1/10 mile
0   100 meters

SHOPPING & ATTRACTIONS

Baron Bliss Memorial **14**
Belize Tourism Village **15**
Bliss Centre for Performing Arts **23**
Commercial Center **21**
Fine Arts **17**
Fort George Lighthouse **13**
Government House **27**
The Image Factory **18**
Marine Terminal **19**
Museum of Belize **8**
Old Belize **30**
St. John's Cathedral **29**
Supreme Court **22**
Traveler's Liquor Heritage Center **32**

Belize City is a good place to walk around, admire the fleet of working wooden fish sloops, do some craft and souvenir shopping, and stock up on Marie Sharp's Hot Sauce to bring home with you.

ORIENTATION

Arriving

BY PLANE

All international flights into Belize land at the **Philip S. W. Goldson International Airport** (© 225-2045; www.pgiabelize.com; airport code BZE), which is located 16km (10 miles) northwest of the city on the Northern Highway. See chapter 3 for details about airlines that service Belize City.

In the baggage claim area, there's an information booth maintained by the **Belize Tourist Board.** This booth supplies maps and brochures, and will often make a call for you if you need a hotel or car-rental reservation. Inside the international departure terminal is a branch of **Belize Bank** (© 225-2107; www.belizebank.com), open Monday through Friday from 8:30am to 4pm. Across the parking lot, you'll find car-rental and tour-agency desks, open daily from 8am to 9:30pm. A taxi into town will cost BZ$50 to BZ$60.

If you fly in from somewhere else in Belize, you'll probably land at the **Municipal Airport** (airport code TZA), which is on the edge of town. A taxi from here costs just BZ$10 to most hotels in the city. There's no bank or any other services at the Municipal Airport, although most car-rental agencies can arrange to have a car there for you. See p. 88 for taxi info.

There is no direct bus service to either airport.

BY CAR

There are only two highways into Belize City: the Northern Highway, which leads to the Mexican border (166km/103 miles away), and the Western Highway, which leads to the Guatemalan border (132km/82 miles away). Both are well-marked and in good driving condition. If you arrive by car from the north, stay on the road into town, paying close attention to one-way streets, and you'll end up at the Swing Bridge. If you're arriving on the Western Highway, stay on it after it becomes Cemetery Road, and you'll end up at the intersection with Albert Street, a block away from the Swing Bridge.

BY BUS

If you arrive in town by bus, you'll probably end up at the main **bus terminal** on West Collet Canal Street. This is an easy walk to downtown, but it is not recommended after dark. A taxi from the bus station to any hotel in town will cost around BZ$8 to BZ$10; see p. 88 for taxi info.

Tip: For excellent info on bus travel around Belize, check out www.belizebus. wordpress.com.

Visitor Information

The **Belize Tourist Board** (© 800/624-0686 toll free in the U.S. and Canada, or 227-2420 in Belize; www.travelbelize.org) has its main office at 64 Regent St., in the heart of the business district of Belize City. If you missed their desk at the airport, they have another information desk here with regional brochures, basic maps, and a score of hotel and tour fliers; the office is open Monday through Friday from 8am to 5pm. Local travel agencies are another good source of information. Two in Belize City to try are **Discovery Expeditions,** 5916 Manatee Dr., Buttonwood Bay (© **223-0748;** www.discoverybelize.com), and **S&L Travel and Tours,** 91 N. Front St. (© **227-7593;** www.sltravelbelize.com).

City Layout

Belize City is surrounded on three sides by water, with Haulover Creek dividing the city in two. The Swing Bridge, near the mouth of Haulover Creek, is the main route between the two halves of the city, as well as the city's principal landmark. At the south end of the bridge is Market Square and the start of Regent Street and Albert Street. This is where you'll find most of Belize City's shops and offices. To the west and east of these two major roads is a grid of smaller roads lined with dilapidated wooden houses. On the north side of the bridge and to the right is the Fort George area. From the southern side of the city, Cemetery Road heads out of town to the west and becomes the Western Highway, while from the northern side of the city, Freetown Road becomes Haulover Road and then the Northern Highway.

The Neighborhoods in Brief

NORTH SIDE

Fort George Anchored by the Fort George Lighthouse and Radisson Fort George Hotel & Marina at the eastern tip of the city, the Fort George neighborhood encompasses the area south of Queen Street, beginning at the northern side of the Swing Bridge, until it ends at Gabourel Lane. This neighborhood is easily the most upscale and picturesque in Belize City, with stately houses and mansions, generally kept in good repair. Most of the best hotels in the city are located here. It also includes the small triangular Memorial Park and the Belize Tourism Village, as well as the lovely seaside Marine Promenade. The area was originally an island, but was deliberately connected to the mainland with landfill. This area should probably be your first choice for a stay in Belize City.

Barracks Road Located a mile or so north of downtown, Barracks Road runs along the Caribbean Sea for a good stretch before curving inland and becoming Princess Margaret Drive. This is where you'll find the Princess Hotel & Casino, as well as

a couple of good restaurants. Much of the land on either side of Barracks Road is set aside as public parkland, while just inland is an area that is made up mostly of modern middle-class homes. While not within easy walking distance of downtown, it's just a very short taxi ride away. The seaside setting and parks make this a relaxing option for those wanting to avoid the bustle of downtown.

SOUTH SIDE

Business District Belize City's downtown business district runs from the south end of the Swing Bridge between East Canal Street and Southern Foreshore Road to the aptly named South Street. In addition to a busy mix of banks and businesses, this area is home to a host of inexpensive hotels, as well as the Supreme Court and the Bliss Institute. Just south of this area, you will find the old Government House and St. John's Cathedral. This is a good option for budget travelers, but those with a little more money to spend will probably head across the river to the Fort George neighborhood.

GETTING AROUND

By Foot

Belize City's downtown hub is compact and easy to navigate on foot. However, the city has a rather nasty reputation for being unsafe for visitors, and you'd be wise to stick to the busiest sections of downtown and obvious tourist districts. You can easily walk the entire Fort George neighborhood, as well as the compact business area just south of the Swing Bridge. If you need to venture any farther, take a taxi. Be careful when you walk, as sidewalks are often in bad shape and sometimes quite narrow. And, don't walk anywhere at night.

 Hauled Over Haulover

Haulover Creek is actually just what locals call the final few miles of the Belize River, before it joins the Caribbean Sea. It got its name as an outgrowth of common usage, as this is the area where goods and cattle used to be "hauled over" by early settlers, before a bridge was built.

By Taxi

Taxis are plentiful and relatively inexpensive. A ride anywhere in the city should cost between BZ$6 and BZ$15. There's no standardized look or color to taxis in Belize. Many are still old, gas-guzzling American models, although newer Japanese sedans are beginning to replace this aging fleet. Most taxis are clearly marked in some form or other, usually with a roof ornament. Very few taxis use meters, so be sure to negotiate your fare in advance. If you need to call a cab, ask at your hotel or try **Cinderella Plaza Taxi Stand** (✆ 223-0371), **Taxi Garage Services** (✆ 227-3031), or **Majestic Taxi** (✆ 203-4465).

By Car

You shouldn't need to navigate Belize City in a car. If you do find yourself driving around Belize City, go slowly, as pedestrians can appear out of nowhere, and pay attention to the general flow of traffic and the wealth of one-way streets. Despite being members of a former British colony, Belizeans drive on the right-hand side of the road, and road distances are listed in miles.

Most rental-car agencies are based at the Philip S. W. Goldson International Airport, although a couple have offices downtown or at the Municipal Airport, and almost all will arrange to deliver and pick up your vehicle at any Belize City hotel. The most reputable rental-car agencies in Belize include **Avis** (✆ 225-2629; www.avis.com), **Budget** (✆ 223-2435; www.budget-belize.com), **Crystal Auto Rental** ★ (✆ 0800/777-7777 toll-free in Belize, or 223-1600; www.crystal-belize.com), **Hertz** (✆ 223-5395; www.hertz.com), and **Thrifty** (✆ 207-1271; www.thrifty.com). Prices run between BZ$100 and BZ$220 per day for a late-model compact to a compact SUV, including insurance. For more information on renting a car in Belize, see chapter 3.

By Bus

While Belize has an extensive network of bus connections to most cities and rural destinations, there is no metropolitan bus system in Belize City.

[Fast FACTS] BELIZE CITY

Airport See "Arriving," above.

American Express American Express Travel Services is represented in Belize by **Belize Global Travel Services Ltd.,** 41 Albert St. (© **227-7185**), which can issue traveler's checks and replacement cards, and provide other standard services. They are open Monday through Friday from 8am to noon and 1 to 5pm, and on Saturday from 8am to noon. To report lost or stolen Amex credit card or traveler's checks within Belize, call the local number above, or call collect to © **336/393-1111** in the U.S.

Babysitters Your hotel front desk is your best bet for finding a babysitter.

Bookstores Bibliophiles will be disappointed in Belize. You'd be best off purchasing any specific reading material, for either pleasure or research, before arriving in the country. Many gift shops carry a small selection of locally produced fiction and poetry, as well as guidebooks and maps. One decent bookstore in Belize City is **The Book Center,** 1 N. Front St. (© **227-7592**), which has reopened in a convenient location downtown, following a March 2008 fire.

Camera Repair Although your chances of having any serious repair

work done are slim, your best bet for camera repair is the **Belize Photo Lab,** at the corner of North Front and Queen streets (© **223-5682**).

Car Rentals See "Getting Around," above.

Cellphones DigiCell (© **0800/DIGICEL** [344-4235]; www.digicell.bz) has a booth at the airport. If you have an unlocked 850/1900MHz GSM phone, they'll sell you a local prepaid SIM chip with a local number. The chip and initial activation costs BZ$50, including BZ$10 of calls. You can buy subsequent minutes in the form of scratch-off cards in a variety of denominations. The SIM chips and calling cards are sold at their desk at the airport or at one of their many outlets around Belize. Their website also has information on setting up your home phone for roaming in Belize. But be careful, the rates are quite high.

Currency Exchange Most banks will exchange money for a small service charge. It is virtually unnecessary to exchange U.S. dollars for Belize dollars while in Belize, as U.S. dollars are universally accepted at the official two-to-one exchange rate. The exception to this is upon leaving the country, when you will want to convert your remaining

Belize dollars. There is a branch of **Belize Bank** (© **225-2107**) at the international airport, open Monday through Friday from 8:30am to 4pm. If you are flying out on a weekend, or outside of these hours, be sure to exchange any Belize dollars beforehand.

Dentists Call your embassy, which will have a list of recommended dentists, or ask at your hotel.

Doctors Contact your embassy for information on doctors in Belize City, or see "Hospitals," below.

Drugstores There are a handful of pharmacies around Belize City. In downtown, try **Brodie James & Co. Ltd.,** Regent Street (© **227-7070**); it's open Monday through Friday from 8am to 6pm and Saturday from 9am to 2pm. Perhaps the best-stocked pharmacy can be found at **Belize Medical Associates ★**, 5791 St. Thomas Kings Park (© **223-0303;** www.belize medical.com); it's open Monday through Friday from 7:45am to 9pm, Saturday from 7:45am to 1pm, Sunday from 10am to noon, and it makes emergency deliveries at any hour.

Embassies & Consulates See "Fast Facts" in chapter 12.

Emergencies In case of an emergency, dial © **90** from anywhere in Belize City. This will connect you to the police, fire department, and ambulance central switchboard. You can also call ☏ **911.**

Express Mail Services Several international courier and express-mail services have offices in Belize City, including **DHL,** 41 Hydes Lane (☏ **223-4350;** www.dhl.com); **FedEx,** 1 Mapp St. (☏ **224-5221;** www.fedex.com); and **Trans Express,** 41 Albert St. (☏ **227-2332**). All can arrange pickup and delivery services to any hotel in town.

Eyeglasses The **Hoy Eye Center** is a small nationwide chain of opticians and eyeglass stores. Their Belize City branch (☏ **223-0994**) is located at the corner of St. Thomas and St. Joseph streets.

Hospitals Belize Medical Associates, 5791 St. Thomas Kings Park (☏ **223-0303;** www.belizemedical.com), is a modern, 24-hour private hospital, with emergency care and numerous private-practice physicians. The city's main public hospital, the **Karl Heusner Memorial Hospital,** Princess Margaret Drive (☏ **223-1548**), is also open 24 hours and has a wide range of facilities and services.

Internet Access Internet cafes are easy to find in Belize City. Rates run between BZ$1 and BZ$8 per hour. Most hotels listed in this chapter have either Wi-Fi or a small business center with Internet

connections. You can also find Internet cafes scattered around the principal business and tourist districts of Belize City. Alternatively, **BTL** (☏ **0800/112-4636;** www.btl.net), the state Internet monopoly, sells prepaid cards in denominations of BZ$10, BZ$25, and BZ$50 for connecting your laptop to the Web via a local phone call. Some knowledge of configuring your computer's dial-up connection is necessary, and be sure to factor in the phone charge if calling from a hotel. The cards are good for only 30 days. In addition, you can buy a 24-hour period of Wi-Fi access from BTL for BZ$30, which will work at a number of hot spots around the city.

Laundry & Dry Cleaning Most folks rely on their hotel's laundry and dry cleaning services, although these can be expensive. Alternatively, you can try **Belize Dry Cleaners & Laundromat,** 3 Dolphin St. (☏ **227-3396;** www.belizedrycleaners.com).

Maps The **Belize Tourist Board** (☏ **227-2430**) can provide you with good maps to both the city and the country either at their kiosk at the international airport, or at their main office at 64 Regent St. Also, most gift shops sell maps of the country.

Newspapers & Magazines Belize has no daily newspaper. There are four primary weeklies: *Amandala* (www.amandala.com.bz), the *Reporter* (www.reporter.bz), *Belize Times* (www.belizetimes.bz), and the *Guardian* (www.guardian.bz). Most come out on Friday, and all are relatively similar in terms of content, although with some differing and usually obvious political leanings. *Amandala* and the *Reporter* actually publish twice weekly, and are my favorites.

Police The main Belize City station is at 9 Queen St.; the tourist police is a division of the small force. Dial ☏ **90** or **911** in the case of emergency. You can also call ☏ **227-2222.**

Post Office The main post office (☏ **227-4917**) is located at 3 N. Front St. It costs BZ$1 to send a letter to the United States, and BZ$1.20 to send a letter to Europe. Postcards to the same destinations cost BZ50¢ and BZ60¢, respectively.

Restrooms There are very few public restrooms in Belize City. The only ones I know of are located at the little cruise ship tourist village on Fort Street in the Fort George neighborhood. However, if you're not a cruise-ship passenger, you must leave an ID at the gate and get a guest pass. Most hotels and restaurants will let travelers use their facilities, although they are happiest about providing the service to clients.

Safety Belize City has a reputation for being a rough and dangerous city. Tourist police do patrol the busiest tourist areas during the day and early evenings. Still, while most populous downtown areas and tourist attractions are relatively safe during the daytime, travelers are strongly advised to not walk around at night, except in the best-lit and most popular sections of downtown. Basic common sense and street smarts are to be employed. Don't wear flashy jewelry or wave wads of cash around. Be aware of your surroundings, and avoid any people and places that make you feel uncomfortable.

Rental cars generally stick out and are easily spotted by thieves, who know that such cars are likely to be full of expensive camera equipment, money, and other valuables. Don't ever leave anything of value in an unattended parked car.

Taxes There is US$39 departure fee that must be paid in cash (in either U.S. or Belize dollars) at the international airport upon departure, although sometimes the fee is already included in your airline ticket; the land exit fee is US$19. There is a 9% hotel tax added on to all hotel bills, and there is a 12.5% GST tax on all goods and services. A 10% service charge is sometimes added on to restaurant bills. Take this into account when deciding how much to tip (if the service is really good, an extra 5%–10% is fine).

Taxis See "Getting Around," above.

Time Zone Belize City is on Central Standard Time, 6 hours behind Greenwich Mean Time. Belize does not observe daylight saving time.

Useful Telephone Numbers For directory assistance, call ✆ **113;** for an international operator, call ✆ **115;** for the exact time, date, and temperature, call ✆ **121.**

Water The water in Belize City is ostensibly safe to drink. However, many travelers react adversely to water in foreign countries, so it's probably best to drink bottled water during your visit to Belize.

Weather The weather in Belize City is subtropical, and generally similar to that of southern Florida. The average daytime temperature is around 80°F (27°C), although it can get considerably warmer during the summer months, while during the winter months, when northern cold fronts extend their grip south, it can get downright nippy. For more details, see "When to Go" in chapter 3.

WHERE TO STAY

Belize City is small, and your options on where to stay are limited. The most picturesque and safest neighborhood by far is the area around the Fort George Lighthouse. Here you'll find most of the city's best shopping, dining, and accommodations. Still, since the city is so compact, and it's not really recommended to walk around anywhere at night, you're best off choosing a hotel that best meets your needs, style, and budget. There are really only three large, modern hotels in town, and they're all listed below. If your tastes tend toward smaller, more intimate lodgings, there are several good options in different price ranges to choose from.

When getting a price quote from or negotiating with a hotel in Belize, be clear about whether you are being quoted a price in Belize or U.S. dollars. There is a 9% tax on all hotel stays in Belize, which isn't included in the rates listed below.

Fort George

EXPENSIVE

The Great House ★   This stately, colonial-style, small hotel is aptly named. Set a block from the water, near the Fort George lighthouse, this three-story converted mansion was originally built in 1927. It has been well maintained and restored. All rooms are on either the second or third floor, and there are no elevators, if that is an issue for you. The rooms on the top floor are my favorites, with high ceilings, wood floors, and a large, shared wraparound veranda. In fact, there are wraparound verandas on both the second and third floors. While the rooms vary in size, most are very spacious; room no. 1 is one of the largest. Room no. 8 is the smallest room, but it just may have the best view. Throughout the building you'll find a mix of wicker, neocolonial, and locally made modern wood furniture.

13 Cork St. (opposite the Radisson Fort George), Belize City. ✆ **223-3400.** Fax 223-3444. www.great housebelize.com. 16 units. BZ$300 double. AE, DISC, MC, V. Free parking. **Amenities:** Restaurant; bar; lounge; concierge; smoke-free rooms. *In room:* A/C, TV, fridge, hair dryer, free Wi-Fi.

Radisson Fort George Hotel & Marina ★★ ☺   Located in the quiet Fort George neighborhood fronting the ocean, out by the lighthouse, just 1 block from the cruise-ship tourist village, this is Belize City's best business-class and luxury hotel. The best rooms are located in the six-story Club Tower; those on the higher floors have the best views. All are spacious and relatively modern, and feature marble floors and plush furnishings. The Colonial rooms, all of which are nonsmoking, are also large and comfortable. Rooms on the ground floor come with a small, private garden terrace, while some of those on the higher floors offer enticing ocean views. The poolside bar here is one of the more popular spots in town, and often features live music. The hotel also features a full-service marina and dive shop. Service here is excellent, and they've got a comprehensive on-site recycling program.

2 Marine Parade, Belize City. ✆ **800/333-3333** in the U.S., or 223-3333 in Belize. Fax 227-3820. www. radisson.com. 102 units. BZ$318–BZ$458 double. Rates slightly lower in the off season. AE, DISC, MC, V. Free parking. **Amenities:** 3 restaurants; 2 bars; lounge; babysitting; concierge; well-equipped exercise room; 2 midsize outdoor pools; room service; smoke-free rooms. *In room:* A/C, TV, hair dryer, minibar, free Wi-Fi.

EXPENSIVE

Chateau Caribbean   This midsize hotel is housed in an old wooden mansion facing the sea. The rooms are all carpeted, with double beds and cable TV. The third-floor deluxe rooms are somewhat misnamed; while they are huge and have excellent ocean views from their private balconies, they're a bit threadbare and Spartan, with too much empty space. The second-floor dining room serves decent, moderately priced meals of Belizean, Chinese, and international cuisine, with a wonderful view of the ocean. Periodic painting and upkeep are performed, but what the hotel really needs is a major overhaul.

6 Marine Parade (P.O. Box 947), Belize City. ✆ **223-0800.** Fax 223-0900. www.chateaucaribbean.com. 21 units. BZ$178 double; BZ$218 deluxe. AE, MC, V. Free parking. **Amenities:** Restaurant. *In room:* A/C, TV.

Barracks Road

EXPENSIVE

Princess Hotel & Casino   This is the largest hotel in Belize City. The massive lobby area lets out into the hotel's casino, two movie theaters, a shopping arcade, an eight-lane bowling alley, a salon, and various restaurants and bars. The hotel is set right on the water's edge on the northern edge of downtown and is built as one long, six-story structure so that every room has an ocean view. The junior suites offer more space and have private oceanfront balconies. The casino is definitely one of the prime nightlife spots in the country, although it attracts far more locals than tourists. The Princess also has a full-service marina and dive shop. The Radisson is definitely more elegant and better maintained, with far more personalized service and ambience, but the Princess does have a bit more in the way of facilities and nightlife.

Barracks Rd., Belize City. © **888/790-4264** in the U.S., or 223-0638 in Belize. Fax 223-3148. www. princessbelize.com. 181 units. BZ$280 double; BZ$300–BZ$600 suite. Rates include breakfast buffet. AE, DISC, MC, V. Free parking. **Amenities:** 2 restaurants; 2 bars; casino; concierge; fitness center; large outdoor pool; room service; smoke-free rooms. *In room:* A/C, TV, hair dryer.

Business District

INEXPENSIVE

Belcove Hotel 🏷 This funky canal-front hotel is my preferred budget choice in town. You just can't beat the charm of grabbing a seat on one of the upstairs balconies overlooking Haulover Creek and the Swing Bridge, especially at these prices. Sure, the rooms are simple and very basic, but they are neatly kept with shiny, varnished wood floors, while the old wooden building is kept in fresh yellow paint with blood-red trim, yet still feels weathered and historic. These folks also offer airport transfers at a better rate than the local taxis.

9 Regent St., Belize City. © **227-3054.** Fax 227-5248. www.belcove.com. 12 units. BZ$68–BZ$110 double. MC, V. Free street parking. *In room:* No phone.

Coningsby Inn 🏷 Housed in a converted old home toward the western end of Regent Street, the rooms here are compact and rather nondescript. Still, they are clean and comfortable. I prefer those on the second floor, although don't choose one of these for the view, which is over an abandoned lot. I would definitely recommend a splurge for one of the air-conditioned rooms. There's a convivial hostel-like vibe to this operation, and the second-floor bar and lounge area is the social hub of the joint.

76 Regent St., Belize City. © **227-1566.** Fax 227-3726. coningsby_inn@btl.net. 10 units. BZ$100 double without A/C; BZ$120 double with A/C. MC, V. Free street parking. **Amenities:** Bar. *In room:* TV.

Hotel Mopan Located a block or so from the water toward the western end of Regent Street, this longstanding and humble little hotel is a good option in downtown Belize City. The rooms are clean and comfortable, and most of them have air-conditioning. It's definitely worth the slight splurge—I'd say it's necessary—for one of the air-conditioned rooms. Those on the third floor are the best, with the end units, nos. 301 and 304, the best of these. There's no true restaurant here, but breakfast is served in the large first-floor dining room and common area, which also serves as the social hub of the hotel throughout the day and as a bar at night.

55 Regent St., Belize City. © **227-7351.** Fax 227-5383. www.hotelmopan.com. 12 units. BZ$90–BZ$150 double. MC, V. Free street parking. **Amenities:** Bar; all rooms smoke-free. *In room:* TV, no phone, free Wi-Fi.

Around Town

In addition to the places listed below, **D'Nest Inn** ★ (© **223-5416;** www.dnest inn.com) is a cute, well-run little bed-and-breakfast located about 4.8km (3 miles) outside of downtown, just off the Northern Highway.

EXPENSIVE

Best Western Belize Biltmore Plaza Located on the northern outskirts of the city, this chain hotel is simple and straightforward. It's a decent choice if you want to be a little closer to the airport and avoid the crowds and commotion of downtown. The rooms are contemporary and comfortable, with tile floors and heavy wood furnishings. All face the hotel's central courtyard and pool area. As at the Radisson and Princess hotels, the bar here is a popular meeting place for locals, after work and on weekends.

Northern Hwy., Mile Marker 3½, Belize City. © **800/528-1234** in the U.S. and Canada, or 223-2302 in Belize. Fax 223-2301. www.belizebiltmore.com. 75 units. BZ$298–BZ$348 double. AE, MC, V. Free parking. **Amenities:** Restaurant; 2 bars; small exercise room; small outdoor pool; room service; smoke-free rooms. *In room:* A/C, TV, hair dryer, free Wi-Fi.

MODERATE

Villa Boscardi ★ This small and elegant bed-and-breakfast is the plushest lodging you'll find near the airport. Housed in a converted private home, the rooms here are spacious and decorated with a sense of style. Most have interesting artwork and headboard treatments over the beds. The best room here is actually a detached cottage. The hotel is located on the northern outskirts of Belize City, in a quiet neighborhood, just a block or so from the water.

6043 Manatee Dr., Buttonwood Bay, Belize City. © **223-1691.** Fax 223-1669. www.villaboscardi.com. 6 units. BZ$130–BZ$158 double. Rates include full breakfast. AE, MC, V. Free parking. **Amenities:** Free Wi-Fi. *In room:* A/C, TV, hair dryer.

Near the Airport

The airport is located just 16km (10 miles) north of downtown Belize City, a 15- to 20-minute drive, depending on traffic. The area around the airport is decidedly undeveloped and of little interest to visitors. Few international flights arrive late enough or leave early enough to necessitate a stay near the airport. While you'll see the large **Global Village Hotel** (© **225-2555;** fax 220-3000; globalhotel@btl.net), right next to the airport, I find this a desultory and unappealing option. I really recommend you take the short taxi ride into Belize City, or stay at one of the places listed below.

The **Belize River Lodge** (© **888/275-4843** in the U.S. and Canada, or 225-2002 in Belize; www.belizeriverlodge.com) is an upscale fishing lodge located on the banks of the Belize River, just a few miles from the airport, while the **Black Orchid Resort** ★ (© **866/437-1301** in the U.S. and Canada, or 225-9158 in Belize; www.blackorchidresort.com) is a small resort hotel, also on the banks of the Belize River near the town of Burrell Boom.

WHERE TO DINE

Despite its small size, Belize City actually has an excellent and varied selection of dining options open to visitors. While Belizean cuisine and fresh seafood are most common, you can also get excellent Chinese, Indian, and other international fare at restaurants around the city.

Note: When the cruise ships are in town, the restaurants in the Fort George area can get extremely crowded, especially for lunch.

Fort George

In addition to the places listed below, you can get good burgers and bar food at the **Bayman's Tavern** at the Radisson Fort George Hotel.

MODERATE

The Smokey Mermaid INTERNATIONAL   I love the open-air brick courtyard setting of this semielegant yet relaxed restaurant. There are a couple of raised decks and gazebos and a few fountains, spread out among heavy wooden tables and chairs under broad canvas umbrellas in the shade of large seagrape and mango trees and a wealth of other lushly planted ferns and flowers. The dinner menu here ranges from Jamaican jerk pork to shrimp thermidor to chicken Kiev. I recommend the yuca-crusted catch of the day. The desserts here are excellent, with their signature sweet being the Decadent Ecstasy, a chocolate-coconut pie swimming in ice cream, nuts, and chocolate sauce. Breakfasts are filling and varied, and there's a lunch menu, with daily specials, and a range of soups, salads, and sandwiches.

13 Cork St., in The Great House. © **223-4722.** www.smokymermaid.com. Reservations recommended. Main courses BZ$24–BZ$82. AE, MC, V. Daily 6:30am–10pm.

INEXPENSIVE

Le Petit Café ★ COFFEEHOUSE   This place does a brisk business for breakfast, especially among local workers. A variety of both sweet and savory baked goods are available, as well as a wide range of coffee drinks. For lunch, you'll find a selection of sandwiches, filled pastries, and a daily special or two. Seating is available in an air-conditioned dining area, as well as an open-air courtyard, under shade trees and flower-covered trellises. These folks also have a small kiosk in the departure lounge of the international airport.

2 Marine Parade, at the Radisson Fort George Hotel. © **223-3333.** Reservations not accepted. Main courses BZ$4–BZ$20. AE, MC, V. Daily 6am–8pm.

Wet Lizard ★ BELIZEAN/INTERNATIONAL   Boasting a prime setting on a second-floor covered deck overlooking the Swing Bridge and Belize City's little harbor, when the cruise ships are in town, this raucous restaurant is the most popular spot in town. The menu here is simple, with an emphasis on sandwiches, burgers, and American-style bar food. Start things off with some coconut shrimp, conch fritters, or fried calamari, before tackling one of the sandwiches or wraps. You can also get tacos, nachos, fajitas, and burritos, as well as a daily special or two. If you like sweets, save room for the banana chimichanga. The best seats here are the small tables and high stools ringing the railing and overlooking the water. Everything is painted in bright primary colors, and the walls are covered with graffiti and signatures from guests.

1 Fort St. © **223-5973.** www.thewetlizard.com. Reservations not accepted. Main courses BZ$10–BZ$30. AE, MC, V. Open only when cruise ships are in port.

Barracks Road

MODERATE

Sumathi ★ 🍴 INDIAN   With a new location near the heart of downtown, this remains the best Indian restaurant in Belize City. The menu features a wide selection of northern Indian and tandoori specialties. If you're familiar with Indian cuisine, you won't be disappointed here. And if you like it hot and spicy, you're in the right place. The weekday lunch special is an excellent deal at BZ$10. This is also an excellent option for vegetarians, who probably won't find as broad a selection to fit their dietary needs in any other restaurant in the city.

No. 31 Eve St. ℭ **223-1172.** Main courses BZ$20–BZ$30. MC, V. Tues–Sun 11am–3pm and 6–11pm.

Business District

In addition to the places listed below, **Nerie's ★**, which has two locations (124 Freetown Rd., ℭ **224-5199**; and at the corner of Queen and Daly sts., ℭ **223-4028**; www.neries.bz), is another restaurant specializing in Belizean cuisine, and it's very popular with locals.

INEXPENSIVE

Big Daddy's Diner BELIZEAN   Located in the two-story concrete Belize City market, just over the Swing Bridge, Big Daddy's is a clean and comfortable cafeteria-style restaurant, and a great place to mingle with some locals. A breakfast here of scrambled eggs and fry jacks is filling and inexpensive. For lunch there are always several salads, rice dishes, vegetables, and main courses to choose from, and the portions are large. There are great views of the sailboats in the river from the restaurant's big windows.

2nd Floor, Commercial Center, Booth 54. ℭ **227-0932.** Main courses BZ$8–BZ$24. MC, V. Mon–Sat 7am–5pm.

Macy's 👙 BELIZEAN   For authentic Belizean cooking and a down-home funky vibe, you can't beat this tiny local place. The food is good, the service is friendly, the prices are right, and the dining room is cool and cozy. Order a fish filet with rice and beans, or curried chicken, or be more daring and try one of their daily wild-game chalkboard specials, which could feature anything from armadillo and deer to wild pig or gibnut. Macy's no longer serves turtle or other endangered species, and there seem to be fewer wild game options than there were in the past. There's only a smattering of tables. Each is set with a plastic tablecloth and plastic place mat, under a strategically placed overhead fan.

18 Bishop St. ℭ **207-3419.** Main courses BZ$10–BZ$32. No credit cards. Mon–Sat 11:30am–9pm.

Around Town

MODERATE

Bird's Isle Restaurant & Bar ★ 👙 BELIZEAN   This relaxed restaurant has arguably the best location in the city, seaside on a small island just over a tiny bridge at the far southern end of Regent Street. The main dining hall is a circular wooden deck under a soaring thatch roof, though I prefer the open-air seats under large shade umbrellas on the wooden deck closer to the water. You can get a range of Belizean staples, fresh seafood, and grilled meats. Portions are hefty. The nightly specials are great deals, especially Wednesdays, with BZ$2.50 burgers. Thursday nights are dedicated to karaoke, while Fridays are turned over to live bands.

Bird's Isle. ℭ **207-6500.** Main courses BZ$10–BZ$16; lobster BZ$24. MC, V. Mon–Tues 10:30am–2:30pm; Wed–Sat 10:30am–2:30pm and 5–10pm (Fri–Sat until midnight or later).

Chon Saan Palace ★ CHINESE   If you're in the mood for Chinese food in Belize City, you can't do better than this local favorite. The room and the menu are immense. You'll find plenty of chow mein and Cantonese dishes, but there's also a substantial Szechuan section and a showstopping sizzling steak that comes hissing and screaming to your table. If you're primed for seafood, you'll love the large fish tanks stocked with live lobster (in season), shrimp, and the daily catch. This is a great place to come with a group, as there are plenty of large, round tables with built-in Lazy Susans, perfect for sharing food and a good time. Don't take the easy way out and head to the more conveniently located New Chon Saan Palace—it's worth the short taxi ride to eat at the original.

1 Kelly St. © **223-3008.** Main courses BZ$12–BZ$40. MC, V. Mon–Sat 11am–3pm and 5–11:30pm (Fri–Sat until midnight or later); Sun 5–11pm.

Riverside Tavern ★★ INTERNATIONAL   One of the most happening spots in Belize City, this large place has both indoor and outdoor seating on a spot overlooking Haulover Creek. The restaurant specializes in hefty steaks and delicious ribs. But you can also get seared tuna, grilled snapper, coconut shrimp, or jerk shrimp. The lunch menu features pizzas, pastas, sandwiches, and rolls. The burgers here—which come in 6-, 10-, and 16-ounce sizes—are rightly famous and served for both lunch and dinner. There are TVs showing sporting events, and at times this place can get quite boisterous.

2 Mapp St. © **223-5640.** Lunch BZ$15–BZ$40; dinner main courses BZ$24–BZ$60. DISC, MC, V. Mon–Wed 11am–midnight; Thurs–Fri 11am–2am; Sat noon–2am.

Old Belize Bar & Grill ☺ BELIZEAN/INTERNATIONAL   What this restaurant lacks in creativity and fancy fare, they make up for in portion size. The servings are huge. There's an emphasis on fried foods here—chicken and shrimp are favorites. But you can also get pizzas, burritos, burgers, hot dogs, and buffalo wings. The best seats are on the long, open-air deck fronting the lagoon here. This is a great spot for lunch. It's also a great spot to bring the kids, as it's part of the Old Belize complex, with an attached museum, beach, and children's play area.

Western Hwy., Mile 5. © **222-4129.** www.oldbelize.com. Main courses BZ$12–BZ$46. AE, MC, V. Daily 11am–10pm.

WHAT TO SEE & DO

There really isn't much reason to take a guided tour of Belize City. The downtown center is extremely compact and lends itself very easily to self-directed exploration. There are only a handful of interesting attractions, and all are within easy walking distance of the central Swing Bridge. Below you'll find reviews of the most interesting attractions, as well as a walking tour of the city.

When cruise ships are in town, you'll find a line of trolley cars and horse-drawn carriages just outside the Belize Tourism Village offering rides around the city. Most of these include a stop, with entrance fee included, to the Museum of Belize (p. 98). If you really feel the need for a guided tour of the city and there's no cruise ship in town, ask at your hotel desk for a recommendation, or call **Belize Horse & Carriage Tours** (© 602-3048), **Discovery Expeditions** (© 223-0748; www.discoverybelize.com), or **S & L Travel and Tours** (© 227-7593; www.sltravelbelize.com). A half-day city tour should cost around BZ$60 to BZ$100 per person, but can easily be combined with a visit to one of the several popular nearby attractions. The latter two above companies offer a whole range of day trips and combinations to the attractions close to the city and even farther afield (see "Attractions Outside Belize City," below, and "Side Trips from Belize City," later in this chapter).

The Top Attractions

Belize City is very light on true attractions. The museums mentioned below are quite quaint and provincial by most international standards, although they are worth a visit if you are spending a day getting to know the city, residents, and local history.

Bliss Centre for the Performing Arts ★   Totally rebuilt and reopened in 2005, the Bliss Institute is a busy little complex that is the cultural heart of Belize City. Housing a performing arts space, rehearsal halls, a cafeteria, the National Institute of the Arts, and a couple of gallery spaces, this is the place to check for live theater, dance, and music performances while you're in town. It's also a good place to stop and see if there's an interesting exhibit of art or photography. The main building's circular design takes advantage of the complex's setting, with large picture windows overlooking the Belize Harbour. The gallery spaces are fairly small, so you will need only about a half-hour, possibly less, to tour the institute.

Southern Foreshore, btw. Church and Bishop sts. Ⓒ **227-2110.** Free admission. Mon–Sat 8:30am–5pm.

The Image Factory ★   This is Belize City's top art gallery. With a large stable of local and regional artists to choose from, this nonprofit gallery and arts organization has regularly rotating exhibitions, as well as a semipermanent collection of art, photography, sculpture, and craft works.

91 N. Front St. ⒸⒸ **223-4093.** Free admission. Mon–Sat 9am–5pm.

Museum of Belize ★★   Housed in what was once "Her Majesty's Prison," this museum features a collection of historical documents, photographs, currency, stamps, and other artifacts, as well as exhibits of Mayan pottery and archaeological finds. Although somewhat small, the collection of Mayan ceramic, jade, and both ornamental and functional pieces is worth the price of admission. There are also traveling exhibits and a room featuring attractively mounted insects from Belize. Just so you won't forget the building's history, a prison cell has been restored to its original condition. The museum takes up the two floors of this historic old brick building. Plan on spending between 1 and 2 hours here.

Gabourel Lane, in front of the Central Bank building. ⒸⒸ **223-4524.** Admission BZ$10 for adults, BZ$4 for students, free for children. Mon–Fri 9am–5pm.

Old Belize ★ ☺   This attraction aims at providing a comprehensive experience of the natural, cultural, and political history of Belize, with exhibits re-creating everything from a rainforest and a Mayan ceremonial cave to a logging camp and a Garífuna home. Admission includes a 45-minute guided tour, but you'll probably want to stay longer to explore some exhibits on your own, visit the gift shop, or eat at the restaurant here (p. 97). There's even a pretty decent little beach here, with a large water slide and children's playground area, and separate zipline cable adventure. Plan on spending between 1 and 2 hours here—more if you're going to eat or hang out at the beach. While it's certainly touristy, if you have only a limited amount of time in Belize City, or the country in general, this place does give a good overview.

Western Hwy., Mile 5. ⒸⒸ **222-4129.** www.oldbelize.com. Admission to full-access package BZ$30 adults, BZ$15 for children 6–12; just to museum BZ$5 adults, BZ$3 children. Tues–Sat 8am–4pm; Sun–Mon 10am–4pm.

St. John's Cathedral ★   This old brick church is the oldest Anglican cathedral in Central America, and the oldest standing structure in Belize. Built in 1812 by slaves using bricks brought over as ballast, it is also the only Anglican church outside of England where kings have been crowned—during the 1800s four Mosquito Indian kings held their coronation ceremonies here. The bell in the high bell tower here was brought over in 1826. In the small yard surrounding the church you'll find a few graves of prominent Anglican clergy.

At the corner of Albert and Regent sts. ✆ **227-3029.** Free admission. Daily 8:30am–5pm.

Traveler's Liquor Heritage Center   Belize's top spirit producer offers the opportunity to learn a bit about the history, lore, and production process of the country's ubiquitous One Barrel Rum at this small museum-like exhibit. You can also get a glimpse into the contemporary production operation at the factory located behind the Heritage Center. At the end of the tour, you can taste various products and shop for bottles, T-shirts, and other souvenirs.

Mile 2½ Northern Hwy. ✆ **223-2855.** www.onebarrelrum.com. Free admission. Mon–Sat 10am–7pm.

A Walking Tour

The following walking tour covers both the north and south sides of Belize City, which together comprise the entire historic downtown center. For most of its length, you'll be either right on the water or just a block or two away. As described, the walking tour should take you anywhere from 2 to 4 hours, depending on how much time you take visiting the various attractions. The only major attraction not right on the route below is the Museum of Belize, although it's only a 4-block detour east from the Swing Bridge. The route laid out on this walking tour is pretty safe during daylight hours, but should not be attempted after dark.

Begin your stroll at the **Fort George Lighthouse** and **Baron Bliss Memorial,** out on the northeastern tip of the city. A small slate stone marks the grave of Henry Edward Ernest Victor Bliss (see "Baron Bliss" on p. 100). After soaking up the view of the Caribbean and some fresh sea air, head toward downtown on Fort Street. On your left, you'll find the **Belize Tourism Village** (✆ **223-2767**), which was built to accommodate the rising tide of cruise-ship passengers. Stop in and shop, or just browse the variety of local and regional arts and crafts. *Note:* If you're not a cruise-ship passenger, you'll have to leave a photo ID at the gate in exchange for a temporary pass to visit the shops and restaurants here.

 Swingin'

The Swing Bridge officially opens twice a day, at roughly 6am and 6pm Monday through Saturday, to let tall masted sailboats pass through. However, if there's no demand, it doesn't open. When it does, the entire process takes around 20 minutes, and in addition to being a minor spectacle, it is a major traffic hassle.

As you continue, Fort Street becomes North Front Street. Just north of the Belize Tourism Village you'll find **Fine Arts** (p. 104) and **The Image Factory** (p. 104), by far the two best galleries and fine arts gift shops in the country. Just before reaching the Swing Bridge, you'll pass the **Maritime Terminal** on your left.

baron BLISS

Henry Edward Ernest Victor Bliss, the fourth Baron Bliss of the Kingdom of Portugal, anchored his yacht, *Sea King*, off of Belize City on January 14, 1926. Within 2 months, the baron would be dead, never having set foot on Belizean soil. Nonetheless, the eccentric Baron Bliss is this tiny country's most beloved benefactor. His time spent anchored in Belize Harbour was enough to convince him to rewrite his will and leave a large chunk of his estate—nearly $2 million at the time—to the country of Belize (then known as British Honduras). The trust he set up stipulated that the principal could never be touched, and only the interest was to be used. The ongoing bequest has funded numerous public works projects around the country, and today it's hard to miss the baron's legacy. There's the Baron Bliss Memorial, Baron Bliss Nursing School, Bliss Institute, and the Bliss (Fort George) Lighthouse. Every year on March 9, a large regatta is held in Belize Harbour in honor of the baron.

Now, cross the **Swing Bridge** and head south. On your left is the **Commercial Center.** Wander through the stalls of fresh vegetables, butcher shops, and fish stands. You'll also find some gift shops and souvenir stands here.

The **Supreme Court building,** off the small **Battlefield Park** (or Market Sq.) just a block south of the Swing Bridge, is a real prize of English colonial architecture with the city's only clock tower. Walk around the four sides and see if any are accurately telling the time.

Down at the southern end of Regent Street, you'll find the **Government House** and **St. John's Cathedral** (p. 99), also known by its more officious-sounding moniker, the Anglican Cathedral of St. John the Baptist. Both of these buildings were constructed with slave labor in the early 19th century, and they remain the most prominent reminders of the 3 centuries of British colonial presence here. The Government House has been converted into a **House of Culture** (© 227-3050), with the mission of encouraging and sponsoring local participation in the arts, music, and dance. You will occasionally find lecture series or an odd concert going on here.

For your return to downtown, head toward the water and come back on the Southern Foreshore Road, stopping in at the **Bliss Institute** (p. 98) to see if there's an interesting exhibit on display or a performance scheduled for later in the evening.

Attractions Outside Belize City

The attractions listed below are within an hour of Belize City; both can be reached by public transportation. In addition, the Mayan ruins of **Altun Ha** ★ and **Lamanai** ★★ and the **Crooked Tree Wildlife Sanctuary** ★ are all easily accessible from Belize City. All are popularly sold as day tours, often in various mix-and-match combinations. If you're interested in visiting one or more of these attractions as part of an organized tour, ask at your hotel, or call **Discovery Expeditions** (© 223-0748; www.discovery belize.com) or **S & L Travel and Tours** (© 227-7593; www.sltravelbelize.com). Prices range from about BZ$100 to BZ$280 per person, depending on the tour, means of transportation, and attraction(s) visited. Tours, especially those to Altun Ha and Crooked Tree, are often combined with lunch and an optional spa treatment at Maruba

Resort Jungle Spa. For more information on Altun Ha, Lamanai, Crooked Tree Wildlife Sanctuary, and Maruba Resort Jungle Spa, see chapter 9.

Belize Zoo ★★   Founded in 1983 as part of a last-ditch and improvised effort to keep and care for a host of wild animals that were being used in a documentary film shoot, the **Belize Zoo,** Western Highway, Mile Marker 29 (✆ **220-8004;** www. belizezoo.org), is a national treasure. Gentle paths wind through some 12 hectares (30 acres) of land, where the zoo houses more than 125 animals, all native Belizean species. According to their own promotional materials, "the zoo keeps animals which were either orphaned, born at the zoo, rehabilitated animals, or sent to the Belize Zoo as gifts from other zoological institutions."

Walking around the zoo, you'll see several species of Belizean cats, April the tapir, and other wild animals in idealized natural surroundings. The animals here are some of the liveliest and happiest looking I've ever seen in a zoo. It's obvious that they're well cared for. All the exhibits have informative hand-painted signs accompanying them. *Tip:* It's best to visit early in the morning or close to closing time, when the animals are at their most active and the Belizean sun is at its least oppressive. In addition, the zoo can get crowded at times; on days when cruise ships are visiting Belize City, busloads of tourists begin to arrive around 10am, but often are packed up and gone by 3pm.

The entrance is a couple of hundred yards in from the Western Highway. Any bus traveling between Belize City and Belmopan or San Ignacio will drop you off at the zoo entrance. Admission is BZ$16 for adults and BZ$8 for children, and the zoo is open daily from 8am to 5pm.

Adjacent to the zoo is a sister project, the **Belize Zoo Jungle Lodge** ★ (✆ **220-8004**). Set on 34 hectares (84 acres) of untouched savannah, the center has a nature trail, an observation platform, a classroom, and a range of guest rooms. An overnight stay here costs between BZ$60 and BZ$144 per person, including hotel taxes, breakfast, and dinner. While most of the beds here are in dormitory-style rooms with shared bathrooms, a few private cabins offer private bathrooms and more space, and are definitely worth the extra dollars. Folks who stay here can take a nocturnal tour of the zoo for BZ$30.

Community Baboon Sanctuary ★   There aren't really baboons in Belize; this is just the local name for the black howler monkeys who reside in this innovative sanctuary. The sanctuary is a community program run by local landowners in eight villages to preserve the local population of these vociferous primates. The howlers found here are an endangered endemic subspecies found only in Belize. There's a visitor's center and natural history museum (✆ **220-2181;** www.howlermonkeys. org) in the village of Bermudian Landing, and it is here that you pay your BZ$10 admission fee, which includes a short guided hike. If you want a longer guided hike, you should hire one of the many local guides for a modest fee. The preserve stretches for some 32km (20 miles) along the Belize River, and there are several trails that wind through farmland and secondary forest. You will undoubtedly hear the whooping and barking of the howler monkeys as they make their way through the treetops feeding on fruits, flowers, and leaves. In addition to the nearly 1,500 howler monkeys that make their home in the sanctuary, there are numerous other bird and mammal species to be spotted here. With your guide's help, you should be able to spot the monkeys and, if you're lucky, any combination of peccaries, anteaters, pacas, and coati-mundi. Bring binoculars if you have them.

At the visitor's center, you can also hire a canoe for a leisurely paddle and float on the Belize River. The cost is around BZ$50 for an hour or so paddle in a canoe that will hold two passengers in addition to the guide. Other guided tours offered include specialized bird-watching excursions and night canoe outings to spot crocodiles. Finally, the several small villages that compose the conservation project are wonderful examples of rural Kriol villages. Be sure to visit one or two, stroll around, talk to the residents, and see what kind of craftwork and food you can find. In each village, there are families that rent out simple rooms. Ask at the museum and information center, or reserve in advance via their website.

Bermudian Landing village, site of the sanctuary's visitor center, is about 32km (20 miles) west of Belize City. If you are driving, head north on the Northern Highway and watch for the Burrel Boom Road turnoff. Buses to Bermudian Landing leave Belize City several times a day. Call the sanctuary's visitor's center (see above) for current schedule and departure point. The one-way fare is BZ$5.

OUTDOOR ACTIVITIES

Due to the crime, chaos, and often oppressive heat and humidity, you'll probably want to get out of the city, or onto the water, before undertaking anything too strenuous. But if you want to brave the elements, there are a few outdoor activities for you to try in and around Belize City. See chapter 5 for more info on adventure sports in Belize.

CAVING   The **Caves Branch ★★★** region is about a 50- to 90-minute drive from Belize City, depending on where you enter the cave systems. Several tour operators offer a variety of hiking and tubing trips through an extensive network of caves here. The **Caves Branch River** is a slow, meandering river that should probably be called a creek. Nevertheless, it passes through a series of long caves, making it perfect for a slow float on an inner tube through this dark and mysterious world. However, I recommend hiking because it allows more time for close examination of the geological formations and Mayan relics than tubing. **Actun Tunichil Muknal ★★**, located near Teakettle Village north of Belmopan, and the **Crystal Cave ★★**, located adjacent to the Jaguar Paw Jungle Resort, are two of the more spectacular caves you will ever visit. Most tour operators and tour desks in Belize City can arrange these trips, or you can call **Ian Anderson's Caves Branch Adventure Company ★★** (© 822-2800; www.cavesbranch.com) directly. These folks run, by far, the most extensive cave adventure tour operation in the country. See "Belmopan" in chapter 10 for more information on the Caves Branch region.

FISHING   While most serious fishermen head to one of the cayes or southern Belize destinations, it's possible to line up fishing charters out of Belize City. The marinas at the **Radisson Fort George Hotel & Marina** (© 223-3333), **Old Belize** (© 222-4129), and **Princess Hotel & Casino** (© 223-2670) all have regular sport charter fleets and can arrange a variety of options. You could also check in with the folks at the **Belize River Lodge** (© 888/275-4843 in the U.S. and Canada, or 225-2002 in Belize; www.belizeriverlodge.com). Expect to pay around US$1,000 to US$1,800 per day for a boat that can accommodate up to four fishermen.

GOLF Your options are limited if you want to hit the links in Belize. There's only one operational golf course in the country, the **Roaring Forks Golf Course** (✆ 820-2131; www.belizegolf.net), a par-64 executive course, located just outside of Belmopan. Greens fees here are just BZ$50 for 18 holes.

JOGGING Belize City is not very amenable to jogging. If you must run, you could try a loop around the Fort George neighborhood, hugging the coast from the Fort George Lighthouse to Memorial Park, then heading to Fort Street, which will bring you back to the lighthouse. It's best to jog very early, before there's much street traffic and before it gets too hot. Another nice stretch for jogging is on the sidewalk and parks that line Barracks Road where it fronts the sea.

SAILING The waters off Belize Harbour are theoretically perfect for day sailing excursions, although currently no one is consistently offering this option. The two main charter companies, **The Moorings** and **TMM Charters,** are both based outside of Belize City, the former in Placencia, the latter in San Pedro. However, if you're interested in trying to line up a day sail, ask at your hotel desk or check in with the marinas at the **Radisson Fort George Hotel & Marina** (✆ 223-3333), **Old Belize** (✆ 222-4129), and **Princess Hotel & Casino** (✆ 223-2670). See chapters 7 and 8 for details on longer charter options.

SCUBA DIVING & SNORKELING The Belize Barrier Reef lies just off the coast from Belize City. It's a short boat ride to some excellent scuba diving and snorkeling. While most serious divers chose to stay out on one of the cayes for really close proximity to the reefs, it is still possible to visit any number of excellent sites on day trips from Belize City, including the Blue Hole and Turneffe and Lighthouse atolls. Check in with **Hugh Parkey's Belize Dive Connection** (✆ 888/223-5403 in the U.S. and Canada, or 223-5086 in Belize; www.belizediving.com).

SPAS & GYMS **Best Western Belize Biltmore Plaza** (p. 94) and **Radisson Fort George Hotel & Marina** (p. 92) have small gym facilities and offer basic spa services. However, only the Radisson allows nonguests use of their facilities, with a daily fee of BZ$20.

SWIMMING Most of the higher-end hotels in Belize City have pools. If yours doesn't, you can head out to the **Cucumber Beach** ★ at Old Belize (p. 98). The beach here has both an open-water section and an enclosed, and hence calmer, lagoon. There are also a water slide and a children's playground, as well as chaise longues and palm-thatch shade shelters. Admission is BZ$5 for beach access, and BZ$10 for both the beach and water-slide privileges. Children are half-price.

SHOPPING

You won't be bowled over by shopping options here in Belize City, and very few people come to Belize specifically to shop. You will find a modest handicraft industry, with different specialties produced by the country's various ethnic communities. The Kriol populations of the coastal area and outer cayes specialize in coral and shell jewelry, as well as woodcarvings with maritime (dolphins, turtles, and ships) themes. The Belizean Mayan population produces replicas of ancient petroglyphs and different modern designs on various-sized pieces of slate. Finally, the Garífuna peoples of the southern coastal villages are known for their small dolls.

My favorite gift item in Belize continues to be **Marie Sharp's Hot Sauce ★★★**, which comes in several heat gradations, as well as some tropical fruit flavors. The original blend of habanero peppers, carrots, and vinegar is one of my all-time favorite hot sauces. The company also produces mango chutney and an assortment of jams. You can pick up Marie Sharp products at any supermarket and most gift shops; I recommend you stick to the supermarkets, though, to avoid price gouging. In addition to Marie Sharp's, Lizette's and Hot Mama brands of locally produced hot sauces are also a good bet.

Please do not buy any kind of sea-turtle products (including jewelry); wild birds; lizard, snake, or cat skins; corals; or orchids (except those grown commercially). No matter how unique, beautiful, insignificant, or inexpensive it may seem, your purchase will directly contribute to the further hunting of endangered species.

The Shopping Scene

Most shops in the downtown district are open Monday through Saturday from about 8am to 6pm. Some shops close for lunch, while others remain open (it's just the luck of the draw for shoppers). Since the cruise ships are such a big market for local merchants, many adjust their hours to specifically coincide with cruise-ship traffic and their particular shore times.

Shopping A to Z

ART

Fine Arts ★★   This is the best gallery and gift shop I've found in Belize City. They have a large selection of original art works in a variety of styles, formats, and sizes. Browse primitivist works by Walter Castillo and Pen Cayetano, alongside more modern abstract pieces, traditional still lifes, and colorful representations of Belize's marine, natural, and human life. 1 Fort St., next to the Belize Tourism Village. ✆ **223-7773.**

The Image Factory Shop ★   Attached to the excellent gallery and exhibition space of the same name, this shop offers up prints, paintings, photographs, and craft pieces by prominent Belizean and regional artists, as well as books, music CDs, and more traditional souvenir items. 91 N. Front St. ✆ **223-4093.**

HANDICRAFTS & SOUVENIRS

By far the largest selection of gift shops and souvenir stands can be found at the **Belize Tourism Village** (8 Fort St.; ✆ **223-2767**).

In addition to housing the best collections of fine art for sale in the city, **Fine Arts** and **The Image Factory Shop** (see "Art," above) also feature some of the best handicrafts and handmade jewelry. The quality and selection are a definite step above what you'll find at most other gift shops and tourist traps in town, and around the country.

Go-Tees ★   This long-standing design and production company has a shop and factory on the northern outskirts of the city, where you'll find an extensive collection of T-shirts, visored hats, and local textiles. They also sell a range of handmade jewelry, Guatemalan textiles, Mexican hammocks, and Belizean crafts. 6238 Park Ave., Buttonwood Bay. ✆ **223-4660.** www.gotees.net.

National Handicraft Center   This place houses a wide selection of local and regional crafts and souvenirs all under one roof, but it's no longer the main game in town. In fact, it's lost a lot of its luster and traffic to the Belize Tourism Village. Still, you'll find a good selection of Mayan stone carvings, coconut shell jewelry, and wooden knickknacks, as well as some oil paintings, prints, and a small selection of books. Moreover, the prices here are slightly better than those at the Belize Tourism Village, and if you see something you really like, you might even be able to bargain for it. 2 S. Park St. © **223-3636.**

JEWELRY

Coral is a very delicate, rapidly disappearing living organism that grows very slowly; please avoid buying coral jewelry, as it just feeds demand and inevitably leads to the destruction of the spectacular Belizean reefs.

Maya Jade ★   This place bills itself as a museum and gallery, and while there is a whole room of museum-style displays explaining the history of Mesoamerican Mayan jade use and artistry, this is nonetheless predominantly a retail operation. That said, the small selection here includes some very well-done necklaces and earrings that you won't find elsewhere. 8 Fort St. © **203-1222.**

LIQUOR

Your best bet for liquor shopping is at local supermarkets, or the duty-free shop at the airport. There are several brands of Belizean rum available; the most popular is **One Barrel,** which has a hint of coconut and vanilla. Other brands produce some more heavily flavored coconut rums. The **Prestige** brand aged rum is pretty good, if you're looking for a straight, dry rum. Belize doesn't produce any wines or other spirits of note, although you may want to pick up a bottle of locally produced wine, or cashew wine, for the sake of novelty.

MARKETS

The only real market of note is the **Commercial Center,** located just over the Swing Bridge, on the southern side of the city. This two-story modern concrete structure houses a mix of stalls and enclosed storefronts. The first floor is predominantly devoted to fresh produce, fish stalls, and butcher shops, but you'll also find stands selling flowers, fresh herbs, and some souvenir shops. There are more souvenir shops and some restaurants, including Big Daddy's, on the second floor. The Commercial Center is open daily from 7:30am to 7pm.

MUSIC

Punta Rock is the most Belizean of music styles. A close cousin to soca and calypso, Punta is upbeat dance music. Popular proponents include Andy Palacios, Chico Ramos, Pen Cayetano, the Garífuna Kids, Travesia Band, and Peter Flores (aka Titiman). For a taste of traditional Kriol folk music, try to track down a copy of *Mr. Peters' Boom & Chime*. You also might be able to find some traditional Garífuna music, which tends to be ceremonial dance music, very similar to traditional West African music.

The best place to find Belizean music is a gift shop. Still, these are very hit or miss. Check at the **Belize Tourism Village** (p. 99). You might also try online music stores; two good sources are **www.stonetreerecords.com** and **www.calabashmusic.com**. I'd avoid the various vendors selling bootleg cassettes and CDs on the side of the road, since the quality can be sketchy, and the artists don't receive a dime.

BELIZE CITY AFTER DARK

Again, Belize City is a small, provincial city in an underdeveloped country, so don't expect to find a raging nightlife scene. The most popular nightspots—for both locals and visitors alike—are the bars at the few high-end hotels in town.

The Performing Arts

It's really the luck of the draw as to whether you can catch a concert, theater piece, or dance performance—they are the exception, not the norm. To find out if anything is happening, ask at your hotel, read the local papers, or check in with the **Bliss Institute** (𝄐 **227-2110**).

The Bar Scene

The bar and club scene in Belize City is rather lackluster. The most happening bar in town is the **Riverside Tavern ★★** (p. 97). This is especially true on weekends, and whenever there's an important soccer, basketball, or cricket match on. The **Bird's Isle Restaurant & Bar ★** (p. 96) is another lively option, with karaoke on Thursday nights and live music on Fridays. For a casual bar scene, you can also try **Thirsty Thursday's** (𝄐 **223-1677**), located out on Newtown Barracks Road. While, for a somewhat refined place to wet your whistle, head to the **Tinto & Blanco Wine Bar** (𝄐 **223-4700**), a small, dimly lit space on the first floor of The Great House (p. 92), which offers up cocktails and a selection of wines by the glass or bottle, and a small selection of dishes to go along with them.

Travelers and locals alike also tend to frequent the bars at the major hotels and tourist traps. The liveliest of these are the bars at the **Radisson Fort George Hotel & Marina** (p. 92), the **Best Western Belize Biltmore Plaza** (p. 94), and the **Princess Hotel & Casino** (p. 92), all of which often have a live band on weekend nights. Of these, I prefer the **Club Calypso ★** (𝄐 **223-2670**), an open-air affair built over the water at the Princess Hotel & Casino, although it's sort of a crapshoot as to which bar will be hopping on any given night.

Casinos

For gaming, the **Princess Hotel & Casino** (p. 92) is the only game in town, and the casino here is large, modern, and well equipped. While it's not on the scale of Vegas or Atlantic City, the casino is certainly respectable, with enough gaming tables, slots, and other attractions to make most casual gamblers quite happy to drop a few dollars.

SIDE TRIPS FROM BELIZE CITY

Given the fact that Belize is so small, it is possible to visit any of the country's major tourist destinations and attractions as a side trip from Belize City. Most are easily reached in less than 2 hours by car, bus, or boat taxi. Other attractions are accessible by short commuter flights. All in all, you can visit almost any destination or attraction described in this book as a day trip, except for the far southern zone.

For a listing of active adventures that make good day trips, see "Outdoor Activities," earlier in this chapter; for a description of the most popular attractions within close proximity to Belize City, see "What to See & Do," earlier in this chapter. Other possible destinations for side trips out of Belize City include **Caye Caulker** and **Ambergris Caye,** dive excursions to the nearby reefs, and even trips to the more isolated dive destinations such as the **Blue Hole** and the **Lighthouse** and **Turneffe atolls ★★**. You can also visit the Mayan ruins of **Altun Ha, Lamanai, Xunantunich, Cahal Pech,** and even **Caracol** and **Tikal.** All of the popular side-trip destinations out of Belize City are discussed in more depth in "What to See & Do," earlier in this chapter, or in the subsequent destination chapters.

Most hotels can arrange any of the day trips suggested above. In addition, you can check in with **Discovery Expeditions** (𝒞 **223-0748;** www.discoverybelize.com) or **S & L Travel and Tours** (𝒞 **227-7593;** www.sltravelbelize.com). **Note:** Most of the tours and activities mentioned here and in "Outdoor Activities," earlier in this chapter, are also sold to visiting cruise-ship passengers. When the cruise ships are in town, a cave-tubing adventure, a snorkel trip to Hol Chan Marine Reserve and Shark-Ray Alley, or a visit to either Altun Ha or Lamanai ruins can be a mob scene. It's often possible to avoid these crowds by starting your tour or activity very early, or in the late afternoon. If you are organizing your tour or activity with a local operator, mention that you want to avoid the cruise-ship groups, if at all possible.

7

THE NORTHERN CAYES & ATOLLS

The cayes (pronounced "keys") are a series of small islands strung along the length of the Belize Barrier Reef, set amid waters that are at once crystal clear and brilliantly turquoise. Seen firsthand, there's something truly mesmerizing and almost unbelievable about the clarity and color of this water. But as they say around here: "You betta Belize it."

With the reef providing protection from the open ocean, the cayes are literally islands of tranquillity in a calm blue sea. Aside from sunbathing and slow strolling, scuba diving, snorkeling, and fishing are the main attractions in the cayes. They are all world-class. From the bustling miniresorts of **Ambergris Caye ★★** to the funky Rastafarian charm of tiny **Caye Caulker ★★★** to the deserted-isle feel of the **Turneffe Islands ★★** and **Lighthouse Reef atolls ★★**, it's the idyllic combination of sun and sea, as well as adventure and relaxation, that attracts and captivates most visitors to Belize. Most of the cayes are small enough to walk from one end to the other in less than 20 minutes. On others, it won't take you nearly as long.

Jacques Cousteau put Belize on the diving map back in 1971, with his explorations of the **Blue Hole ★★**. The country has almost 322km (200 miles) of continuous barrier reefs and visibility of up to 61m (200 ft.) on some days. It's hard to open a diving magazine without finding an article on diving in Belize. For those sticking a little closer to the surface, the snorkeling is just as rewarding, with **Hol Chan Marine Reserve ★★** and **Shark-Ray Alley ★★** considered two of the best snorkeling experiences on the planet.

On the plentiful flats found inside the reefs and up in nearby estuaries, anglers find action with tarpon, snook, permit, and feisty bonefish. There's more tarpon as well as giant snapper and grouper found along the reefs, while out on the open ocean the tackle and game get bigger, with marlin, sailfish, tuna, and wahoo as the principal prey.

The Northern Cayes & Atolls

Shipstern
Lagoon

MEXICO

COROZAL

Deer
Caye

CARIBBEAN
SEA

Blackadore
Caye

*Ambergris
Caye*

LIGHTHOUSE
REEF ATOLL   Sandbore
Caye

Northern
Caye

Maskall

Blue
Hole

Old Northern Hwy.

Caye
Cangrejo

San Pedro

Long
Caye

Half Moon
Caye

0   5 mi

0   5 km

**Caye
Caulker**

Hick's
Caye

Caye
Chapel

Long
Caye

BELIZE

Ladyville

St. George's
Caye

*TURNEFFE
ATOLL*

Drowned
Cayes

**Belize
City**

Spanish Lookout
Caye

To
Lighthouse
Reef Atoll
(see inset)
→

Northern
Lagoon

Blackbird
Caye

Middle
Long
Caye

Southern
Lagoon

Gales Point

Alligator Caye

Deadman's
Caye

----- Reef

0   10 mi

Mullins River

STANN
CREEK

Southern
Long Caye

0   10 km

AMBERGRIS CAYE ★★

58km (36 miles) N of Belize City; 64km (40 miles) SE of Corozal Town

San Pedro is Belize's principal sun-and-fun destination. The compact "downtown" area is a jumble of small hotels, souvenir shops, restaurants, dive shops, and tour agencies. Though San Pedro continues to attract primarily scuba divers and fishermen, it is today popular with a wide range of folks who like the slow-paced atmosphere, including an increasing number of snowbirds, expatriates, and retirees. While certainly not akin to big-city traffic, golf carts and automobiles are proliferating on Ambergris Caye and constantly force pedestrians and bicycle riders to the sides of the road. In fact, the ongoing boom here has actually led to gridlock. During the busy parts of the day, the downtown area of San Pedro is a jumble of golf carts, cars, bicycles, and pedestrians all moving at a rather slow pace. As a separate byproduct of the boom, wooden Caribbean houses are giving way to concrete and cinderblock buildings, and even a small strip mall or two. Development has reached both ends of Ambergris Caye, and steady construction appears destined to fill in the blanks from north to south.

Long before the British settled Belize, and long before the sun-seeking vacationers and zealous reef divers discovered Ambergris Caye, the Maya were here. In fact, the Maya created Ambergris Caye when they cut a channel through the long, thin peninsula that extended down from what is now Mexico. The channel was cut to facilitate coastal trading and avoid the dangerous barrier reef that begins not too far north of San Pedro. Ambergris Caye is 40km (25 miles) long and only .8km (½ mile) wide at its widest point.

Despite the fact that much of the island is seasonally flooded mangrove forest, and despite laws prohibiting the cutting of mangroves, developers continue to clear cut and fill this marginal land. Indiscriminate cutting of the mangroves is already having an adverse effect on the nearby barrier reef: Without the mangroves to filter the water and slow the impact of waves, silt is formed and carried out to the reef, where it settles and kills the coral. There is still spectacular diving to be had just off the shore here, but local operators and long-term residents claim to have noticed a difference and are expressing concern.

Essentials

GETTING THERE & DEPARTING

You've got two options for getting to and from Ambergris Caye: sea or air. The trip is usually beautiful by either means. When the weather's rough, it's bumpy both ways, although it's certainly quicker by air, and you're more likely to get wet in the boat.

BY PLANE There are frequent daily flights between Belize City and San Pedro Airport (airport code SPR) on Ambergris Caye. Flights leave from both Philip S. W. Goldson International Airport and Municipal Airport roughly every hour during daylight hours. Most stop en route at Caye Caulker to drop off and pick up passengers. If you're coming in on an international flight and heading straight for San Pedro, you should book a flight from the international airport. If you're already in Belize City or in transit around the country, it's cheaper to fly from the Municipal Airport, which is also closer to downtown, and quicker and cheaper to reach by taxi. During the high season, and whenever possible, it's best to have a reservation.

Ambergris Caye

ACCOMMODATIONS ■
Azul Resort **9**
Capricorn Resort **8**
Captain Morgain's Retreat **3**
Cayo Espanto **1**
El Pescador **7**
Las Terrazas **5**
Mata Chica **10**
Portofino Beach Resort **11**

DINING ◆
Capricorn Restaurant **8**
Mambo **10**
Rendevous Restaurant
  & Winery **6**
Rojo Lounge **9**

ATTRACTIONS ●
Bacalar Chico National Park
  & Marine Reserve **12**
Butterfly Jungle **4**

NIGHTLIFE ●
The Palapa Bar **2**

MEXICO

Cayo Chelem

Three Cuts

MEXICO
BELIZE

Punta
San Juan

Laguna Cantena

Rock Point

Robles Point

Punta Lemon

Santa Cruz Lagoon

Basil Jones

Punta Azul

Bracilete

Cayo Tostado
(Swab Caye)

Cayo Iguano
(Cayo Pajaro)

Palmetto Point

Cayo Frances

Laguna Cayo Frances

Backadore Caye
(Cayo Negro)

Punta Bajo

Barrier
Reef

Cayo Rosario
(Cayo Guana)

Mexico
Rocks

Chetumal Bay

CARIBBEAN

Punta Arena

SEA

Buena Vista Point

San Pedro Lagoon

San Pedro

Cayo Espanto

Cayo Romero

Cypress Point

San Pedro

Belmopan

BELIZE

Cangrejo

Boca Chica

0   3 mi
0   3 km

However, you can usually just show up at the airport and get a seat on a flight within an hour.

Both **Maya Island Air** (📞 **223-1140** in Belize City, or 226-2435 in San Pedro; www.mayaairways.com) and **Tropic Air** (📞 **800/422-3435** in the U.S. or Canada, or 226-2012 in Belize; www.tropicair.com) have 11 flights daily between Goldson International Airport and San Pedro Airport, and they both follow the same schedule. The flights depart every hour beginning at 7:40am, with the last flight at 5:40pm. Flight time is around 15 minutes; the fare is BZ$126 each way. These flights actually originate at the Belize City Municipal Airport 10 minutes earlier. From the Municipal Airport, the fare is just BZ$70 each way. These flights take around 30 minutes, because they stop en route to pick up passengers at the international airport, and then at Caye Caulker to drop off passengers. When you're ready to leave, flights from San Pedro to Belize City run from 7am to 5pm. Most of these flights stop first at Caye Caulker and then at the international airport before continuing on to the Municipal Airport. Both airlines offer discounts for children.

Almost any of the above Tropic Air and Maya Island Air flights can be used to commute between Caye Caulker and San Pedro. Flight duration is just 10 minutes, and the fare is BZ$70 each way.

Tropic Air has six daily flights between Corozal Town and San Pedro, leaving Corozal Town at 7:30, 9:30, and 11:30am, and at 1:30, 3:30, and 5:30pm. Flights from San Pedro to Corozal Town leave at 7, 9, and 11am, and at 1, 3, and 5pm. The fare is BZ$95 each way.

Maya Island Air (📞 **223-1140** in Belize City, or 422-2333 in Corozal; www.mayaairways.com) has daily flights between Corozal and San Pedro, leaving San Pedro at 7 and 10am and 3 and 4:30pm, and returning at 7:30 and 10:30am and 3:30 and 5pm. Flight duration is 25 minutes. The fare is BZ$85 each way.

Connections to and from all the other major destinations in Belize can be made via the Municipal and international airports in Belize City.

BY BOAT Regularly scheduled boats ply the route between Belize City and Ambergris Caye. All leave from somewhere near the Swing Bridge. Most boats leave directly from the **Marine Terminal,** which is located right on North Front Street just over the Swing Bridge, and the boats are associated with either the **Caye Caulker Water Taxi Association** (📞 **223-5752;** www.cayecaulkerwatertaxi.com) or **San Pedro Belize Express Water Taxi** (📞 **226-3535**). Most are open speedboats with one or two very powerful engines. Most carry between 20 and 30 passengers, and make the trip in about 75 minutes. Almost all of these boats drop off and pick up passengers in Caye Caulker on their way, and on St. George's Caye when there's demand. If you're going to Ambergris or St. George's Caye from Caye Caulker, these boats will pick you up. Find out at the Marine Terminal just where and when they stop. The schedule is subject to change, but boats for Ambergris Caye leave the Marine Terminal roughly every 90 minutes

Add It Up

Because a taxi into Belize City from the international airport costs BZ$50 to BZ$60, and the boat to Ambergris Caye costs BZ$20 to BZ$30, it is only a bit more expensive to fly if you are heading directly to the cayes after arriving on an international flight.

DINING ◆
Ali Baba **22**
Blue Water Grill **24**
Caliente **14**
Caramba **8**
Celi's Deli **17**
Celi's Restaurant **19**
Elvi's Kitchen **11**
Estel's Dine
   By the Sea **13**
Hidden Treasure **29**
Jambel's Jerk Pit **10**
Lily's Treasure Chest **7**
Mickey's **18**
Palmilla **30**
Pinocchio **26**
Red Ginger **4**
Ruby's Café **20**
Sunset Grill **23**
Wild Mangos **21**

ACCOMMODATIONS ■
Blue Tang Inn **3**
Hotel San Pedrano **6**
Mata Rocks **28**
Ramon's Village **25**
Ruby's **20**
San Pedro Holiday Hotel **19**
Sunbreeze **24**
The Phoenix **4**
Tides Beach Resort **1**
Tio Pil's Place **7**
Victoria House **30**
Xanadu Island Resort **27**

San Pedro River
San Pedro Lagoon

$ Bank/ATM
✚ Hospital
ⓘ Information
Ⓟ Police
✉ Post office

Hyperbaric Chamber
San Pedro Airport

CARIBBEAN
SEA

San Pedro

BELIZE
★Belmopan

0 — 1/8 mile
0 — 100 meters

NIGHTLIFE ●
Big Daddy's **10**
Fido's Courtyard **9**
Jaguar's Temple Club **12**
La Playa Lounge **16**
Pier Lounge **14**
The Palace **5**
The Tackle Box **15**
Wet Willy's **2**

7

THE NORTHERN CAYES & ATOLLS | Ambergris Caye

beginning at 8am, with the last boat leaving at 4:30pm. The fare is BZ$30 one-way; BZ$60 round-trip between Belize City and Ambergris Caye; and BZ$20 one-way between Caye Caulker and San Pedro. Children travel for half-price. (See "A Small Caye on the Way," on p. 146, for more details about St. George's Caye.)

It is possible to purchase a seat in advance by visiting the Marine Terminal personally. This is a good idea in the high season, although in most cases, you'll need to purchase the ticket in cash upfront. Some Belize City hotels provide this service or can get you a confirmed reservation by phone.

In addition to the above-mentioned companies, the *Triple J* (© 223-3464) leaves from Courthouse pier near the Marine Terminal every day at 8 and 10:30am, noon, and 3pm, returning from the Texaco dock on Ambergris Caye at 7 and 9am and 1 and 3:30pm. The rates for the *Triple J* are similar to those listed above.

All the boats dock on a pier near the center of town.

GETTING AROUND

The downtown section of San Pedro is easily navigated by foot. Some of the hotels located on the northern or southern ends of the island can be quite isolated, however.

Most hotels arrange pickup and drop-off for guests, whether they are arriving or departing by air or sea. Taxis are waiting for all flights that arrive at the airport, and are available for most trips around the island. If your hotel can't call you one, try **Amber Isle Taxi** (© 226-4060), **Felix Taxi** (© 226-2041), or **Island Taxi** (© 226-3125). Fares run between BZ$6 and BZ$20 for most rides.

Ubiquitous golf carts are available for rent from several outlets on the island. Rates run around BZ$120 to BZ$180 per day for a four-seat cart, and BZ$160 to BZ$280 for a six-seat cart. Hourly rates are between BZ$30 and BZ$50. One of the largest and most dependable outfits is **Moncho's Rental** (© 226-3262; www.monchosrentals.com). Other dependable options include **Cholo's Golf Cart Rental** (© 226-2406) and **Ultimate Cart Rental** (© 226-3326; www.ultimaterentalsbelize.com).

For a more distinctive ride around town, head to **Segway of Belize** (© 226-3344; www.segwayofbelize.com). Rates run BZ$70 per hour, with discounts for half- and full-day rentals.

I personally think the best way to get around is on a bicycle. Most hotels have their own bikes, available for free or for a small rental fee. If your hotel doesn't have a bike, call or head to **Joe's Bike Rental** on the south end of Pescador Drive (© 226-4371). Rates run around BZ$20 to BZ$30 per day.

Depending on where your hotel is located, a water taxi may just be your best means for commuting between your accommodations and the restaurants and shops of San Pedro. **Coastal Xpress** (© 226-2007; www.coastalxpress.com) runs regularly scheduled launches that cover the length of the island, cruising just offshore from north to south and vice versa. The launches are in radio contact with all the hotels and restaurants, and they stop to pick up and discharge passengers as needed. Ferries run at regular intervals, roughly every half-hour, between 5am and 2am. Rates run around BZ$10 to BZ$50 per person for a jaunt, depending on the length of the ride. Chartered water taxis are also available, and usually charge around BZ$80 to BZ$300, depending on the length of the ride and size of your group.

ORIENTATION

San Pedro (the only town on the island of Ambergris Caye) is just three streets wide. The streets, from seaside to lagoonside, are Barrier Reef Drive (Front St.), Pescador Drive (Middle St.), and Angel Coral Street (Back St.). The airport is at the south end of the busy little downtown. The island stretches both north and south of San Pedro. Less than a mile north of San Pedro there is a small channel, or cut, dividing the island in two. The northern section of the island is much less developed, and is where you will find more of the higher-end isolated resorts.

International Costa Maya Festival

Begun as the San Pedro Sea & Air Festival, the annual **International Costa Maya Festival** ★★ is the largest public celebration on Ambergris Caye, even larger and more popular than Carnival. Celebrated from Thursday to Sunday in early August, the festival offers a steady stream of live concert performances, street parades, beauty pageants, and water shows and activities. When the festivities reinvented themselves several years ago, they had been transformed into a regional affair, honoring and inviting the peoples from around the Mayan world. Performers, participants, and festivalgoers come from around Belize, as well as from Mexico, Honduras, El Salvador, and Guatemala, the five countries that compose the Mundo Maya. San Pedro's football field is converted into the fairgrounds, and a large stage is set up at one end. Food stalls and arts and crafts booths are set up as well. Admission to most events is free, and a party atmosphere envelops the entire island.

A bridge connects the northern and southern sections of Ambergris Caye. Pedestrians and bicycles can cross the bridge for free, but golf carts and other vehicles must pay a toll of BZ$5 each way.

FAST FACTS   For the local **police**, dial ✆ **911** or 226-2022; for the **fire department**, dial ✆ **226-2372.** In the case of a medical emergency, call the **San Pedro Health Clinic** (✆ **226-2536**).

Atlantic Bank (✆ **226-2195**) and **Belize Bank** (✆ **226-2450**) are both located on Barrier Reef Drive in downtown San Pedro. The **post office** (✆ **226-2250**) is located on Barrier Reef Drive; it's open Monday through Friday from 8am to noon and from 1 to 5pm. There are plenty of Internet cafes on the island, and most hotels provide connections. One of the best and longest-standing Internet cafes on the island is **Caribbean Connection Internet Café,** 55 Barrier Reef Dr. (✆ **226-2573**).

Most hotels also provide laundry service, but pricing varies widely, so ask first. **Nellie's Laundromat** (✆ **226-2454**) is located on Pescador Drive toward the south end of town. They charge around BZ$12 per load, and they even offer pickup and delivery service.

What to See & Do

Before you book your vacation, you should be aware that there really isn't much beach to speak of on Ambergris Caye: Before you book your vacation, you should be aware that there really aren't any grand beaches on Ambergris Caye. Around most of the island, there's just a narrow band of sand where the land meets the sea. In some spots, even at low tide, it's barely wide enough for you to lay out a beach towel. Some of the beachfront hotels create their own beaches by building retaining walls and filling them in with sand. You'll find the best of these at the resorts on the northern part of the island, and at Victoria House. If your hotel doesn't have a good beach, try walking north or south from town along the water to find a more secluded spot where you can sit and stare out to sea.

Likewise, swimming is not what you might expect. For 100 yards (300 ft.) or more out from shore, the bottom is covered with sea grass. In a smart move that prioritizes the environment over tourism, the local and national government has decided to protect the sea grass, which supports a wealth of aquatic life. Beneath the grass is a layer of spongy roots and organic matter topped with a thin layer of white sand. Walking on this spongy sand is somewhat unnerving; there's always the possibility of a sea urchin or stingray lurking, and it's easy to trip and stumble. Swimming is best off the piers, and many of the hotels here have built long piers out into the sea, with steps down into the water, and usually a roped-off little swimming area. Beyond this, good swimming can be had from boats anchored out in the turquoise waters between the shore and the reef, or by taking a kayak offshore a little way. Take Care

There is a lot of boat traffic (some of it quite fast and furious) running up and down the coast of Ambergris Caye, so do not try to swim or snorkel from shore out to the reef. Unfortunately, over the years, more than one swimmer or snorkeler has been run over by a speeding motorboat.

FUN IN THE WATER
Scuba Diving & Snorkeling

So why do people bother to come here if there is no beach and you can't go swimming right off the shore? They come for the spectacular coral reef, turquoise waters, and seemingly endless visibility. Less than a quarter-mile offshore is the longest coral reef in the Western Hemisphere. The Belize Barrier Reef is second only to Australia's Great Barrier Reef. Snorkeling, scuba diving, and fishing are the main draws here. All are consistently spectacular.

Within a 10- to 20-minute boat ride from the piers lie scores of **world-class dive sites ★★★**, including **Mexico Rocks, Mata Rocks, Tackle Box, Tres Cocos, Esmeralda, Cypress Tunnel,** and **Rocky Point.** A day's diving will almost always feature a mix of steep wall drops and coral caverns and tunnels. You'll see brilliant coral and sponge formations, as well as a wealth of colorful marine life. On good dives, you might see schools of spotted eagle rays, watch an octopus slither among the coral and rocks, or have the chance to swim face to face with a sea turtle. Nurse sharks, moray eels, and large barracuda are also commonly sighted.

There are scores of dive operators in San Pedro, and almost every hotel can arrange a dive trip, because either they have their own dive shop or they subcontract out. Rates are pretty standardized, but you should be able to get deals on multiday, multidive packages. While it's often tempting to purchase all-inclusive dive packages before coming to Belize, this limits your flexibility; for example, if the weather and water are really rough, you're already committed, although you might prefer taking an inland tour to a Mayan ruin over a rough dive.

For reliable scuba-diving service and reasonable rates, contact **Amigos del Mar** (✆ 226-2706; amigosdive@btl.net), **Aqua Dives** (✆ 800/641-2994 in the U.S. and Canada, or 226-3415; www.aquadives.com), **Ecologic Divers ★** (✆ 226-4118; www.ecologicdivers.com), or **Patojo's Scuba Center ★** (✆ 226-2283; patojos@ btl.net). Most of these companies, as well as the individual resorts, charge BZ$140 to BZ$220 for a two-tank dive, with equipment rental included.

For more adventurous and truly top-rate diving, you'll probably want to head out to the **Turneffe Island Atoll ★★, Lighthouse Reef ★★,** and **Blue Hole ★★.** For more information on these sites, see p. 147. Most of the dive operations on the

THE PERFECT plunge

If you're hesitant to take a tank plunge, don't miss a chance to at least snorkel. There's good snorkeling all along the protected side of the barrier reef, but some of the best is at **Shark-Ray Alley** ★★ and **Hol Chan Marine Reserve** ★★, which are about 6.4km (4 miles) southeast of San Pedro. Shark-Ray Alley provides a nice adrenaline rush for all but the most nonchalant and experienced divers. Here you'll be able to snorkel above and between schools of nurse sharks and stingrays. *Hol chan* is a Mayan term meaning "little channel," which is exactly what you'll find here—a narrow channel cutting through the shallow coral reef.

The walls of the channel are popular with divers, and the shallower areas are frequented by snorkelers. Some of the exciting residents of the area are large, green moray eels; stingrays; and nurse sharks (harmless). The reserve covers 13 sq. km (5 sq. miles) and is divided into three zones: the reef, the sea-grass beds, and the mangroves. Most combination trips to Shark-Ray Alley and Hol Chan Marine Reserve last about 2½ to 3 hours, and cost around BZ$60 to BZ$100. There is a BZ$20 park fee for visiting Hol Chan, which may or may not be included in the price of boat excursions to the reserve.

island offer this trip, or will subcontract it out. It's about a 2- to 3-hour ride each way (in a fast boat) over sometimes rough seas. You'll definitely want to choose a seaworthy, speedy, and comfortable boat. Most day trips out to Turneffe Island or Lighthouse Reef and Blue Hole run around BZ$320 to BZ$600 per person, including transportation, two or three dives, and tanks and weights, as well as lunch and snacks. All the above-mentioned operators offer day and multiday trips to the outer atoll islands and reefs. Prices average around BZ$600 to BZ$1,000 for a 2-day trip, BZ$800 to BZ$1,400 for a 3-day trip.

If you've always dreamed of learning to scuba dive and plan on spending any time on Ambergris Caye, you should consider taking a course here. Resort courses will give you a great 1-day introduction into the world of scuba diving, including a very controlled shallow-water boat dive. These courses cost BZ$280 to BZ$360. In 3 to 4 days, however, you can get your full open-water certification. These courses run between BZ$650 and BZ$900, including all equipment rentals, class materials, and the processing of your certification, as well as four open-water and reef dives. All of the above-mentioned dive centers, as well as many of the individual resorts here, offer these courses.

There are a host of boats offering snorkeling trips, and most of the hotels on the island, as well as the above dive operators, also offer snorkel trips and equipment rental. Trips to other sites range in price from BZ$30 to BZ$60 for short jaunts to half-day outings, and BZ$100 to BZ$140 for full-day trips. One of the operators who specializes in snorkeling trips here is the very personable Alfonse Graniel and his launch *Li'l Alfonse* ★ (✆ 226-3136; lilalfonse@yahoo.com). Another good snorkel operator is **Grumpy & Happy** (✆ 226-3420; www.grumpyandhappy.com), a husband-and-wife team that offers private personalized outings. Snorkel gear is available from most of the above operators and at several other sites around town. A full set of mask, fins, and snorkel will usually cost BZ$16 to BZ$30 per person per day.

Rough Seas

The Belize Barrier Reef acts like a giant sea wall. Given the prevailing trade winds, the waters on the inside of the reef are almost always quite calm. However, a quick jaunt outside the reef can bring you into often steep and agitated seas. Most snorkeling trips stick to the smooth waters inside the reef, while scuba trips almost always head for the deeper water on the outside. Always ask about current conditions and where you will be going before you sign up for a trip, and know your abilities and reaction to rough water before venturing out.

Tip: Hol Chan and Shark-Ray Alley are extremely popular. If you really want to enjoy them, try to find a boat leaving San Pedro at or before 8am, and head first to Shark-Ray Alley. Most boats dive Hol Chan first, and this is the best way to get a dive with the greatest concentration of nurse sharks and stingrays. By all means, avoid snorkeling or diving these sites at times when the cruise ships are running excursions there. Alternatively, you may want to consider visiting a different snorkeling site, such as Mexico Rocks Coral Gardens, Tres Cocos, or Mata Rocks, where the snorkeling is just as good, if not better, and you're more likely to have the place to yourself.

COMBINING SNORKELING WITH MANATEE VIEWING Another popular option is a day trip to see manatees and do some snorkeling at a remote caye. These trips include a leisurely tour of famed manatee feeding and mating sites at Swallow Caye on the way to the isolated Goff's Caye, which is little more than a football field–size patch of sand, with a few palm trees. These trips include all transportation, lunch on the caye, and several snorkeling stops, and cost around BZ$120 to BZ$200. Most hotels and tour agencies in town offer this trip; or check with **SEAduced ★** (① 226-2254; www.seaducedbybelize.com) or **Sea-Rious Adventures** (① 226-4202; www.seariousadventures.com).

GLASS-BOTTOM BOATS If you really don't want to take a plunge of any sort, you can still get a good view of the reef and its undersea wonders aboard a glass-bottom boat. There are a few glass-bottom boats working Ambergris Caye. Most hotels and tour agencies on the island can book them for you, or you can contact the *Reef Runner* (① 226-2172) directly. Rates run between BZ$50 and BZ$100, depending on the length of the tour, and whether a meal or drink is involved. Most of the glass-bottom boat tours allow time for a snorkeling break as well.

Sailing

The crystal-clear waters, calm seas, and isolated anchorages and snorkeling spots all around Ambergris Caye make this an excellent place to go out for a sail. Your options range from crewed yachts and bareboat charters for multiday adventures to day cruises and sunset sails. A day cruise, including lunch, drinks, and snorkeling gear, should run between BZ$180 and BZ$300 per person. Most hotels and tour operators around town can hook you up with a day sail or sunset cruise.

Although not a true sailboat, the **Winnie Estelle** (① 226-2427; winnie_estelle@yahoo.com), a 20m (66-ft.) motor-sailer operated by Captain Roberto Smith, does a day cruise to Caye Caulker with several snorkel stops for BZ$110.

There's a lunch stop on Caye Caulker, where you can dine at the restaurant of your choice, on your own account, while snacks and drinks are included on the cruise. This boat can also be chartered for longer trips to the outer atolls, or to southern cayes.

If you're looking for a longer and more adventurous time on the high seas, **TMM** (© **800/633-0155** in the U.S., or 226-3026 in Belize; www.sailtmm.com) is a large-scale charter company with operations on Ambergris Caye. Options include monohulls, catamarans, and trimarans of varying sizes. Given the shallow draft, increased interior space, and reduced drag, a multihull is your best bet. All of the boats are well-equipped and seaworthy. Rates for a weeklong charter run between BZ$3,800 and BZ$18,000, depending on the size of the boat and whether you charter it bareboat or with a crew.

Fishing

Sport fishing for tarpon, permit, and bonefish is among the best in the world around these cayes and reefs, and over the years a few record catches have been made. If you prefer deep-sea fishing, there's plenty of tuna, mahimahi, and marlin to be had beyond the reefs. Both **Fishing San Pedro** (© **607-9967**; www.fishingsanpedro. com) and **Go Fish Belize ★** (© **226-3121**; www.gofishbelize.com) can fix you up with a guide and equipment. A half-day of reef trolling, casting, or fly-fishing for bonefish or tarpon runs around BZ$300 to BZ$600, a full day BZ$600 to BZ$1,000. Deep-sea trolling for larger game costs between BZ$800 and BZ$1,600 for a half-day, and between BZ$1,600 and BZ$3,000 for a full day. These prices are per boat for two to four fishermen and usually include drinks, tackle, and lunch.

Hard-core fishermen might want to check out one of the dedicated fishing lodges, such as **El Pescador ★** (© **800/242-2017** in the U.S. and Canada, or 226-2398; www.elpescador.com) on Ambergris Caye, or **Turneffe Flats ★★** (© **888/512-8812** in the U.S., or 220-4046; www.tflats.com) out on the Turneffe Island Atoll.

Windsurfing, Parasailing & Watercraft

Ambergris Caye is a good place for beginning and intermediate windsurfers. The nearly constant 15- to 20-knot trade winds are perfect for learning on and easy cruising. The protected waters provide some chop, but are generally pretty gentle on beginning board-sailors. If you're looking to do some windsurfing, or to try the latest adrenaline boost of kiteboarding, your best bet is to check in with the folks at **Sail Sports Belize** (© **226-4488**; www.sailsportsbelize.com). Sailboard rentals run around BZ$44 to BZ$54 per hour, or BZ$100 to BZ$140 per day. Kite-board rentals run BZ$110 for a half-day and BZ$164 for a full day. Weekly rates are also available. These folks also rent out several types of small sailboats for cruising around close to shore.

Most resort hotels here have their own collection of all or some of the above-mentioned watercraft. Rates run around BZ$40 to BZ$70 per hour for a Hobie Cat, small sailboat, or windsurfer, and BZ$60 to BZ$80 per hour for a jet ski. If not, **Sail Sports Belize** (see above) is your best bet.

FUN ON DRY LAND
Butterfly Garden

Located about 7.2km (4½ miles) north of the bridge, **Butterfly Jungle ★** (© **610-4026**; www.butterflyjungle.org) is a pleasant little attraction with a butterfly breeding program and covered butterfly enclosure. A visit here includes an informative tour and explanation of the butterfly life cycle, as well as a visit to the enclosure, where anywhere from 15 to 30 species may be in flight at any one time. This place is open daily 10am to 5pm, and admission is BZ$20 for adults, free for children 11 and under.

Spas, Yoga, Fitness & Body Work

While there are no full-scale resort spas or high-end facilities on Ambergris Caye, you can certainly get sore muscles soothed and a wide array of pampering treatments at a series of day spas and independent massage-therapy storefronts. The best of these includes **The Art of Touch,** at the entrance to the Sunbreeze Hotel (© **226-3357;** www.touchbelize.com), and **Asia Garden Day Spa ★** (© **226-4072**), across from the airstrip. Rates run around BZ$160 to BZ$200 for an hour-long massage.

If you want to work out, there's a modest health club and gym at the **San Pedro Family Fitness Club** (see below). These folks also offer aerobic, Pilates, Tae Bo, and yoga classes.

Finally, if you're in the mood for a good yoga session, you'll want to head just north of the bridge to **Ak'Bol Yoga Retreat ★** (© **226-2073;** www.akbol.com), which offers a regular schedule of classes and intensive retreats. They also have rooms and individual cabins, as well as a largely vegetarian restaurant and small spa.

Tennis

This is very far from a tennis destination, and very few hotels have courts. You'll find two lit courts at the **San Pedro Family Fitness Club,** on the west side of San Pedro (© **226-4749;** www.sanpedrofitness.com). You'll want to play early in the morning or late in the afternoon or evening, as it's just too hot to play tennis most days during the heat of the day. This place is a bargain: BZ$30 gets you a full-day pass and access to all their facilities, including the tennis court and complimentary racquet use. If you just want to use the pool here, it will run you BZ$20.

OTHER ATTRACTIONS
Bacalar Chico National Park & Marine Reserve

Occupying the northern end of Ambergris Caye and its surrounding waters, **Bacalar Chico National Park & Marine Reserve ★** (© **226-2833;** www.bacalarchico. org) is a great spot for wildlife viewing. In addition to being home to scores of bird, animal, and plant species (many of which are endemic), the park also features several ancient Mayan ceremonial and trading sites. The ranger station is, in fact, located at the diminutive Chac Balam ruins. Bacalar Chico is the name of the channel cut 1,500 years ago by the Maya to facilitate coastal trading. Just across the channel is Mexico. Nearly 200 species of birds have been spotted here, and the park allegedly contains all five wildcat species found in Belize, including the jaguar—although your odds of seeing a cat are remote at best. However, you've got decent odds of seeing a crocodile or wild deer, and of course numerous bird species. The park is accessible only by boat. All of the local tour outfits offer half- and full-day trips to Bacalar Chico. Depending on your needs, these trips usually provide a mix of bird- and nature-watching, snorkeling, and Mayan ruin explorations. Specialist guides can be hired around San Pedro if you want to focus primarily on any one of these pursuits. Admission to the park is BZ$10.

Excursions Farther Afield

If you've been on the island for a while or just want to see more of Belize, a host of tour operators on Ambergris Caye offer excursions to all of the major attractions and destinations around the country, including Altun Ha, Lamanai, Xunantunich, Mountain Pine Ridge, and even Tikal. You can also go cave tubing in the Caves Branch region. Most of these tours involve a flight in a small charter plane.

One of the most popular day trips is to the Mayan ruins at Altun Ha. This is also one of the most economical, as it doesn't require a flight. This begins on a powerful little boat that will whisk you over to the mainland. You'll then take a taxi to the ruins and have lunch before returning to San Pedro. Most operators offering the Altun Ha trip include a lunch stop at Maruba Resort (p. 201), with the option of adding on a decadent jungle spa treatment. Prices for these trips run around BZ$150 to BZ$300. A similar trip by boat and land is offered to the ruins at Lamanai.

For trips involving a flight, prices range from BZ$250 to BZ$500 per person, depending on the distance traveled and number of activities and attractions crammed into 1 day. Most hotels on the island can book these tours, or you can contact **SEAduced** ★ (© 226-2254; www.seaducedbybelize.com) or **Sea-Rious Adventures** (© 226-4202; www.seariousadventures.com).

For detailed descriptions of these various destinations and attractions, see the respective regional chapters in this book.

Shopping

Most of the shopping on Ambergris Caye is typical tourist fare. You'll see tons of T-shirts and tank tops with dive logos and silk-screen prints of the Blue Hole. Beyond this, the best buy on the island is handmade jewelry sold by local Belizean artisans from makeshift display stands along Barrier Reef Drive. I'd be wary of black coral jewelry, though. Black coral is extremely beautiful, but as with every endangered resource, increased demand just leads to increased harvesting of a slow-growing coral.

Inside Fido's Courtyard at **Belizean Arts** ★ (© 226-3019), you'll find the island's best collection of original paintings and crafts. Of special note are the prints and paintings of co-owner Walter Castillo, a Nicaraguan-born artist whose simple, but bold, style captures the Caribbean color and rhythm of Belize.

---

paint WARS

A modest version of the traditional Caribbean Carnival or Mardi Gras is celebrated in San Pedro—with an odd twist—over the weekend preceding Ash Wednesday and the period of Lent. Sure, there are colorful and lively *comparsa* parades, with marching drum bands and costumed dancers. But over the years a tradition of painting has developed. This tradition predates paintball by decades. In times past, this was a fun and frivolous game between roaming bands of local residents using flour-based homemade "paints." Tourists were usually asked before being painted and their demurrals respected. Over the years, however, the painting fever has skyrocketed and gotten more aggressive: Fresh eggs and the occasional oil-based paint were introduced as weapons, and tourists are now often painted despite pleas to the contrary. It's definitely fun and a good way to meet some locals. If you get to a shower relatively quickly, it'll wash off without much hassle. Still, if you go out during Carnival, expect to get painted, and dress accordingly.

Another shop at Fido's Courtyard worth checking out is **Ambar ★★** (© 226-3101). The owner and artisan here sells handmade jewelry, with a specialty in amber. The stuff here is a significant cut above the wares you'll find in most other souvenir shops and street stands.

To get your fill of jade, head to the small **Ambergris Maya Jade & History Museum,** Barrier Reef Drive (© 226-3311), which has a collection of jade artifacts and jewelry, and really functions as the draw to get folks into their retail store.

Finally, if you just need some reading material for the beach blanket or hammock, head to **Pages** (© 206-2254), with a large selection of new and used books, right on Pescador Drive.

Where to Stay

IN SAN PEDRO

There's a score of hotel options right in the heart of San Pedro town. Most are geared toward budget travelers, although a few of these are quite comfortable and charming. Most of the more upscale resorts are located a little bit farther north or south of town. See below for these options.

Tip: Almost every hotel on Ambergris Caye, and certainly all of the resorts, offers scuba packages. If you plan to do a lot of diving, this is the way to go, as these packages can sometimes provide substantial savings over paying as you go. However, you can also buy dive packages from many of the individual dive operators, either in advance or upon arrival on the caye.

Very Expensive

The Phoenix ★★★   The stark contemporary architecture here is striking. Most units here are two-bedroom/two-bath condo units, although there are a few smaller and a few larger options. All come with full kitchens featuring beautiful granite countertops and stainless steel appliances, a washer and dryer, and large flatscreen televisions in both the living room and the master bedroom. Most have huge balconies that open onto the property's large pool and common area, and the Caribbean Sea beyond. The restaurant here, Red Ginger, is excellent.

Barrier Reef Dr. (P.O. Box 25), San Pedro, Ambergris Caye. © **877/822-5512** in the U.S. and Canada, or 226-2083 in Belize. Fax 226-2232. www.thephoenixbelize.com. 30 units. BZ$650–BZ$900 double. Rates lower in the off season; higher during peak periods. AE, MC, V. **Amenities:** Restaurant; bar; concierge; small contemporary spa and fitness center; 2 outdoor pools; room service. *In room:* A/C, TV/DVD, hair dryer, full kitchen, MP3 docking station, free Wi-Fi.

Expensive

Blue Tang Inn ★   This intimate option features all-suite accommodations. Housed in a three-story oceanfront building, the rooms are comfortable and spacious, and all feature a kitchenette, dining area, and living area with a foldout futon, making them an excellent option for families and extended stays. My favorite feature here is the rooftop deck, which offers wonderful panoramic views and is a great spot to take in the sunset. The hotel is located right on the waterfront, just north of the heart of downtown San Pedro. While there is no restaurant here, they do serve a complimentary continental breakfast. And if you choose to skip cooking on your own, a score of restaurants is just a few steps away.

Sand Piper St. (Box 231), San Pedro, Ambergris Caye. © **866/881-1020** in the U.S. and Canada, or 226-2326 in Belize. Fax 226-2358. www.bluetanginn.com. 14 units. BZ$300–BZ$420 double. Rate includes continental breakfast and San Pedro Airport transfers. Rates lower in the off season; higher during peak periods. AE, MC, V. **Amenities:** Small outdoor pool. *In room:* A/C, TV, kitchenette, no phone, free Wi-Fi.

Ramon's Village ★   The handiwork of local son Ramón Núñez, this place is appropriately named, as there is a small-village feel to the collection of thatch-roofed bungalows and suites. At the center of the complex is a small but inviting free-form pool, surrounded by palm trees and flowering plants. Rooms vary in size and are classified as beachfront, seaside, and garden view, with the beachfront units having the best unobstructed views of the water. All are clean, modern, and comfortable, with colorful-print bedspreads and dark-varnished wood trim. Most have a private or shared balcony with a sitting chair or hammock. There are a few suites, which are larger and provide more room to roam and relax. Room nos. 58 and 61 are large second-floor suites set right near the edge of the sea. Ramon's has one of the longer and prettier beaches to be found in San Pedro.

Coconut Dr. (southern edge of town), San Pedro, Ambergris Caye. © **800/624-4215** in the U.S., or 226-2067 in Belize. Fax 226-2214. www.ramons.com. 61 units. BZ$290–BZ$370 double; BZ$400–BZ$900 suite. Rates slightly higher during peak weeks; lower in the off season. AE, MC, V. **Amenities:** Restaurant; bar; bike and golf cart rental; full-service dive shop; small outdoor pool; room service; watersports equipment rental. *In room:* A/C, hair dryer, no phone.

Sunbreeze ★★   This two-story seafront hotel is built in a horseshoe around a simple garden area, with a small pool at its core. The superior rooms are all spacious and attractively appointed. The standard rooms have slightly small bathrooms, but are otherwise quite acceptable. The five deluxe units feature Jacuzzi tubs and the best views. Room no. 225 is the best of the bunch; a corner deluxe unit with a large balcony facing the Caribbean Sea. On the other end of the horseshoe, no. 201 is the best standard room in the house. This hotel is ideally located in the center of town, with its own dive operation and a small arcade of shops. The hotel's **Blue Water Grill** (p. 129) serves excellent international fare. One of the nicest features here is a covered open-air hammock area built over the restaurant and bar.

Coconut Dr. (P.O. Box 14), San Pedro, Ambergris Caye. © **800/688-0191** in the U.S., or 226-2191 in Belize. Fax 226-2346. www.sunbreeze.net. 42 units. BZ$340 double; BZ$390–BZ$450 deluxe. Rates lower in the off season. AE, MC, V. **Amenities:** Restaurant; bar; bike rental; full-service dive shop; small outdoor pool; room service; smoke-free rooms; watersports equipment rental. *In room:* A/C, TV.

Tides Beach Resort ★   With its wood construction, gingerbread trim, and faded paint, this three-story oceanfront hotel has a worn and weathered feel, although in fact it's not that old. The hotel and sister dive operation are owned and operated by the highly respected and personable local couple of Patojo and Sabrina Paz. All of the rooms are oceanfront and have either a shared or small private veranda or balcony. They feature polished wood floors, simple furnishings, and either two double beds or one king bed. Patojo runs one of the better dive operations on the island, and this place is popular with scuba divers and dive groups.

Boca del Río Dr., San Pedro, Ambergris Caye. © **226-2283.** Fax 226-3797. www.ambergriscaye.com/tides. 12 units. BZ$200–BZ$260 double. Rates include full breakfast. AE, MC, V. **Amenities:** Bar; bike and golf cart rental; full-service dive shop; watersports equipment rental. *In room:* A/C, minifridge, no phone.

Moderate

San Pedro Holiday Hotel ★   You can't miss this brilliantly white three-building complex, with painted purple and pink trim, in the center of town. Every room comes with air-conditioning, and most have excellent ocean views and small refrigerators. Get a room on the second floor, and you'll have a wonderful balcony—you won't want to leave. Celi McCorkle opened this hotel more than 40 years ago, the first on the island, and it's continued to keep pace with the times and tourism boom. A full-service dive shop, a popular bar and restaurant, and a small gift shop round out the amenities. The whole operation has a festive and lively air to it. This hotel lacks some of the amenities of other options in this price range—there's no swimming pool and not all rooms have televisions—but it makes up for that with its lively island vibe and friendly service.

Barrier Reef Dr. (P.O. Box 61), San Pedro, Ambergris Caye. © **713/893-3825** in the U.S., or 226-2014 in Belize. Fax 226-2295. www.sanpedroholiday.com. 17 units. BZ$220–BZ$250 double; BZ$350 apt. AE, MC, V. **Amenities:** 2 restaurants; bar; bike rental; full-service dive shop; watersports equipment rental. *In room:* A/C, no phone.

Tio Pil's Place Formerly known as Lily's, this place is right on the beach, toward the north end of Front Street. The rooms are simple yet well maintained, and feature air-conditioning and minifridges. Not all of the rooms here have a water view—be sure to ask for one. The best rooms are those on the second floor, enjoying a wonderful shared veranda with a sea view. Those on the ground floor also have ocean views, although you need to be prepared for a fair amount of pedestrian traffic, as they are set right on the island's main pedestrian and bicycle thoroughfare. There's a relaxed vibe throughout the operation here, and you'll definitely enjoy the lounge chairs set on the sand for the guests' use.

On the beach, San Pedro, Ambergris Caye. © **800/345-9786** in the U.S. and Canada, or 206-2059 in Belize. Fax 226-2623. www.ambergriscaye.com/lilys. 10 units. BZ$130–BZ$150 double. MC, V. **Amenities:** Restaurant; bar. *In room:* A/C, minifridge, no phone.

Inexpensive

There are quite a few budget options on Ambergris Caye, and almost all of them are concentrated in the compact downtown area of San Pedro. True budget hounds should just walk around and see who's got the best room for the best price. I list a couple of my personal favorites below.

Hotel San Pedrano Although few of the rooms here have ocean views, they are pretty close to the beach and have varnished wooden floors, a single bed and a double bed in every room, and clean bathrooms with tubs. A few of the rooms even have air-conditioning. The best views can be enjoyed from the wide veranda that looks out over the rooftops of adjacent buildings, a great place to gather with fellow travelers or simply sit and read a book.

10 Barrier Reef Dr. (P.O. Box 131), San Pedro, Ambergris Caye. © **226-2054.** Fax 226-2274. www.aguallos. com/hotelsanpedrano. 7 units. BZ$70–BZ$90 double. AE, MC, V. *In room:* No phone.

Ruby's 🔥 Walking toward the ocean and into town from the airstrip, one of the first things you'll see is a three-story whitewashed building with blood-red ginger-bread trim. Most of the rooms at Ruby's overlook the water. The best ones have air-conditioning and a private balcony overlooking the sea. The floors are wooden, the rooms are simply furnished with a couple of beds and little else, and the showers and bathrooms are clean. You can't beat the location at this price in San Pedro. Downstairs you'll find Ruby's Deli, which is a good place for breakfast or a casual midday meal. These folks also have a separate hotel on the lagoon side of the island, with clean, spacious, simple rooms; shared bathrooms; and even lower prices. After years of mixed messages, it seems like the owners here have settled on spelling Ruby's with a "y" and not "ie" at the end.

Barrier Reef Dr. (P.O. Box 56), San Pedro, Ambergris Caye. © **226-2063.** Fax 226-2434. www.ambergris caye.com/rubys. 21 units. BZ$60–BZ$90 double. MC, V. **Amenities:** Restaurant. *In room:* No phone.

SOUTH OF SAN PEDRO
Expensive

Mata Rocks ★ 👔   The blinding white paint and angular architecture of this intimate hotel conjure images of the Greek isles. All of the rooms here have at least a partial ocean view. The best is no. 53, a second-floor unit fronting the sea, with a large private balcony. There are 6 suites and 11 standard rooms; all are clean, modern, and cheery. The suites come with a fully equipped kitchenette, king and sofa beds, and a small sitting area. At the center of the hotel is a small free-form pool that is fed via a small artificial stream, which is in turn fed by a small fountain. Purple and lavender Adirondack chairs provide splashes of color. There is an intimate and relaxed air about the whole operation. A complimentary continental breakfast buffet is served in the open-air beachfront palapa bar, as are snacks and light lunches. This place is located about 2.4km (1½ miles) south of San Pedro town.

Oceanfront, southern end of Ambergris Caye. © **888/628-2757** in the U.S. and Canada, or 226-2336 in Belize. Fax 226-2349. www.matarocks.com. 17 units. BZ$290–BZ$340 double; BZ$390–BZ$420 suite. Rates include continental breakfast. Rates lower in the off season; higher during peak periods. AE, MC, V. **Amenities:** Bar; complimentary bike use; small outdoor pool; free Wi-Fi. *In room:* A/C, TV, minifridge, no phone.

Victoria House ★★★   This elegant and exclusive island retreat features a varied collection of rooms, suites, and villas. Everything is done with a refined sense of style and attention to detail. The resort is set on an expansive piece of land a couple of miles south of San Pedro, with lush tropical gardens and a surprisingly good section of soft white sand fronting it. The plantation rooms and suites are spread through several buildings, and there's a string of individual casitas aligned around a grassy lawn facing the sea. These latter feature high-pitched thatch roofs, tile floors, and wide French doors letting out onto a private balcony. The villas and suites are larger and equipped with flatscreen televisions and plush furnishings. Some have kitchenettes, and others are duplex units that can be joined or rented separately. Service is attentive, yet understated. A full range of tours and activities is offered, and the **Palmilla** restaurant here (p. 131) is one of the finest on the island.

Beachfront, 3.2km (2 miles) south of San Pedro (P.O. Box 22, San Pedro), Ambergris Caye. © **800/247-5159** in the U.S. and Canada, or 226-2067 in Belize. Fax 226-2429. www.victoria-house.com. 42 units. BZ$360 double; BZ$596–BZ$624 casita or plantation room; BZ$740–BZ$1,190 suite; BZ$1,190–BZ$2,320 villa. Rates higher during peak weeks; lower in the off season. AE, MC, V. **Amenities:** Restaurant; bar; free bikes; concierge; full-service dive shop; golf cart rental; 2 midsize outdoor pools; watersports equipment rental; free Wi-Fi. *In room:* A/C.

Xanadu Island Resort ★ ☺   The two- and three-story thatch-roof buildings of this small resort are set in a semicircle around a central pool area. All of the units here are large and loaded with amenities. All are classified as suites, although most have the feel of independent apartments or condo units. This isn't a bad thing, and it makes this a good choice for extended stays and for families. Each unit features a full kitchen or a kitchen and spacious living room. Each comes with a private balcony or front porch. There are single-bedroom as well as two- and three-bedroom units available. The resort has a long pier jutting into the ocean, with a wonderful swimming platform at the end. There's no restaurant here, but several are within close proximity, and the town of San Pedro is just 1.6km (1 mile) away. Xanadu is a certified "Green Globe" sustainable tourism project.

Oceanfront (P.O. Box 109, San Pedro Town), southern end of Ambergris Caye. ⓒ **226-2814.** Fax 226-3409. www.xanaduresort-belize.com. 19 units. BZ$380–BZ$550 double; BZ$550–BZ$800 2-bedroom; BZ$900–BZ$1,200 3-bedroom. Rates slightly higher during peak periods. AE, MC, V. **Amenities:** Free bikes; small outdoor pool. *In room:* A/C, TV, hair dryer, kitchenette, free Wi-Fi.

ON NORTH AMBERGRIS CAYE

This is where you'll find most of the larger, more isolated, and more upscale resorts on Ambergris Caye. If you stay here, you will have to rely on your hotel or on the local water taxis to get to and from San Pedro town.

In addition to the hotels listed below, **El Pescador ★** (ⓒ **800/242-2017** in the U.S. and Canada, or 226-2398; www.elpescador.com) is a lovely and luxurious resort primarily geared toward hard-core fishermen and women.

Very Expensive

Azul Resort ★★ There are only two large villas at this luxury option on the north end of the island. Each is a two-bedroom, two-bathroom affair fronting the sea and sharing a large outdoor pool. The rooms feature bamboo furniture, king-size beds, and Egyptian cotton linens. There's a flatscreen television in the large living room, and each villa comes with a fully stocked kitchen featuring top-line appliances, including a Viking range and fancy espresso machine. My favorite feature here is the massive open-air rooftop patio with fantastic views, a private Jacuzzi hot tub, and a couple of shade-giving gazebos. There's also a smaller wraparound balcony off the second-floor loft bedroom. Each villa has personal concierge services. During most of the year, a 3-night stay is required. The restaurant here, **Rojo Lounge** (p. 132), is one of the best on the island.

Oceanfront, northern end of Ambergris Caye. ⓒ **226-4012.** Fax 220-5058. www.azulbelize.com. 2 units. BZ$1,000 per person. Rates include all meals and snacks, and transfers to and from San Pedro Airport. Rates slightly lower in the off season. AE, MC, V. **Amenities:** Restaurant; bar; complimentary bike and kayak use; outdoor pool; room service; smoke-free rooms. *In room:* A/C, TV, hair dryer, Jacuzzi, full kitchen, minibar, MP3 docking station, free Wi-Fi.

Captain Morgan's Retreat ★ ☺ Captain Morgan's is a large, lively, and well-equipped resort on a long and lovely section of beach. The rooms are either individual beachfront casitas, or one- or two-bedroom villas set in a series of two-story units. All feature thatch roofs and wood construction, as well as attractive Guatemalan bedspreads and varnished wood furnishings. Every room comes with a private balcony or veranda, and all are modern, comfortable, and plenty spacious. I prefer the casitas, which are named after famous pirate captains, for their sense of privacy, although if you want more space and amenities, choose one of the villas. The villas all come with a fully equipped kitchenette. Beach lounge chairs and hammocks are spread along the waterfront and in shady spots on the grounds, and a host of aquatic and land-based activities and tours are offered.

Oceanfront, 4.8km (3 miles) north of the Cut on northern end of Ambergris Caye. ⓒ **888/653-9090** or 307/587-8914 in the U.S., or 226-2207 in Belize. Fax 226-4171. www.belizevacation.com. 26 units. BZ$398 casita; BZ$498 1-bedroom villa; BZ$840 2-bedroom villa. Rates lower in the off season;

higher during peak periods. AE, MC, V. **Amenities:** Restaurant; 2 bars; lounge; complimentary bike use; full-service dive shop; 2 outdoor pools; spa services; watersports equipment rental; free Wi-Fi. *In room:* A/C, minifridge.

Las Terrazas ★★   There's a Greek-isle feel to the collection of whitewashed buildings here. The seafront units are the best, but all are beautifully designed and decorated, and come with top-notch furnishings, fixtures, and amenities. All are condo units with full kitchens, washer/dryer, and at least two flatscreen televisions. The penthouse units come with their own plunge pool. My only quibble is that the ceilings feel a bit low in many units. The restaurant here is elegant and well done, but my favorite hangout is the rooftop lounge and bar above it.

Oceanfront, northern end of Ambergris Caye. ⓒ **800/447-1553** in the U.S. and Canada, or 226-4249 in Belize. Fax 713/780-1786. www.lasterrazasresort.com. 39 units. BZ$490–BZ$990 double. Rates include transfers to and from San Pedro Airport. Rates slightly lower in the off season. AE, MC, V. **Amenities:** Restaurant; bar; outdoor pool; room service; smoke-free rooms; small spa and exercise room. *In room:* A/C, TV/DVD, hair dryer, full kitchen, minibar, MP3 docking station, free Wi-Fi.

Mata Chica ★★★   This boutique resort is hip and chic. Artistic details abound, with an eclectic mix of fabrics, sculptures, ceramics, and paintings from around the world. Every room here is a private bungalow or villa, and all can be considered junior suites or better. My favorites are the casitas, which are the closest to the ocean and feature a large sitting area, a king bed on a raised platform, and an interior garden shower. Set back, but set high on raised stilts, are two very large villas, and one immense mansion. A large outdoor pool sits in the center of the grounds, and there's another smaller pool, as well as a large outdoor Jacuzzi. There's also a small spa, with a full list of treatments and cures, as well as a full-service tour desk. The hotel has an excellent restaurant, **Mambo** (p. 132).

Oceanfront, northern end of Ambergris Caye. ⓒ **223-0002** reservations, or 220-5010 at the hotel. Fax 220-5012. www.matachica.com. 24 units. BZ$390–BZ$880 double; BZ$1,050–BZ$2,090 villa. Rates include continental breakfast and transfers to and from San Pedro Airport. AE, MC, V. **Amenities:** Restaurant; 2 bars; complimentary bike, kayak and watersports equipment use; 2 outdoor pools; small spa; free Wi-Fi. *In room:* A/C, no phone.

Portofino Beach Resort ★★   With thatch-roofed cabins, wood floors, bamboo beds, and large picture windows, this intimate boutique resort has a tropical feel. Every room here is massive. The Tree Top suites are second-floor units with large private balconies, while the VIP suites are large private bungalows closer to the sea. The best room here, the Honeymoon suite, comes with a private Jacuzzi and stunning views from its seafront balcony. Service is excellent, as is the in-house "Le Bistro" restaurant.

Oceanfront, northern end of Ambergris Caye. ⓒ **888/240-1923** in the U.S. and Canada, or 678-5096 in Belize. Fax 226-4272. www.portofino.bz. 16 units. BZ$440–BZ$560 double; BZ$720–BZ$840 suite. Rates include continental breakfast, and transfers to and from San Pedro Airport. AE, MC, V. **Amenities:** Restaurant; bar; complimentary kayak use; outdoor pool; room service; smoke-free rooms. *In room:* A/C, TV/DVD, hair dryer, minifridge, no phone, free Wi-Fi.

Expensive

Capricorn Resort ★   There are just three individual cabins at this intimate little hotel. Each cabin features high-vaulted ceilings, a large tile shower, and a private front deck with a hammock. The walls are painted bold primary colors, and artistic touches—in the form of local, Guatemalan, and other ethnic arts and crafts—abound.

The cabins come with either one queen bed or two full beds; all come with mosquito netting. The restaurant here is excellent.

Oceanfront (P.O. Box 247, San Pedro), 4km (2½ miles) north of the Cut on northern end of Ambergris Caye. ℂ **226-2809.** Fax 226-5091. www.capricornresort.net. 3 units. BZ$370 double. Rates include full breakfast and transfers to and from San Pedro Airport. Rates lower in the off season. AE, MC, V. **Amenities:** Restaurant; bar; complimentary kayak use; room service. *In room:* A/C, no phone.

Moderate

Shirley's Guest House   These picturesque white cabins with green trim are set on well-manicured grounds facing the ocean, just north of the airstrip. They're set on stilts and are shaded by coconut and casuarina palms. The setting is idyllic and quiet. The rooms have varnished floors and quilted bedspreads, and some come with a small refrigerator. Although the rooms are a little on the expensive side for what you get, they are worth it for the location, the space, and the comfort. Note that only adults are allowed to stay here.

Close to the airstrip on the ocean side (P.O. Box 13), Caye Caulker. ℂ **226-0145** or 600-0069. Fax 226-0264. www.shirleysguesthouse.com. 5 units (3 with private bathroom). BZ$100 double with shared bathroom; BZ$130–BZ$180 double with private bathroom. Rates lower in the off season. MC, V. Children not accepted. *In room:* No phone.

AN ISLAND OF YOUR OWN

Cayo Espanto ★★★   Whether you're a bona fide member of the jet set or you just want to pretend, this is the place for you in Belize. Seven bungalows are spread across this small private island. Each is luxurious, elegantly appointed, and set on the ocean's edge. Each comes with a private butler, and all have a private pier jutting out into the ocean. All have wide French doors and windows that open onto private decks and verandas and stunning views. Six of the seven come with a private plunge pool. There's no restaurant or common lounge area here. All meals are served in your villa or out on your private deck or dock area. Service is attentive and pampering, and the food is excellent. Cayo Espanto is located just off the western tip of Ambergris Caye.

Cayo Espanto. ℂ **888/666-4282** in the U.S. and Canada. www.aprivateisland.com. 7 units BZ$2,590–BZ$4,590 double. Rates include 3 meals, all drinks (except wine and champagne), all nonmotorized watersports equipment usage, and transportation to and from San Pedro during daylight hours. Rates slightly higher during peak weeks. AE, MC, V. **Amenities:** Full-service dive operation; small exercise room; 5 small outdoor pools; room service; spa services. *In room:* A/C, TV, hair dryer, minifridge, free Wi-Fi.

Where to Dine

IN SAN PEDRO

Seafood is, of course, the most popular food on the island, and there's plenty of it around all year. However, please keep in mind that there are seasons for lobster and conch (because sea turtles are endangered, never order turtle). Officially, lobster season runs from July 15 to February 14, while conch is available from October 1 to June 30. Local restaurants and fishery officials have struck a deal to allow lobster to be served in the off season. Supposedly this is lobster caught and frozen during the open season, and not while they are mating in the formerly closed season.

If you're staying for an extended period, or have a room equipped with a kitchenette, you'll find several good markets around town. The largest, most modern, and best stocked of these is **Island Supermarket** (ℂ **226-2972**), located on Coconut Drive.

Expensive

Blue Water Grill ★★ INTERNATIONAL/ASIAN   This popular place has a broad and extensive menu, as well as a lovely setting overlooking the ocean and piers from the waterfront in the heart of San Pedro. While there's a good selection of pizzas, pastas, and hearty dishes—such as grilled beef tenderloin with a Creole-mustard and black-pepper sauce and chicken breasts served with fresh herbs, walnuts, and blue cheese—the real reason to come here is for their inspired Asian fare. Start things off with crispy coconut-battered shrimp sticks with a sweet and spicy black-bean dipping sauce. For a main course, I recommend the Japanese spiced grouper with a sesame vinaigrette, or the massive surf and turf. These folks have sushi nights every Tuesday and Thursday. If you come for sushi, be sure to try their spicy scallop hand roll.

At the Sunbreeze Hotel, on the waterfront. ✆ **226-3347.** www.bluewatergrillbelize.com. Reservations recommended. Main courses BZ$32–BZ$65. AE, MC, V. Daily 7–10:30am, 11:30am–2:30pm, and 6–9:30pm.

Red Ginger ★★ FUSION   Housed in The Phoenix hotel and condo complex, this new restaurant serves excellent tropical fusion fare in an understatedly elegant room. When the weather permits, you can dine on a patio just outside. The long menu offers almost too many temptations. Start with some of the grouper ceviche marinated in mango-lime juice and ginger, or the pulled-pork empanadas. For a main, I recommend the grilled snook with a honey-soy glaze. The nightly chef's tasting menu (BZ$80) is a five-course affair with a variety of choices to meet almost any diner's desire. Lunch is an excellent deal here and features rotating daily specials.

At the Phoenix hotel, on the waterfront. ✆ **226-4623.** www.redgingerbelize.com. Reservations recommended. Main courses BZ$34–BZ$74. AE, MC, V. Wed-Mon 11:30am–2:30pm and 6–9:30pm.

Moderate

Celi's Restaurant SEAFOOD/BELIZEAN   This simple restaurant serves dependable local fare in a cheery setting. You can dine either indoors or with your feet in the sand in the restaurant's screened-in outdoor dining area. Stick to the seafood, which is plentiful, reasonably priced, and expertly prepared. Freshly caught fish, shrimp, and conch are prepared in a variety of sauces, and lobster and stone crabs are offered seasonally. For dessert, be sure to try some of Celi's Caye Lime Pie. Across the street, Celi's Deli is a good choice for sandwiches and light meals, especially if you're planning a picnic on some deserted beach or caye. On Wednesday nights they have a popular beach barbecue.

On the beach at the San Pedro Holiday Hotel. ✆ **226-2014.** Reservations recommended. Main courses BZ$18–BZ$32; burgers and sandwiches BZ$14–BZ$16; lobster priced according to size and market. AE, MC, V. Daily 11am–2pm and 5:30–9pm.

Sunset Grill ☺ SEAFOOD/BELIZEAN   Set on a dock over the water on the back side of town, this place serves excellent local fare and fresh seafood in a convivial, yet relaxed, environment. The lunch menu is a bit streamlined, but includes snapper served blackened or with a coconut jerk sauce; however, I recommend the fish or shrimp burgers. For dinner, try the Mango Tango Snapper, which is a grilled filet of fresh-caught fish with a spicy mango glaze and citrus black-bean salsa. A big treat, especially for kids, is the periodic feeding of the massive tarpons who hang around the pier pilings here.

On the lagoon, center of town. ✆ **226-2600.** Reservations recommended for dinner. Main courses dinner BZ$35–BZ$65, lunch BZ$16–BZ$34. AE, MC, V. Daily 11am–11pm.

Wild Mangos ★★ INTERNATIONAL/FUSION   Chef Amy Knox has won the Taste of Belize competition twice. The best seats at this down-home open-air joint are those on the outdoor, covered wooden deck. The menu is fairly broad and very creative. Start things off with the Tres Amigos, a selection of three different ceviches from their ample menu of creative ceviches. For a main course I like the pan-seared filet of fresh-caught Cobia, with a sweet and spicy ancho-honey glaze, or the Conchinita Pibil, a traditional Mayan pork dish slow-cooked in banana leaves. There are often nightly specials, and the desserts are delectable. There's also a somewhat more streamlined lunch menu featuring excellent sandwiches, wraps, tacos, and burritos, as well as salads and other treats.

On the beach, just north of the Sunbreeze Hotel. ✆ **226-2859.** Reservations recommended. Main courses dinner BZ$31–BZ$44, lunch BZ$16–BZ$25. AE, MC, V. Mon–Sat noon–3pm and 6–9pm.

Inexpensive

In addition to the places below, **Ruby's Cafe** and **Celi's Deli,** on the ground floors of Ruby's hotel (p. 124) and across from the San Pedro Holiday Hotel (p. 124), respectively, are good places to pick up a light meal, and both specialize in fresh-baked breads and pastries and sandwiches to go.

Other dependable options include **Micky's** (✆ **226-2223**), which is a popular local joint; **Caramba** (✆ **226-4321**), which serves a mix of Belizean, Mexican, and Caribbean fare; and **Ali Baba** (✆ **226-4042**), which specializes in Middle Eastern cuisine. **Caliente** (✆ **226-2170**) is a good choice for traditional Mexican food, including chicken mole. For a seafront seat in the sand, it's hard to beat **Lily's Treasure Chest** (✆ **226-2650**), which is great for breakfast, lunch, or dinner.

Elvi's Kitchen ★★ BELIZEAN/SEAFOOD/INTERNATIONAL   Local legend Elvia Staines began selling burgers out of a takeout window in 1974. Today, Elvi's is arguably the most popular and renowned restaurant on Ambergris Caye, with a word-of-mouth reputation built on the happy bellies of thousands of diners. The restaurant is a thatched, screened-in building with picnic tables, a large flamboyant tree growing up through the roof, and a floor of crushed shells and sand. You can get everything from Belizean stewed chicken to shrimp in watermelon sauce. For lunch, there are still burgers, including traditional beef burgers, although I prefer the shrimp and fish burgers. There's live music every night, with Caribbean night on Thursday, Mayan night on Friday, and Mexican night on Saturday. Food specials complement the musical selections.

Pescador Dr. ✆ **226-2176.** www.elviskitchen.com. Reservations recommended. Main courses BZ$17–BZ$75; fresh fish, seafood, and lobster priced according to market. AE, MC, V. Mon–Sat 11am–10pm.

Estel's Dine By the Sea ★ SEAFOOD/INTERNATIONAL   If you want to dine right by the water, it's hard to get much closer than Estel's. This casual place has a sand floor with heavy wooden tables and plastic chairs inside the main dining room, and a sand terrace outside with pure plastic patio furniture. A broad range of memorabilia and antiques line the walls, and there's a piano in one corner. This is a popular place to start your day, with excellent huevos rancheros and breakfast burritos. The lunch menu features plenty of fresh seafood and fish simply prepared, as well as a host of Mexican and Belizean standards. Hosts Charles and Estella Worthington are usually on hand—they live upstairs. In general, it's a mellow scene, attracting a convivial blend of locals and tourists.

Barrier Reef Dr. ✆ **226-2019.** Main courses BZ$10–BZ$48. No credit cards. Wed–Mon 6am–5pm.

Jambel's Jerk Pit ★ CARIBBEAN/BELIZEAN   This long-standing beachfront restaurant serves spicy curries and jerk concoctions alongside local specialties. The coconut curry chicken is excellent, and there are several vegetarian options. Still, the spicy Jamaican-style jerk is the signature here, and you can get it served over fish, shrimp, chicken, or conch. Wednesday night features an all-you-can-eat buffet and live reggae music. The restaurant is housed on the second floor of an open-air two-story building just off the town's small central park.

Barrier Reef Dr. ✆ **226-3515.** Main courses BZ$25–BZ$35; lobster BZ$44. MC, V. Daily 10am–10pm.

SOUTH OF SAN PEDRO

In addition to the places listed below, if you're hankering for good Italian food, head to **Pinocchio** (✆ **226-4447;** www.pinocchioitalianrestaurant.com). The owners are from Rome, and everything from the pastas to the wood-oven pizzas is authentic and delicious. Meanwhile, the new **Hidden Treasure** (✆ **226-4111;** www.hiddentreasure belize.com) is earning raves for its creative local and New Latin cuisine.

Very Expensive

Palmilla ★★ INTERNATIONAL/FUSION   This continues to be one of the most elegant and refined dining experiences to be had on Ambergris Caye. The chef here always takes the freshest of local ingredients and prepares them with a creative blend of techniques and spices, influenced by a range of cuisines from around the world. The menu changes regularly, but might include cashew-crusted grouper or a pecan-crusted chicken breast. You can choose a table in the formal dining room, with its orgy of white linens, walls, and orchids, or dine alfresco by candlelight at one of the heavy wooden tables on the outdoor poolside deck. Save room for dessert, as the molten chocolate cake and rum-soaked bread pudding are both to die for.

At Victoria House, south of downtown San Pedro. ✆ **226-2067.** Reservations recommended. Main courses BZ$32–BZ$64. AE, MC, V. Daily 6:30–9pm.

ON NORTH AMBERGRIS CAYE

Despite its relative isolation, the northern section of Ambergris Caye has perhaps the island's greatest concentration of truly excellent eateries. If you're staying in San Pedro or on the southern half of the island, you'll need to take a water taxi. Most of these restaurants will be able to arrange this for you, usually at a reduced rate from the going fare.

Expensive

Capricorn Restaurant ★ INTERNATIONAL/SEAFOOD   Grab one of the outdoor tables here on the wraparound seafront veranda of this boutique hotel's little restaurant. If these are all filled, don't despair, as you'll also be able to watch the water through the wide windows of the small dining room, which are almost always thrown open. Start things off with some fresh ceviche or some peel-and-eat shrimp. Be sure to ask about the nightly specials. For a main, I like the crab cakes made with local Stone Crab claws, although this can also be ordered as an appetizer. There's always fresh fish, and conch, stone crabs, scallops, or lobster depending on season and availability, as well as a selection of steak, chicken, and pork entrees.

At Capricorn Hotel, on northern end of Ambergris Caye. ✆ **226-2809.** www.capricornresort.net. Reservations recommended. Main courses BZ$36–BZ$70. AE, MC, V. Thurs–Tues 8–10am, 11:30am–2pm, and 6–9pm.

Mambo ★★ FUSION/INTERNATIONAL   The eclectic menu here touches on a wide range of world cuisines. From the seared scallops in Jamaican jerk sauce to the filet mignon with blue cheese crust drizzled with an orange-balsamic reduction, the food and presentation here are top-notch. I also enjoyed the mango-and-ginger-glazed pork chops, and the warm chocolate soufflé is one of the best desserts I've tasted in Belize. The restaurant features an excellent and extensive wine list. And for those who want to keep on enjoying the finer things in life after dinner, these folks also offer a selection of Cuban cigars and cognacs. Service is attentive and professional, and the ambience is elegant without being stuffy.

At Mata Chica, on the northern end of Ambergris Caye. ☏ 220-5010. Reservations required. Main courses BZ$32–BZ$64. AE, MC, V. Daily noon–3pm and 6–10pm.

Rendezvous Restaurant & Winery ★★ THAI   This refined restaurant serves excellent French-influenced Thai cuisine. You'll find Thai classics, such as pad Thai and Larb Nua, a delicious cold beef salad, right alongside *Cioppini Exotica,* a Mediterranean-inspired seafood stew. There's a relaxed semiformal air to the whole operation, with subdued lighting and cushioned rattan chairs. For a treat, reserve the chef's table, beside the open kitchen, and order the chef's nightly tasting menu. They produce a few wine varieties right on-site, with imported grape juices. I find these to be pretty immature and thin; you'd do much better to buy an imported bottle off their more traditional wine list.

7km (4⅓ miles) north of Cut, on the northern section of Ambergris Caye. ☏ 226-3426. Reservations recommended. Main courses BZ$38–BZ$68. MC, V. Wed–Mon noon–2pm and 6–9pm.

Rojo Lounge ★★★ 🎁 FUSION   Self-taught chef and owner Jeff Spiegel and his partner Vivian Yu have created an elegant and ultrahip open-air restaurant. There are traditional chairs, as well as couch and plush chair seating, on a broad open deck facing the sea. There's even a table and some bedlike cushions set in a small pool just off the main dining area. It's always wise to try the nightly specials, but whatever you do, don't miss the chorizo, shiitake, and shrimp pot stickers. The guava-glazed baby back ribs are also spectacular. If you're more interested in seafood, there are both crab and grouper cakes, or you could have some homemade conch sausage on a fresh pizza. This place has an extensive wine list, as well as an immense and fabulously stocked bar, and an on-site gourmet market and deli.

At Azul Resort, on the northern section of Ambergris Caye. ☏ 226-4012. www.azulbelize.com. Reservations required. Main courses BZ$36–BZ$68. MC, V. Tues–Sat noon–10pm.

Ambergris Caye After Dark

Ambergris Caye is a popular beach and dive destination, and as such it supports a fairly active nightlife and late-night bar scene. I recommend one of the bars here built out over the water, such as **Wet Willy's** ★ (☏ 226-4136) or **The Tackle Box** (☏ 226-4313), both located off the center of town and both occasionally with live music. Another similar option, **The Palapa Bar** ★★ (☏ 226-3111; www.palapa barandgrill.com), is located about 1.6km (1 mile) north of the Cut on the northern half of the island. This place also sometimes has live music, and boasts a great bar scene both day and night.

Alternately, you might try one of the beachside bars such as the **Pier Lounge** (☏ 226-2002) at the Spindrift Hotel, which features bingo on Tuesday nights, karaoke on Saturday nights, and the famous chicken drop, an island version of roulette, at 6pm every Wednesday night. Another popular choice is **Fido's Courtyard** (© **226-2056**), which has live music every night of the week. For a more chilled-out scene, try the open-air beachfront **La Playa Lounge** (© **206-2101**).

If you're looking for a dance club and late-night action, your best bets are the two traditional San Pedro discos, **Jaguar's Temple Club** (© **226-4077**) and **Big Daddy's** (no phone), which are within a stone's throw of each other on Barrier Reef Drive, near the basketball court and the church, just south of downtown on Coconut Drive.

If you're the betting type looking for a bit more action than the chicken drop, try **The Palace** (© **226-3570**), at the corner of Cari베̃a Street and Pescador Drive.

CAYE CAULKER ★★★

32km (20 miles) N of Belize City; 16km (10 miles) S of Ambergris Caye

While Caye Caulker is no longer the secret hideaway of a few happy hippie backpackers and chosen cognoscenti, it remains the epitome of a small, isolated, and laid-back Caribbean getaway. Unlike neighboring San Pedro, you won't find any gridlock traffic here or be constantly run off the road by cars and golf carts. In fact, golf-cart traffic is relatively light, with flip-flops and bicycles fulfilling most of the transportation needs. Let's hope it stays that way. Still, Caye Caulker has begun to experience some of the effects of the amazing boom going on just to the north on Ambergris Caye. There's more and more development on either end of the island, and the long-neglected northern section of Caye Caulker—across the Split—is even starting to be developed.

Essentials

GETTING THERE & DEPARTING

As with Ambergris Caye, you've got two options for getting to and from Caye Caulker: sea or air. When the weather's rough, it's bumpy both ways, although it's certainly quicker by air, and you're more likely to get wet in the boat.

BY PLANE There are numerous daily flights between Belize City and Caye Caulker Airport (CUK). Flights leave from both Philip S. W. Goldson International Airport and Municipal Airport roughly every half-hour. If you're coming in on an international flight and heading straight for Caye Caulker, you should book a flight from the international airport. If you're already in Belize City or in transit around the country, it's cheaper to fly from the Municipal Airport, which is also closer to downtown and quicker and cheaper to reach by taxi. During the high season, and whenever possible, it's best to have a reservation. However, you can usually just show up at the airport and get a seat on a flight within an hour.

Both **Maya Island Air** (© **223-1140** in Belize City, or 226-2435 in San Pedro; www.mayaairways.com) and **Tropic Air** (© **800/422-3435** in the U.S. and Canada, or 226-2012 in Belize; www.tropicair.com) have 11 flights daily between Goldson International Airport and Caye Caulker, and they both follow the same schedule. The flights depart every hour beginning at 7:40am, with the last flight at 5:40pm. Flight time is around 15 minutes; the fare is BZ$126 each way. These flights actually originate at the Belize City Municipal Airport 10 minutes earlier. From the Municipal Airport, the fare is just BZ$70 each way. These flights take around 20 minutes because they stop en route to pick up passengers at the international airport. When you're ready to leave, flights from San Pedro to Belize City run from 7:10am to 5:10pm. Most of these flights stop first at the international airport before continuing on to the Municipal Airport.

Almost all of the above flights originating in Belize City continue on to San Pedro on Ambergris Caye. Similarly, almost all the return flights originate in San Pedro. The flight between the two islands takes 10 minutes, and the fare is BZ$70 each way.

Connections to and from all the other major destinations in Belize can be made via the Municipal and international airports in Belize City.

BY BOAT   Regularly scheduled boats ply the route between Belize City and Caye Caulker. All leave from somewhere near the Swing Bridge, and the majority leave directly from the **Marine Terminal,** which is located right on North Front Street just over the Swing Bridge; the boats are associated with either the **Caye Caulker Water Taxi Association** (✆ 223-5752; www.cayecaulkerwatertaxi.com) or **San Pedro Belize Express Water Taxi** (✆ 226-3535). Most are open speedboats with one or two very powerful engines, and carry between 20 and 30 passengers, making the trip in about 45 minutes. Almost all of these boats stop to drop off and pick up passengers on St. George's Caye when there's demand. If you're going to Ambergris or St. George's from Caye Caulker, these boats all continue on and will take you there. Find out on Caye Caulker just where and when they stop. The schedule is subject to change, but boats for Caye Caulker leave the Marine Terminal roughly every 90 minutes beginning at 8am, with the last boat leaving at 4:30pm. The fare is BZ$20 one-way; BZ$40 round-trip between Belize City and Caye Caulker; and BZ$20 one-way between Caye Caulker and San Pedro. See "A Small Caye on the Way," p. 146, for more details about St. George's.

In addition to the above-mentioned companies, the *Triple J* (✆ 223-3464) leaves from Courthouse pier near the Marine Terminal every day at 8 and 10:30am, noon, and 3pm, returning from Caye Caulker at 7:30 and 9:30am, and 1:30 and 4pm. The rates for the *Triple J* are similar to those listed above.

It is possible to purchase a seat in advance by visiting the Marine Terminal personally. This is a good idea in the high season, although in most cases you'll need to purchase the ticket in cash, upfront. Some Belize City hotels provide this service, or they can get you a confirmed reservation by phone.

GETTING AROUND

Caye Caulker is small. You can easily walk from one end of the island to the other in around 20 minutes. If you want to cover more ground quickly, a bicycle is your

---

   What's in a Name?

The Spanish called this little island "Cayo Hicaco." *Hicaco* is Spanish for the coco plum palm. Some say the name comes from the fact that ships used to be caulked in the shallow calm waters off the back side of this island, hence Caye Caulker. However, a third theory purports that the island appears as Caye Corker on several early British maps. This line of reasoning claims that early sailors and pirates stopped to fill and then "cork" their water bottles with the abundant fresh water found here.

ACCOMMODATIONS ■
Caye Reef **3**
De Real Macaw **5**
Iguana Reef **8**
Lazy Iguana Bed
 & Breakfast **27**
Maxhapan Cabins **25**
Popeye's Beach Resort **18**
Seaside Cabanas **17**
Tree Tops Guest House **26**
Trends Beachfront Hotel **11**
Yuma's House Belize **10**

DINING ◆
Agave **14**
Amor y Café **19**
Don Corleone **4**
Glenda's **20**
Habaneros **16**
Joe's Habanero **22**
Lazy Lizard **1**
Lighthouse Ice Cream
 Parlour **12**
Marin's Restaurant & Bar **24**
Rainbow Grill & Bar **6**
Rose's Grill & Bar **15**
Sand Box Restaurant **13**
Syd's Restaurant & Bar **21**
Wish Willy's **2**

NIGHTLIFE ●
Barrier Reef Sports Bar
 & Grill **9**
I&I Bar and Cafe **23**
Lazy Lizard **1**
Oceanside Bar **7**

$ Bank/ATM
✚ Hospital
P Police
✉ Post office

Caye Caulker

area of detail

THE SPLIT

CHILDREN'S PARK

FOOTBALL FIELD

Back Dock

Front St.

CENTRAL PARK

Front Dock

Back St.

Middle St.

Caye Caulker

BELIZE

Belize City

Belmopan

Airstrip

CAYE CAULKER MINI-RESERVE

0   1/5 mile
0   200 meters

best bet. Many hotels have their own for guests to use free of charge or for a slight rental fee. If not, you can rent a bicycle in town. There are several places on Front Street that rent bicycles. Rates run around BZ$20 to BZ$30 per day.

While I think it's really unnecessary, you can also rent a golf cart from **Caye Caulker Golf Rentals** (℃ **226-0237**), **C & N Golf Carts** (℃ **226-0252**), or **Jasmine Cart Rentals** (℃ **206-0212**). Rates run around BZ$120 to BZ$180 per day for a four-seat cart. Hourly rates are between BZ$30 and BZ$40.

ORIENTATION

Most boats dock at the pier jutting off Front Street at a spot called Front Bridge—so named because this is the front side of the island facing the reef (east). The town extends north and south from here. As you debark, if you kept walking straight ahead, you'd soon come to the western side of the island and the Back Bridge or dock, where some of the boats dock. Caye Caulker consists of two or three main north–south sand roads, a few cross streets, and numerous paths. The closest street to the water on the east side of the island is Front Street. The next street in is called either Middle Street or Hicaco Avenue, and the next street to the west is called alternately Back Street or Langosta Avenue. The small Caye Caulker airstrip is located on the southern outskirts of the town. At the north end of town, you'll find the Split or Cut, the town's prime swimming and sunbathing spot.

Much of Caye Caulker is uninhabited. The small town and inhabited sections are quite concentrated.

Though Caye Caulker is still a relatively safe place, it is not advisable to leave money or valuables in your hotel room, except in a safe.

FAST FACTS For the local **police**, dial ℃ **911**, or 226-2022; for the **fire department**, dial ℃ **226-0353.** In the case of a medical emergency, call the **Caye Caulker Health Clinic** (℃ **226-0166**).

Atlantic Bank (℃ **226-0207**) is located on Back Street, near the center of the island, and has an ATM that accepts international credit and debit cards. The **post office** (℃ **226-2325**) is also located on Back Street; it's open Monday through Friday from 8am to noon and from 1 to 5pm. There are several **Internet cafes** on the island; just walk along Front Street and find one with an open terminal. I like **Caye Caulker Cyber Café,** which serves drinks—and even has a popular happy hour with reduced rates on drinks and Internet usage. They also have a good book-swap library.

Slow Ride
The unofficial, yet almost universal, motto on Caye Caulker is "Go Slow."

Most hotels provide laundry service, but pricing varies widely, so ask first. There are several coin-operated and full-service **laundromats** on Caye Caulker, all in the central downtown area. Almost all of these are a better deal than going with your hotel's service.

What to See & Do

The main activities on Caye Caulker itself are strolling up and down the sand streets, and swimming and sunbathing off the docks. The most popular spot is at the north end of the island by the **Split ★**. The Split was formed in 1961 when Hurricane Hattie literally split the island in two. You'll find the water's edge rimmed with a nice wooden dock, and there's even a decent little patch of beach and a roped-off swimming area. The water is very calm by the Split, making it a good place to practice if you're an inexperienced snorkeler. Take care when swimming off the docks here. The Split is an active channel with regular boat traffic. At least one swimmer has been killed by a boat, so stick to designated swimming areas, away from obvious boat channels. Also, when the tides are running strong, there's quite a bit of current through the Split, and it's easy to get dragged along for a few hundred yards or so. If you do get caught in this current, treat it like any riptide: Don't panic, and swim diagonally across the current to get out of it.

Aside from the Split, and as on Ambergris Caye, there is not much beach to speak of on the rest of the island. There is a narrow strip of sand for much of the length of the island, where the land meets the sea, but even at low tide it isn't wide enough for you to unroll a beach towel on in most places. In fact, along most of its length this is a small bike and footpath that is probably the busiest thoroughfare on Caye Caulker. Just off the coast, for the first 100 yards (300 ft.) or more out from shore, the bottom is covered with sea grass, which is protected by national law. Beneath the grass is a layer of spongy roots and organic matter topped with a thin layer of white sand. Be careful when walking on this spongy sand, as you might encounter a sea urchin or stingray, and it's easy to trip and stumble.

Several of the hotels have built long piers out into the sea, with steps down into the water, and swimming is best here. Beyond this, some of the best swimming can be had from boats anchored out in the turquoise waters between the shore and the reef, or by taking a kayak offshore a little way.

As on Ambergris Caye, snorkeling, scuba diving, and fishing are the main draws here. All are excellent.

ON & UNDER THE WATER
Scuba Diving & Snorkeling ★★★

There's excellent diving and snorkeling close to Caye Caulker. Within a 5- to 20-minute boat ride from the pier lie some **world-class dive sites ★★**, including **Caye Caulker North Cut, Coral Gardens, Pyramid Flats, Sponge Avenue,** and **Amigos Wreck.** As on Ambergris Caye, a day's diving here will almost always feature a mix of steep wall drops and coral caverns and tunnels. In addition, in Caye Caulker you can dive on the wreck of a 15m (49-ft.) boat and among huge canyons of coral. You'll see brilliant coral and sponge formations, as well as a wealth of colorful marine life. The wreck and canyons are prime spots to spot giant grouper, and rays and turtles are fairly common here as well.

There are several dependable dive operators on Caye Caulker. Rates are pretty standardized, and you should be able to get deals on multiday, multidive packages. The best dive operations on the island are **Belize Diving Services ★★** (© 226-0143; www.belizedivingservice.com), **Big Fish Dive Center** (© 226-0450), and **Frenchie's Diving ★** (© **226-0234;** www.frenchiesdivingbelize.com). Of these, Belize Dive Center is the most up-to-date, with top-notch equipment and mixed-gas and technical diving capabilities. All of these operators charge BZ$100 to BZ$180 for a local two-tank dive, with equipment rental running around BZ$50 to BZ$60 for a complete package and BZ$16 to BZ$30 for a mask, snorkel, and fins.

For more adventurous diving, you'll probably want to head out to the **Turneffe Island Atoll ★★**, **Lighthouse Reef ★★**, and **Blue Hole ★★**. All of the dive operations on Caye Caulker offer this trip or will subcontract it out. It's about a 2- to 3-hour ride each way—depending upon the speed of your boat—over sometimes rough seas. Most day trips out to Turneffe Island or Lighthouse Reef and Blue Hole run around BZ$400 to BZ$500 per person, including transportation, two or three dives, tanks, and weights, as well as lunch and snacks. For more information on these dive sites, see p. 147.

Caye Caulker is another excellent place to learn how to scuba dive. Resort courses will give you an excellent 1-day introduction into the world of scuba diving, including a very controlled shallow-water boat dive. These courses cost BZ$200 to BZ$300. In 3 to 4 days, however, you can get your full open-water certification. These courses cost between BZ$700 and BZ$900, including all equipment rentals, class materials, and the processing of your certification, as well as four open-water and reef dives. All of the above-mentioned dive operations offer these courses.

There are a host of boats on Caye Caulker offering snorkeling trips, and most of the above dive operators also offer snorkeling trips and equipment rental. Snorkeling tours range in price from BZ$30 to BZ$60 for short jaunts to half-day outings, and BZ$100 to BZ$180 for full-day trips—a bit more if you want to jump on a trip all the way out to the Blue Hole. A full set of mask, fins, and snorkel will usually cost from BZ$16 to BZ$30 per person per day.

All of the Caye Caulker dive and snorkel operators offer trips to **Shark-Ray Alley** ★★ and **Hol Chan Marine Reserve** ★★. These trips cost between BZ$90 and BZ$280 per person, depending on whether it is a snorkel or scuba dive trip, how long the tour lasts, and whether there is a stop on Ambergris Caye. Many of these include a stop for lunch and a quick walk around town in San Pedro. See

---

CHOCOLATE & THE manatees

Sure you can get candy bars, cakes, and a whole host of products derived from the fruit of the cacao tree here. But on Caye Caulker, when someone mentions "Chocolate," they are almost inevitably referring to pioneering guide and boat captain Lionel "Chocolate" Heredia. Chocolate began his career as a fisherman, but he soon dedicated himself to the fledgling business of taxiing folks by speedboat back and forth between Belize City and Caye Caulker. This business soon expanded to include guided tours, snorkeling outings, and fishing adventures. Chocolate was also probably the first guide to introduce the popular day trip to see manatees and do some snorkeling at remote cayes. He and his wife, Annie, also led the battle to protect these gentle sea mammals and their feeding grounds, finally seeing the creation of the Swallow Caye Manatee Reserve (www.swallowcayemanatees.org) in 1999.

Chocolate (© **226-0151;** chocolate seashore@gmail.com) still leads manatee and snorkel tours. These tours begin with a stop at the manatee-feeding site on Swallow Caye, before heading to either Goff's or Sergeant's cayes, which are little more than football field–size patches of sand with a few palm trees. The afternoons are usually spent snorkeling in the clear waters off these cayes, and lunching on the sand. These trips, which are also offered by most other tour operators on the island, include all transportation, lunch on one of the cayes, and several snorkel stops, and cost between BZ$120 and BZ$180 per person.

"What to See & Do" on p. 117 for more information and a detailed description of Shark-Ray Alley and Hol Chan Marine Reserve.

One of my favorite options for snorkelers is a day cruise to Shark-Ray Alley and Hol Chan with **Raggamuffin Tours ★** (© 226-0348; www.raggamuffintours.com) aboard a classic wooden Belizean sloop. The trip makes three distinct snorkel stops and includes lunch onboard the boat, snorkeling gear, and the park entrance fee for BZ$90 per person.

Sailing ★★

The crystal-clear waters, calm seas, and excellent snorkeling spots around Caye Caulker make this an excellent place to go out for a sail. Unlike on Ambergris Caye, there are no organized bareboat charters available here, but you can go out on any number of different vessels for a half- or full-day sail, a sunset cruise, a moonlight cruise, or a combined sailing and snorkeling adventure.

A day cruise including lunch, drinks, and snorkeling gear should run between BZ$100 and BZ$240 per person; a half-day tour including drinks, a snack, and snorkeling gear should cost between BZ$70 and BZ$120. Most hotels and tour operators around town can hook you up with an appropriate captain and craft. Or you can head out on the Shark-Ray Alley and Hol Chan tour with **Raggamuffin Tours ★** (© 226-0348; www.raggamuffintours.com). These folks also run a regular 3-day/2-night sailing trip down to Placencia, sleeping in tents on small cayes along the way.

Fishing

Although not nearly as developed or popular on Caye Caulker, sport fishing for tarpon, permit, and bonefish is still excellent around the caye, and on the reefs and flats. There are several dedicated fishing guides on the island, and almost every hotel, tour operator, or dive shop can hook you up with a captain and crew for some angling. If you're a serious fisherman, **Angler's Abroad Fly Shop ★★** (© 226-0303; www.anglersabroad.com) should be your first stop. Other recommended guides on the island include **Porfilio Guzmán** (© 226-0152) and **Esley Usher** (© 669-7585).

A half-day of reef trolling, casting, or fly-fishing for bonefish or tarpon costs between BZ$200 and BZ$400, a full day between BZ$400 and BZ$800. Deep-sea trolling for larger game runs around BZ$800 to BZ$1,200 for a half-day, BZ$1,600 to BZ$2,400 for a full day. These prices are per boat for two to four fishermen and usually include drinks, tackle, and lunch.

Kitesurfing & Sailboarding

With strong, steady, but not overpowering winds, Caye Caulker is a great place to learn or practice kitesurfing. The folks at **Kitexplorer** (© 626-4513; www.kitexplorer.com) rent out both kitesurfing and sailboarding equipment. They also offer an intensive 9-hour course in kitesurfing for BZ$740 that is guaranteed to get you up and skimming across the sea.

Kayaks & Other Watercraft

The calm, protected waters just offshore are wonderful for any number of watersports vehicles. Several hotels and tour operators around Caye Caulker have various types of watercraft for guest use, or general rental. Rates run around BZ$20 to BZ$30 per hour for a kayak; BZ$40 to BZ$60 per hour for a Hobie Cat or small sailboat; and BZ$60 to BZ$80 per hour for a jet ski.

FUN ON DRY LAND

Aside from sunbathing, reading, and relaxing, there's very little to do on Caye Caulker. However, you should be sure to head south of town to the **Caye Caulker Mini-Reserve,** located on the southern outskirts of the town. The term "mini" is certainly fitting. Nevertheless, this local endeavor features a few gentle and well-cleared paths through a small stand of littoral forest. More serious bird-watchers might want to grab a boat and a guide and head to the northern half of the island, where 40 hectares (100 acres) on the very northern tip have been declared the **Caye Caulker Forest Reserve.** In all, more than 130 species of resident and migrant birds have been spotted on and around Caye Caulker. Another option for bird-watchers and nature lovers is to rent a kayak for paddling around on the lagoon and mangrove side of the island. No admission is charged to visit either of these reserves.

EXCURSIONS ON THE MAINLAND

If you've got island fever or Caye Caulker is your only destination, and you want to see more of Belize, several tour operators on Caye Caulker offer excursions to all of the major attractions and destinations around the country, including Altun Ha, Lamanai, Xunantunich, Mountain Pine Ridge, and Tikal. You can also go cave tubing in the Caves Branch region. Most of these tours involve a flight or two in a small charter plane.

The most popular and economical tours are to the Mayan ruins of Altun Ha or Lamanai, or a spa package and lunch at Maruba Jungle Resort. Various operators offer a combined trip visiting both Altun Ha and Maruba. These trips begin with a short boat ride to the mainland, followed by a minibus ride to the selected attraction. Prices for these trips run BZ$140 to BZ$240, although the spa treatments are extra.

For trips involving a flight, prices range from BZ$200 to BZ$400 per person, depending on the distance traveled and the number of activities and attractions crammed into 1 day. Any hotel or tour operator on the island can help you arrange any number of these tours. In most cases, these trips are subcontracted out to an operator based either in Belize City or on Ambergris Caye.

For detailed descriptions of these various destinations and attractions, see the respective regional chapters throughout this book. In addition to the dive and water-sports tour operators listed above, **Tsunami Adventures** (© **226-0462;** www. tsunamiadventures.com) is a good, all-purpose operator with an extensive list of offerings on and under the water, and all around the cayes and mainland too.

Shopping

In terms of shopping, you'll be amazed by the number of small gift shops and makeshift souvenir stands lining the few streets here. As on Ambergris Caye, much of the shopping on Caye Caulker is typical tourist fare. Mostly what you'll be able to buy are T-shirts and jewelry made by local artisans. **Chocolate's Boutique ★** (© **226-0151**) has slightly higher-quality goods, including reasonably priced Guatemalan and Indonesian textiles, as well as some lovely silver and stone jewelry. And yes, the Chocolate of this shop is the same Chocolate discussed in "Chocolate & the Manatee," p. 138.

A couple of good art galleries on the island are **Caribbean Colors Art Gallery** (© **226-0208;** www.caribbean-colors.com), which features some interesting original artwork and hand-painted silk by artist Lee Vanderwalker-Kroll, and **Cooper's**

Art Gallery ★ (© 226-0330; www.debbiecooper.artspan.com), which features the work of local resident Debbie Cooper and other local artists.

As I recommend elsewhere in this book, please avoid buying black coral jewelry. Black coral is extremely beautiful, but as with every endangered resource, increased demand just leads to increased harvesting of a slow-growing coral.

Where to Stay

Accommodations on Caye Caulker have improved over the years, but there are still no resorts or real luxury options to be had. In my opinion, this adds to the charm of the place. Budget and midrange lodging options are abundant, and some of these are quite comfortable.

If you plan on staying for any period of time, you should look into renting a small cottage, condo, or apartment. Look around for signs or bulletin boards, or check with Amanda at **Caye Caulker Rentals ★** (©/fax **226-0029;** www.cayecaulkerrentals.com). Rates begin at around BZ$100 per night, although during the high season rates go up and longer stays are often required. Another option is the fully equipped efficiency units at **Caye Caulker Condos** (©/fax **226-0072;** www.cayecaulkercondos.com), which rent for between BZ$220 and BZ$270 per night.

EXPENSIVE

Caye Reef ★★ Fronting the ocean toward the north end of the caye, the two-bedroom, two-bathroom condo units here are fresh, clean, and well-equipped. Every unit comes with an ocean-facing balcony and is decorated with bright Caribbean colors and original local artwork. The rooftop pool, Jacuzzi, and lounge area is a highlight. Cleaning is only once weekly, but that frequency can be increased for a BZ$20 daily fee. Hot water is solar-heated, and the owners are consciously trying to be sustainable.

Front St. (P.O. Box 31), Caye Caulker. ©/fax **226-0381** or © 610-0240. www.cayereef.com. 6 units. BZ$390 condo; BZ$430 penthouse. Rates slightly higher during peak weeks; lower during the off season. AE, MC, V. **Amenities:** Jacuzzi; outdoor pool. *In room:* A/C, TV, kitchen, free Wi-Fi.

Iguana Reef ★★ This is the closest thing to a resort hotel on Caye Caulker. The spacious rooms are housed in several two-story concrete-block structures. All rooms come with air-conditioning, a stocked minibar, and a programmable safe. The deluxe units have a sitting area, a stereo CD player, and a semiprivate veranda. Iguana Reef, which is on the lagoon or back side of the island, has a large and comfortable sandy area for lounging, with a pier leading off this to a nice swimming spot. This is also arguably the best spot on the island to catch a sunset. The hotel also has a very inviting pool.

Back St. (P.O. Box 31), Caye Caulker. © **226-0213.** Fax 226-0087. www.iguanareefinn.com. 12 units. BZ$270–BZ$330 double; BZ$750 penthouse. Rates include continental breakfast. Rates slightly higher during peak weeks; lower during the off season. DISC, MC, V. **Amenities:** Restaurant; bar; complimentary kayak use; outdoor pool; free Wi-Fi. *In room:* A/C, stocked minifridge, no phone.

MODERATE

In addition to the places listed below, **Popeye's Beach Resort** (𝄢 226-0032; www.popeyesbeachresort.com) is another good option in this price range, with air-conditioned rooms and an oceanfront setting.

Lazy Iguana Bed & Breakfast ★   Housed in an interesting four-story octagonal building, this little bed-and-breakfast offers comfortable rooms in a quiet setting on the back side of the island. Three of the rooms have queen beds, and one comes with two twin beds. All of the rooms are spacious and immaculate. Breakfasts always include a couple of freshly baked items, and plenty of fresh fruit and strong coffee. One of the nicest features here is the open-air fourth-floor thatched terrace, which offers excellent 360-degree views of the island, and has a couple of hammocks perfect for an afternoon siesta. Guests have free use of bicycles, and there's a small lounge with a lending library and cable television.

2 blocks north of the airstrip on the lagoon side (P.O. Box 59), Caye Caulker. 𝄢 **226-0350.** Fax 226-0320. www.lazyiguana.net. 4 units. BZ$210 double. Rates include full breakfast. Rates higher during peak weeks; lower during the off season. MC, V. *In room:* A/C, minifridge, no phone, free Wi-Fi.

Seaside Cabanas ★★   This hotel is built in a horseshoe around a small rectangular pool, with a broad wooden deck around it. All the rooms are spacious and painted in lively yellows and reds, and feature modern decorative touches. Four of the rooms come with private rooftop lounge areas with hammocks strung under an open-air thatch roof. These are by far my favorite rooms, but I also like no. 6, a second-floor unit with a small private balcony. There's no restaurant here, but they have a lively bar and an excellent in-house tour operation.

Front St. (P.O. Box 39), Caye Caulker. 𝄢 **226-0498.** Fax 226-0125. www.seasidecabanas.com. 17 units. BZ$210–BZ$260 double. Rates slightly higher during peak weeks; lower during the off season. No children 9 and under allowed. AE, MC, V. **Amenities:** Bar; bike rental; outdoor pool; free Wi-Fi. *In room:* A/C, TV/DVD, minifridge, no phone.

INEXPENSIVE

There are literally scores of budget options on Caye Caulker. I list my favorite and the most dependable options below. In addition to these, **Yuma's House Belize** (𝄢 206-0019; www.yumashousebelize.com) is your best bet. Formerly known as Tina's Backpacker's Hostel, this place offers clean, basic rooms with an oceanfront location and very lively, hostel-like atmosphere.

De Real Macaw ✒   This place is located just north of the center of town, across from a string of makeshift artisan stalls and streetside restaurants on Front Street. The hotel is its own little compound, around a central sandy garden area, with a few tall shade trees hung with hammocks. The two "beachfront" rooms are the best rooms here, but all are very clean and well kept, with tile floors, tiny television sets, and a front porch or balcony. Most of the rooms come with air-conditioning, but you'll pay a little more for it. The two-bedroom "condo" and separate beach house both come with a full kitchen, and these folks also rent out fully furnished apartments on a weekly basis, located a little bit away toward the center of town.

Front St., north of Front Bridge, Caye Caulker. 𝄢 **226-0459.** Fax 226-0497. www.derealmacaw.biz. 7 units. BZ$50–BZ$110 double with no A/C; BZ$120–BZ$140 double with A/C; BZ$240–BZ$260 condo or beach house. Rates lower in the off season. MC, V. *In room:* TV, minifridge, no phone.

Maxhapan Cabins ★   With just three rooms and expansive grounds located just outside of the "downtown" hustle and bustle, this place feels like a private oasis. Rooms are housed in two yellow wooden cottages set on raised stilts. The best choice is the individual cabin. Everything is simple, but kept immaculate. There's a communal bar area, as well as a two-story open-air structure meant for chilling out. The owner, Louise, is almost always on hand, providing attentive and personalized service.

Just south of town on Center St. (P.O. Box 63), Caye Caulker. ✆ **226-0118.** maxhapan04@hotmail.com. 3 units. BZ$118 double. MC, V. **Amenities:** Complimentary bike use. *In room:* A/C, minifridge, no phone.

Tree Tops Guest House ★ 🔥   It's hard to beat this place for value on Caye Caulker. Set just off the ocean in the heart of town, this converted three-story home offers clean, spacious, and cool rooms. There are four rooms located on the ground floor. Two of these share a common bathroom down the hall, but each has a vanity sink in the room itself. However, the best rooms here are the two top-floor suites. Each of these comes with a king bed and private balcony. The Sunset Suite is the best of these, with the largest balcony and views to both the lagoon and the ocean. If you opt for one of the standard rooms, however, you can still enjoy the view from the rooftop lounge area, which features several hammocks hung under a shade roof.

On the waterfront south of Front Bridge (P.O. Box 29), Caye Caulker. ✆ **226-0240.** Fax 226-0115. www. treetopsbelize.com. 6 units (4 with private bathroom). BZ$100 double with shared bathroom; BZ$138–BZ$196 double with private bathroom. MC, V. *In room:* TV, minifridge, no phone.

Trends Beachfront Hotel   Set right off the water and just off the main pier at Front Bridge, the rooms here are housed in a two-story wooden building painted in tropical pastel colors. The rooms are large, clean, bright, and airy, and it's hard to beat the location. There's also a separate, private bungalow, which is the closest unit to the water, and the best room in the house. These folks also run a separate hotel on Front Street a few blocks away. The rooms here are actually somewhat more modern, and most have air-conditioning; however, they lack the rustic charm and proximity to the water that you'll enjoy at the beachfront option. The Sand Box Restaurant here (p. 144) is one of the most popular on the island.

Beachfront in the center of town, Caye Caulker. ✆ **226-0094.** Fax 226-0097. www.trendsbze.com. 7 units. BZ$60–BZ$100 double; BZ$120 bungalow. AE, MC, V. **Amenities:** Restaurant; bar. *In room:* No phone.

Where to Dine

In addition to the places listed below, if you're hanging out by the Split, you'll probably want to stop in at the **Lazy Lizard** (✆ **226-0368**), a funky bar-restaurant serving cold drinks and a menu of local dishes, sandwiches, and burgers. And be sure to stop in at the **Lighthouse Ice Cream Parlour** on Front Street for a cone or a scoop of some fresh, homemade ice cream.

MODERATE

Agave ★★ INTERNATIONAL   This place serves excellent fusion-inspired contemporary cuisine. Tables are spread around a large, raised, open-air deck fronting Front Street. Inside there's a chill bar and lounge area. Start things off with the excellent crab cakes, served with an orange vodka sauce, or the superb coconut shrimp bisque. For a main course, I like the fresh snapper filet with a spicy papaya glaze. There are also several nightly specials. The owner, Ricael Moran, is actually an accomplished "flair" bartender. If you ask nicely, he may put on a little show.

On Front St., near the center of town. ✆ **226-0403.** Reservations recommended during the high season. Main courses BZ$20–BZ$32. MC, V. Daily 6am–9:30pm.

Don Corleone ★★★ ITALIAN/FUSION Contemporary lighting over the bar, combined with slow-turning ceiling fans and polished concrete floors, with heavy wooden tables set with linen tablecloths and fancy flatware, make this the most elegant restaurant on the island. New chef-owner Luca Michelus, from Trieste, via New York, has taken an already established hit and made it better. You can start with an excellent Caesar salad, or try the Watermelon salad with olives and feta cheese. If you don't opt for one of the nightly specials, I recommend the tagliatelle with shrimp and lobster in a pink sauce finished with brandy; however, everything is done well. The wine list is varied and fairly priced.

On Front St., north of the center of town. ✆ **226-0025.** Reservations recommended during the high season. Pizzas and pastas BZ$22–BZ$34; main courses BZ$28–BZ$50. MC, V. Mon–Sat 5–9:30pm.

Habaneros ★★★ INTERNATIONAL Although the name suggests a Mexican joint, the menu here goes beyond standard Mexican fare. You can get homemade pastas and Thai coconut curries, as well as Brazilian pork. You can also get spicy fajitas made of beef, chicken, or jerk pork. I like to start things off with the Creole Voodoo Cakes, pan-sautéed seafood cakes served with a spicy dipping sauce. The nightly specials tend to be inventive takes on whatever fresh fish and seafood has been caught that day. Heavy wooden tables are spread across the pleasant, open-air, wraparound veranda of this raised-stilt wooden home right on Front Street. There's also indoor seating, but you'll really want to try to grab one of the outdoor spots. Margaritas and sangria are served by the pitcher, and there's a pretty good wine list for Caye Caulker.

On Front St., near the center of town. ✆ **226-0487** or 626-4911. Reservations recommended. Main courses BZ$34–BZ$48. MC, V. Wed–Mon 5:30–10pm.

Rainbow Grill & Bar SEAFOOD/INTERNATIONAL Built over the water near the center of town, this is a great place to dine to the sound of water lapping against the pilings below your feet. A dozen or so wooden tables with plastic chairs are set around the screened-in restaurant. The screen comes in handy, especially when the bugs are biting. Try to grab a table by the outer railing, closest to the water. Chicken, fish, conch, shrimp, and lobster are all offered in a variety of preparations from simply grilled or fried, to served with sauces ranging from lemon-ginger to Cajun. All are very well-prepared and tasty. The lunch menu is much simpler and less expensive. I particularly like the conch fajitas.

Over the water on Front St., near the center of town. ✆ **226-0281.** Reservations recommended during the high season. Main courses lunch BZ$8–BZ$24, dinner BZ$12–BZ$44. MC, V. Tues–Sun 11am–10pm.

Sand Box Restaurant ★ SEAFOOD/INTERNATIONAL This place gets its name from its sand floor, which extends both inside and out. I prefer the outdoor tables in the shade of broad-leafed sea-grape trees. Either way, you'll be able to choose from an extensive menu of Belizean and international dishes. Seafood is the strong suit here, but you can also get chicken or meat dishes. You can have your fresh fish filet served with an almond-and-garlic-butter sauce or spicy banana chutney.

Budget hounds can fill up on burgers, burritos, and quesadillas. The daily happy hour (3–6pm) is quite popular here.

Front St., on the waterfront, near the center of town. ✆ **226-0200.** Main courses BZ$9–BZ$36. AE, MC, V. Daily 7am–9pm.

INEXPENSIVE

In addition to the places listed below, there are several simple local restaurants serving fresh fish, seafood, and Belizean standards at very economical rates. The best of these are **Syd's Restaurant & Bar** (✆ 206-0294) and **Marin's Restaurant & Bar** (✆ 226-0104), both located on Middle Street, near the center of town. However, my favorite of these local joints is **Rose's Grill & Bar** (✆ 226-0407), located on the side street, right next to Habaneros.

For tasty pizzas, burgers, and Tex-Mex at an excellent price, try **Joe's Habanero ★** (✆ 668-8177), a simple joint with a sand floor, run by the folks behind Habaneros (see above).

The best cheap eats on Caye Caulker are the various outdoor grills that set up nightly all along Front Street, offering chicken, shrimp, beef, and lobster (in season) at very reasonable rates.

Amor y Café ★ BREAKFAST   This quaint and simple breakfast joint is still a great place for a breakfast or early lunch. Freshly baked brownies, banana bread, and whole-wheat breads are the mainstay here, served alongside strong coffee, cappuccino, or a fresh-fruit smoothie. You can also get eggs cooked to order or a hefty sandwich. The best thing about Amor y Café, though, is that its few tables are set on an open-air deck overlooking Front Street, so you get to watch Caye Caulker as it slowly wakes up and gets going.

Front St., near the center of town. ✆ **610-2397.** Reservations not accepted. Main courses BZ$4–BZ$12. No credit cards. Daily 6am–noon.

Glenda's BELIZEAN/MEXICAN   This humble establishment is one of Caye Caulker's longest-standing traditions and most popular spots. The menu is written on a chalkboard on your left as you walk up to the open window into Glenda's house. Order here, and the meal will be brought to your table, but don't sit down and expect to be waited on. They specialize in simple Mexican fare, including burritos and rice and beans. Breakfasts feature eggs and johnnycakes, but the star attractions here are the fresh cinnamon rolls and freshly squeezed orange juice. There are only a few wooden tables with either plastic lawn chairs or folding metal card chairs; the best ones are on the small screened-in porch. Come early for breakfast if you want a decent seat.

In back of Atlantic Bank, Caye Caulker. ✆ **226-2148.** Main courses BZ$1–BZ$12. No credit cards. Mon-Fri 7am–3pm.

Wish Willy's ★ FUSION/SEAFOOD   Serving breakfast, lunch, and dinner out of his home's kitchen, Belizean-by-way-of-Chicago chef Maurice Moore has built a reputation for serving excellent fare in a relaxed open-air yard. Tables are long picnic-style affairs that you'll often have to share with others. There's no set menu, but it is always built around the freshest ingredients available, simply grilled, or served with an Asian-fusion flare. Conch may come stir-fried in a teriyaki sauce, or in more traditional Belizean-style fritters. And while there are set opening hours, these may be reduced if Maurice's mood or stamina flag.

A small caye ON THE WAY

Between Belize City and the popular tourist destinations of Caye Caulker and Ambergris Caye lie scores of small islands and cayes. Of these, one is of interest to travelers, **St. George's Caye ★★**.

St. George's is the closest resort caye to Belize City, just 14km (8⅔ miles) offshore. This tiny island played a crucial role in the country's history. From 1650 to 1784, St. George's was the first capital city for the early Baymen colonists, and it was also the site and namesake of the pivotal 1798 sea battle between the Baymen and a hostile Spanish fleet. Today, it is mostly a getaway for a handful of wealthy Belizeans who have vacation cottages on the caye. However, there is one excellent hotel here. **St. George's**

Caye Resort ★★ (© **800/813-8498** in the U.S. and Canada; www.belizeislandparadise.com) is a collection of individual wooden cabins built either facing the sea or on stilts out over the lagoon. The small resort has a pretty pool and extensive tour and activity options, as well as complimentary kayaks and Hobie Cats for guests. This is also a great base for scuba diving, with a dedicated dive shop and excellent operation. You'll feel as if you have the island to yourself, although if you explore, you'll find there's a Belize Army base here. On one end of the island there's a small but excellent private **aquarium ★** (© **662-2170**; daily 11am–5pm; BZ$6) that gives visitors a good look into the local marine life.

On the north end of the island, lagoon side, Caye Caulker. © **660-7194.** Main courses BZ$10–BZ$18. No credit cards. Daily 7am–9pm (although opening hours may vary according to Maurice's stamina).

Caye Caulker After Dark

For evening entertainment, you can stargaze, go for a night dive, or have a drink in one of the island's handful of bars. Periodically, one of the bars will crank up the music, and *voilà*—a disco. In general, the scene is so small that most folks will congregate at one or two bars. Which one or two bars are happening might shift from night to night; ask a local or two, and you'll certainly be directed to the current hot spot. My favorite bar is the open-air **I&I Bar and Cafe ★** (© **625-0344**), which features rustic wooden plank swings for most of its seating. The bar itself takes up the second and third floors of this thatch-roofed wooden structure and is located on a cross street on the southern end of town. Right in the center of town on Front Street, the **Oceanside Bar** (© **226-0233**) often has either live music or karaoke, and the **Barrier Reef Sports Bar & Grill** (© **226-0077**) has a good crowd most nights, with everything from trivia contests to sporting events to live music.

THE OUTER ATOLLS ★★★

40–80km (25–50 miles) E of Belize City

Roughly due east, out beyond the barrier reef, lie two of Belize's three open-ocean atolls, Turneffe Island and Lighthouse Reef. The reef and island rings of tranquillity, in the midst of the Caribbean Sea, are stunning and pristine places. The outer island atolls are popular destinations for day trips out from Belize City, Ambergris Caye, and Caye Caulker. However, if you really want to experience their unique charms, you should stay at one of the few small lodges located right on the edge of one of them, or on one of the live-aboard dive boats that ply these waters.

Getting There & Departing

These are remote and isolated destinations. Aside from the lodges, which all offer their own transportation, there is no regularly scheduled transportation out here. However, private water taxis and charter flights can be arranged.

BY PLANE The only airstrip located on these outer atolls is the private airstrip of the Lighthouse Reef Resort on Big Northern Caye.

BY BOAT Turneffe Island Atoll is a 1½- to 2-hour boat ride from Belize City. The lodges listed below provide their own transportation to and from Belize City as part of their vacation packages.

BY HELICOPTER The quickest and easiest way to get out to these atolls is by helicopter. **Astrum Helicopters** (© **888/278-7864** in the U.S. and Canada, or 222-5100 in Belize; www.astrumhelicopters.com) will take you out here for BZ$2,500 in a helicopter that will hold four passengers, and BZ$5,000 in a six-passenger bird.

Exploring the Atolls

Unlike Pacific Ocean atolls, which are often the crater rings of extinct volcanoes, these atolls were formed over millions of years by a combination of plate tectonics, rising water levels following the last ice age, and millenniums of mid-ocean coral growth. Many of the atoll walls drop off steeply for more than a thousand feet, while in the central lagoons the water depths average only 3 to 12m (10–40 ft.).

Most folks come out here to do one of two things: fish or dive. Some do both. Both activities are truly world-class. In broad strokes, fishermen should head to Turneffe Island Atoll, while dedicated and serious divers would probably want to choose Lighthouse Reef Atoll, although there's great diving to be had off Turneffe.

TURNEFFE ISLAND ATOLL ★★

This is the largest of Belize's three ocean atolls, and the largest in the Caribbean Sea. Both the diving and the fishing here are excellent, but the fishing gets a slight nod. The extensive mangrove and saltwater flats are perfect territory for stalking permit, bonefish, snook, and tarpon. Most fishing is done with fly rods, either wading in the flats or from a poled skiff.

Turneffe Island Atoll also boasts scores of world-class wall, coral, and sponge gardens, and drift dive sites. Most of these sites are located around the southern tip of the atoll. Perhaps the most famous dive site here is **The Elbow ★★★**, a jutting coral point with steep drop-offs, huge sponges, and ample fish life. Another popular site is **Rendezvous Point ★★**, which features several grottoes that divers can swim in and out of, and there's a small modern wreck, the *Sayonara,* sitting in about 9.1m (30 ft.) of water.

LIGHTHOUSE REEF ATOLL ★★

Boasting nearly 80km (50 miles) of wall and reef diving, including some of the best and most coveted dive sites in all of the Caribbean, this is a true scuba-diving mecca. The waters of this atoll, the farthest one from shore, are incredibly clear and pristine. The central lagoon of this atoll is some 48km (30 miles) long and around 13km (8 miles) wide at its widest point. In the center, you'll find the world-famous **Blue Hole ★★**, a perfectly round mid-atoll sinkhole that plunges straight down to a depth of more than 122m (400 ft.). You'll see postcards, photos, and T-shirts all over town showing off aerial views of this perfectly round hole in the ocean. Nearly 305m (1,000 ft.) across, the Blue Hole's eroded limestone karst walls and stalactite formations make this a unique and justifiably popular dive site. However, some of the wall and coral garden dives around the outer edges of the atoll are even better. Of these, **Half Moon Caye Wall ★★** and **North Long Caye Wall ★★** are consistently considered some of the best clear-water coral wall dives in the world.

Toward the southeastern edge of the atoll is **Half Moon Caye National Monument ★★**, a combined island and marine reserve. Half Moon Caye itself is the principal nesting ground for the beautiful and odd-looking red-footed booby. These birds are always here in massive numbers. The island is also a prime nesting site for both hawksbill and loggerhead turtles. **The Belize Audubon Society** (© **223-5004**; www.belizeaudubon.org) has constructed a small visitor center here, and a wonderful viewing platform near the center of the island. They also allow overnight camping with prior arrangement. The admission fee is BZ$20 for Half Moon Caye National Monument and BZ$60 for entrance to the Blue Hole National Monument.

Water conditions here are amazingly consistent, with an average water temperature of around 80°F (27°C), while visibility on the outer atoll walls and reefs easily averages more than 30m (100 ft.).

If you want to stay here as part of a guided tour, I highly recommend **Island Expeditions ★★** (© **800/667-1630** or 604/452-3212; www.islandexpeditions.com), which runs weeklong adventure excursions here based out of a private tent-camp on Half Moon Caye.

Where to Stay & Dine on Turneffe Island Atoll

VERY EXPENSIVE

Turneffe Flats ★★ This is a superbly run fishing resort geared toward dedicated flat-water fly-fishing. Everything here is simple, yet luxurious. The rooms are all beachfront and housed in a couple of long, low buildings raised off the sandy ground just a bit on some wooden pilings. The rooms each come with one queen bed and one twin bed, large bathrooms, and a common shared veranda. Villas come with a living room and satellite television. Meals are served family-style in the main lodge or, weather permitting, outdoors on an open deck off the lodge. The fishing and dive operations here are top-notch. Packages are weeklong affairs, running Saturday to Saturday.

Blackbird Caye, Turneffe Island Atoll. © **888/512-8812** in the U.S. or Canada, or 220-4046 in Belize. Fax 623/298-5008. www.tflats.com. 14 units. BZ$4,050–BZ$4,650 per person per week dive package; BZ$6,280–BZ$7,320 per person per week fishing package. Rates are based on double occupancy and include all meals, round-trip boat transportation from Belize City, and guided daily diving or fishing; drinks, gear rental, and national park entrance fees are extra. Combination packages are available. DISC, MC, V. **Amenities:** Restaurant; bar; full-service dive and tackle shops; free Wi-Fi. *In room:* A/C, no phone.

Turneffe Island Lodge ★★ Located on a tiny private caye at the southern tip of the Turneffe Island Atoll, this is the swankiest outfit on the outer atolls. It even features a small outdoor oceanfront pool, a rare luxury out here. You can either stay in one of the well-appointed lodge rooms or opt for an upgrade to one of their eight private cabanas. One of my favorite features of these cabanas is the private outdoor shower. All rooms come with brightly varnished wood floors, wooden wainscoting and ceilings, and plenty of windows to take advantage of the ample sea breezes. The lodge has some excellent beaches and several long piers built out into the ocean with thatch-roofed open-air hammock huts built at the end. Both the fishing and the dive operations here are excellent.

Little Caye Bokel, Turneffe Island Atoll. © **713/236-7739** in the U.S. and Canada, or 220-4142 in Belize. Fax 713/236-7743. www.turneffelodge.com. 20 units. BZ$4,000–BZ$6,000 per person per week dive package; BZ$4,600–BZ$6,600 per person per week fishing package. Rates are based on double occupancy and include all meals, round-trip boat transportation from Belize City, and guided daily diving or fishing; drinks and gear rental are extra. Combination packages are available. Rates lower in the off season. DISC, MC, V. **Amenities:** Restaurant; bar; full-service dive and tackle shops; small outdoor pool. *In room:* A/C, no phone.

SOUTHERN BELIZE

Southern Belize has only two small cities, **Dangriga** and **Punta Gorda,** and one popular beach village, **Placencia.** This was once the least developed region of Belize, but that's changed dramatically. Placencia is one of the hottest and fastest-growing destinations in Belize. And the tiny Garífuna settlement of **Hopkins Village** is also up-and-coming. Both Placencia and Hopkins Village offer some of the longest and finest sand beaches to be found in the country.

Southern Belize is made up of the Stann Creek and Toledo districts. It is home to the **Cockscomb Basin Wildlife Sanctuary,** a major breeding ground and reserve for the New World's largest cat, the jaguar, as well as several other lesser-known and virtually unexplored forest reserves. It is here you'll find Belize's highest mountain, **Victoria Peak,** which stands at 1,122m (3,681 ft.).

Offshore, you'll find some of Belize's most beautiful cayes and its most remote atoll, **Glover's Reef Atoll ★★**. The cayes and barrier reef down here are as spectacular as those found farther north, yet far less developed and crowded. You can literally have an island to yourself down here. Much of the offshore and underwater wonders are protected in reserves, such as the **Southwater Caye Marine Reserve, Glover's Marine Reserve, Sapodilla Cayes Marine Reserve,** and **Laughing Bird Caye National Park ★★**.

As historically the least developed and colonized region in Belize, the southern zone still maintains ongoing and healthy communities of traditional Mayan and Garífuna peoples. This is one of the few places on the planet where you can comfortably spend a few days in a traditional Mayan or Garífuna village and see how nice it can feel to step away from the 21st century for a bit.

DANGRIGA

116km (72 miles) S of Belize City; 103km (64 miles) SE of Belmopan; 77km (48 miles) N of Placencia

Dangriga, which means "sweet water" in the Garífuna language, was originally called Stann Creek, and you may still hear it referred to as such. The name Stann Creek comes from the Creole version of "Standing Creek," a description of the river's slow-moving waters. As the capital of the Stann Creek District, which is one of the main citrus-growing regions of Belize, Dangriga is an important and vibrant agricultural and fishing community. However, despite its size and almost urban feel, it lacks the seaminess that characterizes Belize City. The town fronts right on the Caribbean and has several waterfront parks, which are surrounded by simple yet attractive residential neighborhoods.

Still, Dangriga is of little interest to travelers. There are no good beaches and few good hotels, and the town can feel stiflingly hot and desolate on most days. Most travelers head farther south to Hopkins Village, Placencia, or Punta Gorda, or out to one of the nearby offshore cayes. Dangriga is the main maritime transportation hub for trips out to Tobacco Caye, South Water Caye, and Glover's Reef Atoll. (See "What to See & Do," below, for more details.)

Dangriga is the largest city in southern Belize and the seat of the country's Garífuna culture. The Garífunas are a proud and independent people, who have managed to maintain their unique language and culture, which dates to the 16th-century intermingling of free Africans and Carib Indians. The only time Dangriga becomes a major tourist attraction is around Garífuna Settlement Day.

Essentials

GETTING THERE & DEPARTING

BY PLANE   There are numerous flights into and out of little Dangriga Airport (DGA) from Belize City. **Maya Island Air** (© **223-1140** in Belize City, or 522-2659 in Dangriga; www.mayaairways.com) has nine flights daily between the Philip S. W. Goldson International Airport and Dangriga. The first flight leaves at 8:10am and the last flight is at 5pm. Flight time is 15 minutes; the fare is BZ$126 each way.

THE garífuna

Throughout the 18th century, escaped and shipwrecked slaves intermarried and blended in with the native Carib Indian populations on several islands in the Lesser Antilles, but predominantly on St. Vincent. The West Africans were a mixed lot, including members of the Fon, Yoruba, Ewe, and Nago tribes. Over the years, the West African and indigenous elements blended into a new people, known first as Black Caribs and today as Garífuna or Garinagu. The Garífuna have their own language, traditions, history, and rituals, all of which blend elements of the group's two primary cultural sources. African-style drumming with complex rhythmic patterns and call-and-response singing accompany ritual possession ceremonies spoken in a language whose entomological roots are predominantly Arawak.

The Black Caribs were fierce warriors and frequently fought the larger colonial powers to maintain their freedom and independence. In 1797, despite the celebrated leadership of Joseph Chatoyer, the Garífuna were soundly defeated by the British forces, who subsequently shipped several thousand of the survivors off to exile on the island of Roatan, in then British Honduras. The Garífuna began migrating and eventually settled along the entire coast of what is present-day Honduras, Nicaragua, Guatemala, and Belize.

The Garífuna reached Belize by 1802. Since the British colonial presence was concentrated in the north, the Garífuna chose to settle in the southern parts of Belize, particularly the Stann Creek and Toledo districts. During the early part of their settlement in Belize, the Garífuna were kept at arm's length by the colonial Baymen, who were still slave owners and feared the influence of this independent free black community. Nevertheless, on November 19, 1832, the Garífuna were officially recognized as members of Belizean society and permitted to participate in the public meetings. For nearly 2 centuries now, the Garífuna have lived quiet lives of subsistence farming, fishing, and light trading with their neighbors, while steadfastly maintaining their language, heritage, and traditions.

The principal Garífuna settlements in Belize include Punta Gorda, Seine Bight, Hopkins Village, Barranco, and Dangriga, the community's unofficial capital. Each year on November 19 (and for several days around the 19th), these communities, and in particular Dangriga, come alive in a riotous celebration of the Garífuna settlement and acceptance in Belize.

ACCOMMODATIONS ■
Bonefish Hotel **6**
Island Expeditions **7**
Pal's Guest House **9**
Pelican Pouch Beach
Resort **1**
Seaclift Bed & Breakfast **8**

DINING ◆
Coconut's Grill & Bar **1**
The King Burger
Restaurant **3**
Riverside Café **4**
Roots Kitchen **11**

ATTRACTIONS ●
Austin Rodriguez' Drum
Shop **2**
Benjamin Nicholas's
Studio **5**
Dangriga Cultural
Center **2**
Drums of My Father
Monument **10**
Gulisi Garifuna Museum **12**

Maya Island Air also has daily flights between Belize City's Municipal Airport and Dangriga at 8 and 10am, noon, and 2:30 and 4:30pm. The fare is BZ$72 each way. These flights take 30 minutes because they stop en route to pick up passengers at the international airport. Maya Island Air flights from Dangriga to Belize City leave between 7:35am and 4:50pm. Most of these flights stop first at the international airport and continue on to Municipal Airport.

Tropic Air (*©* **800/422-3435** in the U.S. or Canada, 226-2012 in Belize City, or 522-2129 in Dangriga; www.tropicair.com) has nine flights daily between Goldson International Airport and Dangriga, with the first flight leaving at 8:15am and the last flight at 5pm. The fare is BZ$126 each way. They also have five daily flights between

Municipal Airport and Dangriga, leaving at 8:30 and 10:30am, and at 12:30, 2:30, and 4:50pm. The fare is BZ$72 each way. Tropic Air flights depart Dangriga for both of Belize City's airports daily between 7:45am and 4:45pm. Flight time runs between 15 and 30 minutes, depending on whether there is an intermediate stop.

Flights to and from Punta Gorda and Placencia on Maya Island Air and Tropic Air stop in Dangriga to pick up and drop off passengers. You can also easily book a flight from Dangriga to either of these onward southern destinations. On both airlines, flights are sometimes added during the high season or suspended during the low season, so check in advance.

BY CAR From Belize City, head west on Cemetery Road, which becomes the Western Highway. Take this all the way to Belmopan, where you will connect with the Hummingbird Highway heading south. Ten kilometers (6 miles) before Dangriga, the Hummingbird Highway connects with the Southern Highway. Follow the signs into Dangriga; you'll be entering from the south end of town.

Alternatively, you can take the unpaved New Belize or Manatee Road, which turns off the Western Highway just past the Belize Zoo, at around Mile Marker 30. The Manatee Road passes by the entrance road to the small Creole village of Gales Point and rejoins the Hummingbird Highway about 14km (8½ miles) outside of Dangriga. This route is shorter as the crow flies, but in worse shape physically, so the going is slower. Either route should take around 2 to 2½ hours from Belize City.

BY BUS James Bus Line (✆ 702-2049) and **National Transport** (✆ 227-2255) have regular service throughout the day between Belize City and Dangriga, roughly every half-hour between 6:30am and 5:30pm from either the main bus terminal on West Collet Canal Street (National Transport) or the nearby Shell gas station on Cemetery Road (James). The fare is BZ$16. The ride takes about 3 hours.

Tip: Most of the buses take the Hummingbird Highway. A few take the coastal Manatee Road. Unless you are heading to Gales Point, I'd try to take the much more comfortable ride on the Hummingbird Highway.

BY BOAT There are no regularly scheduled boats from Belize City to Dangriga, but aside from flying, water is the most direct means of covering the 58km (36 miles) between the two cities. If you want to come by boat, head to the Marine Terminal or ask around the docks in Belize City. Expect to pay from BZ$300 to BZ$500 for a boat that can carry four to eight passengers.

GETTING AROUND

There are no official car-rental agencies, but if you really search, you might be able to find an enterprising local willing to rent you a vehicle. If this is absolutely necessary, your best bet is to have your hotel try to arrange this for you.

Welcome

As you enter Dangriga, you'll come to a traffic circle. Be sure to take a moment to check out the **Drums of My Father** monument here, a larger-than-life bronze casting of three ceremonial *dügü* drums and the maraca-like shaker, or *sísira*. This simple sculpture lets you know right away that you are entering the heartland of Garífuna society and culture.

IF YOU COME TO A fork IN THE ROAD, TAKE BOTH

Given the unique sights offered by the two possible routes down to Dangriga, you might want to consider taking one route on your way south and the other on your way back. The **Hummingbird Highway** passes through some of Belize's most picturesque countryside. The road weaves through jungle mountains and crosses clear streams and small rivers. Admire the forest-covered karst hillsides to the west as you wind your way through mostly uninhabited country. The **Manatee Road** is a red-dirt affair, passing through the forests, lowland swamps, and mangroves that border Belize's large southern lagoon. Still, this route is not for the faint of heart. In the rainy season it can get quite muddy and slick, while in the dry season the dirt can form a hard, jarring washboard and dust can be a problem. In some places you'll have to cross single-lane, rail-less wooden plank bridges that give some drivers vertigo, even though they're not very high.

For a taxi in Dangriga, call **Cacho's Taxi Service** (© 603-4723) or **Star Line Taxi Service** (© 621-9956).

Boats to Tobacco Caye leave from the Gumagurugu River or North Stann Creek in front of the Riverside Café, just below the bridge. The going rate is around BZ$30 to BZ$50 per person one-way. Most of the boats hold between 8 and 10 people, and they leave whenever they fill up. If you already have a group together, you can hire one privately and set a definite return-trip pickup time. Alternatively, you can catch a ride with the folks from **Pelican Pouch Beach Resort** (© 522-2044), who run to Tobacco Caye daily and charge BZ$130 per person each way.

ORIENTATION

The main street through Dangriga is called St. Vincent Street south of the main bridge over North Stann Creek, and Commerce Street north of it. Most of the town's businesses and attractions lie within a few blocks of this bridge in either direction. The airstrip is on the north end of town, near the Pelican Pouch Beach Resort.

FAST FACTS For the **police,** dial © 911 or 522-2022; for the **fire department,** call © 522-2091. The **Dangriga Hospital** (© 522-2078) is located on Courthouse Road, 4 blocks north and 2 blocks east of the main bridge. The **post office** (© 522-2035) is in the southern section of town next to the Bonefish Hotel.

Both of the principal banks in town are on St. Vincent Street: **Belize Bank,** 24 St. Vincent St. (© 522-2903), and **Scotiabank,** 10 St. Vincent St. (© 522-2031). If you need some film or developing, try either **Dangriga Photo Plus,** 64 Commerce St. (© 522-2394), or **Gem's Photo,** 32 Oak St. (© 522-3859).

Finally, if your hotel can't or won't do it for you, take your dirty clothes to **Val's Laundry,** 1 Sharp St. (© 502-3324). They charge around BZ$15 per load, and also offer high-speed Internet connections for a very reasonable rate.

What to See & Do

The main activity in Dangriga is a slow walk up and down the main north–south thoroughfare. If you tire of watching the endless procession of people and listening to the colorful mix of English, Creole, and Garífuna, head a block or two over toward the sea and cop a seat in one of the town's oceanfront parks. If you're looking for a more active adventure, you'll have to head out of Dangriga, but your options are plentiful.

The only true attraction in the area is the quaint little **Gulisi Garífuna Museum** ★ (© 669-0639). Although small, this is worth a visit. You'll find interpretive displays of Garífuna history, culture, and daily life, spread around several rooms here. Three separate documentaries are shown continually on televisions in the different rooms. There's a gift shop, as well as paintings by prominent Garífuna artists such as Benjamin Nicholas and Pen Cayetano. The museum is located 1.6km (1 mile) west of town, on the road out to the Hummingbird Highway. It's open Monday through Friday from 10am to 5pm and Saturday from 8am to noon. Admission is BZ$10.

If you're staying in Dangriga for any period of time, you may also want to visit any number of the relatively nearby attractions, including Guanacaste National Park, Blue Hole National Park, Caves Branch, Hopkins Village, and Cockscomb Basin Wildlife Sanctuary. For more information on the first three attractions, see chapter 10. For details about the rest, see below.

If your hotel can't arrange things for you, contact **C & G Tours and Charters** (© **522-3641;** www.cgtourscharters.com) or the **Stann Creek Tour Guide Association** (© **522-3641**) to set up any number of tours and activities around Dangriga and environs.

FISHING The fishing is excellent out of Dangriga. Most folks head to the flats in search of bonefish, permit, and tarpon. Closer to shore and near the river mouths you can find snook, and beyond the barrier reef lie marlin, sailfish, tuna, wahoo, and dorado. Ask at your hotel, around the docks, or at the **Pelican Pouch Beach Resort** (© **522-2044**). Expect to pay between BZ$800 and BZ$2,400 per day for a full day for several anglers aboard a modern sport-fishing boat. Alternatively, you can line up a lower-tech outing around the docks for around BZ$100 to BZ$400 for a half-day.

KAYAKING You can rent a kayak for paddling around the waters just offshore from the folks at **Island Expeditions** ★★ (© **800/667-1630** in the U.S. and Canada, or 522-3328 in Belize; www.belizekayaking.com). The rates are BZ$70 per day for a single kayak, and BZ$110 for a tandem.

SNORKELING & SCUBA DIVING Dangriga is the jumping-off point for some wonderful small cayes situated right on the edge of the barrier reef, as well as Glover's Reef Atoll. Most of the hotels in town can arrange for a day trip of snorkeling or scuba diving at Tobacco Caye, South Water Caye, or one of the cayes composing Glover's Reef Atoll. Expect to pay from BZ$160 to BZ$240 per person for a full-day snorkel trip out to the reef, including lunch and transportation. Add an extra BZ$120 to BZ$180 if you plan to scuba dive.

ATTRACTIONS ON THE HUMMINGBIRD HIGHWAY

Located just off the highway in the tiny settlement of Pomona Village is one of the most important and renowned factories in all of Belize, **Marie Sharp's.** The factory is small and simple, and depending on the time of year and demand, they may be making any number of their various hot sauces, jams, and chutneys. It's best to call in advance to arrange a tour (© **522-2370;** www.mariesharps-bz.com). If you're lucky, you'll get to meet Marie herself. The tour is free, but you'll want to bring some money to stock up on the sauces.

Tucked a few miles off the highway is **Five Blues Lake National Park ★.** The main feature of this park is a large cenote, whose various hues of blue originally gave the park its name. However, in July 2006, the cenote suddenly and rather inexplicably drained almost completely. By early 2008, the lake had recovered about 75% of its original level, and much of its former beauty. All around the park are forested lands and distinct karst hill formations, with a series of trails leading through them. The park is run by the folks from the local community of Saint Margaret's Village. The park and small village are located on Lagoon Road, just off the Hummingbird Highway around Mile Marker 32. There are about 4.8km (3 miles) of well-marked trails in the park. You can also take a refreshing dip in the lake, or rent a canoe for a leisurely paddle. Admission is BZ$10. Camping is allowed inside the park for BZ$8 per person. Some simple accommodations and restaurants are also available in Saint Margaret's Village.

GALES POINT & THE MANATEES

Gales Point is a small Creole fishing village about 40km (25 miles) north of Dangriga. It is a peaceful little village where you can get in tune with one of Belize's traditional cultures and its slower pace of life. The village stretches along a narrow peninsula that juts into the large brackish **Southern Lagoon,** which is also called Manatee Lagoon because the manatees that inhabit the water of the lagoon bring most people to Gales Point in the first place. Ask at the Manatee Lodge (see below) or around the village, and for BZ$60 to BZ$100 you can hire a small boat to take you out to where the manatees usually feed. The boats generally will hold up to eight people, so the more people you can line up, the less it will cost each of you. You can also ask around in the village about renting a canoe to paddle yourself out to where the manatees feed. I prefer this option, although be sure to get a lightweight modern canoe, as the traditional carved tree-trunk dugout canoes are a bear to paddle. Canoe rentals should run you around BZ$12 to BZ$20 for a half-day. Although once encouraged, swimming with the manatees is no longer allowed. The contact is potentially dangerous for manatees and humans alike, and it's best to just enjoy a pleasant sighting of these gentle water

 On the Road

As you drive the Hummingbird Highway, there are two interesting phenomena to be aware of. Locals swear a local mountain formation looks like a sleeping giant. There are several good views of the "sleeping giant," which is best seen just slightly left of dead ahead as you drive south from Belize City, especially around the Sibun River bridge. Even more mystical and illusive—I've never been able to make it work—is the "antigravity" spot. Stop your car on the gentle hill around Mile Marker 26 and put it in neutral. Locals claim it is ancient earth energy that makes vehicles roll seemingly uphill. I'm guessing it's an optical illusion.

mammals. In addition to the manatees, this is a fabulous bird-watching spot, and if you're lucky you might even see a jabiru stork here.

Other possible trips from Gales Point include visits to the beach or some nearby caves and nighttime turtle walks. The beach on either side of the Manatee River is a major nesting site for the hawksbill turtle. The turtles generally lay their eggs from June to August. These tours generally cost between BZ$60 and BZ$120 for the boat and guide.

Gales Point is one of several villages in Belize to have a community-based ecotourism homestay program (© 209-8031). Rooms in local villagers' homes are very basic and often do not have running water or flush toilets. The rates run around BZ$10 to BZ$16 per person. You can also camp in Gales Point at **Metho's Camping** (© 603-6051) for BZ$10 per person, or stay in their rustic guesthouse for BZ$50.

By far the best lodgings in Gales Point are found at the **Manatee Lodge** ★ (© 877/462-6283 in the U.S. and Canada, or 220-8040 in Belize; www.manatee lodge.com), a tidy little hotel with a fabulous location at the very end of the peninsula. If you decide to eat at any place other than the Manatee Lodge, check out **Gentile's Cool Spot** (no phone).

Gales Point is also home to renowned drum maker **Emmeth Young,** who runs the **Maroon Creole Drum School** (© 603-6051; www.maroondrumschool. com). If you're interested in a lesson, which costs about BZ$10 an hour, or in making your own drum, which will take around 4 days, ask around town for Emmeth.

To drive here from Dangriga, head out of town to the Hummingbird Highway toward Belize City. At the village of Melinda, you'll see the turnoff for Manatee Road and Gales Point.

To get here by bus from Dangriga, you will have to take a Belize City–bound bus using the Manatee Road. These buses do not always enter the village of Gales Point. Ask in advance; if the bus doesn't enter the village, you will have to hike or hitchhike the final 2.4km (1½ miles) out onto the peninsula. From Belize City, you can take one of the Dangriga-bound buses using the Manatee Road. Again, ask in advance whether the bus enters Gales Point village.

Shopping

As the cultural seat of the Garífuna culture, Dangriga is a great place to pick up, or just admire, local arts and crafts.

If you'd like to have a look at some Garífuna paintings, visit the studio of **Benjamin Nicholas** (© 522-2785). Using a Caribbean naïve style, Nicholas paints scenes of traditional Garífuna village life. You'll find his studio on the seafront, just north of Mahogany Street.

If the beat really gets to you, you can buy a handmade wooden drum from **Austin Rodríguez** (© 502-3752), at the **Dangriga Cultural Center** on the oceanfront on the north bank of North Stann Creek. Drums vary in size and cost between BZ$80 and BZ$300. Austin's daughter runs a separate drum shop at 32 Tubroose St. (© 624-6756).

Finally, **Mercy Sabal,** 22 Magoon St. (no phone), has become quite famous for her handcrafted Garífuna dolls. These small dolls are predominantly of female figures in traditional dress, and cost between BZ$30 and BZ$100.

garífuna SETTLEMENT DAY

Each year on November 19, Garífuna Settlement Day is celebrated in Dangriga, with Garífunas coming from around Belize and as far away as Guatemala, Honduras, Nicaragua, and New York. The celebration is a riot of street music and colorful parades. Eating, drinking, and dancing go on well into the night. The Garífuna have their own traditional music, which is based on wooden drums and choral singing. The rhythms and songs have strong African roots, and have given birth to a hybrid pop music called Punta Rock, which is probably the country's most popular music and dance form. If you plan to partake in the festivities, be sure to book far in advance, as every hotel room in Dangriga and the nearby towns and villages sells out early. For more information, contact the **National Garífuna Council of Belize** (© **669-0639;** www.ngcbelize.org).

Tip: Garífuna Settlement Day isn't the only opportunity to experience the full color and vitality of traditional Garífuna culture. At the end of the Christmas and New Year season, on the weekend closest to January 6, the local Garífuna community takes to the streets to enjoy the Wanaragua or John Kunnu dancers. Wearing masks, elaborate costumes, colorful headdresses topped with macaw feathers, and vibrating arrangements of shells and vedas, Wanaragua or John Kunnu dance troupes parade through the streets of Dangriga, accompanied by the beat of traditional drummers.

Where to Stay

MODERATE

Bonefish Hotel   Located a block from the water and across the street from a small park, the Bonefish is an acceptable midrange option right in the heart of Dangriga. The carpeted guest rooms are generally quite large. The second-floor bar and restaurant has a view of the ocean, and serves good local fare and fresh seafood at reasonable rates. This hotel is owned and run by the same folks who have the Blue Marlin Lodge (p. 163) on South Water Caye, and is primarily used as an overnight stop for guests heading out to their island resort.

15 Mahogany St. (P.O. Box 21), Dangriga. © **800/798-1558** in the U.S., or 522-2243. Fax 522-2296. www.bluemarlinlodge.com. 7 units. BZ$100–BZ$180 double. Rates include taxes and service charge. MC, V. Free parking. **Amenities:** Restaurant; bar. *In room:* A/C, TV, minifridge, no phone, free Wi-Fi.

Pelican Pouch Beach Resort ★   This is a comfortable and spacious Caribbean resort, and it's by far the most upscale option right in Dangriga. The rooms range in price, location, and amenities. The best rooms have second-floor ocean views with wonderful balconies, and I think they're worth the splurge. There's no real beach here, but there are plenty of palm trees, lounge chairs, and hammocks spread around, as well as a long dock out into the sea, which is your best bet for swimming. There's a small gift shop featuring Garífuna crafts, Belizean books, and popular wildlife photography. The restaurant serves excellent Belizean and Garífuna meals at reasonable rates. A variety of fishing, diving, and inland tours is available, and Pelican Beach also runs a sister cottage resort, the Pelican's Pouch (p. 164), out on South Water Caye.

North end (P.O. Box 2), Dangriga. ✆ **522-2044.** Fax 522-2570. www.pelicanbeachbelize.com. 17 units. BZ$180–BZ$230 double. AE, MC, V. Free parking. **Amenities:** Restaurant; bar. *In room:* A/C (in 12 units), TV.

Seaclift Bed & Breakfast Set on a quiet residential block fronting a small park and then the ocean, this little converted home offers simple rooms in a homey environment. The furnishings and decor are rather provincial, but the rooms are spacious and cozy. There's a common living room and large ground-floor covered veranda area overlooking the sea.

1738 Southern Foreshore (P.O. Box 177), Dangriga. ✆ **522-3540.** Fax 522-3538. www.seaclift.com. 3 units. BZ$150. Rates include full breakfast. No credit cards. Free parking. *In room:* No phone.

Sea Front Inn As the name implies, this hotel is located right in front of the Caribbean Sea, a few blocks north of the docks. The hotel itself is a large, four-story building with a row of high-pitched gables and expansive seaview windows, balconies, and verandas. The furnishings and decor are quite simple, and rather dated, but most of the rooms are very spacious. Although it's a steep climb up to the fourth floor, the two end units, Seahorse and Conch, are good options with use of a common oceanview balcony. However, the second-floor Manatee room, with its private balcony, is my favorite room in the house. The hallways and common areas feature interesting hand-painted murals of local characters, flora, and fauna. The third-floor restaurant offers fabulous views of the ocean. A wide range of tour and activity options is available. Fully furnished apartments are also available by the week or month.

Front St. (P.O. Box 20), Punta Gorda. ✆ **722-2300.** Fax 722-2682. www.seafrontinn.com. 11 units. BZ$130–BZ$160 double. MC, V. **Amenities:** Restaurant; bar; free Wi-Fi. *In room:* A/C, TV, no phone.

INEXPENSIVE

Pal's Guest House ✦ This budget hotel is down at the south end of town, just off the water, near the mouth of Havana Creek. It's clean and quiet, although the years and constant sea breeze have taken their toll. The rooms with shared bathroom are particularly small and basic. If you have a bit more money to spend, you should opt for one of the second-floor beachfront rooms in a separate building, which have air-conditioning and small private balconies overlooking the sea. The owner, Augustine Flores, is friendly, knowledgeable, and an active member of the local Garífuna community.

868A Magoon St., Dangriga. ✆ **522-2365** or ✆/fax 522-2095. www.palsbelize.com. 19 units (16 with private bathroom). BZ$50 double with shared bathroom; BZ$80–BZ$105 double. MC, V. *In room:* TV, no phone.

Where to Dine

When you're in Dangriga, be sure to sample some of the local Garífuna cooking. One staple you'll find at many restaurants is a bread made from cassava, also known as yuca. The best place in town to look for traditional Garífuna cooking is the down-home **Roots Kitchen** (no phone) on the north side of Havana Creek, at the corner of Ecumenical Drive and Yemery Road. Be sure to try the *hudut,* a dish featuring fresh fish cooked in coconut milk, accompanied by pieces of plantain and cassava.

Up and down the main street through town—St. Vincent Street and Commerce Street—you'll find numerous very basic restaurants. In addition to the restaurant listed below, **The King Burger Restaurant,** 135 Commerce St. (✆ **522-2476**), which is not affiliated with the Burger King fast-food chain, is a local favorite serving simple Belizean meals heavy on the grease. There are also several very basic Chinese restaurants along the main street.

MODERATE

Coconut's Grill & Bar ★ BELIZEAN   Located at the Pelican Pouch Beach
Resort, this is easily the best restaurant in Dangriga. The dinner menu features spicy
curry, served with fish, shrimp, or chicken, as well as thick pork chops in a fruit
glaze. You can also get a real porterhouse steak and several pasta dishes. For lunch
there are burgers, sandwiches, wraps, quesadillas, fajitas, and nachos. Or you can
opt for a salad or more traditional Belizean rice and beans accompanied by fish or
chicken. The best seating is on the open-air patio facing the ocean, although there's
also an indoor dining room for those looking for air-conditioning.

At the Pelican Pouch Beach Resort, north end of Dangriga. © **522-2044.** Reservations not necessary.
Main courses BZ$18–BZ$48. MC, V. Daily 6:30am–10pm.

Taste of India ★ INDIAN   With an extensive menu, fresh ingredients, and a
talented chef-owner, this is my favorite restaurant in Hopkins. While the appetizer
offerings are limited mostly to *samosas, pakoras, and papadum,* the main menu runs
the gamut from curries and *paneers* to *vindaloos* and tandoor specialties. Portions are
good-size, and the spiciness can be adjusted to your taste. I especially like the
shrimp curry and *chana saag,* a spinach and chickpea combination. But the chicken
tikka is also excellent. With a cement floor, exposed beams and electrical work, and
rustic unmatched furnishings, the decor and ambience are rustic, to say the least.
The best tables are actually outside, facing the beach.

Hopkins Village. © **660-0971** or 604-0799. Reservations recommended. Main courses BZ$15–BZ$24.
No credit cards. Daily 5–10pm.

INEXPENSIVE

Riverside Café BELIZEAN   This simple cafe and bar is funky and perennially
pretty run-down. Still, it's popular with the local boatmen and one of the best places
to get travel information in Dangriga. It opens early and serves food throughout the
day. You can get a full meal of fried chicken, beans, and rice for BZ$8. Breakfasts are
hearty and inexpensive. This is the place to ask about rides out to one of the nearby
cayes, to set up a tour around the region, and to pick up some brochures from the
wall-mounted racks. You'll find the cafe just east of St. Vincent Street on the south
side of North Stann Creek.

S. Riverside Dr., Dangriga. © **523-3922.** Reservations not accepted. Main courses BZ$8–BZ$20. MC, V.
Daily 6:30am–9pm.

Dangriga After Dark

There's not much happening in Dangriga after dark. Your best bets would be to see
what's happening at the **Pelican Pouch Beach Resort** (see "Where to Stay,"
above) or the nearby **Malibu Beach Bar** (© **522-3703**).

Beyond Dangriga: Offshore Cayes & Glover's Reef Atoll ★★

The Tobacco Caye range of mangrove cayes lies just 16km (10 miles) east of Dangriga. A little farther south sits South Water Caye. Beyond the barrier reef and farther out to sea is Glover's Reef Atoll.

   Tobacco Caye ★★ itself is just 2 hectares (5 acres) large, with about five different lodging options set more or less side by side. You can walk from one end of the
caye to the other in about 3 minutes, and that's at a leisurely pace.

South Water Caye ★★★ is a little bit larger than Tobacco, but you can still walk from one end to the other in about 5 minutes. Nevertheless, the vibe here is slightly more spacious and luxurious than that on Tobacco Caye, although there's not anything approaching real luxury here, either.

Located just a stone's throw from the south end of South Water Caye, the **Smithsonian Institute of Marine Research** occupies all of the tiny Carrie Bow Caye. Your lodge can make arrangements to visit the caye, meet with resident scientists, and use their beach, which is one of the sandiest in the area.

The largest caye in the area, **Man-O-War Caye** ★★, is a bird sanctuary and major nesting site for the magnificent frigate, or man-o-war. A tour to the caye is an impressive sight, with hundreds of these large seabirds roosting on and circling above the tiny caye. As part of their mating ritual, the males inflate a huge red sack on their throats to attract a mate. In addition to the frigates, the island is home to a large community of brown boobies.

Coco Plum Caye is another isolated and tiny caye in this area, with one small resort that features a handful of individual wooden bungalows spread around the small, sandy island. If you want to stay here, contact **Coco Plum Island Resort** ★ (© **512/786-7309** in the U.S., or 522-2200 in Belize; www.cocoplumcay.com).

A visit to snorkel, dive, or stay out on these cayes usually involves passing through, or staying within, the **South Water Caye Marine Reserve,** which includes Tobacco Caye, Carrie Bow Caye, Cocoplum Caye, and Man-O-War Caye. Admission to the reserve costs BZ$10 per person per day. This fee will be collected by your hotel, boat taxi driver, or tour operator.

To the east of these cayes, and beyond the barrier reef, lies **Glover Reef Atoll** ★★★, a stunning natural coral formation featuring an oval-shaped central lagoon nearly 35km (22 miles) long. Named after the British pirate John Glover, the steep-walled reefs here offer some of the best wall diving anywhere in the Caribbean. The entire atoll is also a marine reserve, and in 1996 it was declared a World Heritage Site by the United Nations. Inside the usually calm lagoon, patch reefs are a wonderland for snorkelers.

Finally, fishing for bonefish, permit, and tarpon is excellent throughout this area. There are no established independent operators. All the local hotels can usually arrange to set up a fishing trip, however.

GETTING THERE

Boats to the outlying cayes leave from the south shore of the Gumagurugu River or North Stann Creek in front of the Riverside Café, just down from the bridge. The going rate is around BZ$30 to BZ$50 per person one-way. Most of the boats hold between 8 and 10 people, and they leave whenever they fill up. If you already have a group together, you can hire one privately and set a definite return-trip pickup time. To rent a whole boat, the going rate is from BZ$400 to BZ$600 round-trip for up to 10 people to Tobacco Caye. The ride takes around 30 to 40 minutes to Tobacco Caye, depending on how fast a boat you book. Add on about 20 to 40 minutes and between BZ$100 to BZ$200 for either South Water Caye or Glover's Reef Atoll. Alternatively, you can catch a ride with the folks from **Pelican Pouch Beach Resort** (© **522-2044**), who run out to South Water Caye daily and charge BZ$130 per person each way.

Paddle to Your Own Drummer

The folks at **Island Expeditions** ★★ (℡ **800/667-1630** in the U.S. and Canada, or 522-3328 in Belize; www.belizekayaking.com) offer sea kayak rental and logistical support for those looking to explore the barrier reef and its many small cayes by kayak. This option is generally for serious paddlers, but can be tailored to suit your needs and abilities. The basic rate is BZ$70 per day and BZ$420 per week for a single kayak, and BZ$110 per day and BZ$700 weekly for a double kayak. Camping gear rental, food supplies, boat transfers to the outer cayes, and other types of logistical assistance can all be added on. And you can combine some independent paddle and camping time with one of their organized tours to Glover's Reef Atoll (see below).

Note: You really should have a reservation before heading out to one of the lodges on these cayes, as there are very limited options and they fill up fast during high season. Try to arrange your transportation when booking a room.

WHERE TO STAY & DINE ON THE OUTER CAYES

All of the options listed below are self-contained lodges and resorts, meaning you will be taking all of your meals at your hotel; all offer fishing, diving, and multiday adventure packages.

In addition to the lodges listed below, **Blue Marlin Lodge** (℡ **800/798-1558** in the U.S., or 522-2243 in Belize; www.bluemarlinlodge.com) is a semiupscale outfit on South Water Caye specializing in dive and fishing packages.

For the more adventurous traveler, **Island Expeditions** ★★ (℡ **800/667-1630** in the U.S. and Canada, or 522-3328 in Belize; www.islandexpeditions.com) and **Slickrock Adventures** ★★ (℡ **800/390-5715** toll free in the U.S. and Canada, or 435/259-4225 in the U.S.; www.slickrock.com) run various multiday kayak and dive tours to small camps and lodges on private, isolated cayes of Glover's Reef Atoll.

Glover's Atoll Resort ★   Located on the private North East Caye, lodging options here range from camping to dorm rooms to simple, rustic cabins with private bathrooms and kitchen facilities. My favorites are the wooden cabins built on stilts over the ocean. The resort also offers large, semipermanent tents, or you can pitch your own. And while they do serve meals, some of the guests actually pack in and cook their own food at the resort's communal kitchen. In addition to what you pack in, fresh fish, lobster, and conch can be purchased on the island, as can drinking water and fresh bread. Most visitors here come as part of the resort's weeklong package, which includes transportation. A meal package will run you around BZ$84 per day.

Glover's Reef Atoll (P.O. Box 563, Belize City). ℡ **520-5016.** Fax 223-5424. www.glovers.com.bz. 11 units. BZ$342 per week camping; BZ$458 per week in dorm room; BZ$574–BZ$688 per person per week in private cabin. Rates include round-trip transportation from Sittee River Village or Dangriga and all taxes. MC, V (add 5% surcharge). **Amenities:** Restaurant; watersports equipment rental. *In room:* No phone.

Isla Marisol Resort ★★   This place offers the plushest accommodations and best dive operation out on Glover's Reef Atoll. A series of raised stilt bungalows are set on the sand under shade trees facing the water. Each comes with a fan and swamp cooler, as well as a small balcony for lazing around on between dives or activities. But the choice digs here are the large reef houses, located on the back side of this tiny island. These are large two-bedroom two-bathroom wooden houses, also on raised stilts, with expansive wraparound balconies and kitchenettes. After dinner, guests tend to congregate at the large bar built on a pier out over the water.

Southwest Caye, Glover's Reef Atoll (P.O. Box 1410, Vashon, WA 98070, USA). © **888/623-5403** in the U.S. and Canada. www.islamarisolresort.com. 14 units. BZ$3,590–BZ$3,990 per person per week, double occupancy. Rates include round-trip transportation from Dangriga, all meals, several daily dive outings, and taxes. MC, V. **Amenities:** Restaurant; bar; full-service dive shop; small spa; watersports equipment rental; free Wi-Fi. *In room:* No phone.

Pelican's Pouch ★★ Run by the folks at the Pelican Pouch Beach Resort in Dangriga, this isolated island getaway is one of the best-run little resorts on these little cayes. The best rooms here are the individual cottages. Set on raised stilts by the water's edge, these wooden cottages vary in size somewhat, but all are very cozy and charming. The Egret and Heron's Hideaway are my favorites of the private cabins. The latter has a delightful private balcony set amid and surrounded by mangroves. The rooms are housed on the second floor of a converted colonial-era convent. Each of these rooms comes with one double bed, two single beds, and a half-bathroom. A couple of communal showers are located on the ground level. The relatively small price difference makes it very worthwhile to book one of the cabins.

South Water Caye (P.O. Box 2, Dangriga). © **522-2044.** Fax 522-2570. www.southwatercaye.com. 13 units (5 with shared shower). BZ$460–BZ$520 double room; BZ$530–BZ$590 double cottage. Rates include 3 meals daily and taxes. AE, MC, V. **Amenities:** Restaurant. *In room:* No phone.

Reef's End Lodge Occupying the southern tip of Tobacco Caye, this rustic lodge offers several distinct rooming options. Most of the rooms here are located in a two-story converted house. Each comes with two twin beds and one full bed. The best of these are on the second floor, especially the corner units. The rooms are Spartan and are geared toward students, groups, and budget travelers. The private cabins are a better bet and not significantly more expensive; however, these also feel rather bare and rustic, although they do have air-conditioning. The best room is the honeymoon suite, which has more contemporary decor, tile floors, and loads of space. The nicest feature here is the restaurant, which is set on stilts, with a deck and some docks out over the water. These folks run the only dive operation on the island.

Tobacco Caye (P.O. Box 299, Dangriga). © **522-2419.** Fax 522-2828. www.reefsendlodge.com. 11 units. BZ$130 double room; BZ$150 double cabin; BZ$390 honeymoon suite. MC, V. **Amenities:** Restaurant; dive operation. *In room:* No phone.

Thatch Caye ★★ 📑 This new boutique resort was built with love, care, and real concern for sustainable development. Accommodations are in spacious individual cabins and casitas and one large family villa. The cabanas are smaller, built over the water, and feature thatch roofs and wonderful oceanfront balconies. The large casitas' best feature is their huge, covered rooftop patios, with a couple of hammocks strung up under a high thatch shade structure on top. The family villa is three connected structures and is great for families or groups of friends. Solar and wind power are used to power the joint, although a backup generator kicks in when necessary, or if guests demand air-conditioning.

Thatch Caye (P.O. Box 133, Dangriga). © **800/435-3145** in the U.S. and Canada, or 603-2414 in Belize. www.thatchcayebelize.com. 10 units. BZ$450–BZ$565 per person per day. Rates include 3 meals daily, and round-trip transportation from Dangriga Airport. MC, V. **Amenities:** Restaurant; bar; complimentary kayak use. *In room:* No phone.

Tobacco Caye Paradise ★ 🔆   This place is at the northern end of Tobacco Caye. The simple wooden cabins are set right at the edge of the ocean, with small private verandas that, in most cases, jut out over the water. These are very basic, with just cold-water showers, minimal furnishings, and a simple floor fan. Still, their location and general vibe are just perfect. There are also five other rooms in a building slightly inland. These are certainly acceptable, but nowhere near as nice as the cabins.

Tobacco Caye (P.O. Box 79, Dangriga). © **520-2742.** bluefield@btl.net. 6 units (4 with private bathroom). BZ$76–BZ$88 double with shared bathroom; BZ$108–BZ$120 double with private bathroom. Rates include 3 meals daily and taxes. MC, V. **Amenities:** Restaurant. *In room:* No phone.

En Route South: Where the Wildcats Roam

Weighing up to 91kg (200 lb.) and measuring more than 1.8m (6 ft.) from nose to tip of tail, jaguars are king of the new-world jungle. Nocturnal predators, jaguars hunt peccaries (wild piglike animals), deer, and other small mammals. The **Cockscomb Basin Wildlife Sanctuary ★★**, established in 1990 as the world's first jaguar reserve, covers nearly 388 sq. km (150 sq. miles) of rugged forested mountains and has the greatest density of jaguars in the world. It is part of the even larger Cockscomb Basin Forest Reserve, which was created in 1984.

The forests within the preserve are home to other wildcats as well, including pumas, ocelots, and margays, all of which are very elusive, so don't get your hopes of seeing them too high. Few people do, but a good guide may be able to find you some tracks. Other mammals that you might spot if you're lucky include otters, coati-mundi, tayra, kinkajous, deer, peccaries, anteaters, and armadillos.

The largest land mammal native to Central America, Baird's tapir, is also resident. Locally known as a "mountain cow," the tapir is the national animal of Belize. A tapir can weigh up to 272kg (600 lb.) and is related to the horse, although its protruding upper lip is more like an elephant's trunk.

Much more easily spotted in the dense vegetation surrounding the preserve's trails are nearly 300 species of birds, including the scarlet macaw, the keel-billed toucan, the king vulture, and the great curassow.

Trails inside the park range from gentle and short to quite arduous and long. Many offer wonderful views of the Cockscomb Mountains and lush forested valleys. There are quite a few waterfalls and swimming holes. During the dry season, you can even climb Victoria Peak, which, at 1,122m (3,681 ft.), is the country's highest mountain. This trip takes several days and requires a permit and local guide. For more information, contact the **Belize Audubon Society** (© **223-5004;** www.belizeaudubon.org). Admission to the park is BZ$10.

Caution should be exercised when visiting the preserve. In addition to jaguars, which can be dangerous, there are poisonous snakes, including the deadly fer-de-lance. Always wear shoes, preferably boots, when hiking the trails here.

The Belize Audubon Society co-manages this park, and even offers a few private cabins and some dormitory sleeping options inside the sanctuary. Rates run between BZ$20 and BZ$30 per person for dormitory-style accommodations, or BZ$120 for one of the cabins, which can sleep up to six persons. Alternatively, you can stay down near the information center near the highway at the **Tutzil Nah Cottages** (© **520-3044;** www.mayacenter.com).

Cockscomb Basin Wildlife Sanctuary is located 9.7km (6 miles) inland from the Southern Highway, some 32km (20 miles) south of Dangriga. The turnoff and entrance to the sanctuary are at the roadside village of Maya Center. This is where you'll find the sanctuary's information center, and where you'll pay your BZ$10 entrance fee. This is also a good place to check out some of the art and craft works at the neighboring shop run by the Maya Center Women's Group and to hook up with a local guide. I've heard great reports about local guide Greg Sho, who can often be found at Greg's Bar, his other business, located right on the side of the highway before the entrance to Maya Center. Any bus heading south to Placencia and Punta Gorda will drop you off at the entrance. From here you'll have to hike the 9.7km (6 miles) or hire a local taxi for around BZ$30 round-trip.

A Nearby Back-Bush Nature Lodge

Nestled at the foot of the Maya Mountains is an interesting little ecolodge, **Mama Noots Jaguar Lodge ★** (©/fax **670-8019;** www.mamanoots.com). With a collection of comfortable rooms, as well as camping and dormitory facilities, the folks at Mama Noots are located in the heart of the **Mayflower Bocawina National Park.** The park protects the small and barely excavated Mayflower Mayan ruins, as well as vast expanses of tropical forests. There's excellent hiking and bird-watching on miles of trails leaving from the resort, including a couple of wonderful waterfalls. All of the electricity is provided by an inventive mix of solar, hydro, and wind generators. A pure mountain spring provides the water. Multiday packages with transportation provided from Dangriga are the preferred means of visiting this little lodge. Contact them for details.

HOPKINS VILLAGE & SITTEE RIVER VILLAGE ★★★

140km (87 miles) S of Belize City; 127km (79 miles) SE of Belmopan; 53km (33 miles) N of Placencia

Hopkins Village is a midsize Garífuna community located on a pretty stretch of white sand beach, 24km (15 miles) south of Dangriga. It is a picturesque village with colorfully painted raised clapboard houses. It is also my preferred destination for getting a true taste of and some direct contact with this unique culture. This is a great place to wander around talking with children, fishermen, and elderly folks hanging out in front of their homes. If you stick around long enough, you may be able to learn a bit about traditional Garífuna lifestyles. Fishing is still the main pursuit of many of the villagers, although tourism is rapidly becoming the main source of employment and income.

Hopkins Village is set on a long, narrow, curving swath of beach, which in addition to Placencia is one of the few true beaches in the country. This white-sand beach is usually quite calm and good for swimming. In recent years, several beach and dive resorts have opened just south of the village, while in the village itself you'll find a hodgepodge of budget lodgings and simple restaurants. Sittee River Village is a few miles south of Hopkins and a mile or so inland, on the banks of the gently flowing Sittee River. This is a tiny little town, but it does have a hotel or two, as well as a good Internet cafe. Fishermen like the quiet riverside setting and access to both fresh- and saltwater angling.

Essentials

GETTING THERE & DEPARTING

BY PLANE The closest airport to Hopkins Village is in Dangriga. See "Dangriga," earlier in this chapter, for flight details. A taxi from Dangriga to Hopkins or Sittee River village should cost BZ$80 to BZ$100 for up to four people. For a taxi in Dangriga, call **Cacho's Taxi Service** (© **603-4723**) or **Star Line Taxi Service** (© **621-9956**).

BY CAR From Belize City, head west on Cemetery Road, which becomes the Western Highway. Take this all the way to Belmopan, where you will connect with the Hummingbird Highway heading south. Ten kilometers (6¼ miles) before Dangriga, the Hummingbird Highway connects with the Southern Highway. Take the Southern Highway toward Placencia and Punta Gorda. About 13km (8 miles) south of this junction, you'll see signs for the entrance to Hopkins Village. From here, it's 6.4km (4 miles) on a graded gravel road. A few miles farther south on the Southern Highway is the entrance to Sittee River Village; however, you can also enter at Hopkins and head south from there along the coast, as it's really just a small loop.

BY BUS Only a couple of the buses each day from Dangriga south make the loop through Hopkins Village and Sittee River. The ride takes between 25 and 35 minutes to Hopkins Village, with Sittee River Village just a few miles farther on the route. The fare is BZ$6 each way. Be sure to ask before you get on the bus if it will drop you off in the village. If not, you will be let off on the Southern Highway, at the entrance to Hopkins, but still some 6.4km (4 miles) away. If this is the case, you will hopefully have arranged pickup with your hotel in advance. Otherwise, you'll have to hitchhike into town. The buses heading back to Dangriga or to points south can be caught in either Hopkins or Sittee River, or better yet, from the Southern Highway. See "Essentials" on p. 152 for details on bus travel between Dangriga and Belize City, and between Dangriga and points south.

GETTING AROUND

Hopkins Village itself is very small, and you can easily walk the entire town. If you're staying south of town or in Sittee River Village, or want to explore, a bicycle is the preferred means of transportation. Most of the hotels will either lend you a bike or rent you one for a few dollars per day.

There are no official taxi services, but if you ask around town or at your hotel, you should be able to hire someone for small trips or excursions. There are also a number of freelance guides in the area who have vehicles and may be willing to provide transportation.

ORIENTATION

The access road from the Southern Highway heads right into the heart of Hopkins Village. If you continued straight, you'd be in the Caribbean Sea. The village itself spreads out for a few hundred yards in either direction. Heading south you'll come to the larger resorts listed below. At the turnoff and entrance to Almond Beach Belize & Jaguar Reef Lodge, the road heads back toward the highway, passing through Sittee River Village. *Note:* It's only a 15- to 20-minute walk from the village to any of the resorts to the south, with the exception of Kanantik, which is farther away.

FAST FACTS   Both Hopkins and Sittee River villages are tiny, and there are no banks or major stores or services. There are, however, Internet cafes in both places, and you can get gas at the little marina in Hopkins.

What to See & Do

This is a very isolated and underdeveloped area. All of the resorts listed below specialize in scuba diving, snorkeling, and, to a lesser extent, fishing. All of them also have a long list of tour options to attractions such as Cockscomb Basin Wildlife Sanctuary, Sittee River canoeing, Blue Hole National Park, the Mayflower Mayan ruins, and cultural tours of Dangriga. If you're staying at one of the lodgings in either of the villages, you'll find numerous local operators offering snorkeling, scuba, and fishing outings, as well as all the above-mentioned tours. One of the better local operators is **Bullfrog Adventures ★** (① **669-0046,** or 665-3043; issymcm@yahoo.com), which employs all local Garífuna guides and boat captains.

If you really want to get a taste of the local culture, sign up for some classes at the **Lebeha Drumming Center ★** (① **608-3143;** www.lebeha.com), which is located on the northern edge of the village. The folks here teach traditional Garífuna drumming and dancing.

SNORKELING & DIVING

Snorkeling and scuba diving are stellar all along the Belize Barrier Reef. The Tobacco Caye range lies just offshore from Hopkins Village, a simple 30- to 40-minute boat ride away, with numerous snorkeling and dive sites. Moreover, the location makes these dive resorts excellent jumping-off points for trips to Glover's Reef Atoll and even Turneffe and Lighthouse Reef atolls. All of the resorts listed below offer multiday dive packages, which are the way to go for serious divers, though we particularly recommend Hamanasi. They also all offer certification classes and advanced open-water courses. If you're not staying at one of the dedicated dive resorts, your best bet is probably to arrange to dive with them, as their equipment and dive masters are generally top-notch, and the price savings of going with a less active operator just aren't worth it. If you're feeling adventurous, for snorkeling excursions, ask around the village and head out with a local boat captain or tour guide. The lower cost and cultural richness might just make up for a slow boat, leaky mask, and loose-fitting fins.

FISHING

There's excellent bonefishing in the inland and barrier reef flats in this area. Anglers can also go for tarpon, permit, and snook, or head offshore for bigger game. Experienced guides can help you track any of the above fish, which you can stalk using traditional casting and trolling techniques, or try catching with a salt-water fly rod and reel. Most of the major lodges and resorts here offer fishing packages and excursions. Well-equipped sport-fishing outings cost between BZ$1,000 and BZ$3,000 per day, depending on the size of the boat, number of anglers, and distance traveled. Alternatively, you can ask around Hopkins Village to line up a more low-tech outing for around BZ$100 to BZ$400 for a half-day.

Shopping

Hopkins Village is a good place to find locally made Garífuna handicrafts. **Rudy Coleman** is a local drum maker, and his drums are excellent. Ask for Rudy around town, or at the **Lebeha Drumming Center.**

Where to Stay

There's a host of lodging options in this area, ranging from simple budget and backpacker hotels in Hopkins Village to upscale dive resorts on the beaches to the south.

VERY EXPENSIVE

In addition to the places listed below, **Belizean Dreams** (© 523-7272; www.belizeandreams.com) is a condo-resort project on the south end of Hopkins Village, featuring a series of large and luxurious fully equipped condo units spread around a grassy lawn and pool area fronting the beach.

Almond Beach Belize & Jaguar Reef Lodge ★★ ☺ This large and lively resort offers the most facilities, lodging options, and tour options in the region. There's a wide range of rooms and suites available here. Some come with kitchenettes, televisions with DVD players, and other amenities that make them good for families and longer stays. The second-floor colonial suites have fabulous ocean-facing balconies. Perhaps the best rooms here are the Almond Beach villas and suites. These all are spacious, are tastefully decorated, and come with a host of amenities. In addition to the on-site activities and services, there's a small, full-service spa. If you just want to hang around the lodge, hammocks and Adirondack chairs are set under the shade of palm trees along the lodge's white-sand beach. There's complimentary use of sea kayaks, Hobie Cats, bicycles, and snorkel gear. There are two freshwater pools as well.

Hopkins Village (P.O. Box 297, Dangriga). © **866/824-1516** in the U.S. and Canada, or 520-7040 in Belize. Fax 520-7091. www.almondjaguar.com. 34 units. BZ$400–BZ$650 double; BZ$540–BZ$3,500 suite. Rates lower in the off season, slightly higher during peak weeks. MC, V. **Amenities:** Restaurant; bar; complimentary bike and kayak use; full-service dive operation; 2 outdoor pools; small spa; watersports equipment rental; free Wi-Fi. *In room:* A/C, hair dryer, stocked minifridge, no phone.

Hamanasi ★★ This well-run dive and adventure resort offers very comfortable rooms in an intimate setting. Diving is the main focus here, and the hotel has an excellent operation. But they have excellent inland tour options as well. The beachfront rooms are housed in a couple of ocean-facing two-story buildings, and I definitely recommend the second-floor rooms for the improved view and privacy of your balcony. There is also a series of "treehouses," spacious individual bungalows set on stilts 3.7m (12 ft.) high in the midst of the hotel's tiny coastal forest, just a few yards behind the main operation. While these don't have an ocean view, they do offer a lush sense of tropical isolation. There are wonderful and artistic tile and woodworking touches in all rooms, and most have quite high ceilings. Hamanasi means "almond" in the local Garífuna language, and you'll see plenty of the namesake *hamans* trees growing around the grounds.

Hopkins Village (P.O. Box 265, Dangriga). © **877/552-3483** in the U.S., or 520-7073 in Belize. Fax 520-7090. www.hamanasi.com. 23 units. BZ$690–BZ$1,030 double. Rates include continental breakfast, taxes, and service charge. Rates lower in the off season. MC, V. **Amenities:** Restaurant; bar; bike rental; full-service dive operation; outdoor pool; room service; all rooms smoke-free; free Wi-Fi. *In room:* A/C, no phone.

Kanantik ★ This small, all-inclusive resort is one of the more luxurious options around. Except for the purchase of a bottle of wine or some top-shelf liquor, little falls outside the all-inclusive price you pay, and this includes all your tours, scuba diving, and dive equipment or fishing gear. The rooms are all individual, hexagonal, thatch-roof cabins, set either right in front of the ocean or slightly back in flowering gardens. Each is spacious and features sapodilla wood floors and driftwood beds. The rooms feature a walk-in closet, and the showers are built of smooth river stones. Meals are served in a large, high-pitched dining room. The owner is Italian, and there's usually an excellent chef on hand serving a mix of local, Italian, and other international cuisine. It is possible to bypass the all-inclusive plan, which may make sense if you don't plan on doing serious diving or fishing.

Southern Hwy., Mile 18.2, south of Hopkins Village (P.O. Box 150, Dangriga). ☎ **877/759-8834** in the U.S., or 520-8048. Fax 520-8089. www.kanantik.com. 25 units. BZ$804 per person double occupancy. Rates include all meals, local drinks and soft drinks, taxes, tips, and activities. MC, V. Kanantik is located 29km (18 miles) south of Dangriga, accessed by a graded gravel road that connects with the Southern Hwy. They also have their own private airstrip, and charter flights directly to the resort can be arranged. **Amenities:** Restaurant; bar; complimentary bike and kayak use; full-service dive operation; midsize outdoor pool w/unheated Jacuzzi; watersports equipment. *In room:* A/C, no phone.

INEXPENSIVE

In addition to the place listed below, there are literally a score (or more) of simple guesthouses and small inns. Some are run by a local renting a spare room, while others are converted houses. Most inns charge around BZ$20 to BZ$30 per person. If you have the time, it might be worth your while to check out a couple before deciding where to stay.

Hopkins Inn 🖋   Located right on the beach, near the center of the village, this little hotel offers clean and comfortable individual cabins at a very fair price. The cabins are all tiled, and feature wood-paneled, pitched roofs. Each has a small front porch. The two units closest to the water have the best views of the sea, but the others are larger and still have good views. A simple continental breakfast is served on your private veranda, and a host of restaurants are within easy walking distance. The owners are very friendly and knowledgeable, and can help arrange any number of tours and adventures.

Hopkins Village (P.O. Box 121, Dangriga). ☎ **523-7283.** www.hopkinsinn.com. 4 units. BZ$100–BZ$200 double. Rates include continental breakfast. No credit cards. **Amenities:** Bike rental. *In room:* Minifridge, no phone.

Jungle Jeanie's by the Sea ★   The individual wooden cabins here are set on raised stilts on the sand. Most have direct views of the ocean, although one large unit with a loft is set back slightly among some trees. All have a private balcony in front, as well as a small refrigerator, microwave oven, and coffeemaker. However, aside from these amenities, the furnishings and decor are quite Spartan. Still, if you're looking for a comfortable cabin on the sand, just steps from the sea, this might be all you need. Some of the cabins are painted in bright primary colors, while others are simply varnished over natural wood. You'll find the hotel right on the beach, at the southern end of town.

Hopkins Village. ☎ **523-7047.** www.junglebythesea.com. 8 units. BZ$110–BZ$240 double. Rates lower in the off season. MC, V. **Amenities:** Restaurant; kayak, windsurfer, and Hobie Cat rentals. *In room:* Minifridge, no phone.

Tipple Tree Beya 🖋   This is an excellent option for budget travelers. With just two rooms in a two-story oceanfront home and one private cabin, this place has a laid-back vibe. Located at the far southern end of the village, literally where the pavement ends, Tipple Tree Beya combines the isolated feel of the more expensive beach resorts here with the convenience and proximity of the in-town options. Right in front of the hotel is an excellent stretch of beachfront. There are hammocks spread on a broad shared veranda, and rustic chairs set out on the sand. The cabin has a small kitchen area, equipped with microwave oven, refrigerator, coffeemaker, and some basic utensils.

Hopkins Village (P.O. Box 206, Dangriga). ℂ/fax **520-7006.** www.tippletree.net. 5 units (4 with private bathroom). BZ$60 double with shared bathroom; BZ$80–BZ$150 double with private bathroom. MC, V. **Amenities:** Bike and kayak rental. *In room:* No phone.

Where to Dine

Even if you're staying at one of the large resorts around here, it's worth heading into town to try a meal at one of the simple, locally run restaurants on the main street. Of these, both **Iris's Restaurant** (ℂ **523-7019**) and **Innies Restaurant** (ℂ **523-7026**) are perennial favorites. Both serve excellent fresh fish and seafood, and will usually have some *hudut* and other Garífuna dishes on hand. Both are very basic, inexpensive, and somewhat funky in decor and vibe. A similar option, which I prefer for its seafront location, is **Laruna Hati** (ℂ **661-5753**), which is located toward the north end of the village.

For excellent grilled fish and seafood, international fare, and tasty bar food, head to the **Barracuda Bar & Grill ★** (ℂ **523-7259**) at the **Beaches and Dreams** hotel, at the south end of the village. And for a relaxed, European-style cafe, try **Thongs ★** (ℂ 662-0110), right on the main road, near the center of the village.

Chef Rob's ★★★ 🍽 FUSION   The profile of an old red car sliced in half serves as a billboard for this little place. After working in the trenches for years as executive chef for some of the better resorts and hotels around Belize, Dutch-born chef Rob has opened his own place. Grab one of the heavy wooden tables on the open-air wood deck under dim, atmospheric lighting with flowing cotton drapes billowing in the breeze. The eclectic menu changes daily but always contains a mix of fresh seafood and quality meats prepared with fresh local ingredients and creative sauces. You might find lamb served with a balsamic vinegar and coconut milk reduction, or the daily catch expertly grilled and topped with a homemade papaya ketchup. Everything is wonderfully prepared by Rob in his small show kitchen. The four-course dinner is a great deal at BZ$55. During high season, lunches are sometimes served.

Hopkins Village. ℂ **670-0445.** Reservations recommended. Main courses BZ$30–BZ$40. MC, V. Tues-Sun 5-9pm.

Driftwood Beach Bar & Pizza Shack ★ PIZZA/SEAFOOD   This place is what a laid-back beach bar and restaurant should be—good food, great prices, cold beer, and a friendly atmosphere. And everything's just steps from the sea. There's a small interior dining room, but you'll want to grab one of the outdoor tables under a thatch-roof shade structure. If you're feeling athletic, there's a beach volleyball court. If you're not feeling athletic, there's a hammock or two on hand. In addition to thin-crust pizzas, there's usually some seafood and a nightly pasta special.

On the beach, north end of Hopkins Village. ℂ **667-4872.** Reservations accepted. Main courses BZ$6–BZ$25. MC, V. Thurs-Tues noon-10pm.

King Kassava 🔲 BELIZEAN/GARIFUNA   Located right at the crossroads entering Hopkins Village, this place is the town's hub on many levels. Locals stop in for a cool one or chat around the outdoor tables under steeply pitched thatch roofs. The food here is fresh and tasty, particularly the seafood. Try the Garífuna-style shrimp, in a slightly spicy red sauce over white rice. Alternatively, you can get some barbecued lobster in season, or whatever fish has just come in off the boats. There's a pool table in a separate room in back, and after about 9pm, the music can get turned up pretty loud.

Hopkins Village. ℂ **608-6188.** Reservations not accepted. Main courses BZ$12–BZ$30. No credit cards. Daily 7am–2pm and 5–11pm.

Hopkins Village After Dark

Aside from the various resort hotels, there is very little in the way of nightlife here— unless you can line up a night dive. Most of the resorts, however, hire local bands and dance troupes to entertain their guests. It's worth combining a dinner at one of these places with the nightly show. Aside from the bar at the **King Kassava** (see above), the liveliest bar on Hopkins Village's main road is **The Watering Hole** (ℂ **614-8686**), which also has a pool table. On full-moon nights, the folks at **Driftwood Beach Bar & Pizza Shack** (see above) host blow-out rave parties, with a live DJ and big bonfire.

PLACENCIA ★★

241km (150 miles) S of Belize City; 161km (100 miles) SE of Belmopan; 89km (55 miles) NE of Punta Gorda

Placencia is still Belize's foremost and fastest-growing beach destination. Located at the southern tip of a long, narrow peninsula that is separated from the mainland by a similarly narrow lagoon, Placencia boasts nearly 26km (16 miles) of white sand fronting a calm turquoise sea and backed by palm trees. Placencia attracts everyone from hippy backpackers and avid naturalists to hard-core divers and upscale snow-birds. The whole peninsula is in the midst of an ongoing major boom, and development currently stretches from the peninsula's southern tip all the way up to Maya Beach on the northern end of the peninsula.

Placencia itself is a tiny Creole village of colorful clapboard houses mostly built on stilts. Once you settle into the slow pace and relaxed atmosphere, it's hard to move on. Placencia is *the* definition of laid-back. For years, the village's principal thoroughfare was a thin concrete sidewalk. Once listed in the *Guinness Book of World Records* as the narrowest street in the world, the sidewalk still runs through the heart of the village parallel to the sea. However, the ongoing construction and development boom have made the main road through town (called "the Back Road") actually the town's busiest thoroughfare most days.

Essentials

GETTING THERE

BY PLANE   There are numerous flights into and out of Placencia's little airport (PLJ). **Maya Island Air** (ℂ **223-1140** in Belize City, or 523-3475 in Placencia; www.mayaairways.com) has 11 flights daily between the Goldson International Airport in Belize City and Placencia. The first flight leaves at 8:10am and the last flight is at 5pm. Flight time is 35 minutes, with a brief stop in Dangriga; the fare is BZ$189 each way. They also have seven daily flights between Belize City's Municipal Airport and Placencia at 8 and 10am, noon, and 2:30 and 4:30pm. The fare is BZ$159 each way.

Placencia

ACCOMMODATIONS ■
Blue Crab Resort **22**
Chabil Mar **17**
Deb & Dave's Last Resort **12**
The Inn at Robert's Grove **20**
Julia & Lawrence's
  Guesthouse **7**
Laru Beya Resort **19**
Lydia's Guesthouse **9**
Maya Beach Hotel Bistro **25**
The Placencia **26**
Ranguana Lodge **8**
Sea Spray Hotel **4**
Singing Sands Inn **23**
Tradewinds **1**
Turtle Inn **18**

DINING ◆
Daisy's **10**
De'Tatch Seafood Beach Bar
  & Grill **5**
Habanero Mexican Café & Bar **21**
Mango's **24**
Mare **18**
Maya Beach Hotel Bistro **25**
Omar's Diner **11**
Pickled Parrot **2**
Purple Space Monkey
  Village **15**
Rumfish y Vino **14**
The Secret Garden **13**
Trattoria Placencia **6**
Tutti Frutti Ice Cream Shop **14**
Wendy's **16**

To Southern Highway

Maya
Beach

False
Caye

CARIBBEAN

SEA

Seine Bight
Village

Placencia Lagoon

Airstrip

Placencia Lagoon

See inset
at right

PLACENCIA
VILLAGE

Placencia
Caye

Belize City
Belmopan
Placencia

✈ Airport
$ Bank/ATM
✝ Church
ⓘ Information
✉ Post office

0   1/2 mi
0   0.5 km

Placencia Village

CARIBBEAN
SEA

Placencia
Lagoon

The Sidewalk

Main
Dock

0   1/5 mi
0   0.2 km

These flights take 50 minutes because they stop en route to pick up and let off passengers at the international airport and in Dangriga. Maya Island Air flights from Placencia to Belize City depart throughout the day, with the first flight at 7:25am and the last flight at 4:50pm. Most of these flights stop first in Dangriga, and then at the international airport, before continuing on to Municipal Airport.

Tropic Air (© **800/422-3435** in the U.S. or Canada, 226-2012 in Belize City, or 523-3410 in Placencia; www.tropicair.com) has 10 flights daily between Goldson International Airport and Placencia, with the first flight leaving at 8:15am and the last flight at 5pm. The fare is BZ$189 each way. They also have five daily flights between Municipal Airport and Placencia, leaving at 8:30 and 10:30am, and at 12:30, 2:30, and 4:50pm. The fare is BZ$159 each way. Tropic Air flights depart Placencia for Belize City's airports daily beginning at 7:25am, with the last flight of the day at 4:25pm.

Flights to and from Punta Gorda on Maya Island Air and Tropic Air stop in Placencia to pick up and drop off passengers. On both airlines, flights are sometimes added during the high season or suspended during the low season, so check in advance. Flight time runs between 25 and 50 minutes, depending on whether there is an intermediate stop or two.

A large new airport located on the northern end of the peninsula is slated to open sometime in early 2011. Big enough to accept commercial jets and charter traffic, it's still unclear whether that traffic will arrive, and whether the local commuter airlines will shift their operations to this facility.

BY CAR   From Belize City, head west on Cemetery Road, which becomes the Western Highway. Take this all the way to Belmopan, where you will connect with the Hummingbird Highway heading south. Ten kilometers (6¼ miles) before Dangriga, the Hummingbird Highway connects with the Southern Highway. Take the Southern Highway toward Placencia and Punta Gorda. After 37km (23 miles) on the Southern Highway, turn left onto the road to Riversdale and Placencia. From this turnoff, it's another 32km (20 miles) to Placencia. The drive from Belize City should take around 2½ to 3 hours.

BY BUS   There is frequent bus service between all major cities in Belize and Dangriga. See p. 154 for more information. Direct buses leave Dangriga for Placencia daily at 10:30 and 11:30am, and at 4 and 5:15pm. The fare is BZ$10. Buses leave Placencia for Dangriga, with onward connection to Belmopan, San Ignacio, and Belize City, daily at 11am and 2 and 4:40pm. If you're heading south, you'll want to get off the bus as soon as it hits the Southern Highway and flag down the next southbound bus.

However, many independent and bus travelers also reach Placencia via Independence Village and Mango Creek, using the *Hokie Pokie* ferry (© **523-2376**). This 15-minute boat ride used to cut a lot of bumpy, dusty miles off the road trip; however, now that the road is paved, this is no longer necessary. Still, if you're heading south, this is the best way to go. The ferry fare is BZ$12. All north- and southbound bus traffic along the Southern Highway stops in Independence Village, near the ferry dock. Ferries between Placencia and Independence Village leave regularly throughout the day, with at least six trips in each direction. See p. 154 for information on buses making the run between Belize City and the southern reaches of Belize.

GETTING AROUND

Placencia Village itself is tiny, and you can walk the entire length of the sidewalk, which covers most of the village, in about 10 to 15 minutes. If you need a taxi, call **S & M Taxi** (℃ **602-4768**) or **Tuff Gong Taxi** (℃ **523-3323**). Fares within the village run BZ$6 for one person, and BZ$3 per person for two or more people. A trip from the airstrip to the village costs BZ$12 for one person, and BZ$6 per person for two or more people.

If you want to rent a car or golf cart while in Placencia, **Barefoot Rentals** (℃ **523-3438** or 629-9602; www.barefootrentals.net) is the best option, charging around BZ$120 per day for a golf cart, and between BZ$150 and BZ$180 per day for an SUV.

If you want to explore more, a scooter is a good way to get around. Several hotels and operators in the area rent scooters. Rates run around BZ$60 to BZ$80 for a half-day and BZ$100 to BZ$120 for a full day.

If you want a little more exercise, a bicycle is a decent option. The terrain is flat, although it can get hot on the main road, and there aren't really any trails or off-road options. Many hotels have bikes either free for guests or for rent. Several shops around town also rent out bicycles. A relatively modern bike in good shape should cost between BZ$20 and BZ$30 per day.

ORIENTATION

For most of the peninsula there is only one road. As the road reaches the end of the peninsula and the village of Placencia, it basically dead-ends at the Shell station and some boat docks. Just before this, a dirt spur turns right just beyond the soccer field and heads for a few hundred yards toward the lagoon. Once you've arrived, your main thoroughfare will hopefully be the beach and the sidewalk, which run parallel to each other starting near the docks and heading north.

Hotels and resorts are spread all along the length of the Placencia peninsula. To make it easier to understand where a hotel or resort is, the peninsula is broken up into three broad sections: Maya Beach, Seine Bight, and Placencia Village. Maya Beach is the northernmost section of the peninsula, and the hotels and resorts here are quite spread out, with few other services or businesses. More or less anchoring the center of the peninsula is the tiny Garífuna village of Seine Bight. Just to the north and south of Seine Bight village are several other isolated resorts. Down at the southern end of the peninsula is Placencia Village itself.

The very helpful **Placencia Information Center** (℃ **523-4045;** www.placencia. com) is located toward the end of the road in a tiny mini-mall just across from the soccer field.

FAST FACTS   For the local **police,** dial ℃ **911** or 503-3142; you can also reach the newly formed **tourist police** at ℃ **603-0374.** If you need any medical attention, the **Placencia Medical Center** (℃ **523-3326**) is located behind the school in the center of the village.

There's a **Scotiabank** (℃ **523-3277**) on the main road near the center of the village, as well as an **Atlantic Bank** (℃ **523-3431**). Scotiabank has an ATM that accepts international cards. There's a **pharmacy** attached to Wallen's Market (℃ **523-3346**) in the center of the village. The **post office** is located above the Fishermen's Co-op, near the start of the sidewalk.

There are a couple of gas stations in Placencia. You'll find the Shell station where the road hits the end of the peninsula in the heart of the village. There's also a Texaco station at the Inn at Robert's Grove Marina.

If you need to use the Internet, there's a host of options. If you want Wi-Fi or some food or drink to go along with your surfing, I recommend the **De Tatch** (© 503-3385). The **Placencia Office Supply** (© 523-3205), which is on the main road and has high-speed connections, is another good option.

Fun On & Off the Beach

You just can't help slowing down and relaxing in Placencia. Sit back, sip a seaweed shake, and forget your cares. Nobody ever seems to get up early (except maybe the fishermen), and most people spend their days camped in the sand reading books and eating seafood. The beach, although narrow in places, is arguably the best in Belize. You can walk for miles and see hardly a soul. Still, if you need more activity and adventure, there's a host of options.

WATERSPORTS EXCURSIONS

SNORKELING & SCUBA DIVING   There's often decent snorkeling right off the beach, especially if you head north a mile or so. The water's clear and you'll see plenty of fish and bottom life in the sea grass and along the sand bottom.

One of the more popular snorkel excursions is to the nearby **Laughing Bird Caye** (© 523-3565; www.laughingbird.org). Located just a few miles offshore from Placencia, Laughing Bird Caye is a national park. It's a tiny little island measuring roughly 11×107m (35×350 ft.). There's good snorkeling and swimming offshore, and a beautiful little beach. Many tour operators take folks here and then serve a picnic lunch on the beach or head to nearby **Little Water Caye.**

However, if you're serious about diving or snorkeling, you'll want to get out to the **barrier reef** and its dozens of little offshore cayes. It's between 16 and 40km (10–25 miles) out to the reef here, making it a relatively quick and easy boat ride. Diving here is as spectacular as at other more popular dive destinations in Belize, and you'll often have far fewer fellow divers around.

 Gentle Giants

From late March to early July—especially just before, during, and after the full moons—the waters offshore from Placencia are a world-renowned place to spot and dive with mammoth **whale sharks** *(rhincodon typus),* the largest fish in the sea. Whale sharks can reach lengths of up to 12m (40 ft.) and weigh in at more than 20 tons. It's about a 30-minute boat ride to Gladden Spit, an offshore, deepwater site where tens of thousands of cubera snapper come to spawn right around the full moons. No dummies, the whale sharks come to feed on the nutrient-rich snapper spawn. And not only whale sharks. During these peak feeding periods, you are also likely to see dolphins, bull sharks, and sea turtles, as well as the massive schools of snapper. *Note:* Even during peak periods, whale shark sightings on these dives are far from guaranteed. If you sign up for one of these dives, you must be very prepared for the possibility that you'll see little more than some snapper and jack.

BYO

While most hotels and all of the dive shops in town have snorkeling and diving gear for rent, you might consider bringing your own. If nothing else, bring your own mask and snorkel. Fins are a lesser concern, as most operators should have fins to fit your feet. However, faces vary vastly, and a tight-fitting mask is essential to an enjoyable snorkel experience. If you plan on going out snorkeling or diving more than a few times, the investment will more than pay for itself.

Most of the larger resorts have their own dive operations, and these tend to be some of the better operations on the peninsula. There is also a handful of independent operators in the village servicing folks at the rest of the hotels. If you're not staying at a hotel with a dedicated dive operation, check in with the folks at **Avadon Divers** ★★ (© 888/509-5617 in the U.S. and Canada, or 503-3377 in Belize; www.avadondiversbelize.com) or **Seahorse Dive Shop** ★ (© 523-3166; www.belizescuba.com).

A snorkeling trip should cost between BZ$60 and BZ$160, depending on the distance traveled and whether lunch is included. Rates for scuba diving run between BZ$120 and BZ$300 for a two-tank dive, also depending on the length of the journey to the dive site and whether gear and lunch are included. Equipment rental should cost from BZ$15 to BZ$30 for a snorkeler, and BZ$30 to BZ$60 for a scuba diver.

FISHING Fishing around here is some of the best in Belize. There's excellent bonefishing in flats in this area. Anglers can also go for tarpon, permit, and snook, or head offshore for bigger game, including grouper, yellowfin tuna, king mackerel, wahoo, mahimahi, and the occasional sail or marlin. Most of the hotels and resorts on the peninsula offer fishing packages and excursions. Well-equipped sport-fishing outings run between BZ$1,200 and BZ$3,000 per day, depending on the size of the boat, number of anglers, and distance traveled. However, you can hire a smaller open-air skiff perfectly suited for fly-casting for bonefish, permit, or tarpon for between BZ$400 and BZ$1,000 per day. The folks at **Tarpon Caye Lodge** ★ (© 523-3323; www.tarponcayelodge.com), who have a small fishing lodge on the remote Tarpon Caye, have some of the more experienced fishing guides in town, specializing in fishing for permit and tarpon. You can also try **Trip 'N Travel** (© 523-3614), another long-standing local operation with well-regarded guides.

KAYAKING Several hotels and tour operators in town rent out sea kayaks. The waters just off the beach are usually calm and perfect for kayaking. However, the lagoon is probably a better choice, offering more interesting mangrove terrain and excellent bird-watching opportunities.

Rates for kayak rental run around BZ$10 to BZ$20 per hour, or BZ$60 to BZ$80 for a full day. A guided tour of the mangroves or a combined snorkeling and kayak tour offshore should cost between BZ$80 and BZ$150 per person.

If you're looking for a guided tour, the best kayak operator in Placencia is **Toadal Adventure** ★ (© 523-3207; www.toadaladventure.com). These folks offer several different multiday kayaking trips, both out on the ocean and on inland rivers. Custom trips can also be designed.

SAILING The crystal-clear waters, calm seas, and isolated islands surrounding Placencia make this an excellent place to go out for a sail. Your options range from crewed yachts and bareboat charters for multiday adventures to day cruises and sunset sails.

The Moorings ★ (☎ 888/952-8420 in the U.S. and Canada, or 523-3351 in Belize; www.moorings.com) is a large-scale charter company with its Belizean operations based out of Placencia. Options include monohulls, catamarans, and trimarans of varying sizes. Given the shallow draft, increased interior space, and reduced drag, a multihull is your best bet. All of the boats are well-equipped and seaworthy. Rates for a weeklong charter run between BZ$4,000 and BZ$18,000, depending on the size of the boat and whether you charter it bareboat or with a crew.

A day cruise, including lunch, drinks, and snorkeling gear, should cost between BZ$160 and BZ$300 per person. Most hotels and tour operators around town can hook you up with a day sail or sunset cruise, or you can simply head to the docks or check in with the folks at **Next Wave Sailing** (☎ **661-3744**).

GUIDED DAY TRIPS

While the ocean and outlying cayes are the focus of most activities and tours in Placencia, there are a host of other options. The most popular of these include tours to Cockscomb Basin Wildlife Sanctuary (see "Dangriga," earlier in this chapter), the Mayan ruins of Lubaantun and Nim Li Punit (see "Punta Gorda & the Toledo District," later in this chapter), and up the Monkey River. Day trips can run between BZ$100 and BZ$300 per person, depending on the distance traveled and the number of activities offered or sites visited. Almost every tour agency in town offers these trips, or ask at your hotel for a recommended guide or operator.

Monkey River ★ Perhaps the most popular "inland" trip offered out of Placencia is up the Monkey River, and most of it is actually on the water, anyway. Located about a half-hour boat ride down the coast and through the mangroves, the Monkey River area is rich in wildlife. If you're lucky, you might spot a manatee on your way down. Once traveling up the Monkey River, you should keep your eyes peeled for crocodiles, green iguana, wild deer, howler monkeys, and the occasional boa constrictor. In addition, you're likely to see scores of bird species. These tours can be done entirely in a motor launch or may allow you to kayak on the Monkey River portion; I recommend the latter. Most tours include lunch in the quaint little Creole fishing village of Monkey River itself, as well as a short hike through a forest trail. Monkey River trips cost between BZ$90 and BZ$120 per person.

SPAS & BODY WORK

If you're looking for a little pampering while in Placencia, there are several options. Most of the big resorts, such as Turtle Inn and The Inn at Robert's Grove, have their own spas, which you may be able to book even if you're not a guest there. Alternatively, there are a couple of day spas right in the village. The **Secret Garden Day Spa** (☎ **523-3420**) is located behind Wallen's Market near the center of the village, while **Siripohn's Thai Massage & Oriental Spa** (☎ **620-8718**) is located in the Placencia Village Square, next to the Tutti Frutti Ice Cream Parlor. An hour-long massage should cost you between BZ$140 and BZ$200.

If you want to have an acupuncture treatment or stretch out some, head to the **Acupuncture Center** (☎ **523-3172**), which is also near Wallen's Market. These

Sidewalk Fair

Most days, the Placencia sidewalk is a lazy affair. However, on the second weekend of February, it comes alive with the annual **Placencia Sidewalk Arts Festival.** Local artists show their wares, and a host of restaurants set up outdoor booths. There are also games, events, and raffles. For more information, contact the **Placencia Information Center** (✆ **523-4045; www.placencia.com).**

folks offer traditional acupuncture, various massage and herbal treatments, and regular yoga classes.

Shopping

Simple souvenir shops are abundant in Placencia. Located right on the main road near the Scotia Bank, the **Beach Bazaar ★** (✆ **523-4309**) is the best of the bunch. They've got a selection of traditional souvenirs, as well as some higher-end ceramic, wood, and metal artworks.

If you're looking for some finer art, stop in at **Art 'N Soul** (✆ **503-3088**), which is on the sidewalk about 91m (300 ft.) north of the pier and features paintings and prints by local artists. While farther north, in Seine Bight, you should definitely stop in at **Lola's Art Gallery ★** (✆ **523-3342**), which features the colorful acrylic paintings of owner Lola Delgado. These paintings come in a wide range of sizes and prices.

Tip: Be on the lookout for locally produced organic chocolate. Marketed under the brand name **Goss** (www.gosschocolate.com), these milk and dark-chocolate bars are sold at stores around town. If you don't pick up any here, they are also on sale at the international airport.

Where to Stay

There is a host of accommodations options in and around Placencia. In general, the town's budget hotels and guesthouses are located in the village proper, either just off the sidewalk or around the soccer field. As you head north to the broader and more isolated beaches, prices tend to rise.

VERY EXPENSIVE

Chabil Mar ★★ This upscale option features a collection of mostly two-bedroom, two-bathroom condo units in a series of two-story buildings with blue roofs spread around lushly planted grounds, toward the southern end of the Placencia peninsula. All units feature Mexican-clay tile floors and lively, tropical decor. Most have spacious private balconies or verandas, and all come with full kitchens featuring granite countertops. A long dock leads out to a large deck area covered with a thatch-roofed shade structure, and there are two midsize pools to choose from. Service is very attentive and accommodating.

Placencia Village, on the beach just north of the center of the village. ✆ **866/417-2377** in the U.S., or 523-3606 in Belize. Fax 523-3611. www.chabilmarvillas.com. 22 units. BZ$700–BZ$1,020 double. AE, MC, V. **Amenities:** Restaurant; bar; complimentary bike and kayak use; concierge; 2 outdoor pools; room service; all rooms smoke-free; free Wi-Fi. *In room:* A/C, TV, minifridge.

The Placencia ★   This large resort and condo project dwarfs everything else on the Peninsula. The multilevel pool, with a swim-up bar and separate children's section, is the largest in Belize. The rooms and apartments feature marble floors throughout, as well as high-def flatscreen TVs and contemporary decor. Most of the master bedrooms come with Jacuzzi tubs. A series of three-story buildings forms a rough horseshoe shape around and behind the aforementioned pool. Oceanfront rooms are at a premium. If you can't land one of these, try for a second- or third-floor unit with a sea-facing balcony. The resort sits on an excellent long stretch of white-sand beach, with the requisite wooden dock jutting out into the sea, featuring a bar, some chaise longues, hammocks, and a swimming ladder on the end of it.

Maya Beach. ✆ **520-4110.** Fax 520-4112. www.theplacencia.com. 92 units. BZ$410–BZ$500 double; BZ$540–BZ$630 2-bedroom villa. Rates higher during peak weeks. AE, MC, V. **Amenities:** 2 restaurants; 3 bars; babysitting; complimentary bikes and kayaks; concierge; full-service dive shop; large outdoor pool; room service; small spa; free Wi-Fi. *In room:* A/C, TV, hair dryer, minibar.

Turtle Inn ★★★ 📖   This is Francis Ford Coppola's fanciest resort in Central America. You get your choice of a one- or two-bedroom private villa here. All have plenty of space, including a large living room and a spacious bathroom that lets out onto a private interior rock garden, with its own open-air shower. Tons of beautiful woodwork and a heavy dose of Asian decor and furnishings dominate the rooms. All of the villas are set on the sand just steps from the beach, but not all have ocean views. The Coppola Pavilion is a two-bedroom unit set on the beach a little off the main resort, with its own pool and a kitchen, wine cellar, and steam bath/shower in each of the two bathrooms. There's a small spa and a full-service dive operation across the street on the lagoon side of the peninsula.

Placencia Village, on the beach north of the center of the village. ✆ **800/746-3743** in the U.S., or 824-4912 central reservation number in Belize, or 523-3244 at the hotel. Fax 523-3245. www.turtleinn.com. 25 units. BZ$700–BZ$960 1-bedroom double; BZ$1,080–BZ$1,350 2-bedroom double; BZ$3,700 Coppola Pavilion. Rates include continental breakfast. Rates lower in the off season; higher during peak weeks. AE, MC, V. **Amenities:** 3 restaurants; 2 bars; babysitting; complimentary bikes and kayaks; concierge; full-service dive shop; 2 outdoor pools; room service; watersports equipment rental; free Wi-Fi. *In room:* Hair dryer, minibar.

EXPENSIVE

The Inn at Robert's Grove ★★★ ☺   This boutique resort boasts two restaurants, three pools, an in-house spa, professional dive and fishing operations, and a tennis court. Rustic red-tile floors, Guatemalan textiles, and Mexican ceramic accents abound. All rooms come with a private balcony, hung with a hammock. Many of the suites come with fully equipped kitchenettes, and all have a large living room and a large balcony. There are six—count 'em—six Jacuzzis spread around the resort. The rooftop ones are particularly inviting for late-night stargazing and soaking. Guests enjoy unlimited free use of the hotel's sea kayaks, windsurfers, Hobie Cat sailboats, tennis court, and bicycles, as well as free airport transfers. The hotel also owns and manages two small private islands, Ranagua Caye and Robert's Caye. You can take a day trip to these tiny offshore cayes, or spend a night or two in a simple yet comfortable cabin.

Placencia, on the beach north of the airstrip. ✆ **800/565-9757** in the U.S., or 523-3565 in Belize. Fax 523-3567. www.robertsgrove.com. 52 units. BZ$378–BZ$418 double; BZ$520–BZ$920 suite. Rates lower in the off season; higher during peak weeks. AE, MC, V. **Amenities:** 2 restaurants; 3 bars; lounge; babysitting; concierge; full-service dive shop; exercise room; 3 outdoor pools; room service; small spa;

lit outdoor tennis court; complimentary watersports equipment and bike use; free Wi-Fi. *In room:* A/C, TV, hair dryer, minifridge.

Laru Beya Resort ★★ ☺

This resort offers roomy, bright, and well-designed rooms and condo units on a great patch of Placencia's pristine white beach. You have the choice of one-bedroom rooms, or one-, two-, and three-bedroom condo units. The better rooms are higher up, with great ocean views, and all but a few more budget options come with televisions. The penthouse suites come with their own rooftop Jacuzzis. All the furnishings and decor are top-notch. Kayaks, Hobie Cats, and bicycles are available free for guests, and there's even a small miniature golf course, which is a hit with the kids.

Placencia, on the beach north of the airstrip. ☎ **800/890-8010** the U.S. and Canada, or 523-3476 in Belize. Fax 523-3483. www.larubeya.com. 24 units. BZ$240–BZ$500 double; BZ$700 2-bedroom condo; BZ$800 3-bedroom. Rates lower in the off season; higher during peak weeks. AE, MC, V. **Amenities:** Restaurant; bar; complimentary bikes; outdoor pool; smoke-free rooms; complimentary windsurfers and Hobie Cats. *In room:* A/C, hair dryer, kitchenette, free Wi-Fi.

Singing Sands Inn ★

This place has the most lush gardens and grounds in the area. The six individual thatch-roofed wooden cabins are set in a row perpendicular to the beach, with cabin nos. 1 and 2 closest to the ocean. You'll still get something of an ocean view from cabin nos. 3, 4, and 5, while no. 6 is set amid the flowers and foliage. Each has a small porch with a couple of chairs. In addition to the cabins, there are a couple of larger, fully equipped apartments with kitchenettes. There's a midsize outdoor pool and a large open-air deck area facing the ocean, and there's a long dock built out into the sea with a shaded palapa at the end of it. The restaurant here is quite good, with oceanfront open-air seating either under the stars or protected by a thatch roof.

Maya Beach. ☎ **888/201-6425** in the U.S. and Canada, or ☎/fax 520-8022 in Belize. www.singingsands.com. 10 units. BZ$280–BZ$340 double. Rates lower in the off season. MC, V. **Amenities:** Restaurant; bike and kayak rental; outdoor pool; smoke-free rooms; free Wi-Fi. *In room:* No phone.

MODERATE

In addition to the places mentioned below, The Maya Beach Hotel (☎ **520-8040;** www.mayabeachhotel.com) offers five clean, cozy beachfront rooms and a cool pool, and is home to **Maya Beach Hotel Bistro** (see below), one of the best restaurants on the peninsula.

Blue Crab Resort

There's a relaxed and laid-back atmosphere at this small beachfront hotel north of Seine Bight village. The rooms are all simple and clean, and they're housed in several separate wooden buildings set on stilts a few feet above the sand. The air-conditioned rooms are located in a fourplex building. I'd try to get one that faces the beach. The two older individual cabanas are actually closer to the water, but are a bit smaller and lack air-conditioning. Of these, cabana no. 1 is your best bet, as it's closest to the sea and gets good cross-ventilation. The tiny restaurant here is locally famous for its cuisine, as the owner was born in Taiwan, and she serves an enticing mix of Asian, international, and local fare. The folks here make the excellent organic Goss chocolate you'll see around Belize.

Seine Bight, on the beach north of the village. ☎ **523-3544.** Fax 523-3543. www.bluecrabbeach.com. 6 units. BZ$180–BZ$200 double. Rates include airport transfers. Rates lower in the off season. MC, V. **Amenities:** Restaurant; free Wi-Fi. *In room:* No phone.

Ranguana Lodge ⚓ The five individual cabins at this small family-run hotel are all clean and cozy. In the two older cabins, nearly everything is made of hardwood—walls, floors, ceilings, even the louvered windows. These rooms feature a full kitchenette. The three oceanfront cabins are right in front of the sea and have air-conditioning; however, they are a little smaller and have a little less character. All of the cabins are just steps from the ocean, and all come with a private balcony or porch area. All are painted a blinding pure white, with a different primary or Day-Glo color used for trim.

Placencia Village, on the beach in the center of the village. ℂ **523-3112.** Fax 523-3451. www.ranguana belize.com. 5 units. BZ$160–BZ$176 double. Rates include taxes. AE, MC, V. *In room:* TV, minifridge, no phone.

INEXPENSIVE

If the places listed below are full, you can simply walk around the village and see what's available, or head to either **Julia & Lawrence's Guesthouse** (ℂ **503-3478;** www.juliasrooms.com) or **Deb and Dave's Last Resort** (ℂ **523-3207;** deband-dave@btl.net), both located just off the sidewalk toward the center of the village.

Lydia's Guesthouse ⚓ This is one of the longest-running and most popular budget options in Placencia, and it's fitting that this classic two-story converted home survived Hurricane Iris. The rooms are simple and clean, although a few can be a bit cramped. The shared bathrooms and showers are kept immaculate, and guests have free use of the kitchen that takes up the ground floor of the amiable Lydia Villanueva's private home next door. You'll find a convivial hostel-like atmosphere—travelers from around the world make up the guest list. There's even a good ocean view from the shared balcony on the second floor, a real steal in this price range. Lydia also rents various houses around the village for longer stays.

Placencia Village, toward the northern end of the sidewalk. ℂ **523-3117.** Fax 523-2335. www.lydias guesthouse.com. 8 units, all with shared bathroom. BZ$40–BZ$60 double. MC, V. *In room:* No phone.

Sea Spray Hotel Rooms and prices vary substantially in this perennial budget and backpacker favorite. The economy rooms are a bit cramped and dark. Most rooms are in a two-story building built perpendicular to the sea. The four deluxe rooms are in a separate two-story building fronting the sea, and these come with televisions and kitchenettes, as well as comfortable private oceanview balconies. There's also a separate, fully equipped beachfront cabana, although I think the deluxe rooms are a better and more comfortable choice. The attached De'Tatch Seafood Beach Bar & Grill serves hearty local fare at very reasonable prices, and also has an Internet cafe. As at Lydia's (above), there's a convivial hostel-like atmosphere here.

Placencia Village, on the beach toward the middle of the sidewalk. ℂ **523-3148.** Fax 523-3364. www. seasprayhotel.com. 21 units. BZ$50–BZ$130 double. AE, DISC, MC, V. **Amenities:** Restaurant. *In room:* Minifridge, no phone.

Tradewinds You can't beat the setting of Tradewinds. Perched right on the ocean's edge toward the southern end of the village, the individual cabins here are just a few feet from the water. All are roomy, though rather Spartan, and come with a very inviting porch hung with a hammock overlooking the waves, where we predict you'll spend most of your time. The less expensive rooms here are set a bit farther back from the sea in a simple triplex building, although each comes with its own little veranda. Everything is painted in lively pastels, and there's a friendly, family-like vibe to the whole operation.

Placencia Village, on the beach, south end of the village. © **523-3122.** Fax 523-3201. www.placencia. com. 9 units. BZ$80–BZ$140 double. Rates slightly lower in the off season; higher during peak weeks. MC, V. *In room:* Minifridge, no phone.

Where to Dine

In addition to the places mentioned below, the restaurant at **The Inn at Robert's Grove** (p. 180) is consistently top-notch. On the other end of the spectrum, **Wendy's** (© **523-3335**) is a popular, low-key spot serving excellent Belizean, Mexican, and international fare, located on the main road, at the southern end of town, almost by the pier.

Finally, as you wander around town in the heat of the day, be sure to stop in at **Tutti Frutti Ice Cream Shop** for some fresh, homemade ice cream or gelato. Tutti Frutti is on the main road in the Placencia Village Square shopping center, across from the soccer field. **Daisy's,** located on the main road near the center of town, also serves fresh homemade ice cream, as well as breakfast, lunch, and dinner.

There are also several grocery stores in the village, in case you want to put together a picnic lunch.

EXPENSIVE

Mare ★★★ ITALIAN/SEAFOOD   This is a great choice for a romantic dinner. The lighting at night is subdued, and tables are adorned with candles and flowers. The restaurant looks out over the hotel's pool and onto the sea, and the setting is also wonderful during the day for lunch. The kitchen serves expertly prepared Italian cuisine and fresh seafood. I like to start things off with the *insalata de pesce,* which features fresh red snapper smoked on the premises. In addition to nightly specials, there are delicious thin-crust wood-oven pizzas, a selection of pastas, and several hearty main dishes. Whole, freshly caught fish are roasted in the wood oven, as are lobster tails in season. Most of the herbs and vegetables served are grown right here at the hotel's organic garden. The wine list features a range of fine wines from Francis Ford Coppola's own vineyard.

At Turtle Inn, on the beach north of the center of the village. © **523-3244.** www.turtleinn.com. Reservations recommended. Main courses BZ$40–BZ$92. AE, MC, V. Daily 11am–3pm and 6:30–9pm.

Maya Beach Hotel Bistro ★★★ FUSION/SEAFOOD   This is my favorite restaurant on the Placencia peninsula. There's nothing fancy about the decor or ambience at this open-air beachfront restaurant, but the food and service are consistently top-notch. You can start things off with their trio or quartet of starters. Some of the top choices here are the fish cakes, coconut shrimp, and roasted pumpkin, coconut, and green-chili soup. Signature main dishes here include the cacao-dusted pork chop served on a risotto cake, and the nut-encrusted fresh catch served with a papaya-pineapple salsa. The coconut ribs and pork burger are also excellent.

At Maya Beach Hotel, on Maya Beach. © **520-8040.** www.mayabeachhotel.com. Reservations recommended. Main courses BZ$28–BZ$56. AE, MC, V. Tues–Sun 7am–9pm.

MODERATE

In addition to the places listed below, **Mango's** (© **600-2040;** www.mangosbelize. com) is a lively beachside bar and restaurant up in Maya Beach. The bar food here runs from burgers and shrimp po' boy sandwiches to burritos and quesadillas.

De'Tatch Seafood Beach Bar & Grill ★ BELIZEAN/SEAFOOD   This funky and friendly open-air beachfront joint is one of the most popular spots in town. Traditional Belizean breakfasts here are hearty and inexpensive. You can get excellent seafood or shrimp burritos or tacos for lunch, and a selection of tasty meat, poultry, and seafood offerings for dinner. I like the seafood gumbo and Belikin-battered conch steak. The second-floor open-air deck can get hot in the daytime, but it is especially nice on starry nights.

Placencia Village, on the ocean just off the Sea Spray Hotel toward the center of the village. © **503-3385.** Reservations not accepted. Breakfast and lunch main courses BZ$6–BZ$16; dinner main courses BZ$12–BZ$36; lobster BZ$32–BZ$50. AE, DISC, MC, V. Daily 7am–10pm.

Habanero Mexican Café & Bar ★ MEXICAN   Set on the lagoon side of the peninsula beside the marina at Robert's Grove, this restaurant serves a mix of Tex-Mex and traditional Mexican fare. When the bugs aren't biting, you'll want to grab a table outdoors on the deck overlooking the water. This is also a great spot to catch the sunset. When the bugs are biting, you can seek refuge in the screened-in main dining room. My favorite dishes here are the garlic shrimp tacos and the spicy fish chimichanga. For those looking for a fiesta, you can order sangria and margaritas by the pitcher.

At the marina across from The Inn at Robert's Grove, north of the airstrip. © **523-3665.** Reservations recommended. Main courses BZ$16–BZ$34. AE, MC, V. Daily noon–10pm.

Rumfish y Vino ★★ SEAFOOD/FUSION   This is the hippest and most sophisticated joint in Placencia. Offering a wide-ranging menu of fusion fare, bar food, and tapas, this is a great place to come for a long evening of wining and dining. Start off with the succulent conch fritters or some of their homemade fish pâté, and then move on to one of their nightly specials. Standout options include their gourmet mac 'n' cheese and the Jamaican jerk pork chops. For lunch, I love the fish tacos. The wine list here is unique for Belize, featuring a broad selection of Italian and California wines that they import themselves, and there are also several local beers on tap.

Placencia Village Sq., on the main road, across from soccer field. © **523-3293.** www.rumfishyvino.com. Reservations recommended. Main courses BZ$14–BZ$27. MC, V. Daily 11am–midnight.

Trattoria Placencia PASTA   There's not much besides pasta and some simple salads and appetizers on the menu, but the folks here make a massive batch of fresh fettuccine daily, and they offer a long list of sauces to have with it. My favorites include the eggplant, capers, and fresh tomatoes, although the marinara sauce is also excellent and loaded with fresh shrimp, fish, conch, and lobster (in season). They also make their own pesto and have Belizean-made Italian sausage. Heavy wooden tables are spread widely on a covered porch and a screened-in dining room.

Placencia Village, on the oceanfront about midway along the sidewalk. © **623-3394.** Main courses BZ$28–BZ$40. V. Mon–Sat 5–9:30pm.

INEXPENSIVE

Omar's Diner ♦ BELIZEAN/MEXICAN   There's no assembly-line production, Styrofoam wrappings, or U.S.-style short-order cook here. Sometimes the speed of service doesn't live up to diner norms. Still, this long-standing restaurant consistently serves hearty and tasty local fare at great prices. I recommend some fresh fish or shrimp in the Belizean creole, Cajun, or curry sauce. Omar isn't afraid to spice up

Lobster season opens each year on June 15, and Placencia pulls out all the stops to celebrate the culinary possibilities of this underwater arthropod. In addition to concerts, games, and sidewalk booths hawking all sorts of goods and treats, you'll be able to sample everything from lobster fritters and lobster quiche to lobster bisque and beyond. If it can be made with lobster, you'll probably find it here. The Placencia Lobster Festival is held in late June each year. For more information and exact dates, contact the **Placencia Information Center** (🕻 **523-4045;** www.placencia.com).

his cooking. There's a homey, welcoming vibe to the whole operation, which is located streetside on the main road. If there's no free table, you'll be able to take a seat with another fellow traveler who has room.

Placencia Village, on the main road in the center of the village. 🕻 **523-4094.** Breakfast and lunch main courses BZ$5–BZ$14; dinner main courses BZ$10–BZ$24; lobster BZ$30–BZ$40. MC, V. Daily 7am–10pm.

Pickled Parrot ★ INTERNATIONAL   This popular place serves a mix of quality bar food, pizzas, and a nightly range of main dishes and specials. The bulk of the menu is made up of pizzas, burgers, subs, and burritos. Dinner specials range from mango-rum glazed chicken to lobster curry. There's a relaxed, informal atmosphere at this open-air sand-floored restaurant, and the bar can get rowdy at times, especially after folks have downed a few rounds of Parrot Piss, the bar's signature mixed drink.

Placencia Village. 🕻 **624-2651.** www.pickledparrotbelize.com. Reservations not accepted. Main courses BZ$10–BZ$30; pizzas BZ$34–BZ$44. V. Mon–Sat noon–9pm.

Purple Space Monkey Village INTERNATIONAL   This place, well-located in the heart of the village, has risen from the ashes twice, once after Hurricane Iris and then again after a devastating fire. The heavy wrought-iron tables and chairs are a rainbow of primary colors. The food is well-prepared, abundant, and reasonably priced. I like to start the day with their fry jacks stuffed with eggs and cheese. The lunch menu tends toward burgers, sandwiches, wraps, and burritos, whereas their dinner menu gets more creative and extensive. Specialties here include fresh blackened fish, as well as fish, chicken, or shrimp served in a mango-teriyaki sauce. There's free Wi-Fi throughout, as well as four complimentary computer workstations and a lending library.

Placencia Village, in front of the soccer field. 🕻 **523-4094.** Breakfast and lunch main courses BZ$10–BZ$16; dinner main courses BZ$26–BZ$46. MC, V. Daily 7am–10pm.

The Secret Garden ★ 🏠 INTERNATIONAL/COFFEE HOUSE   The name of this quiet and cozy little spot is appropriate. Reached over a small yellow bridge, it has a few outdoor tables on a wood deck in a shady garden. A few more tables are located on a covered veranda, and a couple more are inside the small restaurant. Dinner choices change regularly, but might feature fresh grilled red snapper with a roasted red pepper sauce or some spicy shrimp "Diablo" served over linguine. There's always fresh fish, conch, and lobster in season, and even some vegan options. In many ways, this place is similar to the Purple Space Monkey (above), including the free Wi-Fi access and lending library, but with a much mellower and more refined vibe.

Placencia Village, behind Wallen's Market. ☎ **523-3420.** Main courses breakfast BZ$8–BZ$14, dinner BZ$18–BZ$32. MC, V. Tues–Sat 7:30–11am and 5–9pm.

Placencia After Dark

Placencia is a quiet and remote beach destination, which is why my favorite late-night activity here is simply taking a stroll on the beach and stargazing. Still, there are a few bars in the village, and some of the larger resort hotels have lively nightlife scenes.

Two of the most popular spots in town are the **Barefoot Beach Bar** ★ (☎ **523-3515**) and the **Tipsy Tuna Sports Bar** (☎ **523-3089**), two neighboring establishments; I prefer the relaxed vibe and outdoor setting of the Barefoot Beach Bar, while the Tipsy Tuna is more of a late-night place, with pool tables and regular live music and karaoke.

For real late-night action, there's the **D'Eclipse Entertainment Club** (☎ **523-3288**), just north of the airstrip. This place is in a location where noise pollution wouldn't bother existing hotels and houses. However, it's yet to really catch on with any local or visiting crowd.

PUNTA GORDA & THE TOLEDO DISTRICT ★

330km (205 miles) S of Belize City; 161km (100 miles) S of Dangriga

Punta Gorda, or simply "P.G.," is Belize's southernmost town. This is the end of the road and feels a bit like the end of the world. P.G. is a quiet place with clean, paved streets, few cars, lush vegetation, and a very slow pace. Although it is right on the Caribbean, there is no beach to speak of, and the water just off town is rather uninviting. However, there are several wonderful offshore cayes within easy reach that have excellent beaches and serve as bases for equally excellent snorkeling, scuba diving, and fishing. Inland from P.G., the surrounding scenery is as verdant as you'll find anywhere in Belize (due to nearly 508cm/200 in. of rain a year). The surrounding Toledo District is home to various Mayan ruins and numerous villages that are still peopled by Kekchi and Mopan Maya Indians, who have been migrating here from Guatemala over the past century.

Settled by Garífunas in 1823, Punta Gorda was accessible only by boat for decades, and even though the Southern Highway is now paved and easily connects the town with points north, there's still a sense of this being a distant frontier. As the administrative center for the Toledo District, Punta Gorda has an active market and bus services to the many surrounding Mayan and Garífuna villages, although connections are not very frequent. Most travelers do little more than pass through Punta Gorda on their way to or from Guatemala by way of the Puerto Barrios ferry. However, there is plenty to keep the adventurous traveler busy for several days, including fishing, scuba diving, rainforest hiking, and bird-watching.

Punta Gorda

Hospital
Police
Bank/ATM
Post office

0   1/10 mile
0   100 meters

Airstrip

Belize City
Belmopan
B E L I Z E
Punta Gorda

Sports ground

North St
King St
Queen St
Prince St
Far West St
West St
Back St
Clements St
Church St
Main St
Front St
George St
Victoria St
Cemetery Lane

Gas Station

■ **Bus Station**

Town Hall

Pier

Gulf of Honduras

■ **Bus Station**

ACCOMMODATIONS ■
Blue Belize **14**
Coral House Inn **15**
Charlton's Inn **3**
Hickatee Cottages **15**
Nature's Way Guest
 House **12**
Sea Front Inn **2**
Tate's Guesthouse **8**

DINING ◆
Emery's **4**
Earth Runnin's Café **6**
Gomier's Foods **1**
Grace's Restaurant **5**
Marrenco's Ice Cream
 Parlour **11**
Marian's Bayview **13**
The Snack Shack **7**

NIGHTLIFE ●
Bukut Bar **6**
PG Sports Bar **9**
Reef Bar **10**

Essentials

GETTING THERE & DEPARTING

BY PLANE   There are several daily flights into and out of Punta Gorda's little airport (PND). **Maya Island Air** (© **223-1140** in Belize City, or 722-2856 in Punta Gorda; www.mayaairways.com) has four flights daily between Belize City and Punta Gorda. These flights leave from the Municipal Airport at 8 and 10am and 2:30 and 4:30pm. Most of these flights stop 15 minutes later at the Goldson International Airport to pick up passengers. The fare is BZ$204 each way from Municipal Airport, and BZ$240 each way from the international airport. When you're ready to leave, Maya Island Air flights from Punta Gorda to Belize City depart at 6:45, 9:30, and 11:30am, and at 4pm. Most of these flights stop first in Placencia and Dangriga, and then at the international airport, before continuing on to Municipal Airport.

Tropic Air (© 800/422-3435 in the U.S. or Canada, 226-2012 in Belize City, or 722-2008 in Punta Gorda; www.tropicair.com) has five daily flights from Goldson International Airport to Punta Gorda at 8:15 and 10:20am, and at 12:20, 2:20, and 5pm. These flights stop 15 minutes later at the Municipal Airport to pick up passengers. The fare is BZ$204 each way from the Municipal Airport, and BZ$240 each way from the international airport. Tropic Air flights depart Punta Gorda for Belize City's airports daily at 7, 9:40, and 11:35am, and at 1:35 and 4pm.

Flight times run between 55 minutes and 1 hour and 20 minutes, depending on the number of stops, since most flights to and from Punta Gorda on Maya Island Air and Tropic Air stop in Placencia and Dangriga to pick up and drop off passengers. On both airlines, flights are sometimes added during the high season or suspended during the low season, so check in advance.

BY CAR It is a long way to Punta Gorda. However, the Southern Highway, which starts just outside of Dangriga, is paved the entire 161km (100 miles) to Punta Gorda, where it ends. Coming from Belize City, head first to Belmopan and turn south on the Hummingbird Highway. Just before Dangriga, the Hummingbird Highway connects with the Southern Highway, which takes you all the way to Punta Gorda. Alternatively, you can take the Manatee Road turnoff just past the Belize Zoo, although the Manatee Road is a washboard dirt-and-gravel road for most of its length. See "By Car" in "Essentials" on p. 154 for more information. It should take between 4 and 5 hours to drive between Belize City and Punta Gorda.

BY BUS James Bus Line (© 207-3937 in Belize City, or 702-2049 in Punta Gorda) and **National Transport** (© 227-2255) have regular service throughout the day between Belize City and Punta Gorda. Buses leave at irregular intervals between 4:30am and 5pm, with at least 15 buses making the run throughout the day. In Belize City, National Transport buses leave from the main terminal on West Collet Canal, while James buses leave from nearby, near the Shell gas station on Cemetery Road. It's worth getting an express bus, which should take only a little more than 5 hours. However, there are far more frequent nonexpress buses. On these, the trip takes 6 hours or more. In some cases, you may have to change buses in Belmopan or Dangriga. The one-way fare is BZ$24.

Departing buses begin running at 3am, with the last bus leaving at 4pm. All buses, even the express buses, stop in Belmopan, Dangriga, and Independence. However, the express buses are not supposed to stop along the route to pick up and drop off passengers at intermediary points.

BY BOAT Several boats run daily between Punta Gorda and Puerto Barrios, Guatemala. If there's enough demand, the boats may stop in Livingston, Guatemala, as well. Expect to pay between BZ$30 and BZ$40 per person. The boats leave from the main pier in Punta Gorda. **Requena's Charter Service,** 12 Front St. (© 722-2070; watertaxi@btl.net), is one of the more dependable operators. When the seas are calm, the crossing takes about 1 hour. Departures for Guatemala tend to leave between 8:30 and 9am, although there are often afternoon departures as well. The boats tend to return from Puerto Barrios between 2 and 4pm. You'll have to pay the BZ$7.50 in exit taxes. *Note:* When coming and going, be sure to get your passport stamped at the immigration office just up from the dock.

Celebrating the Sweet

Each year in late May, P.G. pulls out all the stops for the **Toledo Cacao Fest** (www.toledochocolate.com). The festival, which runs over a weekend, includes a wide range of events and activities, including live concerts, fireworks, cacao farm tours, and of course plenty of opportunities to taste all sorts of dishes and creations made from or with cacao and chocolate. See the above website for exact dates.

GETTING AROUND

Punta Gorda is a very small and compact town, and you should be able to get around primarily on foot. If you're just too hot or tired, or you're heading farther afield, have your hotel call a cab, or call **Galvez's Taxi Travel & Tour Service** (℃ 722-2402) or the **Roots & Herbs Taxi Service** (℃ 722-2834).

Another option for getting around is to rent a bike. Ask at your hotel, and they should be able to help you find one for rent, or head to **Sykes Bicycle Rental** (℃ 626-6269) at 42 Prince St.

ORIENTATION

Punta Gorda is a small coastal town, and the road into town runs right along the water before angling a bit inland. There's a tiny triangular park at the center of the town. On one side is the Civic Center, or Town Hall. On one corner is a cute little clock tower, and the Belize Bank anchors another corner. Still, much of the town's activity is water based, and many of the most important businesses, hotels, restaurants, and government offices are located on Front Street, which runs along the waterfront. The town's main pier is off the center of Front Street. On the western edge of town, only 6 blocks from the water, is P.G.'s airstrip.

The **Belize Tourist Industry Association** (℃ 722-2531), in conjunction with local hotels and tourism operators, runs a well-staffed and helpful information center on Front just north of the main pier. This is a good place to come to find current transportation schedules, book a tour, or arrange a homestay.

FAST FACTS   For the local **police,** dial ℃ 911 or 722-2022, and for the **fire department,** call ℃ 722-2032. If you need medical attention, go to the **Punta Gorda Hospital** on Main Street, toward the southern end of town (℃ 722-2026). The **post office** (℃ 722-2087) is on Front Street across from the main pier. **Belize Bank,** 30 Main St. (℃ 722-2324), can handle most of your banking needs.

There's a **Texaco** gas station (℃ 722-2926) out toward the northern end of Front Street and a Shell station out by "The Dump." Finally, if your hotel can't or won't do it for you, take your dirty clothes to **Punta Gorda Laundry Services,** on Main Street across from the Belize Bank, which charges around BZ$15 per load.

What to See & Do

There's very little in the way of attractions right in town. A stroll through Punta Gorda is the best way to enjoy the Caribbean atmosphere. If you get a little antsy at such a slow pace, there are plenty of cultural wonders and natural adventures within easy reach of Punta Gorda. There are a host of tour operators and guides in P.G. Your hotel and the information center listed in "Essentials," above, can probably hook you up with a good guide or adventure operator. Alternatively, you can check in with the folks at **Tide Tours ★** (📞 **722-2129;** www.tidetours.org), a local ecotourism initiative that integrates environmentally and socially aware practices with their wide range of tour and adventure options.

REACHING THESE ATTRACTIONS Most of the villages and attractions discussed below (such as Nim Li Punit) are located along the highway and have regular bus service every day. Buses to and from the other villages and attractions generally run at least once daily. Buses tend to leave for the villages from Punta Gorda between noon and 2pm, depending on which village or destination you are traveling to. These buses all leave from the market area in front of the Civic Center along Queen Street.

The time of departure from the villages to P.G. varies but is usually early in the morning, sometimes right around dawn. There's often only one bus per day, but some villages have two or more daily buses. Ask in P.G., or in the actual village, as schedules are subject to change. Fares run around BZ$2 to BZ$8 per person each way.

Another alternative is to hire a taxi or go on an organized trip. Ask at your hotel or the information center, and you should be able to set up a trip. You can usually hire a car and driver/guide for BZ$180 to BZ$360 per day. This price will usually cover a group of four.

The truly adventurous might want to tour this area by mountain bike. You can reach most of the above sites and villages in an athletic couple of hours of riding. Leave early to avoid the oppressive midday heat, and expect slow going and lots of mud in the rainy season.

MAYAN RUINS

None of Belize's southern ruins is as spectacular or actively restored as the more famous sites in the northern and western parts of the country. Still, the ancient Maya did have substantial cities and trading posts all up and down the Belizean coast, and several impressive reminders can be found near Punta Gorda. Travelers interested in the ongoing Mayan tradition will find themselves in a region of numerous small Kekchi and Mopan Maya villages, many of which have taken tentative steps to enter the tourism industry with homestay programs or basic guesthouses.

Lubaantun   The largest of the nearby Mayan ruins is **Lubaantun.** The name, which means "Place of the Fallen Stones" in Yucatec Maya, was given to the site in 1924 and it was descriptive of the state of the buildings at that time. This Late Classic Maya ruin is unusual in that the structures were built using a technique of cut-and-fitted limestone blocks rather than the usual rock-and-mortar construction technique used elsewhere by the Mayans. Set on a high ridge, the site features five plazas and two ball courts. The highest temple here rises just 15m (50 ft.) or so, and it's still mostly in ruins, with trees growing out of the rubble. Although largely unexcavated, the ancient city's center has been well cleared, and the surviving architecture and urban outline give a good sense of the former glory of this Mayan ceremonial center.

Lubaantun is perhaps most famous as the site where a crystal skull was allegedly discovered by a young Canadian woman in 1926. There's much debate as to the origin and age of the skull, which some say was planted as a surprise present for

Anna Mitchell-Hedges, who just happened to discover the carved skull on her 16th birthday while accompanying her father, who just happened to be leading the archaeological expedition. Others claim that the skull was a plant that had actually been purchased in London by Mitchell-Hedges. There are also claims that the crystal skull is the work of extraterrestrials, and that it has shown remarkable healing powers. The skull is currently kept in a vault in Canada.

Lubaantun is located about 32km (20 miles) northwest from Punta Gorda, about 11km (7 miles) from the well-marked turnoff on the highway near Big Falls, and 1.6km (1 mile) from the small Mayan village of San Pedro Columbia. Admission is BZ$10.

Nim Li Punit ★ Nim Li Punit, meaning "Big Hat" in Kekchi Mayan, features 26 steles, including the largest Maya carved stele in Belize, measuring almost 9m (30 ft.) tall. This stele bears the depiction of a local ruler wearing a large, broad diadem, or "big hat," hence the name of the site. Discovered only in 1976, Nim Li Punit is a relatively small site, with four compact plazas and one very well-preserved ball court, with a stone marker in its center. One of the plazas served as an astronomical observation area, with a platform and stone markings indicating the point where the sun rises on the equinoxes. There are three Royal tombs that have been discovered and partially excavated, and you can peer down into two of them. However, overall, very little excavation or restoration has been undertaken. Nonetheless, the eight carved steles, and in particular, stele 14, make this a worthwhile stop. The best-preserved steles, including stele 14, are currently housed at the small museum and visitor center at the entrance to the site.

Nim Li Punit is set on a high hilltop, and on a clear day, you have a great view over the flat southern plains, all the way to the Caribbean Sea. It is believed that this Late Classic city had close ties to Copan, Honduras. If you can visit only one of the Mayan sites in southern Belize, I recommend Nim Li Punit over Lubaantun.

Nim Li Punit is located about 3.2km (2 miles) off the Southern Highway, near the village of Indian Creek, 40km (25 miles) north of Punta Gorda. A dirt road leads from the highway to a parking area near the visitor center. Admission is BZ$10.

Other minor ruins in the area include **Uxbenka** near Santa Cruz and **Pusilha** near Aguacate.

PLACES FOR A DIP

Mayan culture, past and present, may be the main attraction of Punta Gorda, but it also boasts plenty of natural attractions. In the forested hills south of San Antonio is one of the most beautiful swimming holes in all of Belize. Flowing out of a cave in a limestone mountain, the aptly named **Blue Creek ★★** is a cool stream with striking deep turquoise water. Lush rainforest shades the creek, creating an idyllic place to spend an afternoon. You can cool off by swimming up into the mouth of the cave from which the stream flows. Blue Creek is also known locally as Ho Keb Ha, which means "the place where the water flows from." During the dry season, you can actually hike about 8km (5 miles) through the cave to an aboveground exit. The village of Blue Creek is reached from a turnoff about 2.4km (1½ miles) east of San Antonio. From here it's another 4km (2½ miles) south on a rough dirt road. The creek runs right through the little village, but the best swimming holes and the cave source of the creek are about a 10- to 15-minute hike upstream.

Just off the Southern Highway, near the village of Big Falls, there is a natural **hot spring** that's billed as the only such hot spring in Belize. You can have a refreshing swim in the river at the falls and then warm your muscles in the hot spring. This is a popular spot for locals on weekends.

There are also some attractive small waterfalls near the village of San Antonio, with inviting pools for a refreshing dip.

WATERSPORTS

The fishing, scuba diving, and snorkeling to be had off Punta Gorda are world-class. Kayaking on the ocean or up the Moho River is also excellent. Most tour operators and hotels in town can offer or line up a snorkel, dive, or fishing expedition to the very underexplored Sapodilla Cayes.

If you want to do an extended dive trip, or some volunteer work in marine conservation, check in with the folks at **Reef Conservation International ★** (✆ 702-0229 or 629-4266; www.reefci.com). These folks have cabins and campsites, as well as research and dive facilities on the idyllic Frank's Caye, which is part of the Sapodilla Marine Park.

For fishing, I recommend you check in with **Dan Castellanos** at Blue Belize (see below) or with **Garbutt's Fishing Services** (✆ 722-0070). Both know the waters and fishing grounds around here, and can guide you in pursuit of tarpon, bonefish, and permit.

Deer Dance

The Mopan Mayan village of San Antonio is the site of the Deer Dance, a 9-day traditional Mayan cultural celebration that takes place in late August and early September. Although this traditional cultural ceremony coincides with a Catholic religious holiday, the Feast of San Luis, its roots are traditional Maya.

A BOTANICAL GARDEN

The **Toledo Botanical Arboretum ★** (✆ 722-2470) is a sustainable farm and botanical garden project that accepts day visitors. In addition to a broad variety of ornamental flowers and orchids, tropical palms and bromeliads, they grow more than 100 varieties of tropical fruit, and something is always ripe for a just-picked treat. The Toledo Botanical Arboretum is close to both the Kekchi Maya village of San Pedro Columbia and the Lubaantun ruins. A 2-hour guided tour of the facility costs around BZ$10. Visits and transportation should be arranged in advance.

STAYING IN A MAYAN VILLAGE

Many people who make it as far as Punta Gorda are interested in learning more about Mayan village life. Though the ruins were abandoned centuries ago, Maya Indians still live in this region. The villages of the Toledo District are populated by two main groups of Maya Indians, the Kekchi and the Mopan, who have different languages and agricultural practices. The Mopan are upland farmers, while the Kekchi farm the lowlands. Both groups are thought to have migrated into southern Belize from Guatemala less than 100 years ago. Four decades of political violence and genocide in neighboring Guatemala have bolstered this migration.

San Antonio, the largest Mopan Maya village, is in a beautiful setting on top of a hill, with an old stone church in the center of the village. Steep streets wind through the village, dotted with both clapboard houses and traditional Mayan thatched huts. In addition to the Deer Dance, the nearby village of San Pedro is known for its annual festival on June 13 in honor of that village's patron saint. This festival includes masked dances and other Mayan rites mixed with more traditional Catholic themes and celebrations. Beyond San Antonio and San Pedro, there is a host of even smaller and more remote traditional Mayan villages.

The Maya Village Homestay Network (© 722-2470; demdatsdoin@btl. net) provides accommodations directly with families in the Mayan villages. There's a BZ$10 registration fee for any stay, and then accommodations cost BZ$20 per person per night, and meals are BZ$8 per person per meal. These fees are paid directly to your host family. Accommodations during a homestay can range from a hammock to a simple bed, and almost all families have some sort of bathroom or latrine. Currently, the villages involved in the homestay program include Aguacate, Na Luum Ca, and San José.

If you opt for this program, you can expect plenty of close contact with the local villagers. You will be eating what the locals eat, which in most cases means plenty of beans and tortillas, as well as the occasional chicken soup or meat dish. One of the highlights for many guests is participating in the cooking chores and learning the simple art of tortilla making.

STAYING WITH A GARÍFUNA FAMILY

Those seeking a unique Caribbean cultural experience can also look into staying with a local Garífuna family. Just 18km (11 miles) south of Punta Gorda lies the small Garífuna village of Barranco. With a little more than 100 residents, Barranco is a quintessential quiet Garífuna village. However, this is the hometown of one of Belize's most famous and beloved musicians, Andy Palacio (p. 29), and the town's little House of Culture is a great place for a quick visit to learn a little about the history, traditions, and culture of the Garífuna people of this area. Although the road to Barranco is usually passable during the dry season, it's best to get there by boat. Ask around at the Punta Gorda pier whether there's any regular ferry service. If not, you should be able to hire a ride for about BZ$80 to BZ$120 per boat.

Shopping

Wednesday and Saturday are market days around the small market square in front of the Civic Center and along the waterfront. This is a great time and place to find local and Guatemalan handicrafts, as well as fresh fruit and produce. If the outdoor market isn't happening, you can find most of the same items at either the **Southern Frontier Giftshop,** 41 Front St. (© 722-2870), or the **Fajina Craft Center ★**, on Front Street next to the post office (© 722-2470), which is a cooperative of Mayan women from the area.

Where to Stay

VERY EXPENSIVE

Machaca Hill Lodge ★★★ 🎁 With beautiful private cabins, stellar personalized service, and excellent cuisine, this is the most luxurious option in the Toledo area and one of the top hotels in the whole country. The 12 large individual bungalows are set on a high hillside of rich forest above the Río Grande. Each features a huge shower made of smooth river stone. The kidney-shaped pool has a broad and inviting stone deck area around it, and it's also set on one of the highest points on the property, giving it excellent views all around. A tramway connects the lodge to the river below, where there's a wonderful dock and bar area. This place was originally geared toward fishermen and is still an excellent base for fishing. Much of the food served here comes from the hotel's expansive organic gardens.

P.O. Box 135, Punta Gorda. © **722-0050.** Fax 722-0051. www.machacahill.com. 12 units. BZ$620–BZ$880 double. Rates include breakfast, afternoon tea, on-site activities, and all taxes. Fishing and all-inclusive package rates are also available. AE, DISC, MC, V. **Amenities:** Restaurant; bar; lounge; concierge; outdoor pool; small luxurious spa. *In room:* A/C, hair dryer, no phone, free Wi-Fi.

EXPENSIVE

Located on a bend in the Moho River, about a 20-minute drive outside P.G., the **Cotton Tree Lodge ★** (© **866/480-4534** in the U.S. and Canada, or 670-0557 in Belize; www.cottontreelodge.com) offers almost a dozen large, individual wood and thatch bungalows.

The Lodge at Big Falls ★ This comfortable nature lodge caters to ecotourists and those looking to explore the nearby Mayan ruins and villages, and is set on the banks of the Río Grande, just outside the village of Big Falls. The six individual octagonal cabins all overlook the river and feature high thatched ceilings, large windows providing plenty of cross-ventilation, and cool rustic tile floors. Each comes with a large covered veranda equipped with a hammock for lazing away and watching the river flow. Named after birds, my favorite cabins are Trogon, Aracari, and Tiger Heron, the closest ones to the river. Although there's electricity here, at night the light is provided by kerosene lanterns. There's a good-size outdoor pool on the broad lawn outside the main lodge, and a host of tour options is available, including lazy inner tube floats on the river right here.

Near the village of Big Falls, 29km (18 miles) north of Punta Gorda (P.O. Box 103, Punta Gorda). © **671-7172.** www.thelodgeatbigfalls.com. 6 units. BZ$280–BZ$360 double. MC, V. **Amenities:** Restaurant; bar; kayak and mountain bike rentals; outdoor pool; free Wi-Fi. *In room:* No phone.

MODERATE

In addition to the places listed below, **Beya Suites** (© **722-2956;** www.beyasuites. com) is a small hotel with well-equipped, tidy rooms; an on-site restaurant; and a rooftop patio, located just across from the bay, just north of town.

Blue Belize ★ Rooms here are found in two neighboring houses connected by an elevated wooden walkway and stairs. All are cheery, with contemporary decor and lots of natural light. My favorites are those on the second floor of the newer building. These share a huge wraparound veranda and also come with flatscreen televisions. The owners here run an excellent tour operation, and Dan Castellanos, one of the owners, is considered one of the area's top fishing guides.

139 Front St. (P.O. Box 37), Punta Gorda. © **722-2678.** www.bluebelize.com. 5 units. BZ$140–BZ$190 double. Rates include continental breakfast. MC, V. **Amenities:** Free Wi-Fi. *In room:* Kitchenette, no phone.

Coral House Inn ★ This homey bed-and-breakfast is my favorite option right in P.G. The rooms are simple affairs, with firm beds and cable televisions. The rooms are all on the second floor, with a large shared balcony overlooking the sea. There's a refreshing lap pool set at an angle off the main building, and an artsy open-air cement door leading to a lawn and gardens that run off to the sea. The gardens also provide innovative wastewater treatment. The owners are a cheerful and helpful couple, and they provide free bicycles for use during your stay. These folks also rent out a separate, private little cottage. The hotel borders the town cemetery, so consider yourself forewarned if that spooks you.

151 Main St. (P.O. Box 43), Punta Gorda. 📞 **722-2878.** Fax 722-2682. www.coralhouseinn.net. 5 units. BZ$165–BZ$200 double. Rates include continental breakfast. MC, V. **Amenities:** Bar; lounge; complimentary bike use. *In room:* A/C, TV, no phone, free Wi-Fi.

Hickatee Cottages ★ 📷 This cozy retreat features a small collection of rooms set under tall trees among flowering gardens. It's located just a mile or so from downtown, but you'll feel a world apart nonetheless. All the rooms are quite spacious, with varnished wood floors, furniture made by Belizean Mennonites, a separate sitting area, and a front veranda strung with a hammock. The suite comes with a flatscreen television and DVD player. There's no regular programming, but the hotel has a DVD lending library. There's a small creek running through the property, and you can hike trails through thick forest and brush here. The bird-watching is excellent, and you're very likely to see, or at least hear, howler monkeys. If the heat of the day gets to you, there's a small but refreshing plunge pool. The owners, who met on the Green Tortoise bus, got off the bus to set up this little place.

Ex-Serviceman Rd. (P.O. Box 148), Punta Gorda. 📞 **662-4475.** www.hickatee.com. 5 units. BZ$150–BZ$220 double. Rates include continental breakfast and round-trip transfer to P.G. airport or bus station. MC, V. **Amenities:** Restaurant; bar; small plunge pool; free Wi-Fi. *In room:* No phone.

Sirmoor Hill Farm ★ 📷 This converted plantation home is a unique lodging choice in the area. There are only two rooms for rent, and they share a bathroom. Each room features soaring ceilings, wood floors, and whitewashed wooden walls. The place is best suited to be taken over by a couple of friends or a small family. Located a few miles outside of town, you drive up to the house via a long driveway lined on either side with towering royal palm trees. The working farm still has cattle and horses, as well as teak and mahogany groves. There's also the ruins of an old rum distillery on-site. Guests get the run of the old home, which includes large common living areas, a screened-in veranda, a massive kitchen, and a beautiful infinity pool.

New Road MLS3, Punta Gorda. 📞 **722-0052.** www.sirmoorhillfarm.com. 2 units. BZ$220 1 room; BZ$380 both rooms. Rates include full breakfast. MC, V. **Amenities:** Outdoor pool; free Wi-Fi. *In room:* No phone.

INEXPENSIVE

Punta Gorda has a host of budget lodgings. In addition to the place listed below, you could check out **Charlton's Inn,** 9 Main St. (📞 **722-2197**), or **Tate's Guesthouse,** 34 José María Núñez St. (📞 **722-0147**).

And, for an ecolodge experience at pretty budget prices, check out **Sun Creek Lodge** (📞 **604-2124;** www.suncreeklodge.com), a delightful collection of individual cabins, at Mile 14 on the Southern Highway.

Nature's Way Guest House 🏄 Located 3 blocks south of the central park and across the street from the water, Nature's Way is a longtime favorite of budget travelers. There's a variety of room, bathroom, and bed configurations, from bunk beds to a mix of twins and matrimonials. Still, everything is quite basic and rustic. Even though most rooms do not have private bathrooms, everything is kept tidy, and the shared bathrooms are large and clean. Only breakfast is served here, though it is hearty and plentiful, and the hotel is close to downtown and other dining options. The guesthouse is operated by an American named William "Chet" Schmidt, who moved down here some 40 years ago to promote sustainable agricultural and tourism practices.

65 Front St., Punta Gorda. ℂ/fax **702-2119**. 6 units (1 with private bathroom). BZ$30–BZ$60 double. No credit cards. *In room:* No phone.

Where to Dine

Dining options are far from extensive in Punta Gorda. In addition to the restaurants listed below, check out **Grace's Restaurant,** at the corner of Main and King streets (ℂ **702-2414**), for good local fare.

Out a little bit north of town, just across from and facing the bay, **Waluco's Cool Spot** (ℂ **670-3672**) is a good place for fish, pasta, or rotisserie chicken. The open-air restaurant has a great view and a friendly, casual vibe. And even a bit beyond Waluco's, you'll find the **Mangrove Inn ★** (ℂ **722-2270**), which serves a limited nightly menu in an intimate setting with personalized service.

For a cool treat on a hot day, head to **Marenco's Ice Cream Parlour,** 57 Main St. (ℂ **722-2572**).

Earth Runnins' Café ★ BELIZEAN/INTERNATIONAL   Owned and run by the very personable Giovanni Foster, this place serves a broad and creative menu ranging from local classics to Cajun-style blackened fish and Thai shrimp curry. The whole fish is excellent. The heavy wood tables and chairs, as well as the massive wood bar, were built by Giovanni himself. There's a stage on one side of the room, and the bar here is one of the more lively in town. The hours listed below are not strict by any means, so it always pays to check in advance to see if they'll be open.

13 Main Middle St. ℂ **702-2007**. www.earthrunnins.com. Main courses BZ$10–BZ$18. No credit cards. Wed–Sun 7:30am–2pm and 5–11pm.

Emery's BELIZEAN   This is a good bet for simple, fresh, local cuisine. I prefer the tables in a large, open-air, thatch-roof structure off the small wooden building that has the kitchen, bar, and small screened-in dining area. This large dining area has half-walls of bamboo and a series of floor fans cooling things off. There's a chalkboard menu with the standard fare and daily specials. Offerings range from stew chicken and pork to whole fried snapper and snook filets. Everything is well-prepared, and the prices are right.

North St. ℂ **722-2317**. Main courses BZ$8–BZ$30. No credit cards. Daily 8am–10pm.

Gomier's Foods BELIZEAN/VEGETARIAN   This should definitely be the first stop for any vegetarian or health-food nut. While the menu at this place features plenty of traditional locally prepared food and dishes, this is the only place in P.G. to find stir-fried tofu and a wide range of vegetarian entrees. Most of the herbs and vegetables are organically grown by owner Gomier himself. Again, this is predominantly a one-man show, and the hours listed below are somewhat optimistic, so be sure to check first whether this place is open or have a backup plan if you go.

At the corner of Vernon and Front sts. ℂ **722-2990**. Main courses BZ$8–BZ$20. No credit cards. Tues–Sat 8am–2pm and 6–9pm.

Marian's Bayview ★ INDIAN/BELIZEAN   For years, Marian made a name for herself selling authentic East Indian food out of a simple stall at the small market in downtown Punta Gorda. She's got her own digs now, and you can sit at a table and enjoy your meal. Granted, the tables are rather rickety, the chairs are plastic, and the third-floor dining area has an unfinished feel to it, with bare cement on the floors and some of the walls. Still, the food is delicious. Every day, Marian makes a limited menu that usually includes a mix of Indian and Belizean fare, and a mix of seafood and meat options.

At the corner of Vernon and Front sts. ☎ **722-0129.** Main courses BZ$8–BZ$18. AE, MC, V. Mon–Wed and Fri–Sat 11am–2pm and 6–10pm; Thu 11am–2pm; Sun noon–2pm and 6–10pm.

The Snack Shack ★ ◢ INTERNATIONAL This simple, open-air spot is a great place for a cool drink on a hot day. It's also a top choice for breakfast or a light lunch. Heavy wooden tables are spread around a wooden deck surrounded by heliconia and red ginger flowers, and large tree-trunk columns support the corrugated tin roof. In addition to standard breakfast fare, you can get a range of fresh-baked goodies. For lunch there are a selection of filling salads, as well as burgers, chicken sandwiches, tuna melts, and BLTs.

On Main St., between King and Queen sts. ☎ **702-0200.** Main courses BZ$5–BZ$10. MC, V. Mon–Fri 7am–3pm; Sat 7am–2:30pm.

Punta Gorda After Dark

Overall, Punta Gorda's a pretty quiet town. The most dependable spot for any action is the **PG Sports Bar** (☎ 722-2329), which only very occasionally has sporting events on the tube. Instead, this is really an all-purpose nightspot with occasional live bands, DJs, and karaoke nights. It's located on Main Street at the southern edge of the little central park. Another good spot to meet and mingle with locals is the **Bukut Bar** at Earth Runnins' (see above), which also has live music every now and again. I personally like the view and breeze at the **Reef Bar** (☎ 702-0154) for a quiet place to get a drink and have a conversation. Finally, you can try heading out north of town to **Waluco's** (see above), where there are occasionally live music jam sessions, a local Punta Rock band, or a Garífuna drumming outfit.

NORTHERN BELIZE

With few exceptions, Northern Belize is overlooked by most tourists who fly into the country and head quickly to the cayes, the Cayo District, the southern beaches, or the Mayan Mountains. Even those who enter by land from Mexico frequently make a beeline to Belize City and bypass this region. Still, northern Belize has its charms, not least of which is its undiscovered and undeveloped feel. It's here that you'll find some of the country's larger biological reserves, including the **Crooked Tree Wildlife Sanctuary,** the **Shipstern Wildlife Reserve,** and the **Río Bravo Conservation Area.** With more than 430 species of birds and 250 species of orchids, this region should be especially attractive to naturalists.

9

The region was also an important and strategic part of the Mayan Empire, and ancient ruins abound. Most notably, it is here that you will find the **Altun Ha** and **Lamanai** ruins, two of the country's most popular and important Mayan sites. Lesser sites such as **Cuello, Cerros, Santa Rita,** and **Noh Mul** are also possible stops for true aficionados. Finally, northern Belize is home to three unique and isolated lodges: **Maruba Resort Jungle Spa, Chan Chich Lodge,** and **Lamanai Outpost Lodge,** all of which are described in detail in this chapter.

For our purposes, "northern Belize" refers to the northern section of the Belize District, as well as the entire Orange Walk and Corozal districts. The land here is low and plain, with massive sugar cane, citrus, soybean, and pineapple plantations set amid large swaths of forests; swamps; lagoons; and slow, steamy jungle rivers. Belize's Northern Highway runs from Belize City to the Mexican border, a little more than 161km (100 miles) away. The road is not in good shape, and the scenery tends to be flat and monotonous. There are few people and fewer population centers. There are only two cities of any note along the way, and both are actually designated as towns, **Orange Walk Town** and **Corozal Town.** Of these, only Corozal, with its seaside setting and proximity

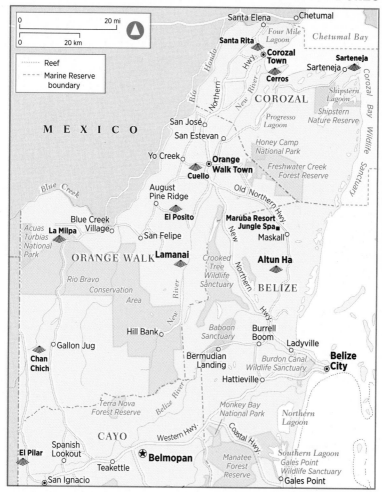

to the Mexican border and Shipstern Wildlife Reserve, is a destination with much appeal to travelers. Orange Walk, for its part, serves mainly as a gateway to the Lamanai ruins and the Río Bravo Conservation Area.

Much of this area was originally settled by immigrants fleeing southern Mexico's Yucatán peninsula during the Caste Wars of the mid–19th century. This is undoubtedly the most Spanish region in Belize. However, it is also the region with the largest concentration of Mennonite communities. Members of this somewhat radical and oft-persecuted Christian order have thrived in this farming area. You can't miss the Mennonites in their distinctive, heavy, home-sewn garb and horse-drawn carriages.

ALONG THE OLD NORTHERN HIGHWAY

The Old Northern Highway is in rough shape. The narrow, paved road is perennially in dire need of repair; it's riddled with potholes and washed out in many sections. Still, it is the only route to one major attraction and one unique resort. Aside from these two places, there's not much else along this highway, except for a few tiny communities and the occasional roadside restaurant or bar. To get here, take Freetown Road out of Belize City to connect with the Northern Highway. The turnoff to the Old Northern Highway is to the right just past Sand Hill; watch for signs for Altun Ha and Maruba Resort Jungle Spa.

Altun Ha ★

Altun Ha is a small, well-preserved Mayan ruin. Only a few of the most imposing temples, tombs, and pyramids have been uncovered and rebuilt; hundreds more lie under the jungle foliage. Still, there are two large central plazas surrounded by mid-size pyramids and mounds, as well as the beginnings of the excavation of residential areas. While nowhere near as extensive as some other sites, Altun Ha offers admirable quality and detail of excavation and restoration. Sections of different structures have been left in various states of repair and restoration, which gives a good sense of the process involved. Moreover, while the climb to the top of the tallest pyramids here is rather easy by Mayan standards, the views are still wonderful. The site was named after the village in which it's situated—Rockstone Pond, the literal Mayan translation meaning "stone water." At the back of the site, behind Plaza B, is the namesake pond. Archaeologists theorize that the pond is an example of a pre-Columbian waterworks project and a demonstration of the ingenuity of Mayan engineering.

Despite its somewhat diminutive size, Altun Ha was a major trade and ceremonial center. In its prime, during the Classic Period, Altun Ha supported a population of about 10,000. Many jade, pearl, and obsidian artifacts have been discovered here, including the unique jade-head sculpture of **Kinich Ahau** (the Mayan sun god), the largest well-carved jade from the Mayan era. Today, it's kept in a bank vault in Belmopan, out of public view, although you can see a replica at the Museum of Belize (p. 98). Some of the pieces found here show a direct link to the great Mexican city of Teotihuacán.

The largest (though not the tallest) temple here is the **Temple of the Masonry Altars,** which fronts Plaza B. It has been well-restored, and the pathway to the top is well-maintained and even features handrails. However, if you're fairly fit and not acrophobic, I recommend you climb the almost entirely unrestored **Temple A-6,** which is truly the tallest building here. A climb to the top of Temple A-6 affords an excellent panorama of the entire site. Be careful climbing down; the Mayans were a society run by priests and holy men, not lawyers. A more litigious society would have never permitted the construction of such steep and treacherous stairways.

The site is open daily from 9am to 5pm. Admission is BZ$10 for adults, free for children 11 and under. There is no public transportation to Altun Ha, so you'll need to take a tour, a taxi, or your own wheels, or hitchhike. If you're driving, Altun Ha is located about 48km (30 miles) north of Belize City on the Northern Highway. Once

Altun Ha

To parking lot and
Northern Highway

Visitor's Center

A-6

A-7

**Temple
of the
Green
Tomb**

A-1 Pavilion

PLAZA A

A-5

A-2

A-4 B-1

A-3

**Temple of the
Masonry Altars**

B-4

PLAZA B

B-2

B-3

B-5 B-6

Altun Ha

Belize City

Belmopan

BELIZE

you're on the Old Northern Highway, it's 18km (11 miles) to the Altun Ha road. From the highway, it's another bumpy 3.6km (2¼ miles) to the ruins.

Half-day tours to Altun Ha from Belize City cost between BZ$80 and BZ$160. Full-day tours can be combined with visits to Crooked Tree Wildlife Sanctuary (see "En Route North: Crooked Tree Wildlife Sanctuary," below) or the Community Baboon Sanctuary (see "What to See & Do" in chapter 6), and should run between BZ$150 and BZ$280. Many of the tours include lunch and an optional spa treatment at Maruba Resort Jungle Spa.

An Isolated Jungle Spa

Maruba Resort Jungle Spa ★★ 🎁 Decadent, sensual, and exotic are words often used to describe this boutique resort, and for good reason. The whole place is an imaginative jungle fantasy where health, hedonism, and happiness are the primary goals. The accommodations are a collection of uniquely designed and decorated rooms and private villas, set in a patch of densely planted gardens and forest. Artistic touches abound and range from the many interesting architectural details to the eclectic mix of decorations and furnishings from Africa, Asia, the Caribbean, the Middle East, and, of course, Belize. The best rooms here are the private suites. The standard rooms are certainly up to snuff, but I think it's worth the splurge for one of the suites.

There are two outdoor pools here, as well as a separate hot mineral pool. The spa facilities and services are wonderfully done. The Mood Mud Massage is their signature offering, and I highly recommend it. The food at the restaurant here is excellent, featuring a creative mix of international and fusion cuisine. This place is popular with day-trippers from the cayes and Belize City, as well as cruise-ship passengers. Luckily, one of the pools is reserved for hotel guests, and once the day tours clear out, you'll have the place to yourself. In addition to the spa treatments, a host of tours, activities, and adventures is offered here. If you're in the mood for some serious imbibing, don't miss a taste of their home-brewed Viper Rum and Scorpion Stinger.

Old Northern Hwy., Mile Marker 40½, Maskall Village. © **800/627-8227** in the U.S., or 225-5555 in Belize. Fax 225-5506. www.maruba-belize.com. 18 units. BZ$310 double; BZ$378 junior suite; BZ$630 suite. AE, MC, V. **Amenities:** Restaurant; bar; lounge; 2 outdoor pools; spa; free Wi-Fi. *In room:* A/C, hair dryer, no phone.

EN ROUTE NORTH: CROOKED TREE WILDLIFE SANCTUARY ★

53km (33 miles) NW of Belize City

Crooked Tree Wildlife Sanctuary is a swampy lowland that is home to more than 260 resident species of birds and serves as a resting spot for scores of migratory species. During a visit here, you are sure to spot any number of interesting water birds, including kites, hawks, ducks, grebes, pelicans, ospreys, egrets, and herons. However, the preserve was established primarily to protect Belize's main nesting site of the endangered jabiru stork, the largest bird in the Western Hemisphere. The jabirus arrive every November and pass the winter in these warm lowland climes. The jabiru is an impressive bird, standing nearly 1.5m (5 ft.) tall, with a wingspan that can reach up to 3.7m (12 ft.). Crooked Tree has rapidly become known as an excellent place to spot other endangered wildlife as well. Crocodiles, iguanas, coati-mundi, and howler monkeys are all frequently sighted. There are six major lagoons here connected by a series of creeks, rivers, and wetlands.

The small Creole village of Crooked Tree is the gateway to this wildlife sanctuary. The village is reputed to be some 300 years old, and one of the oldest ongoing settlements in Belize. If you poke around, in addition to the sanctuary's visitor center, you'll find the church, the school, the soccer field, a few general stores, and a couple of simple guest houses.

The best way to explore the preserve is by dugout canoe. Ask in town or at the visitor center and administrative building for a local who will paddle you around in a dugout for a few hours. The going rate is around BZ$20 to BZ$40 per person for a 2- to 3-hour paddle tour of the lagoons. Or, if you're in the mood for a little exercise, Bird's Eye View Lodge (see below) offers canoe rental for BZ$10 per person per hour. If you're looking for a good local bird guide, contact **Sam Tillet** (© **220-7026;** www.crookedtreebelize.com), who also runs a simple guest house. All visitors must first register at the visitor center and pay the BZ$8 admission fee. The Crooked

Tree Wildlife Sanctuary was set up and is still administered by the **Belize Audubon Society** (✆ **223-5004;** www.belizeaudubon.org).

If you'd like to spend the night, accommodations can be arranged with a local family for around BZ$30 to BZ$80 double occupancy. Meals should run you an additional BZ$30 to BZ$50 per person per day. Or, if you want to stay in a comfortable lodge right on the edge of a lagoon, check out the **Bird's Eye View Lodge** ★ (✆ **225-7027;** www.birdseyeviewlodge.com), where a double costs between BZ$160 and BZ$240.

Crooked Tree is located 53km (33 miles) northwest of Belize City. If you are driving, head up the Northern Highway and watch for the turnoff to Crooked Tree. From the turnoff, it's another 4.8km (3 miles) on a well-graded dirt road.

Jex & Sons (✆ **225-7017**) direct buses leave for Crooked Tree Village Monday through Saturday from a bus terminal on Regent Street West in Belize City at 10:50am; Monday through Friday from a terminal at Pound Yard Bridge at 5:15pm; and from Crooked Tree for Belize City at 6:30 and 7am. The fare is BZ$7 each way. Alternatively, you can take any bus heading to Orange Walk Town, Corozal, or the northern border and ask to be dropped off at the entrance to Crooked Tree. From here you'll have to walk or hitchhike, or get really lucky and find a cab patrolling around. If you're staying at a hotel in the village, they will usually pick you up.

Half-day tours to Crooked Tree from Belize City or the northern cayes cost between BZ$80 and BZ$160. A full-day trip combining Crooked Tree and Altun Ha, including transportation, guide, and lunch, should cost between BZ$160 and BZ$300.

> ### Going Nuts
>
> Crooked Tree is also home to a thriving cashew industry. Each year during the first weekend of May, Crooked Tree village hosts its annual Cashew Festival, where you can sample raw and roasted nuts and taste some cashew wine, cashew jelly, and a whole plethora of dishes cooked around or including the local nut.

ORANGE WALK TOWN

89km (55 miles) N of Belize City; 50km (31 miles) S of Corozal

Between Belize City and Corozal Town, the only settlement of any size is Orange Walk Town, a bustling agricultural and business community with a population of some 18,000. This is the heart of Belize's sugar cane industry, and some locals still call the town "Sugar City." Originally called Holpatin by the ancient Maya, the town's riverside location has ensured its status as a trade center for more than 2,000 years. The town's current name comes from the many citrus groves once planted alongside the New River here. Orange Walk Town's residents are a very heterogeneous mix of mestizos, Mayans, Chinese, and Black Creoles. There's not too much of interest to travelers in the town, but this is the gateway to several of

> ### What's in a Name?
>
> "Orange walk" is the Creole term for "orange orchard" or "orange grove," just as "sugar walk" would be the Creole version of "sugar plantation."

the surrounding attractions of note, including the Lamanai ruins and the Río Bravo Conservation Area to the west.

Essentials

GETTING THERE & DEPARTING

BY PLANE Although there's a small airstrip here, no regularly scheduled commuter traffic arrives in Orange Walk Town. The closest active airports are those in Corozal Town (see "Corozal Town," later in this chapter) and the Philip S. W. Goldson International Airport outside of Belize City (see chapter 6).

BY CAR Orange Walk is on the Northern Highway about 89km (55 miles) from Belize City. Take Freetown Road out of Belize City to connect with the Northern Highway. The highway is also known in this area as the Belize-Corozal Road, and Queen Victoria Avenue right in the heart of town. After passing through the small downtown section of Orange Walk Town, the highway continues north to Corozal.

There's a tollbooth where the Northern Highway crosses the New River a few miles south of Orange Walk Town. The fee is BZ75¢ per car.

BY BUS Buses (© 227-2255 in Belize City, or 302-2858 in Orange Walk Town) leave throughout the day, roughly every half-hour between 5:30am and 7:30pm. Morning buses leave from the main bus terminal on West Collet Canal Street. Catch any

mennonites IN BELIZE

Mennonites are a Protestant branch of the 16th-century Anabaptist movement, which also gave birth to the Amish and Hutterites. Believing that the New Testament is the sole word of God and that children should not be baptized, the Mennonites also believe that true Christians should not hold political or public office or serve in the military. Modern Mennonites are somewhat split as to the use of electricity and the internal combustion engine.

Mennonites get their name from Menno Simons, a Dutch Catholic priest who converted to Anabaptism and went on to lead the budding movement. From the start, the Anabaptists were severely persecuted and repeatedly forced into exile. Mennonites first migrated to Belize from Mexico in 1958. While the initial wave of immigrants was small, the Mennonites quickly settled in, buying large tracts of land and establishing very successful dairy

farming and agricultural enterprises. The early Mennonite settlers were successful in negotiating certain strategic concessions and guarantees from the government, including that of religious freedom and exemption from military service and some forms of taxation.

While there are Mennonites throughout Belize, the Orange Walk District and northern Belize have one of the highest concentrations in the country, with large communities in Shipyard, Blue Creek Village, Little Belize, and Spanish Lookout. Most Mennonites, even in Belize, speak an archaic form of German. They are easily recognized, with their fair skin and blond hair, especially when they're traveling in their low-riding, horse-drawn carriages. The women often wear puffy cloth bonnets and simple cotton dresses, while the men sport broad-rimmed straw hats, dark jeans, and distinctive full beards with no moustache.

Orange Walk Town

ACCOMMODATIONS ■
D*Victoria Hotel **7**
Hotel De La Fuente **4**
St. Christopher's Hotel **3**

DINING ◆
El Establo Bar & Grill **1**
Nahil Mayab Restaurant **6**

ATTRACTIONS ●
Banquitas House of
  Culture **2**
La Inmaculada Church **5**

bus going to Corozal Town or Chetumal. The Orange Walk Town bus station is right on the Northern Highway in the center of town near Town Hall. You can pick up a return bus here to Belize City, or continue onward to Corozal. Buses can be either direct or local, and they vary in age and comfort. You'll pay more for a comfortable direct or express bus. The fare is BZ$5 to BZ$8 between Belize City and Orange Walk Town, and BZ$6 to BZ$10 between Orange Walk Town and Corozal Town.

GETTING AROUND
Orange Walk is pretty compact, and the city center is just a few blocks wide in either direction. Still, a few taxis can be had around town. If you can't flag one down, call ✆ **322-2050,** or head to the little park across from Town Hall.

ORIENTATION
The Northern Highway runs right through the heart of Orange Walk Town. However, there is also a bypass that skirts the city proper, for those in a rush to get to Corozal. Several gas stations are located on the outskirts of either end of town. As

you're traveling north, the New River and "downtown" district will be to your right, while the Town Hall and Sports Ground are on the highway, on your left.

FAST FACTS   If you need to call the **police,** dial ✆ **911** or 322-2022; for the **fire department,** dial ✆ **322-2090;** and for medical emergencies, call the **Northern Regional Hospital** at ✆ **322-2072.**

There's a **Belize Bank** (✆ **322-2019**) at the corner of Main and Park streets, and a **Scotia Bank** (✆ **322-0866**) down the block on the corner of Park Street and Lover's Lane. The **post office** (✆ **322-2345**) is located on the north end of Main Street.

Seeing the Sights

If you're staying in Orange Walk Town, you might want to visit the **Banquitas House of Culture,** at Main Street and Banquitas Plaza (✆ **322-0517**), which is set just off the river on some expansive and manicured grounds. The House of Culture itself features a small collection of artifacts and historic displays from the Mayan, logging, and colonial eras. There's also a small amphitheater here that very occasionally may have live music, theater, or dance. In the center of town you'll find **La Inmaculada Church** (✆ **322-2043**), one of the few colonial Spanish churches in the country.

You might also want to stop at **Godoy's Orchid Garden,** 4 Trial Farm Rd. (✆ **322-2969**). Commercial growers and exporters, the Godoy family also offers visitors a stunning and informative tour of their extensive collection.

Two of the most popular tours out of Orange Walk Town are to **Crooked Tree Wildlife Sanctuary** (see "En Route North: Crooked Tree Wildlife Sanctuary," earlier in this chapter) and the **Lamanai ruins** (see "The Submerged Crocodile: Lamanai," below).

If you're looking for some nearby outdoor adventure and a refreshing dip, head to **Honey Camp Lagoon,** which features an unlikely sandy beach ringed by palm trees next to a spring-fed freshwater swimming hole. Honey Camp Lagoon is located about a 20-minute drive south from Orange Walk Town, via the Old Northern Highway.

> **Fun Fact**
>
> The original Mayan name for the New River, Dzuilhuinicob, translates roughly as "River of Strange People."

If your hotel can't hook you up and you want a local guide for any of the aforementioned tours or trips to any of the nearby ruins or up to Lamanai (see below), call **J. Avila & Sons River Tours,** 42 Riverside St. (✆ **322-3068**), or **Jungle River Tours ★**, 20 Lovers Lane (✆ **302-2293**), which is run by the very personable and knowledgeable Wilfrido Novelo.

A COUPLE OF MINOR MAYAN SITES NEARBY

Cuello   This small site is located just more than 4.8km (3 miles) from Orange Walk Town, near the Cuello Rum Distillery. It is named after the family that owns the land and distillery, and permission to visit the site must be obtained in advance. While very small and little excavated, Cuello is nonetheless one of the oldest-known Mayan sites in Belize, showing evidence of occupation as far back as 2600 B.C., in the early Pre-Classic Period.

There are two main plazas on the site, surrounded by small temples and ceremonial structures. Very little has been excavated and restored so far. Evidence exists that this minor ceremonial city was razed on more than one occasion during distinct warring periods.

You can obtain permission to visit Cuello by stopping at the rum distillery at the entrance to the site, or by calling in advance (✆ 322-2183). If you ask, you will probably be able to get a quick tour of the distillery as well. You might also be able to arrange for a guided tour by asking around Orange Walk Town. To get here, take the San Antonio Road out of Orange Walk Town toward Yo Creek.

Noh Mul Noh Mul means "great mound," and this site boasts the largest Mayan structure in the Orange Walk District. Noh Mul was active in two distinct periods, the late Pre-Classic era from around 350 B.C. to A.D. 250, and during the late Classic era from A.D. 600 to 900. At the time, it was a major ceremonial center and supported a massive residential community that extended for nearly 21 sq. km (8 sq. miles). One of the more interesting features here is the fact that the two major ceremonial plazas are connected by a raised walkway, or *sacbe*. Crude excavation techniques, pillaging, and local agriculture have combined to limit the amount of restoration and conservation in evidence at Noh Mul.

Noh Mul is located about 1.6km (1 mile) west of the small village of San Pablo, which itself is about 14km (8⅔ miles) north of Orange Walk Town. Any nonexpress bus running the northern line to Corozal and Chetumal can drop you off at San Pablo. However, your best bet for visiting Noh Mul is to try to arrange a tour in advance in Orange Walk Town or Belize City. You should have permission to visit Noh Mul; to get permission in San Pablo, check in with **Esteban Itzab** (no phone), whose house is located across from the water tower in the heart of the village. There are no facilities on-site, so bring some food and water with you.

Where to Stay & Dine

There are few good dining options in Orange Walk Town. Your best bet is **Nahil Mayab Restaurant ★**, on the corner of Santa Ana and Guadalupe streets (✆ 322-0831; www.nahilmayab.com), an excellent all-purpose restaurant and bar serving a range of local dishes. The best seats here are located in a pretty garden patio, where you'll also find a small children's playground. These folks also offer free Wi-Fi. Another good option is **El Establo Bar & Grill,** Northern Highway (✆ 322-0094), a tidy roadside joint on the main highway just north of town.

INEXPENSIVE

D*Victoria Hotel For years, this was the hotel of choice in Orange Walk Town, but I much prefer the two newer options Hotel De La Fuente (see below) and St. Christopher's Hotel (see below). You'll still find spacious, clean rooms here, but the decor is definitely dated and the hotel sits right on the side of a dreary section of the Northern Highway. You'll also find a cool swimming pool with a tiled patio around it. The higher-priced rooms feature air-conditioning. The restaurant serves decent Belizean and Chinese food at reasonable prices. Between the raucous bar here on weekends and the everyday street noise, this is not exactly a quiet spot.

40 Belize-Corozal Rd., Orange Walk. ✆ **322-2518.** Fax 322-2847. www.dvictoriabelize.com. 31 units. BZ$60–BZ$90 double. Rates include taxes. MC, V. **Amenities:** Restaurant; bar; small outdoor pool; room service. *In room:* TV, no phone.

Hotel De La Fuente ★ This is easily the best hotel option in Orange Walk Town. Located just north of the St. Christopher, this place offers more amenities than any other hotel in town. Even the budget rooms here feature televisions, air-conditioning, free Wi-Fi, minifridges, and in-room coffeemakers. The pricier rooms are larger and come with a kitchenette.

14 Main St., Orange Walk. ℂ/fax **322-2290.** Fax 322-3651. www.hoteldelafuente.com. 22 units. BZ$70–BZ$140 double. MC, V. **Amenities:** All rooms smoke-free. *In room:* A/C, TV, minifridge, free Wi-Fi.

St. Christopher's Hotel Named after the patron saint of world wanderers, this is a dependable option in Orange Walk Town. The rooms and bathrooms are spacious, clean, and comfortable, and the hotel is on a quiet street, just up from the New River. Most of the rooms here have air-conditioning, although a few less expensive rooms come with just fans.

10 Main St., Orange Walk. ℂ/fax **302-1064** or 322-2420. www.stchristophershotelbze.com. 25 units. BZ$50–BZ$96 double. MC, V. *In room:* TV, no phone.

THE SUBMERGED CROCODILE: LAMANAI ★★

Lamanai is one of the more interesting and picturesque Maya ruins to visit in Belize. Set on the edge of the New River Lagoon, it is one of the largest Maya sites in Belize and features three large pyramids, a couple of residential areas, restored steles, and open plazas, as well as a small and unique ball court that featured a large round stone set flush in its center. In addition, nearby are the ruins of two churches built by the Spanish during the 16th century; just off these ruins are the rusting remains of an abandoned sugar mill, which was set up and settled by U.S. Confederate soldiers who chose exile after the Civil War.

Lamanai was occupied continuously from around 1500 B.C. until the Spanish arrived in the 16th century, and it supported non-Maya populations into the 19th century. Because it was still occupied by the Maya when the Spanish arrived, Lamanai is one of the few sites to retain its traditional name. Lamanai translates as "submerged crocodile" in Mayan; one of the principal rulers here was Lord Smoking Shell, who claimed he was the descendant of the spirit of a crocodile. Numerous crocodile images have been found in the steles, carvings, and pottery here. And there are still plenty of live crocs in the lagoon.

Lamanai was an important and powerful Pre-Classic trading city. As at Altun Ha, relics here can be traced to various cities throughout the early Mayan, Aztec, and Olmec worlds. It's a steep and scary climb to the top of the **High Temple,** but the view over the treetops and the lagoon is well worth it. The site's most striking feature just may be the **Mask Temple,** which features a series of 3.7m-high (12-ft.) stone-and-mortar faces set into its sides. One of these faces is well-restored and shows a distinct Olmec influence.

While many of the temples and ruins here have been cleared and restored to varying degrees, they are still surrounded by dense rainforest. The trails leading between temples offer excellent bird- and wildlife-watching opportunities.

There's a modern visitor center and museum here. The collection, though small, is quite interesting as it shows chronologically the distinct styles and influences present over the long history at Lamanai.

Lamanai is open daily from 8am to 4pm. Admission is BZ$10. Although you can drive or fly here, the most common and scenic way to reach Lamanai is via boat up the New River. A host of different boats leave from docks just south of Orange Walk. The trip on the river is an hour of naturalist heaven as you cruise between narrow and densely forested banks and alongside flooded marshes and wetlands. Eventually, the river opens onto the New River Lagoon, with the ancient Mayan city perched strategically atop some small limestone cliffs.

Most of the year it's possible to drive to Lamanai if you have a four-wheel-drive vehicle. During the heavy part of the rainy season, the road may become impassable. To drive here, take the Northern Highway into Orange Walk Town. Turn left near the center of town onto San Antonio Road. Follow signs to Yo Creek and San Felipe. There's an intersection at San Felipe; follow the signs to Indian Church and Lamanai. The total distance from Orange Walk Town is just about 48km (30 miles), but it will take you at least an hour to drive there on the rough dirt road. There's also a small airstrip in the neighboring village of Indian Church, and charter flights can be arranged through Lamanai Outpost Lodge.

With the rise in cruise-ship traffic, many of the new operators run massive speedboats between Orange Walk and Lamanai. Not only are these noisier and more impersonal, but they also remove almost all of the opportunity to enjoy the bird- and wildlife-viewing along the way. Be sure to try to book a smaller, slightly slower boat—you'll enjoy the trip much more.

While most folks either go on a guided tour or have a reservation at the Lamanai Outpost Lodge (see review below), you can drive yourself to the boat docks, just south of the Toll Hill Bridge over the New River a few miles before Orange Walk, and pick up a boat there. Expect to pay around BZ$70 to BZ$80 per person for a boat to take you upriver to the ruins and back. The boats tend to leave for Lamanai between 8 and 10am, returning between 2 and 5pm. Many are booked in advance by large tour groups, although it's almost always possible to find a few spaces available with a boat departing in short order. Parking is safe near the docks, and the boat companies will usually watch your car for free or a nominal fee. If you want to set up the trip in advance, I recommend you book with **Jungle River Tours ★**, 20 Lovers Lane (𝄐 **302-2293**).

A Neighboring Nature Lodge

Lamanai Outpost Lodge ★★ 👔 This rustic yet very comfortable lodge is set on a gentle hillside on the banks of the New River, about a mile from the Lamanai ruins. The rooms here are all large and made of heavy local hardwoods, with high thatch roofs. A ceiling fan is all you have—and all you will need—to cool things off. All the rooms have a private or semiprivate balcony or veranda; most of which come with a hammock all ready for your afternoon siesta. While all the rooms are very similar in comfort and design, you'll want to ask for a riverfront room to be able to catch the sunrise from your front porch. A wide range of tours and activities is available here, and the guides are excellent. Down by the river there's a swimming and sunbathing dock. There are also canoes here that guests can take out on the New River at any time.

Indian Church Village, on the New River (P.O. Box 63, Orange Walk). 𝄐 **888/733-7864** in the U.S., or 672-2000 in Belize. Fax 727/864-4062 in the U.S. www.lamanai.com. 20 units. BZ$292–BZ$680 double. Rates include tax. Multiday and all-inclusive packages available. AE, MC, V. **Amenities:** Restaurant; bar; lounge; smoke-free rooms; free Wi-Fi. *In room:* Minifridge, no phone.

GOING WEST

The far western section of Orange Walk District is a wild area of virgin forest, remote farmlands, and underexplored Mayan ruins. It is also home to one of the country's premier and most unique nature lodges, Chan Chich Lodge.

Río Bravo Conservation Area ★

Administered by the nonprofit **Programme for Belize,** this 105,218-hectare (260,000-acre) tract is a mix of virgin forest, sustainable-yield managed forest, and recovering reforestation areas. The goal of the project is to combine sustainable management techniques with educational and tourism uses in a model that can prove the practical benefits of forest preservation and conservation. The land is home to nearly 400 bird species and more than 200 species of tropical trees. It also supports a healthy population of most of the new-world cat species, and is one of the best areas in the Americas for spotting a jaguar—although these sightings are far from common or easy to come by.

LA MILPA ★

Located inside the Río Bravo Conservation Area, La Milpa is the third-largest Mayan site in Belize, behind Caracol and Lamanai. Enshrouded in jungle and just barely beginning to be excavated, La Milpa is a great site for budding archaeologists and those looking for a sense of what it must have been like to discover and begin uncovering an ancient Mayan city. Set on a high ridge, La Milpa was once a great ceremonial city. So far, at least one **Great Plaza,** numerous smaller plazas and courtyards, and two ball courts have been uncovered. The main plaza is one of the largest such public spaces yet discovered in the Mayan world. Polychrome pottery from various periods as well as numerous carved steles have been uncovered. In 1996, excavation of a royal tomb here revealed a male skeleton buried with an elaborate and beautiful jeweled necklace. Ongoing archaeological research is being led by Boston University, in conjunction with the National Geographic Society and Programme for Belize.

A visit to La Milpa ruins is usually combined with a stay at **La Milpa Field Station** (see below), although it is possible to do it as a day trip from Orange Walk or on your way driving to or from Chan Chich Lodge. In any event, you will need permission and a reserved guide arranged in advance by calling the **Programme for Belize** (✆ **227-5616;** www.pfbelize.org).

Where to Stay

INSIDE RIO BRAVO

La Milpa Field Station   Run by the Programme for Belize, this simple lodge is located in the heart of the wild Río Bravo Conservation Area and just 4.8km (3 miles) from La Milpa ruins. This working biological and archaeological field station also offers rooms, meals, and tours for travelers, students, and volunteers. The private thatch-roof cabins, while still relatively rustic, feature private bathrooms and a sense of being at a more typical nature lodge. For their part, the dormitory rooms and shared bathrooms are kept quite clean, and would certainly please even the most discerning backpacker or budget traveler. The dorm rooms and shared bathrooms use solar power and high-tech composting toilets. Guided tours are always available, and educational packages, sometimes including fieldwork, are often offered.

La Milpa section of Río Bravo Conservation Area, Orange Walk district. ✆ **227-5616.** Fax 227-5635. www.pfbelize.org. 8 double-room cabins, 30 dormitory beds. BZ$300 per person for cabins; BZ$260 per person for dormitories. Rates, based on double occupancy, include 3 meals, taxes, and 2 guided tours daily. MC, V. **Amenities:** Restaurant; lounge; smoke-free rooms. In room: No phone.

RUINS OF YOUR OWN

Chan Chich Lodge ★★ 🛈🛈   Set in the central plaza of a small Mayan ceremonial city, Chan Chich is one of the most unusual jungle lodges in Mesoamerica. The low hills that surround 12 individual bungalows are all unexcavated pyramids and temples. The rooms feature high-pitched thatch roofs and wraparound wooden decks, and are all spacious, clean, and quite comfortable. Most come with two queen beds made up with heavy comforters and lots of pillows. My only complaint is that given the restricted size of the central plaza, most of the bungalows are quite close to each other. The deluxe bungalows are slightly larger, especially in the bathroom area, and feature king-size beds and some Japanese-style decor. There's also a luxurious two-bedroom villa, with its own Jacuzzi and expansive living areas, well suited for families.

Behind one of the overgrown temple mounds, there's a screened-in pool and Jacuzzi area with its own bar. Some 14km (8.65 miles) of well-groomed trails lead off from the central plaza, and a host of guided tours and hikes is available. Wildlife viewing here is excellent, with more than 350 bird species identified nearby. They also claim to average 50 to 80 daylight jaguar sightings per year. You can go horseback riding, visit nearby agricultural communities, or canoe and swim at Laguna Verde. Day trips to Lamanai, La Milpa, and other Mayan sites can also be arranged. The food here is excellent, which is a good thing, since you have no other options.

Gallon Jug, Orange Walk District (P.O. Box 37, Belize City). ©/ **800/343-8009** in the U.S., or ©/fax 223-4419 in Belize. www.chanchich.com. 13 units. BZ$500–BZ$600 double; BZ$1,790 villa. Rates lower in the off season. A meal package will run you an extra BZ$140 per day. Multiday all-inclusive packages are available. AE, MC, V. You can either drive here or take a charter flight to nearby Gallon Jug; if you choose the charter, Chan Chich can arrange the flight and pick you up at the airport. If you choose to drive, it takes about 4 hr. from Belize City, much of it on dirt roads, so a 4-wheel-drive vehicle is recommended. If you are driving here, you will need permission to pass through the Programme for Belize's lands; call the lodge in advance to arrange this. **Amenities:** Restaurant; bar; lounge; Jacuzzi; small pool; smoke-free rooms. *In room:* No phone.

barry bowen, BELIKIN BEER, COCA-COLA & CHAN CHICH

Building a modern nature lodge in the central plaza of an ancient Mayan ceremonial city is bound to be controversial. Some see it as a desecration and outrage. However, most recognize that the construction and operation of Chan Chich Lodge has served as an important safeguard against looters, and a strong tool for raising awareness and money to support conservation and excavation efforts.

First discovered in 1938 by J. Eric Thompson, the site was originally named Kaxil Uinic, before being renamed by Barry Bowen in 1987. Bowen, owner of the Belikin Beer company and exclusive distributor for Coca-Cola in Belize, bought more than 303,514 hectares (750,000 acres) of land (about one-sixth of the country) in the western Orange Walk District in 1984. When Bowen and his workers rediscovered Chan Chich, the site had been severely looted, and many of the mounds and temples showed signs of active looting trenches.

Chan Chich sits on some 101,171 hectares (250,000 acres) of private reserve, and is bordered to the north by the 106,028 hectares (262,000 acres) of the Río Bravo Conservation Area. Since Bowen bought the land, a total hunting ban has been enacted, and if these protected lands are connected to the Kalakmul Reserve in Mexico and the Maya Biosphere Reserve in Guatemala, they may one day form a major Mesoamerican environmental and archaeological megareserve spanning three countries.

In February 2010, Bowen was killed, when the small plane he was piloting crashed just before landing in San Pedro.

COROZAL TOWN

13km (8 miles) N of Belize City; 50km (31 miles) N of Orange Walk Town; 13km (8 miles) S of the Mexican border

Corozal is a quiet seaside town, located just south of the Río Hondo (Hondo River), which forms the border between Mexico and Belize. Set on a crystal-clear bay, Corozal was an important point on the early Mayan trading routes, and the evidence remains in the ruins of **Cerros** and **Santa Rita.** During the mid-1800s the modern town was settled with a large population of refugees from Mexico's Caste War. In 1955, Hurricane Janet paid a visit and left few of the town's wooden buildings standing. The rebuilding relied heavily on cement and cinderblock construction. Today, Corozal is home to a growing expatriate community. While not part of the traditional tourist circuit, Corozal Town makes a good base for fishing excursions in the calm bay; bird- and wildlife-viewing tours into nearby **Shipstern Nature Reserve;** shopping trips to neighboring **Chetumal, Mexico;** and explorations of the aforementioned Mayan ruins. New attractions in this area are a couple of swank casinos and shopping centers located just on the Belizean side of the Mexico–Belize border.

Essentials

GETTING THERE & DEPARTING

BY PLANE   Most flights to and from Corozal Airport connect through San Pedro Airport on Ambergris Caye. There are numerous flights connecting San Pedro to both of Belize City's airports, as well as other destinations around the country.

Maya Island Air (© 223-1140 in Belize City, or 422-2333 in Corozal; www. mayaairways.com) has daily flights between Corozal and San Pedro, leaving San Pedro at 7 and 10am and at 2 and 4:30pm, and returning at 7:30 and 10:30am and at 2:30 and 5pm.

Tropic Air (© 800/422-3435 in the U.S. or Canada, 226-2012 in Belize City, or 422-0356 in Corozal; www.tropicair.com) has direct flights between San Pedro and Corozal, leaving every 2 hours between 7am and 5pm. The flights return to San Pedro following a similar schedule between 7:30am and 5:30pm.

On both airlines, the flight duration is 25 minutes, and the fare is BZ$95 each way.

See chapters 6 and 7 for more information on flights between San Pedro and Belize City, and other destinations around the country.

BY CAR   Corozal Town is the last town on the Northern Highway before you reach the Mexican border. Take Freetown Road out of Belize City to connect with the Northern Highway. If you're driving in from Mexico, you'll reach a fork in the road 4.8km (3 miles) from the border; bear left and follow the signs to reach Corozal Town.

BY BUS   Buses (© 227-2255 in Belize City, or 402-3034 in Corozal) leave Belize City for Corozal and the Mexican border throughout the day, roughly every half-hour between 5:30am and 7:30pm from the main terminal on West Collet Canal Street. Catch any bus going to Corozal Town or Chetumal. The Corozal Town bus station is located 2 blocks west of the small central plaza and Town Hall. You can pick up a return bus here to Belize City, or onward to the Mexican border and Chetumal. The fare is BZ$16 to BZ$20 between Belize City and Corozal Town, BZ$6 to BZ$10 between Orange Walk Town and Corozal Town, and around BZ$6 between Chetumal and Corozal Town.

BY BOAT   The *Thunderbolt* (☎ 226-2904 in San Pedro, or 422-0026) has two daily boats running between San Pedro on Ambergris Caye and Corozal. The boats leave each destination at 7am and 3pm and cross paths about midway. The trip takes around 90 minutes. Fare is BZ$60 one-way.

GETTING AROUND

Corozal Town is very compact, and it's easy to walk anywhere in the entire downtown and waterfront areas. However, if it's just too hot, you're too tired, or you're heading farther afield, you can have your hotel call a taxi. Or try **Corozal Bus Terminal Taxi Union** (☎ 422-3194) or **Corozal Taxi Association** (☎ 422-2035).

If you're looking to rent a car up here, contact **Corozal Car Rentals** (☎ 422-3339; www.corozalcars.com).

ORIENTATION

Corozal is located right on a beautiful section of Corozal Bay. The town is laid out more or less in a grid, with avenues running roughly north–south and streets running east–west. The avenues run up numerically in order beginning with the waterfront 1st Avenue. The streets run in parallel but separate numerical order north and south from the town's central plaza, so that 3rd Street North and 3rd Street South are two distinct roads, one located 3 blocks north of the central plaza, the other 3 blocks south. The Northern Highway from Belize City and Orange Walk enters the town from the south. If you bear right and stay close to the water, you will be on 1st Avenue. If you bear left, you will be on 7th Avenue, the town's busiest thoroughfare, which skirts the western edge of downtown before passing the bus terminal and continuing on to Chetumal and the Mexican border.

The **post office** (☎ 422-2462) and Town Hall front the small central plaza. Most banks and businesses are within a 2-block radius in either direction.

FAST FACTS   If you need to call the **police,** dial ☎ 911 or 422-2202; for the **fire department,** dial ☎ 422-2105; and for medical emergencies, call the **Corozal Hospital** at ☎ 422-2076.

There are several banks in Corozal Town: **Atlantic Bank,** 1 Park St. (☎ 422-3473); **Scotiabank,** 4th Avenue (☎ 422-2322); and **Belize Bank,** 5th Avenue and 1st Street South (☎ 422-2087). All of these change U.S. dollars, Belize dollars, and Mexican pesos, as well as provide cash advances on your credit card.

If your hotel doesn't have a tour desk or good connections, and you want to visit any of the sites mentioned below or take an organized tour in this region, call **Belize VIP Transfer & Tours** (☎ 422-2725; www.belizetransfers.com).

What to See & Do

There isn't much to see or do in Corozal Town. It's mostly just a stopping point for weary travelers. However, it sits on the shores of a pretty, quiet bay with amazing turquoise-blue water that is officially the **Bay of Chetumal,** but locally dubbed **Corozal Bay.** If you want to split hairs, the small bay just off Corozal Town could be considered a separate entity from the larger Bay of Chetumal that it sits in.

If you've just come from Mexico, you can take a day or two to walk around town and marvel at the difference between Mexican culture and Belizean culture. The countries are so close and yet worlds apart. Belize is truly a Caribbean country, with frame houses built on high stilts to provide coolness, protection from floods, and shade for sitting.

Corozal Town

ACCOMMODATIONS ■

Almond Tree Hotel Resort **8**
Casa Blanca Hotel **1**
Copa Banana **8**
Corozal Bay Inn **7**
Hok'ol K'in Guesthouse **5**
Mirador Hotel **3**
Tony's Inn & Beach Resort **6**

DINING ◆

Cactus Plaza **5**
Patty's Bistro **2**
Y-Not Bar & Grill **6**

↖ To Santa Rita and
Mexican border

Bus station ■

Town Hall ■

Pier

Bay of Chetumal
(Corozal Bay)

To
Corozal
← Airport

0   1/10 mile
0   100 meters

ⓘ Information
🅿 Police
✉ Post office

Corozal Town

Belize City ●
⊛
Belalmopan

B E L I Z E

The heart of Corozal Town is the small plaza between 1st Street North and 1st Street South and 4th and 5th avenues. This is a good place to grab a bench and watch the locals go about their daily business. However, if you want a really inviting park bench, I recommend heading a couple of blocks east to tiny parks and public lands you'll find all along the bayfront.

MAYAN RUINS

If you haven't yet had your fill of Mayan ruins, there are a couple to visit in the area. If you look across the water from the shore in Corozal Town, you can see **Cerros** or **Cerro Maya** on the far side of the Bay of Chetumal. "Cerro" means hill in Spanish, and the site is that little bump in the forest you can see across the bay. (Up close it seems much larger.) Cerros was an important coastal trading center during the late Pre-Classic Period. Some of the remains of this city are now under the waters of the bay, but there's still a 21m-tall (69-ft.) **pyramid** built right on the water's edge that you can climb for a wonderful view of the bay. Ask around town to find someone willing to take you by boat to the ruins. Or you can drive, by heading out of town to the south and catching the free ferry across the New River; this will connect you with the road to Cerros.

Right on the outskirts of town, you'll find some of the remains of another ancient city many believe was the Mayan trading center of **Chactemal (Chetumal).** It is currently called **Santa Rita.** Corozal Town is actually built on the ruins of Santa Rita, which was an important late Post-Classic Mayan town and was still occupied at the time of the Spanish Conquest. The only excavated building is a small temple across the street from the Coca-Cola bottling plant. To reach it, head north past the bus station and about a kilometer (⅔ mile) later, at the sharp curve to the right, take the road straight ahead that leads up a hill. You'll see the building 1 block over to the right.

TWO NEARBY NATURE RESERVES

Bird-watchers and naturalists will want to visit the nearby **Shipstern Nature Reserve ★** (www.shipstern.org). The reserve's 8,903 hectares (22,000 acres) protect a variety of distinct ecosystems and a wealth of flora and fauna. Managed by the Swiss International Tropical Conservation Foundation, Shipstern Nature Reserve is home to more than 250 bird species, and its mangroves, lagoons, and flat wetlands are excellent bird-watching sites. The massive network of lagoons and wetlands is home to manatees and Morelet's crocodiles. The reserve also has lowland tropical dry forest unique to Belize, as well as a butterfly breeding project. The reserve is open daily from 8am to 4pm. Admission is BZ$10 per person and includes a short guided hike. It is possible to spend the night in some simple accommodations or pitch a tent inside of Shipstern Nature Reserve; rates are around BZ$30 to BZ$40 per person for a room and BZ$10 per person for camping. There's no restaurant here, but kitchen facilities are available at the rooms. To make a reservation, call the ranger station at ⓒ **423-2247.**

Tip: The wetlands here are a major insect breeding ground. This is a bonanza for the birds and bats, but you might want to bring along plenty of insect repellent, and probably lightweight long-sleeved shirts and pants.

Five kilometers (3.1 miles) beyond Shipstern Nature Reserve, on the edge of the peninsula, lies the tiny lobster and fishing community of **Sarteneja.** In Sarteneja, the best place to stay is **Fernando's Seaside Guesthouse** (ⓒ **423-2085;** www.cybercayecaulker.com/sarteneja.html). Fernando is an excellent guide, and he can arrange everything from fishing or snorkeling trips to Mayan ruin excursions and night tours of the Shipstern Nature Reserve.

To drive to Shipstern Nature Reserve and Sarteneja, you used to have to first drive down to Orange Walk Town and take the Sarteneja Highway through San Estevan and Little Belize. There is now another route that cuts some time and distance off this trip. Heading south out of Corozal, stick close to the bay. Just outside of Corozal, take the small barge ferry over the New River, which then connects to the roads to Copper Bank, Progresso, Shipstern, and on to Sarteneja.

Several buses daily connect Shipstern Nature Reserve and Sarteneja to Orange Walk, Corozal Town, Chetumal, and Belize City. Alternatively, you can hitch a ride on the *Thunderbolt* (see "By Boat" under "Essentials," above) heading to San Pedro, or hire a boat on the docks in Corozal for around BZ$160. The price is for the entire boat, and most boats can carry as many as 10 passengers.

The **Bacalar Chico National Park & Marine Reserve** lies about an hour's boat ride away from Corozal Town. This is a great spot for snorkeling and wildlife

CROSSING INTO mexico

While Corozal Town is a sleepy little burg with a village feel to it, Chetumal, its nearby Mexican neighbor, is a small, bustling border city with a lively shopping and nightlife scene. Chetumal is also the gateway to the beaches and Mayan ruins of the Yucatán Peninsula.

Chetumal is the capital of Quintana Roo, the Mexican state that makes up much of the Yucatán Peninsula, and is home to the resort towns of Cancún, Cozumel, Playa del Carmen, and Isla Mujeres, as well as the Mayan sites of Tulúm and Cobá.

Most Belizeans come to Chetumal to take advantage of the town's "free zone," an area with scores of duty-free shops, modern multiplex cinemas, restaurants, and a couple of casinos. You can also visit the **Museo de la Cultura Maya** ★, Avenida de los Héroes, between avenidas Colón and Ghandi (© **983/832-6838**), which offers a much more extensive museum representation of Mayan history, art, and archaeology than you will find anywhere in Belize. The museum is open Tuesday through Sunday from 9am to 7pm (it stays open 1 hr. later Fri–Sat). Admission is around US$4.

Just 40km (25 miles) north of Chetumal lies the beautiful **Bacalar Lagoon.**

This natural area is also known as Las Lagunas de los Siete Colores (The Lagoons of Seven Colors), and is a good place to have lunch and admire the views.

Frequent buses run between Corozal and Chetumal. The ride takes about 1 hour, including the formalities of the border crossing. The actual border is at the Belizean city of Santa Elena on the Hondo River, 13km (8 miles) north of Corozal Town. You don't need a visa in advance, but you will have to pay BZ$38 in departure fees. The bus fare runs around BZ$12 one-way.

Alternatively, you can head to Chetumal by boat, a quick 10-minute hop away. If you depart Belize by boat, your departure fee is just BZ$7.50.

Tip: Your best bet for changing money from U.S. or Belize dollars into Mexican pesos are the money-changers on the Belize side. Alternatively, there's widespread compatibility between ATMs in Chetumal and other Mexican destinations and most PLUS and Cirrus debit and credit cards.

For more on the area, pick up a copy of *Frommer's Cancún, Cozumel & the Yucatán* or *Frommer's Mexico.*

viewing. Ask around town or at the docks; you should be able to hire a boat for around BZ$240 to BZ$300, and the snorkeling equipment and a bag lunch will probably run an extra BZ$30 to BZ$50 per person. For more information on Bacalar Chico National Park & Marine Reserve, see chapter 7.

Where to Stay

MODERATE

Almond Tree Hotel Resort ★★   Located right on the water, toward the southern end of Bayshore Drive, sometimes referred to as "Gringo Lane," this small hotel has the best rooms and pool in town. All of the rooms are on the second floor, and feature Mexican-tile floors and high ceilings. Half of them come with televisions, and two feature fridges. The pool is set amid well-tended and flowering gardens, and there's also a small patch of beach on the bay side.

Bayshore Dr., Corozal District. ✆ **628-9224.** www.almondtreeresort.com. 6 units. BZ$170–BZ$250 double. MC, V. **Amenities:** Restaurant; outdoor pool; smoke-free rooms. *In room:* A/C, no phone, free Wi-Fi.

Casa Blanca Hotel   This is a good place to come if you really want to get away from it all. Casa Blanca is located in Consejo Village, a small retirement and vacation community located on Corozal Bay about 11km (7 miles) north of Corozal Town. All of the rooms are located on the second floor. The doors are all hand-carved with Mayan motifs in local mahogany. The restaurant serves good American, Belizean, and international fare. The best things here are a couple of large thatch palapas built fronting a long dock that juts out into the bay. Here you'll find hammocks, and tables and chairs; either option is well-suited for hanging out in the cool shade and reading a book or watching the water.

Consejo Village (P.O. Box 212), Corozal District. ✆ **423-1018.** Fax 423-1003. www.casablancabelize. com. 10 units. BZ$150–BZ$190 double; BZ$300 suite. AE, MC, V. **Amenities:** Restaurant. *In room:* A/C, TV, no phone.

Corozal Bay Inn   Ten individual thatch-roof cabins are spread around the grounds of this seaside hotel. If you're looking for amenities, this is the place to stay in Corozal. Each room has two double beds under mosquito netting, as well as a 27-inch flatscreen TV, and the entire grounds are wired for Wi-Fi. The bathrooms are large, and each room comes with a small refrigerator and a hand-painted Mexican ceramic sink in a nook off the main bedroom.

Bayshore Dr. (P.O. Box 1), Corozal Town. ✆ **442-2691.** Fax 800/836-9188 in the U.S. and Canada. 10 units. BZ$160 double. Rates include full breakfast. AE, MC, V. **Amenities:** Restaurant; outdoor pool. *In room:* A/C, TV, hair dryer, minifridge, no phone, free Wi-Fi.

Tony's Inn & Beach Resort ★   This beachfront hotel has long been the lodging and meeting place of choice in Corozal. The rooms are all housed in a two-story L-shaped building and feature clean tile floors, one king bed or two double beds, a small sitting area, and a 27-inch TV. The second-floor rooms are all nonsmoking and have a shared veranda overlooking a grassy garden area. As at the neighboring Corozal Bay Inn, there's a sandy area by the water's edge here that can sort of be considered a beach, although the best swimming is off the end of the private pier. The Y-Not Bar & Grill ★ (p. 219) serves lunch and dinner, and breakfast is served in a dining room just off the hotel lobby.

Bayshore Dr. (P.O. Box 12), Corozal Town. ✆ **800/447-2931** in the U.S. and Canada, or 442-2055. Fax 422-2829. www.tonysinn.com. 24 units. BZ$150–BZ$170 double. AE, MC, V. **Amenities:** Restaurant; bar; room service; free Wi-Fi. *In room:* A/C, TV, hair dryer.

INEXPENSIVE

Copa Banana ✐   The five suites here are actually located in two side-by-side residential-style homes. Each has a full-service communal kitchen for guest use, and if you take two or three (or five) rooms, you can have one or both of the houses to yourself. Rooms are clean, bright, and spacious, and come with either one queen bed or two twin beds. Several have sea views, although the hotel is located across a small street and vacant lot from the water. Both houses have large living rooms, and one has a dining room if you decide to cook dinner. Guests have free use of the hotel's bicycles, which is a nice plus.

409 Bayshore Dr. (P.O. Box 226), Corozal Town. ✆ **422-0284.** Fax 422-2710. www.copabanana.bz. 5 units. BZ$110 double. MC, V. **Amenities:** Complimentary bike use; all rooms smoke-free. *In room:* A/C, TV, no phone, free Wi-Fi.

Hok'ol K'in Guesthouse   There are a handful of budget hotels right in Corozal Town, but this is the best of the bunch. The rooms here are located in a two-story building located right across the street from the bay and its little seaside promenade. Rooms are simple and most are a bit cramped, but everything's kept sparkling clean. Those on the second floor have small private balconies, most with pretty sea views. Some of the rooms have air-conditioning, although you'll pay a little more for it. The restaurant here serves good American and Belizean fare at very reasonable prices.

89 4th Ave. (P.O. Box 145), Corozal Town. ✆ **442-3329.** Fax 422-3569. www.corozal.net. 11 units. BZ$94–BZ$110 double. MC, V. **Amenities:** Restaurant. *In room:* TV, no phone, free Wi-Fi.

Mirador Hotel ★   This hotel has a commanding location, fronting Corozal Bay in the heart of Corozal Town. The imposing four-story concrete building, with a curved facade, seems a bit out of place. Rooms are spotless and simply appointed. About half of the rooms face town, so be sure to request an oceanview or cornerview room. The best feature here is the large rooftop terrace, with a covered area hung with a couple of hammocks. The hotel's restaurant serves local and Chinese fare.

2nd St. S. and 4th Ave., Corozal Town. ✆ **442-0189.** www.mirador.bz. 24 units. BZ$70–BZ$80 double; BZ$100–BZ$180 double with A/C. AE, MC, V. **Amenities:** Restaurant; room service. *In room:* TV, free Wi-Fi.

Where to Dine

In addition to the places listed below, the restaurant at the **Almond Tree Resort** is also quite good, and a popular hangout for the local expatriate community.

MODERATE

Y-Not Bar & Grill ★ BELIZEAN/INTERNATIONAL   This open-air joint is the principal restaurant and bar at Tony's Inn & Beach Resort. It has a lovely setting on the water's edge under a high-pitched thatch roof. There's a loft area with seating in the main restaurant, but my favorite tables on a warm starry night are located on an uncovered little wooden deck built right over the water. Start things off with some coconut shrimp or conch fritters. The chicken and beef fajitas are the most popular items here, but if you want something more substantial, try a T-bone or rack of barbecue ribs. There's also always plenty of fresh seafood and shrimp served in a variety of sauces. I recommend the chipotle-glazed grouper.

At Tony's Inn & Beach Resort (p. 218), Corozal Bay Rd. ☎ **422-2055.** Main courses BZ$14–BZ$35. AE, MC, V. Daily 11am–11pm.

INEXPENSIVE

Cactus Plaza 🌶 MEXICAN   Serving basic Mexican fare in a pleasant open-air setting, this is perennially one of the most popular restaurants in Corozal Town. The menu here is simple: Get some tacos, tostados, or *salbutes* (a disk of fried cornmeal, somewhat thicker than a traditional tortilla, usually topped with some shredded chicken, refried beans, or a cabbage salad), and maybe a side of rice and beans. My favorite seats are on the canvas-shaded rooftop patio, although you can also grab a seat at the small counter or at heavy tables on the ground floor. On weekend nights, the bar here is pretty lively.

6 6th St. S. ☎ **422-0394.** Reservations not accepted. Main courses BZ$2–BZ$12. MC, V. Tues–Sun 11:30am–10pm.

Patty's Bistro ★★ 🌶 BELIZEAN/INTERNATIONAL   This quaint little joint is a local favorite for lunch, but it's also open for dinner and does a brisk business in takeout as well. The menu here ranges from Belizean staples such as stew chicken and *escabeche* (a local chicken soup) to coconut curry shrimp and chicken mole. Brave souls might start things off with the cow-foot soup, but I prefer the shrimp and conch ceviche. There are daily chalkboard specials. The air-conditioned dining room features yellow and salmon painted walls, kitschy art, and tables with table-cloths covered in plastic and set with Mexican or Guatemalan place mats.

13 4th Ave. ☎ **402-0174.** Reservations not accepted. Main courses BZ$8–BZ$15. MC, V. Daily 11am–9pm.

Corozal Town After Dark

Corozal Town is a pretty quiet place. If you're looking for anything resembling action, forget about it. If you want to meet some locals, fellow travelers, or expatriates, head to the bars at either **Tony's Inn & Beach Resort** (p. 218) or the **Corozal Bay Inn** (p. 218). They're side by side, so if one's not happening, you can just walk next door. On Friday and Saturday nights, you can also try the bar at **Cactus Plaza** (p. 220).

If you're in the mood to try your luck, head north of town to the free zone and hit the tables at the **Princess Casino** (☎ **423-7652**) or the **Golden Princess Casino** (☎ **423-7680**).

THE CAYO DISTRICT & WESTERN BELIZE

Western Belize, from the capital city of Belmopan to the Guatemalan border, is a land of rolling hills, dense jungles, abundant waterfalls, clear rivers, extensive caves, and numerous Maya ruins. This region was the heart of the Belizean Maya world, with the major ruins of **Caracol, Xunantunich,** and **El Pilar,** as well as lesser sites such as **Cahal Pech.** At the height of the Classic Maya Period, there were more residents in this area than in all of modern Belize.

Today, the area around Belmopan and extending throughout the Cayo District is the heart of Belize's ecotourism industry. There are a host of national parks and protected areas, including the **Guanacaste** and **Blue Hole National parks,** the **Mountain Pine Ridge Forest Reserve,** and the **Chiquibil National Park.** The pine forests and rainforests here are great for hiking and bird-watching; the rivers are excellent for canoeing, kayaking, and inner tubing; and the dirt roads are perfect for horseback riding and mountain biking.

The cave systems of the Cayo District were sacred to the ancient Maya, and many of them are open for exploration by budding and experienced spelunkers alike. Some of the more popular underground attractions include **Actun Tunichil Muknal, Barton Creek Cave, Chechem Ha, Crystal Cave,** and the **Río Frío Cave.** Of particular interest is the **Caves Branch River,** which provides the unique opportunity to float on an inner tube, kayak, or canoe through a series of caves.

The Western Highway runs through the heart of the Cayo District all the way to the Guatemalan border, and serves as the gateway to side trips into Guatemala's Petén Province and the majestic Mayan ruins of **Tikal** (see chapter 11).

BELMOPAN

84km (52 miles) W of Belize City; 32km (20 miles) E of San Ignacio; 161km (100 miles) NW of Placencia

Belmopan is a rather desultorily planned city and the official capital of Belize. After Hurricane Hattie devastated Belize City in 1961—not the first time a storm leveled or flooded the city—government officials figured enough was enough and decided to move the country's capital safely inland. A host of government buildings, including the National Assembly, are laid out according to a master plan, surrounded by residential areas, with everything connected by a ring road. Unfortunately, the planners who designed it didn't count on the people's resistance to moving here. Belmopan is an example of what happens when you build it and no one comes. In fact, many government workers make the daily commute from either Belize City or San Ignacio—both are easy rides on well-paved roads.

Unless you are coming to Belize on government business, you will probably want to avoid Belmopan entirely. However, if you are traveling around by bus, you will at least pass through it. If you get into town late at night, don't despair—you can easily spend the night and make an early onward connection in the morning. The area around Belmopan is chock-full of natural wonders, including **Guanacaste** and **Blue Hole National parks,** as well as the **Caves Branch River** and its network of hollowed-out limestone caves. There are also several very comfortable and interesting nature lodges in close proximity to Belmopan.

Essentials

GETTING THERE & DEPARTING

BY PLANE Tropic Air (© 800/422-3435 in the U.S. or Canada, or 226-2012 in Belize; www.tropicair.com) flies to Belmopan's small airport (BCV) Monday, Wednesday, and Friday. Flights leave from San Pedro at 8am and 3pm, but only the 3pm flight picks up passengers in Belize City. Return flights leave Belmopan at 9am and 4pm, and both of these will stop in Belize City if there's demand. One-way fares are BZ$95 between Belmopan and Belize Municipal Airport; BZ$126 between Belmopan and the Belize City International Airport; and BZ$165 between Belmopan and San Pedro.

BY CAR From Belize City, take Cemetery Road to the Western Highway. At Mile 50 you'll see the well-marked turnoff for the Hummingbird Highway and Belmopan. Turn left here and follow signs to the entrance to Belmopan, about 3.2km (2 miles) beyond the turnoff. It should take about 1 hour to drive from Belize City to Belmopan.

BY BUS Belmopan has very frequent bus service from Belize City. Nearly all buses heading west and south from Belize City stop in Belmopan. Buses to Belmopan leave roughly every half-hour from the main bus station on West Collet Canal Street between 5am and 7pm. Return buses to Belize City leave the main bus station in Belmopan about every half-hour between 5am and 7pm. The fare each way is BZ$6. The trip takes 1½ hours. From Belmopan, there are also frequent onward connections to Dangriga, Placencia, Punta Gorda, and other points south, as well as to San Ignacio, Benque Viejo, and the Guatemalan border.

GETTING AROUND

Belmopan is an extremely compact little city. You can easily walk to most places around the central hub. If you need a taxi, there are always taxis near the bus station and central market. Alternatively, you can call **Elvi's Taxi Service** (© 802-3732)

Western Belize

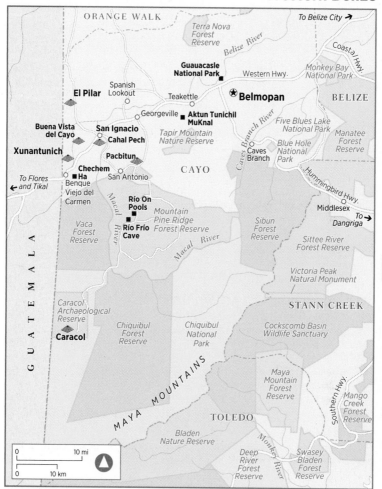

or **Market Square Taxi Service** (© 822-0371). A taxi ride anywhere in town should cost around BZ$6 to BZ$10.

ORIENTATION

Belmopan is a planned city with a ring road and broad streets. The city itself is located just off the Hummingbird (Southern) Highway, 3.2km (2 miles) south of the Western Highway. The bus station and small central market area are the heart of the town, and you will hit them soon after heading in off the highway. Within a 2-block radius, you'll find a couple of banks, two gas stations, and a few small strip malls. At the center of the city's radius, just off the market and bus station, is Independence

Plaza, which houses the post office and prime minister's office. Sidewalks cut through Independence Plaza in various directions, making most of downtown Belmopan easily accessible by foot.

FAST FACTS   All of the principal banks in town, **Atlantic Bank,** Garden City Plaza (② 822-0693), **Scotiabank,** Ring Road (② 822-1412), and **Belize Bank,** 60 Market Sq. (② 822-2341), are located close to the central market and bus station.

For the **police,** dial ② 911, or 822-2220; for the **fire department,** dial ② 822-2311. The **Belmopan Hospital** (② 822-2264) is located on Constitution Drive, a block north of its intersection with the North Ring Road.

The **Market Square Drug Store** (② 822-0045) is a well-stocked pharmacy located just off the Market Square.

What to See & Do

Perhaps the biggest attraction close to Belmopan is the **Belize Zoo,** Western Highway, Mile Marker 29 (② 220-8004; www.belizezoo.org). For more information on visiting the zoo, see p. 101.

If you're spending any time in Belmopan, it pays to see if anything is happening at the **George Price Centre for Peace & Development** (② 822-1054; www.gpcbelize.com). Primarily geared toward providing the local community with a library, classes, computer facilities, and meeting facilities, this place often hosts traveling art and museum exhibits, as well as movie showings, concerts, dance recitals, and theater performances.

Caves Branch River Cave System ★★★

The Caves Branch River is a gently flowing body of water coming down off the Mountain Pine Ridge. It really should be called a creek in most places. However, what makes the Caves Branch River unique is the fact that it flows in and out of a series of long limestone caves that are easily navigable on inner tubes and in kayaks.

There are two major entry points along the river for visits to the Caves Branch caves: One is at and around **Ian Anderson's Caves Branch** jungle lodge (p. 230), and the other is just above **Jaguar Paw,** a hotel built on the banks of the river. In general terms, travelers looking for more adventurous and extensive trips

---

The Underworld

The ancient Maya believed that caves were a mystical portal between the world of the living and the underworld of spirits and the dead. From their earliest days, there is evidence that the Mayans made extensive use of caves for ritual purposes, as well as for more mundane and rudimentary things such as keeping dry, storing grains, and gathering water. They called this mystical realm **Xibalba.**

Belize is literally riddled with caves. In almost every explored cave to date, some evidence of use by the Mayans has been uncovered. Fire pits, campsites, burial mounds, and ritual altars have all been found. Numerous pieces of pottery and abundant bones and artifacts have also been encountered. Belize offers many unique and easily accessible opportunities to explore this fascinating world, on foot, by kayak or canoe, or by floating on an inner tube. Don't miss it.

Belmopan

ACCOMMODATIONS ■
Belmopan Bed & Breakfast **7**
Bullfrog Inn **4**
El Rey Inn **3**
ATTRACTIONS ●
George Price Centre for
    Peace & Development **6**

DINING & NIGHTLIFE ◆
Bullfrog Inn Restaurant **4**
Chon Saan Palace **2**
Pasquale's Pizza
    & Wings **1**
Perk Up Coffee Shop **5**

($) Bank/ATM
✚ Hospital
(i) Information
P Police
✉ Post office

into the caves should head to Ian Anderson's place; those seeking a gentler tour into the underworld or who sign up for a guided excursion out of any of the country's major tourist centers will inevitably be doing the tour out of the Jaguar Paw entrance.

By far, most visitors either go directly through Jaguar Paw or use the same section of the river. There's a government-operated parking area about a kilometer (⅔ mile) downriver from Jaguar Paw and a host of operators running the tubing tour from here. Either way, you will have to hike upstream to a put-in. Depending on the tour you choose and the amount of hiking you want to do, you will eventually climb into your inner tube and begin a slow float through anywhere from one to four caves. You will be equipped with a headlamp and little else. If your group is small enough, I recommend you coordinate and all shut off your headlamps for a period of time. It's quite a spooky sensation to be floating in total darkness, wondering where the walls and ceilings are and whether you'll ever emerge into daylight again.

Most of the caves here contain Mayan pottery and artifacts, although you won't see them on the majority of tube trips, unless your guide stops for a short hike.

The Caves Branch River cave system is a very popular tourist attraction, and it can get crowded at times, especially in the three caves closest to Jaguar Paw and the public entrance. When the cruise-ship groups are in the caves, it's downright overcrowded. Whatever tour operator you use, try to time it so that you avoid other large groups if possible. I also highly recommend hiking the extra 15 minutes or so upstream to get to the fourth cave. However, if you choose to do the tour with Ian Anderson's Caves Branch outfit, you are assured of avoiding the crowds. Also, wear plenty of insect repellent, as the mosquitoes can be fierce here (only on the hike—once you're in the caves there are none).

Cave tubing tours cost between BZ$60 and BZ$240, depending on the length of the tour. The most inexpensive way to go is to drive yourself to the government parking area mentioned above and hire one of the local guides there for around BZ$30 to BZ$50. However, you'll generally get better guides, better service, and better equipment if you go with one of the more established operators.

Actun Tunichil Muknal ★★★

Actun Tunichil Muknal means "Cave of the Crystal Sepulcher," and the site was featured in the 1993 National Geographic Explorer film *Journey Through the Underworld*. This is one of the most adventurous and rewarding caves you can visit in Belize. The trip involves a 45-minute hike and three shallow river crossings through dense forest to the entrance of the cave. A midsize stream flows out of the beautiful entrance. From here you wade, crawl, swim, and scramble, often up to your waist in water. There are some tight squeezes. Inside, you'll come to several ceremonial and sacrificial chambers. Fourteen skeletons and burial sites have been found inside here, as well as numerous pieces of pottery and ceramic shards. There are even two rare slate steles, believed to have been used by Mayan religious and political leaders for ritual bloodletting ceremonies. Many of the skulls, skeletons, and pieces of pottery have been encased in calcium, creating an eerie effect, while others are very well maintained, making it hard to imagine that they are more than a thousand years old. Moreover, given its remote location and relatively recent discovery, Actun Tunichil Muknal has been spared much of the serious looting that has plagued many other Mayan cave sites. Only licensed guides can take visitors into this cave. Most hotels and tour agencies in the Cayo District can arrange these tours.

Note: You will get wet on this trip. Make sure your guide has a dry bag for your camera, and be sure to pack a change of clothing for when you get back to your transportation.

Zipline Canopy Tour ★

The folks at **Jaguar Paw** (© **820-2023;** www.jaguarpaw.com) have set up an "Aerial Trek Canopy Tour," in which visitors get to strap on a climbing harness and glide along steel cables, or ziplines, from one treetop platform to another, above and through the forest canopy. There are a total of eight platforms. At its highest, you are some 24m (80 ft.) above the forest floor. The 2-hour trip costs BZ$110 per person, and can easily be combined with their cave tubing excursion (see above) for a full-day adventure outing.

NATIONAL PARKS

Guanacaste National Park ★, a 20-hectare (50-acre) park located where the Hummingbird Highway turns off of the Western Highway, about 3.2km (2 miles) north of Belmopan, is an excellent introduction to tropical forests. The park is named for a huge old guanacaste (or tubroos) tree that is found within the park. Guanacaste trees were traditionally preferred for building dugout canoes, but this particular tree, which is about 100 years old, was spared the boat builders' ax because it has a crooked and divided trunk that makes it unacceptable for canoe building. More than 35 species of epiphytes (plants that grow on other plants), including orchids, bromeliads, ferns, mosses, lichens, and philodendrons, cover its trunk and branches.

There are nearly 3.2km (2 miles) of well-marked and well-maintained trails in the park, with several benches for sitting and observing wildlife. The park is bordered on the west by Roaring Creek and on the north by the Belize River. Among the animals you might see are more than 120 species of birds, large iguanas, armadillos, kinkajous, deer, agoutis (large rodents that are a favorite game meat in Belize), and jagarundis (small jungle cats). Bring along a bathing suit in case you want to take a refreshing dip in the Belize River. This park is administered by the **Belize Audubon Society** (© 223-5004; www.belizeaudubon.org) and is open daily from 8am to 5pm. Admission is BZ$5.

The Maya Mountains are primarily limestone and laced with caves, which is why this region of Belize is also known as Cave Branch. About 19km (12 miles) south of Belmopan on the Hummingbird Highway, you'll find **Blue Hole National Park** ★★. The first signs you see of the park will be the parking area, visitor center, and trail entrance to **St. Herman's Cave,** although I recommend you continue on to the park's principal entrance. If you do stop here, it's less than a .8km (½-mile) hike from the road to one of the largest and most easily accessible caves in Belize. You'll need a good flashlight and sturdy shoes to explore this undeveloped .8km-long (½-mile) cave.

A little farther on down the Hummingbird Highway, you'll come to a principal entrance to **Blue Hole National Park** ★★. The park gets its name from a crystal-clear pool, or cenote, formed in a collapsed cavern. A short, well-marked trail leads to the main attraction here. Dense jungle surrounds a small, natural pool of deep turquoise. A limestone cliff rises up from the edge of the pool on two sides. The water flows for only about 30m (100 ft.) on the surface before disappearing into a cave and flowing on underground to the Sibun River. This is a great place for a quick dip on a hot day because the water is refreshingly cool and clear. It can get crowded here on weekends, but early in the morning during the week, you may have the place almost to yourself. You can clearly see fish swimming around the edges of the Blue Hole. A 2.4km (1.5-mile) trail connects the Blue Hole pool with St. Herman's Cave. This trail passes through lush and beautiful primary and secondary tropical forests that are rich in flora and fauna. More than 200 species of birds have been recorded here. Be sure to wear plenty of insect repellent or long-sleeved clothing, as the mosquitoes can be fierce. *Tip:* If you're interested in only the pool, be sure to continue on the Hummingbird Highway, and don't park at the St. Herman's Cave entrance.

With a guide hired at the park entrance, you can explore the **Crystalline Cave** here. This cave system goes on for miles and features beautiful geological structures and formations, Mayan relics, and some calcified skeletons. The park, which is administered by the **Belize Audubon Society** (© 223-5004; www.belizeaudubon.org), is open daily from 8am to 5pm, and admission is BZ$8. A self-guided trail map and a brochure about the park are available at the small visitor center. And if the park ranger is available, he'll usually throw in a brief guided tour for free. You'll have to pay an additional BZ$30 for a 1½- to 2-hour guided tour of the Crystalline Cave.

A PRIVATE PARK & EDUCATIONAL CENTER

Located just inland from Mile Marker 31 on the Western Highway is **Monkey Bay Wildlife Sanctuary** (© **820-3032;** www.monkeybaybelize.org), a private reserve and environmental education center comprising some 433 hectares (1,070 acres) of varied natural habitat. There's a visitor center, and a range of tours is offered. This place specializes in hosting student groups, but anyone can visit for the day, or even stay in accommodations that range from somewhat plush private rooms to a dormitory-style bunkhouse to camping. In all cases, be forewarned: The showers are cold water only, and the bathrooms are outdoor latrines. Tours include guided hikes, bird-watching expeditions, cave explorations, and canoe outings on the Sibun River. With the addition of the neighboring 911-hectare (2,250-acre) **Monkey Bay Nature Reserve,** this is a very large protected area, with more than 250 recorded bird species.

While walk-ins can often be accommodated, it's best to contact them in advance before coming for any tour or stay. Rates run around BZ$16 per person for camping; BZ$30 per person for a dorm bunk and shared bathroom; and BZ$90 for a double room with private bathroom. Meals cost between BZ$16 and BZ$20. A guided 3-hour paddle on the Sibun River costs BZ$60 per person.

Golf

Belize's only operational golf course is located on the outskirts of Belmopan. The **Roaring River Golf Course** (© **820-2031;** www.belizegolf.net) is a par-64, 18-hole executive course. Greens fees run BZ$50 for 18 holes, and there's no charge for a set of clubs if necessary. A 9-hole round will run you BZ$35. The course is open every day of the year from dawn to dusk.

Shopping

Located just a mile or so outside of Belmopan, on the way to Belize City, **Art Box** ★★ (© **822-2233;** www.artboxbz.com) is an excellent gift shop spread over two floors, with an extensive collection of souvenirs, art and craft works, T-shirts, books, and other assorted Belizean-made gift items. There's also a pleasant coffee shop on the premises, with free Wi-Fi to go along with your cappuccino or latte.

Where to Stay

In addition to the places listed below, there are four well-equipped individual cabins at the **Roaring River Golf Course** (© **820-2031;** www.belizegolf.net) on the outskirts of Belmopan. All come with a riverview private patio and run BZ$190 per night.

IN BELMOPAN
Moderate

Bullfrog Inn   This is the most modern and comfortable hotel in Belmopan. Rooms are spacious and come with one king bed or two queen beds, air-conditioning, and cable television. Most rooms have a small private balcony with a wrought-iron railing overlooking a small patch of grass and the ring road. This place is justifiably popular with business travelers, as it's really the only game in town. The restaurant here is one of the more dependable in town, and the bar can actually get hopping.

25 Half Moon Ave. (P.O. Box 28), Belmopan. ℂ **822-3425.** Fax 822-3155. www.bullfroginn.com. 25 units. BZ$170 double. MC, V. **Amenities:** Restaurant; bar. *In room:* A/C, TV.

Inexpensive

In addition to the places listed below, you could also try the **Belmopan Bed & Breakfast** (ℂ **822-0176;** www.belmopanbedandbreakfast.com), which is located at 8 Trio St. and rents two neat rooms in a residential home with a swimming pool. Rates run around BZ$110 for a double, including breakfast, taxes, and free Wi-Fi.

El Rey Inn ✦   If you're looking for a clean, inexpensive place to spend the night, try this small hotel located in a residential neighborhood just off the north ring road. The rooms are fairly basic, but the rates are some of the best in Belmopan. This little hotel has a simple restaurant serving reasonably priced meals, and a host of tours can be arranged. El Rey Inn is about a 10-minute hike or a short taxi ride from the bus station. These folks also have a sister property, **Hibiscus Hotel** (ℂ **822-1418**), closer to the center of town, government offices, and bus station, with rooms that feature air-conditioning and televisions.

23 Moho St., Belmopan. ℂ **822-3438.** Fax 822-2682. www.belmopanhotels.com. 12 units. BZ$46–BZ$80 double. MC, V. **Amenities:** Restaurant. *In room:* No phone.

Where to Dine

In addition to the place listed below, Belmopan now has a branch of the ever-popular and ever-expanding local Chinese franchise, **Chon Saan Palace,** 7069 George Price Blvd. (ℂ **822-3388**), where you can get a host of well-prepared Cantonese and Szechuan favorites. The restaurant at the **Bullfrog Inn,** 25 Half Moon Ave. (ℂ **822-3425**), which serves a mix of local and international cuisine, is another of the better restaurants in the city proper. While just outside of town, the restaurant at **Roaring River Golf Course** (ℂ **820-2031;** www.belizegolf.net) is garnering praise for its hearty and tender steaks. Budget travelers and those looking for some local flavor should probably grab food from the various vendors and stalls at the central market. But this option is not for those with delicate digestive tracts.

A couple of other options lie just outside of the city, about 26km (16 miles) east along the Western Highway at Mile Marker 32, where you'll find a pair of popular roadside restaurants and bars: **Cheers** (ℂ **822-8014**) and **Amigos** (ℂ **802-8000**). Both are large and lively spots serving local fare, grilled meats, seafood, and typical bar food such as nachos and burgers.

Pasquale's Pizza & Wings PIZZA/INTERNATIONAL   I like the casual vibe of this local favorite. The best tables are those on an open-air wooden deck. These are picnic tables with vinyl tops stapled in place. The menu features a range of pizzas, pastas, and submarine sandwiches, as well as the namesake wings, which come in spicy and mild variations. If you want something more substantial, try the chicken cacciatore or vodka shrimp.

Corner of Forest Dr. and Slim Lane, Belmopan. ℂ **822-4663.** BZ$12–BZ$20. MC, V. Mon–Sat 11am–9pm; Sun noon–8pm.

Perkup Coffee Shop ★ 🏠COFFEE SHOP/INTERNATIONAL   This new joint has quickly become one of the best and most popular spots in all of Belmopan. Serving a range of coffee concoctions, as well as a limited menu of soups, salads, sandwiches, and wraps, this is a great place any time. They also have quesadillas and several flavors of chicken wings. Those hearty enough to attempt their spiciest wings can win a spot on the restaurant's "Wall of Flame." In the evenings, it earns the distinction of being Belmopan's only wine bar, and it's a free Wi-Fi hot spot.

No. 4 Shopping Center (across from Brodie's), Belmopan. ✆ **822-0001.** www.perkupcoffeeshop.com. BZ$12–BZ$18. MC, V. Mon–Wed 11am–8pm; Thu–Fri 11am–9pm; Sat 10am–6pm.

Serendib Restaurant BELIZEAN/SRI LANKAN/CHINESE   This pleasant little restaurant is another good choice in the tiny town of San Ignacio. Former owner Hantley Pieris came to Belize from Sri Lanka years ago with the British army. Hantley has sold the place, and the menu now features a lot more local fare and Chinese cuisine, but you can still can get beef or chicken curry with yellow or fried rice and potato salad. Sandwiches, burgers, chow mein, stew chicken, and fried fish also make appearances on the menu. The best seats are in the courtyard out back.

27 Burns Ave. ✆ **824-2302.** Main courses BZ$10–BZ$24. MC, V. Mon–Sat 7:30am–3pm and 6–10pm.

Belmopan After Dark

For a mellow scene, you can head to the **Perkup Coffee Shop ★** (see above) for a glass or bottle of wine. Their Thursday-evening open-mic night is quite fun, and there's live music most Friday nights. The most happening spot in town is the **VIP Lounge** (✆ **802-0060**), located right on Market Square. The **Bullfrog Inn** (see above) is another of the city's more popular watering holes, and they frequently have raucous karaoke nights. The restaurants out on the Western Highway mentioned above are another good bet for an evening out.

Lodges Near Belmopan

While Belmopan itself is of very little interest to most travelers, several of the country's best and most interesting nature lodges are located within close proximity to the capital city. All of the places below have their unique charms.

Banana Bank Lodge ★ ☺   Owners John and Carolyn Carr moved to Belize almost 30 years ago. Carolyn is an artist and John is a cowboy from Montana. Together, they operate one of the oldest cattle ranches in Belize and one of the original ecolodges in the country. Options range from two-bedroom cabanas that are well-suited to families to lodge rooms to the large Chateau Brio suites. Several suites have full kitchenettes. The rooms and suites have air-conditioning, while the cabanas come only with fans. Horseback riding is the most popular attraction here, but canoeing, visits to Maya ruins, and other day and overnight trips can all be arranged. On the grounds, you can visit Carolyn's studio and get close to the Carrs' pet jaguar, Tika Two. Cruise-ship passengers come here frequently for day trips, and it can get a little crowded and hectic when they're around.

Western Hwy., Mile Marker 47 (P.O. Box 48, Belmopan). ✆ **820-2020.** Fax 820-2026. www.banana bank.com. 14 units. BZ$260–BZ$350 double. Rates include full breakfast. AE, MC, V. **Amenities:** Restaurant; bar; large outdoor pool; smoke-free rooms; free Wi-Fi. *In room:* No phone.

Ian Anderson's Caves Branch ★★ ☺   Originally a rustic camp for hard-core adventure travelers, this place has added some very comfortable accommodations. Set on the banks of the Caves Branch River amid dense forest, the most luxurious options here are the jungle suites and bungalows, and these are in fact quite plush for jungle lodgings. The latter feature red-tile floors, large verandas, and a beautiful shower with a large screened window opening up to the forest. Folks choosing to stay in the jungle cabanas or bunkhouse share common bathroom and shower areas. These open-air showers are quite fun, as the shower heads are just old buckets with nail holes perforating them. Perhaps my favorite accommodations here are the "tree-house" suites, overlooking the river. A wide range of cave explorations, hiking, mountain biking, and kayaking tours are offered here, including overnight cave tours and jungle treks. These folks sit in the middle of a massive private nature reserve and are actively involved in local conservation programs.

Hummingbird Hwy., Mile Marker 4½ (P.O. Box 356, Belmopan). © **822-2800.** www.cavesbranch.com. 20 units. BZ$30 per person bunkhouse; BZ$196 double cabana; BZ$330–BZ$570 double suite or bungalow. MC, V. **Amenities:** Restaurant; bar; Jacuzzi; two-tier pool; smoke-free rooms. *In room:* No phone.

Pook's Hill ★ ♟♟   This isolated jungle resort is set on the grounds of a small Maya ruin in the midst of a lush forest and a 121-hectare (300-acre) private reserve. The individual thatch-roof cabins are set on a hillside just off the ancient central plaza. Those highest up the hill have the best views of the surrounding forest, but they're a little bit smaller and slightly less luxurious than the units a little lower down. My favorite cabin is Kinkajou, which is tiled with river stones. Two cabins are located below the main lodge and across a small creek; they are built on raised stilts 3.7m (12 ft.) above the ground. These two cabins have large decks and are great for bird-watching. Above the dining area is the open-air lounge and bar, which is lit by kerosene lanterns at night and buzzes with hummingbirds during the day.

Western Hwy., Mile Marker 52½ (P.O. Box 14, Belmopan). ©/fax **820-2017.** www.pookshillbelize.com. 11 units. BZ$406–BZ$472 double. Rates lower in the off season. A full meal plan here costs BZ$102 per person per day. MC, V. Turn south off Western Hwy. at Mile Marker 52½ at Teakettle Village. Follow signs on the dirt roads 9.7km (6 miles) until you reach the lodge. **Amenities:** Restaurant; bar; laundry service. *In room:* No phone.

SAN IGNACIO ★★

116km (72 miles) W of Belize City; 32km (20 miles) W of Belmopan; 13km (8 miles) E of the Guatemalan border

In the foothills of the mountains close to the Guatemalan border lie the sister towns of Santa Elena and San Ignacio, which are set on either side of the beautiful Macal River. For all intents and purposes, San Ignacio is the more important town, both in general terms and particularly for travelers. Just north of town, the Macal and Mopan rivers converge to form the Belize River. San Ignacio is the business and administrative center for the Cayo District, a region of cattle ranches and dense forests, of clear rivers and Mayan ruins. It is also the second-largest metropolitan center in the country. Still, you won't find any urban blight here. If you've come from Guatemala, you'll sense immediately that you are now in a Caribbean country. If you've come up from the coast, you might be surprised by how cool it can get up here in the mountains. Despite the similarity in the sound of their names, the Cayo District and the

For Short
The name "Cayo" is used to refer to both the Cayo District and the city of San Ignacio.

cayes are worlds apart. While the cayes cater to those looking for fun in the sun, Cayo caters to those interested in nature, outdoor adventures, and Mayan ruins. This area makes a great first stop in Belize; you can get in a lot of activity before heading to the beach to relax.

Essentials

GETTING THERE & DEPARTING

BY PLANE   While there is an airstrip in San Ignacio (SQS), none of the local commuter airlines has regular service here.

BY CAR   Take the Western Highway from Belize City. It's a straight shot all the way to San Ignacio. You'll come to the small town of Santa Elena first. Across the Macal River lies San Ignacio. If you're heading to San Ignacio and points west, a well-marked detour will lead you through the town of Santa Elena to a Balley bridge that enters San Ignacio toward the north end of town. The more prominent and impressive Hawksworth Bridge is solely for traffic heading east out of San Ignacio toward Santa Elena, Belmopan, and Belize City.

BY BUS   San Ignacio has very frequent bus service from Belize City. Buses to San Ignacio leave roughly every half-hour from the main bus station on West Collet Canal Street between 5am and 8pm. Return buses to Belize City leave the main bus station in San Ignacio roughly every half-hour between 4am and 6pm. The fare is BZ$10. The trip takes 2½ hours. Most of the western-bound buses continue on beyond San Ignacio to Benque Viejo and the Guatemalan border.

GETTING AROUND

The downtown center of San Ignacio is quite compact and easily navigated by foot. If you want to visit any of the major attractions listed below, you'll probably have to find transportation. Frequent buses (see above) will take you to the entrances to most of the hotels listed below on Benque Viejo Road, as well as within walking distance of the Xunantunich ruins. Infrequent buses (ask around town or at the bus station; ✆ 824-3360) do service the Mountain Pine Ridge area. However, if you don't have your own vehicle, you will probably need to take some taxis or go on organized tours.

As in the rest of Belize, roads are minimal, and almost everything can be found on or just off the Western Highway, or the road through Mountain Pine Ridge. Numerous buses ply the main road between Belmopan and San Ignacio, continuing on to the border town of Benque Viejo del Carmen. If you want to drive yourself, particularly anywhere off the main highway, a four-wheel-drive vehicle is recommended.

You can rent a car from **Cayo Rentals** (✆ 824-2222; www.cayoautorentals.com) or **Matus Car Rental** (✆ 824-2005; www.matuscarrental.com). A small four-wheel-drive vehicle here should run you around BZ$120 to BZ$240 per day.

If you need a cab, call the **Cayo Taxi Association** (✆ 824-2196). Taxi fares around the Cayo District should run you as follows: BZ$6 to BZ$10 around town, BZ$20 between San Ignacio and Bullet Tree Falls, and BZ$50 between San Ignacio and Chaa Creek or duPlooy's. Collective taxis run regularly between downtown San Ignacio and the border at Benque Viejo; the fare is BZ$8 per person.

San Ignacio

Belize City • ⊛**Belmopan**
• San Ignacio

B E L I Z E

- $ Bank/ATM
- ✚ Hospital
- P Police
- ✉ Post office

← To Parrot's Nest,
Bullet Tree, El Pilar,
& Cohune Palms

The Savannah

Macal River

Hawksworth Bridge

Maya St.
Blancaneaux St.
Simpson St.
Burns Ave.
George St.
West St.
Hospital St.
Waight's Ave.
Church St.
Far West St.
Hudson St.
Old Benque Rd.
Melhado St.
Buena Vista Rd.
Awe St.
George Price Ave.

SANTA ELENA

To Xunantunich,
Benque Viejo del Carmen
& Guatemalan border

0 — 1/10 mile
0 — 100 meters

ACCOMMODATIONS ■
Casa Blanca Guest House **12**
Hi-Et **5**
Martha's Guest House **8**
Midas Tropical Resort **1**
New Balmoral Hotel **7**
Plaza Hotel **10**
San Ignacio Resort Hotel **13**

DINING ◆
Amore Mio **6**
Erva's **3**
Eva's Restaurant & Bar **4**
Ko-Ox Han-Nah **11**
Hode's Place Bar & Grill **1**
Martha's Restaurant
& Pizza House **8**
Maxim's Chinese
Restaurant **9**
Mr. Greedy's Pizzeria **2**
Running W Steak House
& Restaurant **13**

NIGHTLIFE ●
Hode's Place Bar & Grill **1**
Mr. Greedy's Pizzeria **2**
Princess Casino **13**
The Stork Club **13**

ORIENTATION

San Ignacio is on the banks of the Macal River, on the western side of an old metal bridge across from its sister city of Santa Elena. Across the single-lane Hawksworth Bridge is a traffic circle and a Shell gas station. Downtown San Ignacio is to the north on Burns Avenue, and the San Ignacio Hotel is located south up a steep hill on Buena Vista Road. Most of the hotels and restaurants in town are on or within a block of Burns Avenue. The road to Benque Viejo del Carmen, Xunantunich ruins, and the Guatemalan border branches off Buena Vista Road. This is actually a continuation of the Western Highway.

FAST FACTS There are several banks located right in the heart of downtown San Ignacio: **Atlantic Bank,** at Burns Avenue and Columbus Park (✆ 824-2347); **Scotiabank,** at Burns Avenue and Riverside Street (✆ 824-4190); and **Belize Bank,** 16 Burns Ave. (✆ 824-2031).

To reach the **police,** dial © **911** or 824-2022; for the **fire department,** dial © **824-2095.** The **San Ignacio Hospital** is located on Simpson Street, on the western side of town (© **824-2066**). The **post office** (© **824-2049**) is located on Hudson Street, near the corner of Waight's Avenue.

The succinctly named **The Pharmacy** (© **824-2510**) is located on West Street. If you need eyeglass repair or help, head to the **Hoy Eye Center,** 4 Far West St. (© **824-4101**). If you need laundry done and your hotel doesn't offer the service or charges too much, you can drop off your dirty clothes at **Martha's Guesthouse,** 10 West St. (© **804-3647**), for same-day service at about BZ$15 per load.

What to See & Do

The Cayo District is Belize's prime inland tourist destination. There's a lot to see and do in this area, from visiting Mayan ruins and caves to engaging in a broad range of adventure activities. In addition to the tours, activities, and attractions listed below, all of the listings in the Mountain Pine Ridge section (later in this chapter) and in the Belmopan section (earlier in this chapter) are easily accessible from San Ignacio.

Some of the tours, activities, and attractions listed below can be done on your own, but others will require a guide or adventure tour operator. Most hotels in the area either have their own tour operations or can arrange to hook you up with a reputable local operator. In addition, there are several long-standing tour agencies based in San Ignacio. Some of the best of these are **Cayo Adventure Tours** (© **824-3246;** www.cayoadventure.com), **Pacz Tours ★★** (© **824-2477** or 824-0536; www.pacztours.net), and **Yute Expeditions ★** (© **824-2076;** www.inland belize.com). All of these companies offer virtually all of the options listed in this chapter and more, including multiday tours, treks, and adventures.

In addition, serious bird-watchers might want to sign up for a tour with **Birding in Belize ★** (© **824-2772;** www.birdinginbelize.com).

MAYAN RUINS

The Cayo District is in the heart of the Mayan highlands, with several major ruins and cave systems used by the ancient residents of this region. The most impressive are **Xunantunich ★★** (on Benque Viejo Rd.), **El Pilar ★★** (near Bullet Tree Falls Village), and **Caracol ★★** (deep in the Mountain Pine Ridge area; see "Mountain Pine Ridge & Caracol," later in this chapter), but true Maya-philes can keep busy visiting a host of sites in this area. Close by, in Guatemala, lies **Tikal ★★★**, perhaps one of the best excavated and most impressive Mayan cities in Mesoamerica. See chapter 11 for complete coverage.

CAHAL PECH High on a hill to the southwest of downtown San Ignacio are the Mayan ruins of **Cahal Pech.** Although compact, there are actually seven plazas here, as well as numerous residences, temples, and a couple of ball courts. Formerly the home of Mayan royals, this site has received some meticulous restoration. The restoration created a bit of controversy in town because parts of the ruins were restored to an approximation of the way they were supposed to have looked when they were first built, which is a bit more polished and modern-looking than most people like their ruins. However, the setting is beautiful, with tall old trees shading the site's main plaza and pyramid. *Tip:* Be sure to climb the small B4 pyramid, on your left near the entrance to the site. Though diminutive, it offers excellent views of the Macal River.

The name Cahal Pech means the "Place of the Family of Pech" (*Pech* means "tick" in Mayan). The name was given to the site in the 1950s when there were quite a few ticks in the area. The ruins date back to between 650 and 900, though many think that the site was used prior to this time as well.

At the entrance, you'll find a small museum that displays a collection of artifacts recovered from the site and provides insight into the Cahal Pech social structure. It also has a small model of the old city, as well as a skeleton recovered from one of the graves here.

Admission to the museum and ruins is BZ$10, and the site is open daily from 8am to 5pm. Be sure to ask for a copy of the informative guide to the site. To reach Cahal Pech, walk or drive up toward the San Ignacio Resort Hotel (p. 240), continuing on around the curve for a few hundred yards until you pass the soccer field. Turn left here and climb the hill toward the ruins. The entrance to the ruins is beyond a large thatched building that houses the Cahal Pech disco. It's about a 20-minute walk.

Xunantunich ★★ Although you may have trouble pronouncing it (say "Zoo-nahn-too-*neetch*"), Xunantunich is an impressive, well-excavated, and easily accessible Mayan site. The name translates as "Maiden of the Rocks." The main pyramid here, **El Castillo,** rises to 39m (128 ft.) and is clearly visible from the Western Highway as you approach. It's a steep climb, but the view from the top is amazing—don't miss it. You'll be able to make out the twin border towns of Benque Viejo, Belize, and Melchor de Menchos, Guatemala. On the east side of the pyramid, near the top, is a remarkably well-preserved stucco frieze.

Down below in the temple forecourt, archaeologists found three magnificent steles portraying rulers of the region. These have been moved to the protection of the small on-site museum, yet the years and ravages of weather have made most of the carvings difficult to decipher. Xunantunich was a thriving Mayan city about the same time as Altun Ha, in the Classic Period from about 600 to 900.

The visitor center at the entrance contains a beautiful scale model of the old city, as well as a replica of the original frieze. Open daily from 8am to 4pm, the site charges an admission of BZ$10. Xunantunich is located 10km (6¼ miles) past San Ignacio on the road to Benque Viejo. To reach the ruins, you must cross the Mopan River aboard a tiny hand-cranked car-ferry in the village of San José Succotz. You may be able to watch colorfully dressed women washing clothes in the river as you are cranked across by the ferryman. After crossing the river, it is a short, but dusty and vigorous, uphill walk to the ruins. If you've got your own vehicle, you can take it across on the ferry and drive right to the ruins. To get here by bus, take any bus bound for Benque Viejo and get off in San José Succotz. You'll see a small line of makeshift souvenir stands lining the road, just beside the ferry crossing.

Chechem Ha ★ This ancient Mayan burial cave was discovered by accident when a local hunter, Antonio Morales, went chasing after his errant dog. When the cave was explored, a cache of Mayan artifacts, including many large, fully preserved pots, was discovered. Archaeologists estimate the relics could have been placed here more than 2,000 years ago. This cave is one of only two in the area with an elaborate altar used for ceremonial purposes by the religious and ruling classes.

The cave is located 16km (10 miles) south of Benque Viejo, on a dirt road that is recommended only for four-wheel-drive vehicles. Chechem Ha, which means "Cave of Poisonwood Water," is privately owned by the Morales family, and admission is allowed only with a prearranged guided tour. Ideally, you should make a reservation in advance, although it's often hard to contact and confirm with the Morales family; their phone number is ✆ **820-4063.** If you receive no response, you can usually drive out to the entrance any morning and arrange the tour directly with the Morales family beforehand. The cost of a 45-minute tour is BZ$60 for up to three people if you book directly. Local hotels and tour companies also offer this trip, but charge a little bit more. You can also visit Chechem Ha on an organized tour with one of the local agencies working with the Morales family. Almost every hotel and tour agency in the area can arrange this for you, although they tend to charge a little bit more for their efforts.

A short hike from the entrance, the Chechem Ha Falls make a refreshing spot to wash and cool off after clambering around inside the caves. Also close to Chechem Ha is **Vaca Falls,** a beautiful and remote waterfall that's often combined with a visit to the cave, though it's a destination in its own right.

RIVER TOURS

For much of Belize's history, the rivers were the main highways. The Maya used them for trading, and British loggers used them to move mahogany and logwood. If you're interested, you can explore the Cayo District's two rivers—the Macal and Mopan—by canoe, kayak, and inner tube. Throughout most of the year, the waters in these rivers are easily navigable both up- and downstream. However, during the rainy season, things can change drastically—and fast. I've heard of a few flash floods, and even one story of water nearly reaching the road on the Hawksworth Bridge.

Still, for the most part, trips are leisurely, with plenty of places to stop for a quick swim or land excursion. During the rainy season (July–Sept), white-water kayaking is available, although it's not very consistent. Inflatable kayaks are a much more common and dependable option, not requiring nearly as much technical proficiency or water.

Most tours put in upstream on the Macal River somewhere around Chaa Creek (p. 244) or duPlooy's (p. 245) and then float leisurely downstream. The trip can take anywhere from 1 to 3 hours, depending on how much time you spend paddling, floating, or stopping to hike or swim. All of the local riverside hotels offer this service, as well as a host of operators in San Ignacio. For its part, the Mopan River is more easily accessible in many ways, since Benque Viejo Road borders it in many places. The Mopan is well-suited for inflatable kayaks and inner tubes.

In addition to most of the tour operators listed above, you can contact **David's Adventure Tours** (✆ 824-3674). If you want to go inner tubing, contact the folks at the **Trek Stop** (✆ 823-2265; www.thetrekstop.com).

Both of Cayo's principal rivers are great for swimming. On the Macal River you can join the locals right in town, where the river is treated as a free laundry, car wash, horse and dog wash, and swimming hole. However, you'll do better to head upstream. The farther upstream you head, the more isolated and clear the swimming holes become.

Another alternative is to head downriver about 2.4km (1½ miles) to a spot called **Branch Mouth,** where the different-colored waters of the Macal and Mopan rivers converge. Branch Mouth is a favorite picnic spot, with shady old trees clinging to the riverbanks. There's even a rope swing from one of the trees. The road is dusty, so you'll be especially happy to go for a swim here. Farther upstream, on both the Macal and Mopan rivers, are numerous swimming holes.

GROUP B

GROUP A

To Succotz's →
Ferry

El Castillo

GROUP C

Belize City
Belmopan
Xunantunich
BELIZE

0   50 yards
0   50 meters

10

THE CAYO DISTRICT & WESTERN BELIZE

San Ignacio

OTHER ADVENTURE ACTIVITIES & NATURAL WONDERS

Belize Botanic Gardens ★★   Located next to duPlooy's (p. 245) and run by the same family, the Belize Botanic Gardens (© 824-3101; www.belizebotanic.org) is a sprawling collection of local and imported tropical fauna. They have an excellent mix of fruit trees, palms, bromeliads, and bamboos, all well laid out whether you are taking a self-guided or guided tour. The orchid house is not to be missed, with its beautiful collection of orchids and sculpted waterfall wall. The gardens are open daily from 7am to 5pm. Admission is BZ$10, and includes a helpful self-guided tour booklet. Guided tours cost BZ$15 per person, including the entrance fee.

While it's still possible to navigate the Belize River all the way to Belize City—the Macal and Mopan rivers join and become the Belize River—this is not generally something tourists get to do. Still, each year in early March, scores of three-person canoe teams undertake the long 290km (180-mile) paddle from San Ignacio to Belize City in the **Ruta Maya Belize River Challenge.** Teams gather in San Ignacio below the Hawksworth Bridge on March 5, and thousands of people line the banks of the river for the start. The finish line, fittingly enough, is the Swing Bridge in Belize City. It takes between 3 and 4 days to complete the course, with the teams scheduled to arrive in Belize City on or around Baron Bliss Day, on March 9.

Barton Creek Cave ★   This is one of the area's more relaxing caves to explore. The trip is conducted entirely by canoe, and while there are a few tight squeezes and areas with low ceilings, in general you won't get as wet (you'll stay dry, in fact) or claustrophobic here as you will at many of the other caves in Belize. Located beside a small Mennonite community, Barton Creek is navigable for nearly a mile inside the cave. Along the way, by the light of headlamps and strong flashlights, you'll see wonderful natural formations, a large gallery, and numerous Mayan artifacts, including several skeletons, believed to be the remains of ritual sacrifices. One skull sits so prominently atop a natural bridge that it's likely that a local tour operator moved it there to heighten the dramatic effect. You can climb along the dry edges of the cave in certain parts.

There's a BZ$10 fee to visit the site, but that doesn't include the canoe trip or transportation. If you drive there yourself, you can hire a canoe that holds two passengers, plus the guide, for around BZ$30 to BZ$40. Tours out of San Ignacio average around BZ$100 to BZ$150 per person, including the entrance fee. Barton Creek Cave is located several miles down a side road off the Pine Ridge Road, about 6.4km (4 miles) from the Western Highway. Visits to Barton Creek Cave are often combined with a stop at the Green Hills Butterfly Ranch (see "Mountain Pine Ridge & Caracol," later in this chapter).

Horseback Riding   If you enjoy horseback riding, there's some wonderful terrain in this area. Rides can be combined with visits to jungle waterfalls and swimming holes, as well as nearby Mayan ruins. Most of the hotels in the area offer horseback riding tours.

Alternatively, you can contact the folks at **Mountain Equestrian Trails** (© **669-1124;** www.metbelize.com), who have one of the better stables and horse-riding operations in the Cayo District. Also, keep in mind that most lodges in the area offer horseback riding, so ask at your hotel or lodge first.

The Rainforest Medicine Trail ★   Located directly between Chaa Creek and the Macal River Jungle Camp, this is the former Ix Chel Farm, which was set up by Dr. Rosita Arvigo and Dr. Greg Shropshire. Rosita studied traditional herbal medicine with Don Elijio Panti, a local Mayan medicine man and a folk hero in Belize. Panti died in February 1996 at the estimated age of 104. Here on the farm, they built a trail through the forest to share with visitors the fascinating medicinal values of many of the tropical forest's plants.

The farm boasts a small gift shop that features local crafts, T-shirts, and several relevant books, including a couple by Arvigo. You'll also find Ix Chel's line of herbal concentrates, salves, and teas called Rainforest Remedies.

Self-guided visits to the Medicine Trail, along with a tour of Chaa Creek Natural History Museum and a visit to their Blue Morpho Butterfly Breeding project, cost BZ$20. You can easily spend 3 hours visiting all three attractions. Guided tours of the Medicine Trail are also available. Call © **824-2037** for reservations.

Mountain Biking If your preferred activity is mountain biking, you can go on an organized tour or rent bikes in San Ignacio. From San Ignacio, a great ride is out to El Pilar ruins. You can also ride out to Xunantunich; however, that ride is mostly on the main highway. Mountain bikes are available for rent at various hotels and tour agencies around San Ignacio and should cost around BZ$6 to BZ$10 per hour, or BZ$30 to BZ$60 per day.

Be careful—the hills here are steep, and the heat and humidity can be overwhelming. Take (and drink) lots of water, and try to avoid pedaling during the middle of the day.

A Spa If you want some serious pampering, or a soothing massage after some hard-core adventure, head to the **Spa at Chaa Creek** ★★ (© **824-2037;** www.chaacreek.com). A wide range of treatments is offered, including a hydrating manicure, a variety of facials, and a range of full-body massage treatments. Full-day and multiday spa packages are also available. The spa itself is quite lovely, set on a high hill above the Chaa Creek hotel (p. 244), and the equipment and facilities are top-notch. It's usually open daily 8am to 4pm.

Tropical Wings Nature Center ★ Located just off the main road, at Mile Marker 71½ near the village of San José Succotz, is this small attraction. You'll find an enclosed butterfly garden with scores of brightly colored and varied species flitting about. There's also a butterfly breeding center, as well as an open-air medicinal-plant nature trail. Hummingbird feeders ensure that you'll be buzzed by these frenetic, flighty creatures. This place is open daily from 9am to 5pm; admission is BZ$6. Call © **823-2265** for more information.

Shopping

Orange Gift Shop & Gallery is the best-stocked gift shop in this region and can be found at **Caesar's Place** (© **824-2341;** www.orangegifts.com) about 11km (7 miles) east of San Ignacio. However, I find the prices a bit high, and similar goods can be found less expensively at other shops. A good alternative in town is **Arts & Crafts of Central America,** 24 Burns Ave. (© **824-2253**).

Throughout Belize, and especially in Cayo, you will see slate carvings of Mayan hieroglyphs. If you're in the area, it's worth a visit to one of the sources, the **García Sisters** ★★. This family of artisans runs an interesting little museum-cum-craft shop (p. 252). It's located outside of San Antonio village on the road to Mountain Pine Ridge (see "Mountain Pine Ridge & Caracol," later in this chapter, for more information).

Where to Stay

VERY EXPENSIVE

Ka'ana ★★★ This boutique hotel is stylish and chic. All of the art and furniture on hand are produced within a 65km (40-mile) radius of the hotel. If you want all the trappings of a modern luxury hotel, this should be your top choice in the area. Rooms all come with 40-inch plasma televisions, MP3 docking stations, a stocked minibar, and a personal espresso machine. While the rooms are nice enough, you'll definitely want to splurge on the larger, private casitas, which feature small decks in both the front and the back. The bathrooms here feature a wall of glass tiles in the large showers, letting in natural light. In addition to the excellent restaurant here (p. 242), they have a well-stocked wine cellar and cigar bar. This place is a member of the Small Luxury Hotels of the World group. Ka'ana is located about 3km (2 miles) southwest of downtown, on the road out to Benque Viejo.

Mile 69¼ on the road to Benque Viejo (P.O. Box 263, San Ignacio), Cayo District. ✆ **877/522-6221** in the U.S. and Canada, or 824-0430 reservations office in Belize, or 820-3350 at the hotel. Fax 824-2041. www.kaanabelize.com. 15 units. BZ$500 double; BZ$700 casita. AE, MC, V. **Amenities:** Restaurant; bar; lounge; concierge; outdoor pool; room service; smoke-free rooms; small spa. *In room:* A/C, TV, hair dryer, minibar, MP3 docking station, free Wi-Fi.

EXPENSIVE

San Ignacio Resort Hotel ★★   This is easily the most comfortable and luxurious option in town. Set on a high ridge above the Macal River, the rooms are all spacious, modern, and smartly designed. The standard rooms come with a private balcony or patio letting out onto gardens. I actually prefer them to the Regal suites, which are somewhat larger but lack the balcony. The plushest room here is a large second-floor master suite, with a private Jacuzzi tub on its large balcony. In addition to the pool, there are jungle trails, a small iguana farm, a riverside beach and swimming hole, and a medicinal plant trail. There's one lighted tennis court, and an excellent restaurant and bar with great views from its terrace. The casino and Stork Club bar and lounge (p. 244) are equally popular with locals and guests.

18 Buena Vista St. (P.O. Box 33), San Ignacio, Cayo. ✆ **800/822-3274** in the U.S., or 824-2125. Fax 824-3362. www.sanignaciobelize.com. 24 units. BZ$340 double; BZ$400 Regal suite; BZ$600 master suite. Rates slightly lower in the off season. AE, MC, V. **Amenities:** 2 restaurants; bar; lounge; casino; concierge; midsize outdoor pool; room service; small full-service spa; lit tennis court. *In room:* A/C, TV, hair dryer, free Wi-Fi.

MODERATE

In addition to the place listed below, **The Rolson Hotel** (✆ 824-2730; www.rolsons. com) offers clean, business-class-style rooms with televisions, air-conditioning, and free Wi-Fi.

Cahal Pech Village Resort 🗲   Set on a hillside on the outskirts of town, this hotel has a wonderful view of San Ignacio and is a stone's throw away from the Cahal Pech ruins. Accommodations can be had either in the main building or in one of the thatch-roof individual cabanas. All are clean, spacious, and well-maintained, and feature carved Mayan wall hangings and colorful Guatemalan bedspreads. The rooms have larger bathrooms, and they are higher up and thus have better views from their private balconies—particularly the rooms on the third floor. On the other hand, the cabanas offer a greater sense of privacy and feature large screened-in porches. There's a large, open-air restaurant on the second floor of the main building, where guests gather for meals and to trade travel tales, and a two-tiered midsize outdoor pool set on a high spot near the main building with a great view over the town and valley.

Cahal Pech Hill, San Ignacio, Cayo District. ☏ **824-3740.** Fax 824-2225. www.cahalpech.com. 42 units. BZ$158 double; BZ$198–BZ$238 suite and family cabanas. MC, V. **Amenities:** Restaurant; bar; lounge; mountain bike rental; outdoor pool; free Wi-Fi. *In room:* A/C, TV, no phone.

Martha's Guest House   This cozy guesthouse is located in the heart of San Ignacio, above a popular little restaurant. The vibe here is somewhere between that of a homestay and that of a youth hostel. All of the rooms are immaculate. The more expensive rooms are larger and have minifridges and coffeemakers. There are also a couple of common lounge and balcony areas, where guests can hang out and read a book or chat. The fourth-floor First Lady suite is huge, and it features a large balcony with wonderful views of the town. It also comes with its own kitchenette, making it a good option for families. These folks also have a separate option a few blocks away that they are calling The Inn at Martha's, with fully equipped studio apartments.

10 West St. (P.O. Box 140), San Ignacio, Cayo District. ☏ **804-3647.** Fax 824-2917. www.marthasbelize. com. 10 units. BZ$120 double; BZ$140–BZ$160 suite. AE, MC, V. **Amenities:** Restaurant; bar. *In room:* TV, no phone; free Wi-Fi.

INEXPENSIVE

San Ignacio is a very popular budget travel destination, and there are plenty of good options in town. During the high season, reservations are recommended for the more popular places. At other times, backpackers might prefer to arrive in town early enough to visit a few places, and see which place gives the best bang for the buck. Of the backpacker-geared options, I like the **Hi-Et,** 12 West St. (☏ **824-2828;** thehiet@yahoo.com), with its hostel-like vibe and playful name. Those looking for accommodations with the trappings of a business-class hotel but at budget prices could also check out the **New Balmoral Hotel,** 17 Burns Ave. (☏ **804-3502**), or the **Plaza Hotel,** 4A Burns Ave. (☏ **824-2040**).

   Cosmos Camping (☏ **824-2116;** cosmoscamping@btl.net) is a campground on the road leading out toward Branch Mouth and Las Casitas, where you can pitch your tent for BZ$10 per day. There are showers and communal bathrooms that are kept clean, and the river is just across a field. This place is about a 15-minute hike from downtown San Ignacio, doable for a backpacker. They have some simple cabins here as well.

Casa Blanca Guest House   This centrally located hotel has won a loyal following in a short period. The rooms are all located on the second floor of a building set in the heart of the city's commercial core. The compact rooms all come with a television, ceiling fan, private bathroom, and air-conditioning, although you'll have to pay more for the A/C. There's a large common sitting area and a communal kitchen where you're always likely to bump into fellow travelers. There's also a small common balcony overlooking the hustle and bustle of Burns Avenue.

10 Burns Ave., San Ignacio, Cayo District. ☏/fax **824-2080.** www.casablancaguesthouse.com. 8 units. BZ$60 double; BZ$100 double with A/C. MC, V. *In room:* A/C, TV, no phone.

Midas Tropical Resort ★ 🍷   Located a short walk from downtown San Ignacio, Midas feels a world away. The round Mayan-style cottages have thatch roofs and screen walls, and there are also wood cabins on raised stilts with corrugated roofs. All are comfortable, clean, and spacious, with ceiling fans and plenty of screened windows for ventilation. Some come with air-conditioning and televisions, and you'll pay just a little more for the perks. The newer "King deluxe" rooms are the best bets here and an excellent value. The hotel has ample grounds with plenty of shady trees. The Macal River is only a stroll away down a grassy lane, and you can spend the day lounging on the little beach on the riverbank. If you don't want to swim in the river, these folks offer use of a pool at their in-town sister, Venus Hotel.

Branch Mouth Rd., San Ignacio, Cayo District. *©* **824-3172** or 824-3845. www.midasbelize.com. 13 units. BZ$108–BZ$128 double; BZ$158–BZ$178 king deluxe. MC, V. To reach Midas, walk north out of town on Savannah St., which is 1 block east of Burns Ave. The hotel is about .8km (½ mile) from the center of town. **Amenities:** Restaurant; free Wi-Fi. *In room:* No phone.

Where to Dine

In addition to the places listed below, **Maxim's Chinese Restaurant,** 23 Far West St. (*©* **824-2283**), is the place to go for Chinese food, while **Amore Mio** (*©* **602-8365**), fronting the bus station, is an excellent little Italian restaurant. You might also want to take the adventure of finding **Sanny's Grill,** 23rd Street (*©* **824-2988**), which is tucked away in a residential neighborhood and serves excellent seafood and grilled meats. For inexpensive eats in a large outdoor setting, you can try **Hode's Place Bar & Grill** (*©* **804-2522**), located out on the northern end of town.

EXPENSIVE

La Ceiba ★★★ 🍴 BELIZEAN/FUSION This resort restaurant is one of my favorite restaurants in the country, and a not-to-miss spot if you're staying in the region. Chef Sean Kuylen shows a deft hand, combining contemporary techniques with local ingredients, many harvested from the organic gardens here. Try the fresh red snapper marinated in herbs and wine and then baked in a salt crust, or the jerk chicken served in a coconut curry stew. I especially like the creative interpretations of Belizean classics, which often show up as daily specials and might feature a version of the seafood stew sere, or a jazzed-up stew beans and rice. However, for lunch you can always find the local pork sausage served in Dukunu—a roasted corn tamale recipe that dates to Mayan times—accompanied by a chipotle, guava, and tomato chutney. The wine selection here is excellent, well-priced, and expertly stored.

At Ka'ana resort, mile 69¼ on the road to Benque Viejo. *©* **820-3350.** Reservations recommended. Main courses BZ$24–BZ$66. AE, MC, V. Daily 7am–10pm.

MODERATE

Running W Steak House & Restaurant ★★ STEAKHOUSE/BELIZEAN This restaurant is located in the San Ignacio Resort Hotel and is affiliated with Belize's largest beef and cattle operation, its namesake. Try the Mayan Steak, marinated strips of tenderloin grilled and served with fresh tortillas. If you want something more traditional, order the 16-ounce porterhouse. There are also fish and chicken dishes, as well as some Belizean standards. The dining room is large and comfortable, with plenty of varnished wood. A few wrought-iron tables line an outdoor patio and make a great place to have lunch with a jungle view or dinner under the stars.

18 Buena Vista St., in the San Ignacio Resort Hotel. *©* **824-2034.** Reservations recommended. Main courses BZ$20–BZ$60. AE, MC, V. Daily 7am–11pm.

INEXPENSIVE

Erva's BELIZEAN/MEXICAN There are scores of places in San Ignacio serving local cuisine, but this place is a long-standing favorite. Erva is an excellent cook and congenial hostess. In addition to traditional Belizean and Mexican standards, you can get pizza and some seafood dishes here. Still, it's the stew chicken and rice and beans that brings folks in the door—and keeps them (and me) coming back for more. Erva's is located on the ground floor of the Pacz Hotel.

4 Far West St. ✆ **824-2821.** Main courses BZ$8–BZ$20. MC, V. Daily 7am–10pm.

Eva's Restaurant & Bar 👔 BELIZEAN/INTERNATIONAL Eva's is now a couple blocks off of Burns Avenue, and not quite a bustling hub of tourist activity, but you can still get hearty servings of well-prepared Belizean and Mexican standards. The *escabeche,* a traditional soup or stew, is excellent, as are the stew beans and rice.

Corner of Waights Ave. and Far West St. ✆ **600-0793.** Main courses BZ$6–BZ$18. MC, V. Daily 6:30am–9pm.

Ko-Ox Han-Nah ★ INDIAN/PAN-ASIAN This place is also known simply as Hannah's. Don't be put off by the humble decor, with simple furniture and half walls with steel grating substituting for windows. The menu is massive, with a host of curries, vindaloos, and other Indian staples, mixed with a hefty dose of Chinese and Thai cuisine. Heck, you can even get burgers, burritos, Belizean fare, and big breakfasts here. Still, I recommend you come for the Indian cooking. The chef here is not shy to spice things up. The vindaloos and other spicy dishes can blow your head off if you're not accustomed to authentic cooking. This is a great restaurant for vegetarians, with ample options to choose from.

5 Burns Ave. ✆ **824-3014.** Main courses BZ$16–BZ$48. MC, V. Daily 6am–9pm.

Martha's Restaurant & Pizza House BELIZEAN/PIZZA The restaurant at this popular budget hotel is equally popular. The homemade pizzas are excellent. You have your choice of a variety of toppings, and you can build your own. You can also get everything from burgers to burritos to vegetarian entrees, as well as local Mayan specialties such as chaya tamales, made from cornmeal and a locally grown green. This is a great place for breakfast, including the typical Belizean breakfast of fry jacks, eggs, and beans, as well as excellent huevos rancheros and strong coffee. This is a good place to grab a free Wi-Fi connection as well. Try to snag one of the outdoor tables, and be sure to thank Martha herself.

10 West St. ✆ **804-3647.** Main courses BZ$16–BZ$44. MC, V. Daily 7am–10pm.

Mr. Greedy's Pizzeria ★★AMERICAN/PIZZA This place may just serve the best pizza in Belize. Grab a table on a wooden deck fronting the street, or toward the rear of the restaurant where the floor is actually made up of sand. In addition to the pizzas, they serve a long list of bar food, including excellent burgers, and pasta dishes. For a main dish, I recommend the chicken Parmesan. This place opens early for breakfast, where you can get the day going with a breakfast burrito or breakfast burger, in addition to more traditional morning fare. The bar can get popular at night, and they also offer free Wi-Fi.

34 Burns Ave. ✆ **804-4688.** Main courses BZ$15–BZ$30. MC, V. Daily 6am–midnight.

San Ignacio After Dark

San Ignacio is a pretty sleepy town. Several bars line Burns Avenue in the downtown area, though. I like the relaxed pub vibe at **Mr. Greedy's** ★ (see above). On weekends, the most happening spot in town can often be found up the hill at **The Stork Club** (📞 824-2034), which is located in the San Ignacio Resort Hotel. This place has karaoke on Thursday nights, and live bands often on the weekends.

On the north end of town, **Hode's Place Bar & Grill** (📞 804-2522) is a massive spot that is very popular with locals. They have a tiny casino, as well as a large video arcade, and a pool and foosball tables. Alternatively, you can find out if there's live music at **Caesar's Place** (📞 824-2341), which is the home turf of the Mango Jam band, a local jazz outfit. Caesar's is located out on the Western Highway, about 11km (7 miles) east of San Ignacio.

If you're the gambling type, you'll want to head to the **Princess Casino** (📞 824-4099), which is also located at the San Ignacio Resort Hotel. I'd definitely choose this one over the very little casino at **Hode's Place** (📞 804-2522).

Nearby Lodges & Retreats

ON THE ROAD TO BENQUE VIEJO & THE GUATEMALAN BORDER

While San Ignacio is the regional hub and does make a good base for side trips, the real attractions in western Belize are up the rivers and in the forests. Within a few miles of San Ignacio are several lodges set somewhat off the beaten path, where you can canoe down clear rivers past 1.2m (4-ft.) iguanas sunning themselves on the rocks; ride horses to Mayan ruins; hike jungle trails, and spot scores of beautiful birds and, occasionally, other wild animals. Out on the road to Caracol and Mountain Pine Ridge, there are more of these lodges. Except for the true budget traveler, I highly recommend that you stay at one of the lodges listed below while you're in the area. A few of the lodges can be reached by public bus from San Ignacio, though you may have up to a 20-minute walk after getting off the bus, so consider taking a taxi or arranging pickup in town. All the lodges offer a wide range of active adventures and tours to all the principal sites in the area.

Very Expensive

In addition to the places listed below, **Ek' Tun** ★ (📞 820-3002; www.ektunbelize. com) is a unique, isolated, and gorgeous retreat with just two individual cottages set on the banks of the Macal River. It can be reached only by boat.

Chaa Creek ★★★ ☺   Located on a high, steep bank over the Macal River, this is one of the top hotels in the country. All of the thatched-roof cottages are artistically decorated with local and Guatemalan textiles and handicrafts. Each comes with a quiet porch or balcony area set amid the flowering gardens. My favorite rooms are the large treetop suites, which feature a queen bed, a sunken living-room area, and a wraparound deck fitted with a sunken Jacuzzi. The lodge has a lovely full-service spa, and a host of on-site attractions, including a natural history museum, a Blue Morpho butterfly breeding project, a medicinal plant trail, and a beautiful pool. Canoes and mountain bikes are available, and horseback rides can always be arranged. Mick and Lucy Fleming, who originally began farming this land in 1977, are the engaging hosts, and much of the food served in the restaurant is organically grown on the hotel's own farm.

Off the road to Benque Viejo (P.O. Box 53, San Ignacio), Cayo District. 📞 877/709-8708 in the U.S. and Canada, or 824-2037 reservations office in Belize, or 820-4010 at the lodge. Fax 824-2501. www.chaacreek. com. 23 units. BZ$540–BZ$700 double; BZ$800–BZ$1,150 suite or villa. Rates include breakfast. AE, MC,

On November 2, the residents of Benque Viejo del Carmen celebrate **Los Finados**, a local version of El Día de los Muertos (The Day of the Dead), or All Souls' Day. Families visit the local cemetery, where graves are spruced up and adorned with flowers and votive candles. Many families set up a makeshift altar for their dead at home or on the front lawn. *Bollos* are prepared from cornmeal dough stuffed with chicken and a local purple bean, the *ixpelon*. Local children make jack-o-lanterns out of hollowed-out squash or even grapefruit. At night the cemetery is alight with the flicker from hundreds of candles.

V. To reach Chaa Creek, drive 8km (5 miles) west from San Ignacio and watch for the sign on your left. It's another couple of miles down a rough dirt road from the main highway. **Amenities:** Restaurant; bar; lounge; bike rental; concierge; large outdoor pool; smoke-free rooms; small well-equipped spa; free Wi-Fi. *In room:* No phone.

Mopan River Resort ★ This all-inclusive resort is set on the banks of the Mopan River across from the border town of Benque Viejo. You can reach the hotel only by crossing the river in the resort's little diesel-powered ferry. The individual bungalows are spread along the banks of the river, and all have a view of the flowing water. The bungalows are spacious, with high-pitched thatch roofs and varnished wood floors and walls. I find the bathrooms a tad small and the decor and furnishings a bit dated. Quite a few of the units come with two twin beds, so if you want a true king-size bed, be sure to specify. Aside from a limited number of entrance and border-crossing fees (if you go to Tikal) and top-shelf liquor or wine, you should have virtually no out-of-pocket expenses, as all food, drinks, tips, tours, taxes, and transfers to and from the international airport are included.

Riverside North, Benque Viejo del Carmen, Cayo District. ✆ **823-2047.** Fax 823-3272. www.mopanriver resort.com. 12 units. BZ$2,050–BZ$2,256 per person for a 3-night package, double occupancy. Rates are all-inclusive. Rates higher during peak periods. Minimum 3-night stay. MC, V. The resort is closed July 1–Oct 27. **Amenities:** Restaurant; bar; lounge; outdoor pool; smoke-free rooms; free Wi-Fi. *In room:* A/C, TV, hair dryer, minibar, no phone.

Expensive

duPlooy's ★ This family-run lodge overlooks the Macal River, with jungle-covered limestone cliffs opposite. This stunning location, combined with personalized attention, makes duPlooy's one of Cayo's more popular jungle lodges. My favorite rooms are the spacious bungalows, which come with a king-size bed, futon couch, and large wooden veranda. Another option is the Belize River House, two separate multiroom suites that can be rented separately, or as one huge unit sleeping up to 14 people. The lodge's open-air bar features a spacious deck overlooking the river. There's a beach on the river, as well as several trails through the forest. One of the nicest features here is an elevated walkway running at the level of the forest canopy, which connects much of the complex and also juts out into the forest, offering wonderful opportunities for bird-watching. The neighboring **Belize Botanic Gardens** ★★ provides even more bird-watching opportunities, in addition to an abundance of tropical flora.

Off the road to Benque Viejo (P.O. Box 180, San Ignacio), Cayo District. ⓒ **824-3101.** Fax 824-3301. www.duplooys.com. 19 units. BZ$390 double; BZ$500–BZ$630 casita or suite. Rates include continental breakfast and unlimited entrance to the Belize Botanic Gardens. MC, V. To get here, head out of town on the road to Benque Viejo; the turnoff for duPlooy's is the same as that for Chaa Creek, and it is well marked. DuPlooy's is a bit farther on the same dirt road, but be sure to take the right fork and follow the signs. **Amenities:** Restaurant; bar; lounge; small spa; free Wi-Fi. *In room:* No phone.

Moderate

Black Rock Jungle River Lodge ★ 🏕 So, you *really* want to get away from it all? Well, this is the place. The setting, on a high bluff overlooking the Macal River, is one of the most stunning in the area. The individual cabins here are lovely. The better ones feature large private balconies and fabulous views of the river and/or canyon cliffs. Meals are served in the large open-air dining room and main lodge area, which also has a fabulous view of the river below and forests all around. Much of the fresh produce is organically grown on-site, and electricity is provided by a combination of solar and hydro power sources. Swimming and inner tubing on the river from the lodge are excellent.

Off the road to Benque Viejo (P.O. Box 48, San Ignacio), Cayo District. ⓒ **820-4049** reservations office, or 820-3929 at the lodge. www.blackrocklodge.com. 13 units. BZ$210–BZ$240 double; BZ$300–BZ$360 deluxe. Rates lower in the off season; higher during peak periods. MC, V. If you're driving, take the turnoff for Chaa Creek and duPlooy's, and then follow the signs to Black Rock. **Amenities:** Restaurant. *In room:* No phone.

Clarissa Falls Resort Situated on a 324-hectare (800-acre) working cattle ranch, this modest resort boasts a range of accommodations from deluxe suites to individual cabins to campsites. The thatch-roof cabins are fairly basic, with cement floors, bamboo walls, simple beds, and little else. The suites are nicely done and feature a full kitchen and dining area. The open-air restaurant here serves excellent Belizean and Mexican cuisine for very reasonable prices, and sits atop a small Mayan ruin. Owner Chena Gálvez is extremely personable, and staff members can help arrange boats and inner-tube rentals; horseback riding is also available. If you'd like to just visit for the day, you can swim in the river and picnic for BZ$2, which is a very popular activity on weekends (if you crave peace and tranquillity, visit on a weekday).

Benque Viejo Rd., Mile Marker 70½ (P.O. Box 44, San Ignacio), Cayo District. ⓒ/fax **824-3916.** www.clarissa falls.com. 12 units. BZ$150 double; BZ$350 suite; BZ$15 per person to camp. AE, DISC, MC, V. Clarissa Falls Resort is about 1.6km (1 mile) down a dirt road, off the highway about 6km (4 miles) west of San Ignacio. The bus to Benque Viejo will drop you at the turnoff. **Amenities:** Restaurant. *In room:* No phone.

Macal River Jungle Camp ⚑ Run by the folks at Chaa Creek, this deluxe campsite is a great choice for those who want to be close to nature but like to have a few frills and easy accessibility. The spacious tent units are all set on raised platforms among the forest trees. Each comes with two to four single beds, as well as a couple of kerosene lanterns. There's a small sitting area or front porch, with an oil lamp and a couple of chairs. Meals are served in a central, open, thatched-roof structure, which also has some hammocks for hanging out. The communal bathroom and shower areas are clean and well-maintained. The river is down a short path from the campsite; Rainforest Medicine Trail and Chaa Creek are nearby. Guests at the tent camp can rent canoes, head over for meals a la carte, or sign up for any tours offered at Chaa Creek.

Off the road to Benque Viejo (P.O. Box 53, San Ignacio), Cayo District. ⓒ **877/709-8708** in the U.S. and Canada, or 824-2037 reservations office in Belize, or 820-4010 at the lodge. Fax 824-2501. www. belizecamp.com. 10 tents. BZ$110 per person. Rates include breakfast and dinner. Rates slightly lower during the off season. AE, MC, V. **Amenities:** Restaurant. *In room:* No phone.

Inexpensive

The Trek Stop This rustic little outpost is geared toward backpackers and adventure travelers. The accommodations here are spread around a broad garden and backed by dense forest, and they range from campsites to simple cabins to a couple of newer cabins with private bathrooms. Most of the wooden cabins are quite small, but they do come with a private little front porch, where you can sit and read. Guests can either eat at the little restaurant here or cook their own food in the communal kitchen. A wide range of tours and activities is offered, and inner tubing on the Mopan River is one of their specialties. They even have a 9-hole Frisbee golf course. This place is very close to the ferry over to Xunantunich. The Trek Stop is located next to the Tropical Wings Nature Center, just off the main road about 9.7km (6 miles) west of San Ignacio.

Benque Viejo Rd., Mile Marker 7½, San José Succotz, Cayo District. ©️ **823-2265.** www.thetrekstop. com. 10 units (8 with shared bathroom). BZ$76 double cabin; BZ$48–BZ$56 double with shared bathroom; BZ$10 per person camping. MC, V. **Amenities:** Restaurant; mountain-bike rental; free Wi-Fi. *In room:* No phone.

ON THE ROAD TO BULLET TREE FALLS

El Pilar ★★ (©️ **824-3612;** www.marc.ucsb.edu/elpilar) was discovered in the 1970s, but real excavation and exploration didn't begin for another 20 years, and in fact it's still in its nascent stages. The site sits on a high hill some 274m (900 ft.) above the Mopan River and is one of the largest Mayan settlements in Belize. Some say it even rivals Caracol. This ancient ceremonial city featured more than 25 known plazas and covered some 40 hectares (100 acres), straddling the Belize and Guatemala border. The site is quite large, but most visitors concentrate on Xaman Pilar (North Pilar) and Nohol Pilar (South Pilar). Pilar Poniente (West Pilar) is in Guatemala, a little less than a mile away. There are several well-marked and well-maintained trails throughout the site. While you can explore El Pilar by yourself—you can even download a very informative trail map from the above website—I still recommend hiring a local guide. Plan on spending at least 3 hours here, though you could easily spend a full day or two exploring this site. The sunsets from Plaza Ixim looking west to Pilar Poniente and the forested hills of Guatemala are spectacular.

El Pilar is located about 19km (12 miles) north of San Ignacio, past the village of Bullet Tree Falls. In addition to driving your own vehicle, several tour agencies in San Ignacio offer horseback or mountain-bike tours out to El Pilar.

A Couple of Places to Stay in Bullet Tree Falls

To get to the hotels mentioned below, take Waight's Avenue west out of the center of San Ignacio. This turns into Bullet Tree Falls Road. Follow the flow of traffic to the village of Bullet Tree Falls. The whole trip is just more than 2 miles. If you arrange it in advance, the hotels will provide pickup, or a taxi should cost you around BZ$20.

Cohune Palms River Cabañas ★ 👜 The individual thatch-roof cabins here are beautifully done. Each features a private little balcony, strung with a hammock. Loft sleeping areas make this a great choice for families. The grounds are lush and lead down to the Mopan River, where you'll find a lovely covered thatch-roof ranch house, open-air dining room, and large wooden deck, where you can lounge around and watch the water flow. When you're ready to cool off, plunge in using the nearby rope swing, or ask for an inner tube for a leisurely float.

Bullet Tree Falls (P.O. Box 198, San Ignacio), Cayo District. ✆ **820-0166** or 609-2738. www.cohune palms.com. 4 units. BZ$138–BZ$198 double. MC, V. **Amenities:** Restaurant; mountain-bike rental; free Wi-Fi. *In room:* No phone.

Parrot's Nest Just upstream from Cohune Palms, the Parrot's Nest is set on a 2-hectare (5-acre) tropical plant farm on the banks of the Mopan River. This simple lodge consists of a few rustic wooden cabins; two of these are set high on stilts, among the branches of a huge guanacaste tree. Only one of the units has a private bathroom, but the shared showers and toilets are kept immaculate. A host of tours and activities can be arranged. You can also take an inner tube right from the lodge and spend some time floating on the river.

Bullet Tree Falls (P.O. Box 198, San Ignacio), Cayo District. ✆ **820-4058.** www.parrot-nest.com. 6 units (5 with shared bathroom). BZ$90 double. MC, V. **Amenities:** Restaurant; mountain-bike rental. *In room:* No phone.

MOUNTAIN PINE RIDGE & CARACOL ★★

111km (69 miles) W of Belize City

South of San Ignacio and the Western Highway, and east of the Macal River, lies the Mountain Pine Ridge region of Belize. Few people think of pine trees when thinking about the tropics, but you'll see plenty of them in these rugged mountains. This area is a natural wonderland of spectacular waterfalls, wild orchids, parrots, keel-billed toucans, and other exotic flora and fauna. **Mountain Pine Ridge Forest Reserve, Hidden Valley Falls** (also called Thousand Foot Falls), **Five Sisters Falls,** and the **Río on Pools** and **Río Frío Caves** are all located in this area.

Continuing on through the Mountain Pine Ridge, you'll eventually come to **Caracol,** which is the largest of the Belizean Mayan ruins. Caracol was a major Classic Mayan center, rivaling and frequently battling nearby Tikal. Excavation is still in its infancy here, but the site is nonetheless impressive. At nearly 42m (138 ft.), the main pyramid at Caracol remains the tallest manmade structure in Belize.

Pine beetle infestations and forest fires have periodically ravaged the forests of the Mountain Pine Ridge reserve, leaving broad swaths totally barren for miles. However, the forests here tend to recover well, and quickly.

Essentials

GETTING THERE & DEPARTING

BY PLANE The nearest airport to this region is in San Ignacio. Although it gets no regularly scheduled commuter traffic, there is a private airstrip at Blancaneaux Lodge (p. 252) for charter flights to that hotel.

BY CAR If you're driving to the Mountain Pine Ridge area from Belize City along the Western Highway, the first turnoff is at Georgeville, around Mile Marker 61. This is the quickest route if you're going deep into the Mountain Pine Ridge area and to Caracol. There's another turnoff in the town of Santa Elena that will take you through Cristo Rey and San Antonio villages, as well as to some of the lodges listed below. Whichever of these routes you take, the roads merge around Mile Marker 10, where you will come to the entrance to the Mountain Pine Ridge Forest Reserve.

ACCOMMODATIONS ■
Black Rock Jungle River
  Lodge 9
Blancaneaux Lodge 19
Chaa Creek 7
Crystal Paradise Resort 4
duPlooy's 8
Five Sisters Lodge 20
Hidden Valley Inn 16
Ka'ana 3
Macal River Jungle Camp 7
Mopan River Resort 1
Mountain Equestrian Trails 12
Mystic River Resort 6
Pine Ridge Lodge 18
Table Rock Camp & Cabañas 5
The Trek Stop 2

ATTRACTIONS & SHOPPING ●
Barton Creek Cave 15
Belize Botanical Gardens 8
Calico Jack's Village 14
Caracol 24
Five Sisters Falls 21
Green Hills Butterfly Ranch
  & Botanical Collection 13
Hidden Valley Falls 17
Magaña Zaac Tunich
  Art Gallery 11
Río Frío Cave 22
Río on Pools 23
Tanah Mayan Art Museum 10

The guard will ask you where you are going, and whether you have a reservation, but there is no fee to enter the reserve.

These roads can get pretty muddy and slick in the wet season and are bumpy and rugged in the dry season, so I recommend you have a four-wheel-drive vehicle, if nothing else, for the extra clearance it will provide. Even though the distances seem relatively slight in terms of mileage, the going can be slow, so allow plenty of driving time if you plan on visiting this area.

Tip: The difference in time and distance between these two turnoffs is negligible, as they meet up about 14km (8⅔ miles) in from the Western Highway (19km/12 miles if you're coming via Cristo Rey Village and San Antonio Village).

BY BUS There is no regular direct bus service to the Mountain Pine Ridge area from Belize City.

GETTING AROUND

Your best bet for getting around this area is to have your own vehicle. Short of that, you can rely on your hotel or organized tours. Taxis can be called from San Ignacio

10

THE CAYO DISTRICT & WESTERN BELIZE

Mtn Pine Ridge & Caracol

and Santa Elena. For a cab, call **Cayo Taxi Association** at © **824-2196.** A cab from San Ignacio to any of the hotels in this area costs around BZ$80 to BZ$120, and a cab from Philip S. W. Goldson International Airport in Belize City to a hotel in this area costs between BZ$250 and BZ$300.

ORIENTATION

Once the two entrance roads join up, there is basically one "major" road leading through the Mountain Pine Forest Reserve and on out to the Caracol ruins. This rough dirt road is alternatively known as the Pine Ridge Road or the Chiquibil Road. Caracol, the Río on Pools, Río Frío Cave, and Five Sisters Falls are located either right on or just off this road. Various spurs and assorted lesser roads head off toward some of the other attractions and destinations listed below. Everything is fairly well-marked and signposted.

There are no major settlements in this area. The only town of any size and note is San Antonio Village, a quaint little Maya village.

What to See & Do

The easiest way to visit Mountain Pine Ridge and its many attractions is on a guided tour out of San Ignacio or one of the nearby lodges. These tours average between BZ$60 and BZ$120 per person for a half-day tour of Mountain Pine Ridge and a visit to one of the waterfalls, and about BZ$180 to BZ$300 for a full-day guided trip to Caracol with lunch. If you're staying in Mountain Pine Ridge, just arrange the tour with your hotel. If you're in San Ignacio, check in with **Pacz Tours ★★** (© **824-2477** or 824-0536; www.pacztours.net) or **Yute Expeditions ★** (© **824-2076;** www.inlandbelize.com).

HORSEBACK RIDING The terrain here is wonderful for horseback riding. Most horseback tours will take you to one or more of the major attractions in this area, or at least to some quiet swimming hole or isolated waterfall. Most of the hotels out here offer horseback riding tours. Alternatively, you can contact the folks at **Mountain Equestrian Trails** (© **669-1124;** www.metbelize.com), who have one of the better stables and horse-riding operations in the Cayo District. A half-day trip including lunch costs BZ$122 per person; a full-day trip costs BZ$166.

MOUNTAIN BIKING This region lends itself equally well to mountain biking. The same trails and dirt roads that are used by cars and horses are especially well-suited for fat-tire explorations. Most of the hotels in the region have bikes for rent or free for guests. If not, you'll probably have to have them arrange it for you, or contact an agency in San Ignacio (see "San Ignacio," earlier in this chapter).

ZIPLINE CANOPY & CAVE TOURS ★ The folks at **Calico Jack's Village** (© **820-4078;** www.calicojacksvillage.com) have opened up a multiadventure sport attraction in the hills and forests just outside the village of El Progresso. The main attraction here is a zipline canopy tour, in which you use a climbing harness and pulley system to glide along steel cables from one treetop platform to another. There are a total of six platforms here, connected by five cables. The longest cable is some 427m (1,400 ft.). The roughly hour-long trip costs BZ$110 per person. While here you can also take a guided tour of one of their on-site caves (BZ$90) or hike their jungle trails (BZ$80). Combination packages with lunch are available, and they have a few onsite villas for those looking to stay.

WILL NATURAL WONDERS NEVER CEASE?

WATERFALLS   Waterfalls are abundant in this region. Perhaps my favorite are the falls found at the **Río on Pools ★★**. This is a series of falls and pools somewhat reminiscent of Ocho Ríos in Jamaica. There's a little entrance hut and parking lot when you enter the area. From here, some concrete steps lead straight down a very steep hill to the base of the falls. While the views and swimming are fine at the bottom, it's a very strenuous hike back up, and I personally think you'll find better pools and views by hiking a few minutes upstream. Here you'll find numerous pools and rapids flowing between big rocks. Many of these rocks are perfect for sunbathing. This place can get crowded on weekends, when locals come for family picnics and getaways. The Río on Pools are located at around Mile Marker 18½ of the Pine Ridge Road. There is no entrance fee.

You can also visit the **Five Sister Falls ★★**, a lovely series of cascading falls that divides into five distinct side-by-side cascades just above the riverside beach and bar area of the Five Sisters Lodge (p. 255). If you are not staying at the lodge, you may visit the falls for BZ$10. It's 290 steps, almost straight down, to the water and the base of the falls. Luckily, you don't have to hoof it, unless you want to, since they have a little funicular. For an extra charge of BZ$8, the funicular will take you to and from the base of the falls, where the hotel has a little beach area and several natural swimming holes. There are some nature trails you can hike, and a small snack bar, restrooms, and changing facilities. You'll even find a wonderful open-air thatch palapa on the banks of the river strung with hammocks—a compelling spot for an afternoon siesta.

RIO FRIO CAVE   This high, vaulted cave is about 183m (600 ft.) long and open at both ends, with a lazy creek flowing through it. There's a path leading through the cave, and several hiking trails run through the forests surrounding it. This is a good cave for those who might normally find the thought of spelunking too claustrophobic for comfort. The views looking out from within the cave are gorgeous. Along the neighboring trails you will find other caves that you can venture into. However, be careful and be sure to have a good flashlight. To reach the Río Frío Cave, drive the Pine Ridge Road to Douglas Da Silva Village at about Mile Marker 24. Do not follow the turnoff for Caracol, but head into the little village. Here you will see signs for the turnoff to the cave. The cave is about 1.6km (1 mile) outside the village. There's a small parking area very close to the mouth of the cave and a couple of picnic tables and benches along the river. No admission is charged to visit here.

BUTTERFLIES   The **Green Hills Butterfly Ranch & Botanical Collection ★** (*(C* **820-4017;** www.green-hills.net) is a lovely little project affording you the chance to see numerous butterfly species and a range of tropical flora. These folks raise dozens of local species of butterflies, and visitors get to see them up close and personal. This place is located at around Mile Marker 8 of the Pine Ridge Road, across from Mountain Equestrian Trails. Guided tours (BZ$25) are offered daily, between 8am and 3:30pm. Reservations are recommended.

CARACOL ★★

Caracol (www.caracol.org) is the largest known Mayan archaeological site in Belize, and one of the great Mayan city-states of the Classic era (A.D. 250–950). At one point, Caracol supported a population of more than 150,000. Caracol, which means "shell" in Spanish, gets its name from the large number of snail shells found here during early explorations. So far three main plazas with numerous structures and two ball courts have been excavated.

Caracol has revealed a wealth of informative carved glyphs that have allowed archaeologists to fill in much of the history of this once powerful city-state. Glyphs here claim Caracol defeats of rivals Tikal in A.D. 562 and Naranjo in 631. One of the earliest temples here was built in A.D. 70, and the Caracol royal family has been officially chronicled since 331. The last recorded date on a glyph is 859, and archaeologists conclude that by 1050 Caracol had been completely abandoned.

Caracol is located deep within the Chiquibil Forest Reserve. The ruins are not nearly as well-cleared or excavated as Tikal or Xunantunich. However, this is part of the site's charm. There is great bird-watching and the chance to see other wild fauna out here. Moreover, the area has been declared the **Caracol Archaeological Reserve,** and excavation and restoration are ongoing. A visit to Caracol is often combined with a stop at the Río on Pools or one or more of the other attractions in the Mountain Pine Ridge area.

> ### Sky Scraper
>
> The largest pyramid at Caracol, **Caana** or "Sky Palace," stands some 41m (135 ft.) high, and is the tallest Maya building in Belize, and still the tallest man-made structure in the country (the Radisson Fort George in Belize City is the only modern structure that even comes close).

Caracol is open daily from 8am to 4pm; admission is BZ$15. There's a small visitor center at the entrance, and a guide can sometimes be hired here, although most visitors come with their own guide as part of an organized tour. Caracol is about 80km (50 miles) along a dirt road from the Western Highway. Actually, the final 16km (10 miles) into the park are paved. Plan on the drive taking about 2 hours, a little more if the road is in bad shape.

Shopping

If you're in the area, be sure to stop at the **Tanah Mayan Art Museum** ★ (② 824-3310; daily 8am–5pm), run by the García sisters, some of the premier artisans working in carved slate. While it's a stretch to call their little shop and showroom a museum, you will find a nice collection of the García sisters' carvings, as well as other Maya artifacts and handicrafts. This place is located at about Mile Marker 8 of the Cristo Rey Road, about a mile before you reach the village of San Antonio. On the other side of the village, you should stop at the **Magaña Zaac Tunich Art Gallery** (no phone), which carries a range of local craftworks and specializes in woodcarvings.

Where to Stay & Dine

VERY EXPENSIVE

Blancaneaux Lodge ★★★ This remote ecolodge, another of Francis Ford Coppola's properties, is set on a steep, pine-forested hillside, overlooking the Privassion River and a series of gentle falls. The individual cabanas here are all cozy and intimate. Most of these are "riverfront" units, although a couple are termed "garden view." My favorites are the riverfront "honeymoon" units, which have private plunge pools. Most of the villas are two-bedroom, two-bathroom affairs. The best feature of

Caracol

these is their large, open-air central living area, which flows into a forest- and river-view deck. Villa 7 is Coppola's private villa whenever he visits, and it features some of the director's photo memorabilia, as well as a painting by his daughter and fellow director Sofia Coppola. You can rent it whenever he's not around, and it comes with a private plunge pool and a personal butler. The luxurious "Enchanted Cottage" is a short distance from everything else, and has a great view, an infinity pool, and personal butler service, as well.

Mountain Pine Ridge Reserve (P.O. Box B, Central Farm), Cayo District. ✆ **800/746-3743** in the U.S., 824-4912 reservations office in Belize, or 824-3878 at the lodge. Fax 824-3919. www.blancaneaux.com. 20 units. BZ$560–BZ$1,000 double cabin; BZ$1,080–BZ$1,450 2-bedroom villa; BZ$2,800 Enchanted Cottage. Rates include continental breakfast. Rates lower in the off season; higher during peak weeks. AE, MC, V. Blancaneaux has its own airstrip, and charter flights from Belize City can be arranged. **Amenities:** Restaurant; bar; lounge; bike rental; horse stables; 2 outdoor pools; small spa. *In room:* Free Wi-Fi.

EXPENSIVE

Hidden Valley Inn ★★ This isolated mountain resort has a beautiful setting on more than 2,833 hectares (7,000 acres) of private land. The individual bungalows are all plenty roomy, and come with either one queen bed or two twin beds, as well as cool red-tile floors, high ceilings, and a working fireplace. Deluxe units feature beautiful claw-foot bathtubs and outdoor waterfall showers. The outdoor pool and Jacuzzi are surrounded by a beautiful slate deck. This is the closest hotel to the Hidden Valley, or Thousand Foot Falls, the tallest waterfall in Belize, a semistrenuous 2-hour hike from the hotel. However, there are actually several other, much more easily accessible, jungle waterfalls and swimming holes right on the property. The property boasts an extensive network of trails, and the bird-watching is excellent. The coffee you're served at breakfast is grown right here, as are many of the fruits and vegetables.

Mountain Pine Ridge (P.O. Box 170, Belmopan), Cayo District. © **866/443-3364** in the U.S., or 822-3320 in Belize. Fax 822-3334. www.hiddenvalleyinn.com. 12 units. BZ$390 double; BZ$500 deluxe. Rates slightly lower in the off season; higher during peak periods. MC, V. **Amenities:** Restaurant; bar; lounge; free mountain bike use; Jacuzzi; small outdoor pool; free Wi-Fi. *In room:* No phone.

Mountain Equestrian Trails (MET) ★ The folks here are some of the best horse- and adventure-tour operators in the area. The rooms are decidedly rustic and a bit pricey for what you get. Housed in a series of duplex buildings, all feature high thatched roofs, cool tile floors, queen beds hung with mosquito netting, and plenty of windows for cross-ventilation. The rooms do feature colorful Guatemalan bed-spreads and indigenous arts and crafts on the walls. There's no electricity in the rooms, and kerosene lanterns provide light. A large open-air palapa serves as the lodge's restaurant, bar, and meeting area. While horses and horseback riding tours are the principal draw here, a whole range of tours and activities is offered. The owners at MET helped create the private Slate Creek Preserve, a 1,214-hectare (3,000-acre) tract of land bordering the Mountain Pine Ridge Preserve. A meal package runs BZ$78 per person per day.

Pine Ridge Rd., Cayo District. © **800/838-3918** in the U.S. and Canada, or 669-1124 in Belize. www.metbelize.com. 10 units. BZ$264 double. Rates lower in the off season. AE, MC, V. **Amenities:** Restaurant; bar. *In room:* No phone.

Mystic River Resort ★★ Perched on a hill overlooking the Macal River, every room here is a private little cabin, with high wood ceilings, a working fireplace, a small sitting area with a divan, and a cozy, private balcony for peering through the trees to the river below. Furnishings and decor are tasteful. The small plunge pool is only .6m (2 ft.) deep, but features a central fountain and an adjacent shade area with chaise longues and a nearby bar, making it a popular place to hang out. Creative meals are served in the large open-air dining room.

Mile 6, Cristo Rey Rd., Cayo District. © **678-6700.** www.mysticriverbelize.com. 11 units. BZ$350–BZ$450 double. AE, MC, V. **Amenities:** Restaurant; bar; free canoe use; small plunge pool; smoke-free rooms; free Wi-Fi. *In room:* A/C, MP3 docking station, no phone.

Table Rock Camp & Cabañas ★ 🎁 This intimate resort is a great choice in the region. Rooms feature high-pitched thatch roofs, plenty of louvered windows for ventilation, cool tile floors, and pretty showers built with smooth, local river stones. Two of the rooms are part of a duplex building, with small private decks off the front. But the Mot Mot cabin here is the top choice, with more space and a spacious private veranda. It's a short hike down to the Macal River, where the lodge keeps several canoes and has built an open-air octagonal hammock hut beside a pretty patch of beach. Much of the land here is devoted to organic gardens and citrus groves. Meals and service are top-notch.

Mile 5, Cristo Rey Rd. (P.O. Box 179), Cayo District. © **670-4910.** www.tablerockbelize.com. 6 units. BZ$270–BZ$310 double. Rates lower in the off season; higher during peak periods. AE, MC, V. **Amenities:** Restaurant; bar; free bike use; free canoe use; all rooms smoke-free; free Wi-Fi. *In room:* No phone.

MODERATE

Crystal Paradise Resort   The nicest thing about this little family-run resort is probably the Tut family that runs it. Most of the rooms are in thatch-roof duplex buildings, with tile floors, ceiling fans, and private verandas. The best rooms face the Macal River Valley, with beautiful views of the surrounding forests. One popular feature here is the on-site bird-watching platform built to blend in with the forest canopy. A host of tours is offered, and the in-house guides—most of them family members—are excellent. The restaurant serves wonderful Belizean cuisine, and there's always a convivial vibe in the open-air dining room, bar, and lounge areas. This place is located on the road to Mountain Pine Ridge, near the tiny Cristo Rey Village.

Cristo Rey Village (P.O. Box 126), Cayo District. ©/fax **824-2772** reservations office or 820-4014 at the lodge. www.crystalparadise.com. 20 units. BZ$118–BZ$158 double. AE, MC, V. **Amenities:** Restaurant; bar; lounge. *In room:* No phone.

Five Sisters Lodge ★   This hotel is located in the heart of the Mountain Pine Ridge Reserve, about 61m (200 ft.) above its namesake Five Sisters Falls, a beautiful and rambling series of waterfalls and swimming holes. The individual cottages have palmetto stick walls, thatched roofs, and beds hung with mosquito netting. Some have polished wood floors, while others feature cool Mexican tiles. All have a mix of local and Guatemalan furnishings and decor, as well as a screened-in veranda hung with a hammock. The junior suites feature excellent waterfall views, king-size beds, and large tubs. The standard rooms are comfortable enough, but most lack a view or balcony. The best room here, although it's a good distance from the main lodge, is the Riverside Villa, a luxurious cabin set down by the river and falls.

Mountain Pine Ridge (P.O. Box 173, San Ignacio), Cayo District. © **800/447-2931** in the U.S. and Canada, or 820-4048 in Belize. Fax 820-4024. www.fivesisterslodge.com. 19 units. BZ$210–BZ$230 double; BZ$300 junior suite; BZ$500 Riverside Villa. Rates include continental breakfast. Rates lower in the off season. AE, MC, V. **Amenities:** Restaurant; bar; lounge. *In room:* No phone.

Pine Ridge Lodge   This rustic little lodge is located in the heart of the Mountain Pine Ridge area, close to all attractions. Most of the rooms are in duplex units, with polished concrete floors, simple wooden furniture, and local and Guatemalan crafts and textiles completing the decor. Light in the rooms is provided by kerosene lanterns, and the showers are heated by on-demand butane heaters. The grounds are loaded with a wide variety of orchids and attract an equally wide variety of bird species. The lodge is set on the banks of a small creek, and the best rooms are close to and overlooking this creek. There's also a small waterfall an easy hike from the lodge. Meals, which feature organic fruits and vegetables grown on-site, are served family-style in the small screened-in dining room and bar area.

Mountain Pine Ridge (P.O. Box 128, San Ignacio), Cayo District. © **800/316-0706** in the U.S., or 606-4557. www.pineridgelodge.com. 6 units. BZ$178 double. Rates lower in the off season. Rates include continental breakfast. No credit cards. **Amenities:** Restaurant; bar. *In room:* No phone.

11

TIKAL & GUATEMALA'S PETÉN

Bordering Belize, Mexico, and Honduras, and occupying the entire northeastern section of Guatemala, the Petén is Guatemala's largest and least populated province. Most of the Petén is forest—thick tropical rainforest. It is a lush and wild landscape that contains some of Mesoamerica's richest archaeological treasures. In 1990, the government of Guatemala officially established the **Maya Biosphere Reserve,** a tract of 1 million hectares (2.5 million acres) that includes most of the Petén Province. Moreover, the Maya Biosphere Reserve adjoins the neighboring **Calakmul Biosphere Reserve** in Mexico and the **Río Bravo Conservation Area** in Belize, comprising a joint protected area of more than 2 million hectares (5 million acres).

The Petén Province is home to perhaps the most impressive and best preserved of the ancient Mayan ceremonial cities, **Tikal.** It is also home to numerous other lesser, and less excavated, sites. In addition, the area is a rich and rewarding destination for bird-watchers and ecotourists. Given the close proximity of Tikal to the Belize border (and the long distance between Guatemala City and the Petén), it is in some ways more convenient to visit Tikal from Belize than it is from Guatemala. This chapter will give you all the necessary information to plan a visit to this fascinating destination, whether you want to take a quick 1-day tour of the ruins at Tikal or a multiday adventure exploring the region.

TIKAL ★★★

100km (62 miles) NW of the Belize border; 65km (40 miles) N of Flores

Tikal is one of the greatest of the surviving Classic Maya cities. It is estimated that Tikal once supported a population of about 100,000 people.

Archaeologists have identified more than 3,000 structures, and in its heyday, the city probably covered as much as 65 sq. km (25 sq. miles). Tikal is far more extensively excavated than any ruins in Belize, and unlike the grand cities and excavations in Mexico, Tikal rises out of dense jungle. The pyramids here are some of the most perfect examples of ceremonial architecture in the Maya world. Standing atop Temple IV, you are high above the rainforest canopy. The peaks of several temples poke through the dense vegetation. Toucans and parrots fly about, and the loudest noise you'll hear is the guttural call of howler monkeys.

Tikal is within easy reach of Belize's western border, and scores of organized tour groups and independent travelers from Belize visit the site every day.

Essentials

GETTING THERE & DEPARTING

BY PLANE **Tropic Air** (© **800/422-3435** in the U.S. or Canada, 226-2012 in Belize City, or 502/7926-0348 in Flores; www.tropicair.com) has two daily flights to Flores Airport (FRS) from Goldson International Airport in Belize City, at 7:45am

Tikal

ACCOMMODATIONS ■
Jaguar Inn **2**
Jungle Lodge **1**
Tikal Inn **3**

DINING ◆
Comedor Imperio Maya **5**
Comedor Tikal **4**

Complex P

Group H

Complex M

MALER CAUSEWAY

MAUDSLAY CAUSEWAY

Complex R

Complex O

Temple IV

North
Acropolis

WEST
PLAZA

Sweat
House

TOZZER CAUSEWAY

Temple II

Complex N

Temple III

GREAT
PLAZA

EAST
PLAZA

Temple I

Bat
Palace

Central
Acropolis

Temple V

Pyramid

El Mundo
Perdido

South
Acropolis

*PLAZA OF THE
SEVEN TEMPLES*

Sylvanus G. Morely Museum

Campground

Visitor's Center

Complex Q

Lithic Museum

Entrance

Map■

Group F

To Flores

◀ — — Walking Tour

0   1/10 mile

0   100 meters

MENDEZ CAUSEWAY

Temple VI
(Temple of the inscriptions)

Telephone Tip

Guatemala's country code is **502** (Belize's is 501). Guatemala uses an eight-digit phone numbering system. Nonetheless, to avoid confusion between Belizean and Guatemalan telephone numbers, we have included the country code in the Guatemalan numbers, whereas in this section and throughout the book, we've omitted the Belizean country code in phone number listings.

and 3pm. The flights return at 8:45am and 4:15pm. Flight duration is 45 minutes; it costs BZ$228 each way or BZ$447 round-trip.

Leaving Belize, you will have to pay a total of BZ$79 in departure taxes. Leaving Guatemala, there is a US$30 departure tax for international flights, as well as a US$3 Guatemalan tax on all flights to and from Flores.

The airport is on the road to Tikal, about 2.4km (1½ miles) east of Santa Elena. A taxi from the airport into Santa Elena or Flores should cost you around Q25 (25 quetzales; see p. 264). Or you can take a local bus (usually an old Bluebird school bus) for around Q1. Collective taxis and minivans to Tikal are usually waiting at the airport and charge around Q50 per person each way. You can sometimes bargain, and you can often get a slight discount if you purchase a round-trip fare right from the start. A private taxi can be hired for the drive for around Q400.

BY CAR Driving from Belize City, take the Western Highway to San Ignacio, and continue on to the border town of Benque Viejo del Carmen. From Benque, follow the signs to the border at a bridge over the Mopan River, a little more than 1.6km (1 mile) out of town.

The border crossing and formalities are very similar to those described below in "By Bus." You will be corralled by touts on the Guatemalan side offering all sorts of aid and services, and demanding all sorts of fees and duties. By law you are supposed to have your tires fumigated. This should cost only a U.S. dollar or two. You should not have to pay any additional fees. Whether you are driving your own car or a rental car, be sure to have all your current registration, title, and insurance papers.

Once across the border, follow signs out of Melchor de Mencos toward Flores and Tikal. It's about a 1-hour drive to the crossroads at Ixlú, also known as El Cruce. If you are going to El Remate or Tikal, you will turn right here. If you are going to Flores or Santa Elena, you will continue on straight. From Ixlú, it's about 25 to 30 minutes either way to Santa Elena/Flores or the ruins at Tikal. The entrance to Tikal National Park is located 18km (11 miles) south of the visitor center and true entrance to the ruins and its network of trails. Here you will have to pay the Q150 entrance fee. The entrance is open daily from 6am to 6pm. If you arrive after 3pm, tell them you plan to visit the ruins the following day, and they will stamp your ticket to that effect. If you plan to spend more than a day here staying at one of the hotels or campsites near the ruins, advise them and try to pay your entrance fee for subsequent days in advance, as sometimes they send people all the way back to the entrance gate to buy a subsequent day's ticket.

If you're traveling in a rental car, be sure that the company you rented from in Belize allows the car to cross into Guatemala. **Crystal Auto Rental** (✆ 0800/777-7777 in Belize; www.crystal-belize.com) does.

Beware: It is strongly advised that you do not travel at night. It is a sad fact that armed groups occasionally set up roadblocks along these isolated yet frequently trafficked roads.

BY BUS   If you're traveling from Belize City by bus, you can take one of two daily buses. These buses run between Belize City and Santa Elena, not the Tikal ruins. If you're coming from Belize City, you'll have to get further transportation to visit Tikal. The buses leave at 9:30am and 2:30pm from right in front of the Marine Terminal in downtown Belize City. The fare is BZ$60 one-way. The trip takes around 5 to 6 hours. The return buses leave Flores/Santa Elena at 5 and 7:30am. Two separate bus lines make this trip run: **Línea Dorada** (📞 **502/7926-0070;** www.lineadorada.info) and **San Juan Travel** (📞 **502/5847-4738**). Both can be booked in Belize by **Mundo Maya Travels** (📞 **223-0457;** mundomayatravels@yahoo.com).

Alternatively, you can take one of the many buses from Belize City (or from San Ignacio) to the Guatemalan border. Buses to San Ignacio leave roughly every half-hour from the main bus station on West Collet Canal Street between 5am and 8pm. Return buses to Belize City leave the main bus station in San Ignacio roughly every half-hour between 4am and 6pm. The fare is BZ$10. The trip takes 2½ hours. Most of the western-bound buses continue beyond San Ignacio to Benque Viejo and the Guatemalan border. Some of these leave you in Benque Viejo, while others go all the way to the border crossing, a little more than 1.6km (1 mile) away. There are numerous taxis at the Benque Viejo bus station that will take you to the border for BZ$8.

On the Belize side, you will have to fill out a departure card, have your passport stamped, and pay the departure tax of BZ$30, plus the BZ$7.50 PACT tax. Just over the bridge lies the Guatemalan border town of Melchor de Mencos. When you pass through Guatemalan immigration, you will be provided with a tourist card good for up to 90 days. Theoretically this card is free. However, border formalities in Guatemala are often open to corruption, with border officials and local touts looking to glean some extra money. Moreover, Guatemalan border formalities change from time to time, and there is a long-running dispute between Guatemala and Belize (Guatemala claims that all of Belize is actually part of Guatemala, dating back to the mid–19th c.), so it always pays to check with the Guatemalan Embassy in your home country if you are certain you will be traveling there. The border crossing can take from 20 minutes to more than an hour, depending on the crowds.

Once you're finished with the border formalities, it is a simple matter to find onward transportation to Tikal or Flores and Santa Elena. The least expensive means of transport is the local bus; however, none of the local buses goes directly to Tikal. Instead, they head to Flores and Santa Elena, but they will drop you off at Ixlú (El Cruce), where you can flag down one of the many minivans and collective taxis going from Flores and Santa Elena to the ruins. Be forewarned that while local buses are very inexpensive (around Q3–Q8), they can be overcrowded and very slow. They stop almost constantly along the way to pick up and discharge passengers and their cargo. I recommend you take one of these buses only if you're interested more in the local color and adventure of the trip than in a speedy arrival at the ruins.

A much better bet is to take one of the collective taxis or minivans that leave right from Melchor de Mencos. Most of these wait just outside the border station and leave as soon as they fill up. Some go to Flores and Santa Elena, while others go directly to Tikal. Most charge Q80 to Q160 per person.

Finally, if there are no collective taxis or minivans available, you can hire a taxi that will carry up to six people for between Q400 and Q600.

Tip: If you are only going for the day, try to arrange a round-trip fare with your taxi or minivan driver, with a specific departure time from Tikal. Usually, it's best to leave Tikal by 4pm, so as to drive during daylight and arrive at the border with plenty of time.

BY ORGANIZED TOUR   Organized day trips leave daily for Tikal from Belize City, San Ignacio, San Pedro, Caye Caulker, and Placencia. Costs for these all-inclusive trips are approximately BZ$200 and BZ$400 by land (from Belize City, or

safety IN GUATEMALA

Over the past 50 years, Guatemala has had an ongoing history of political and civil violence and repression. Crime, both petty and violent, is a problem throughout Guatemala. The Guatemalan police and judiciary are underfunded, understaffed, and largely ineffectual. Decades of civil war, genocide, and paramilitary activity, in addition to historic poverty and underdevelopment, have created a dangerous climate where lawlessness is rampant. Foreign nationals—as well as everyday Guatemalans—are the targets of robberies, kidnapping, murders, and rapes. The U.S. State Department strongly cautions visitors to Guatemala and keeps a relatively up-to-date analysis of the situation at **http://travel.state.gov**.

Luckily, the Petén District, where Tikal is located, is a largely isolated and forgotten section of eastern Guatemala. The most common attacks against tourists visiting Tikal occur on the road between the Belizean border and Flores. Taxis, local buses, and air-conditioned minivans have all been targeted. These highway robberies tend to occur in waves, and are by far the exception and not the norm. In almost all known cases, the attacks are armed but nonviolent robberies. If you plan to visit Tikal for a few days as a side trip from Belize, it is often a good idea to find a hotel safe in Belize that will guard any valuables you do not need with you while in Guatemala.

Still, hundreds of tourists visit Tikal and Flores every day, and the vast majority of them have no problems whatsoever. Be sure to take all necessary precautions. Never travel alone or at night, and stick to the most popular and populous tourist destinations and attractions. If you are driving, stop only for people holding guns; do not try to run blockades. Common wisdom cautions against using the low-fare Guatemalan buses and tour agencies; however, high-end tour groups in fancy air-conditioned microbuses do attract the attention of organized criminal gangs. Some tour groups travel with armed guards. This may or may not increase your sense of security and your actual security, to boot. (As far as I'm concerned, the jury is out on that one.) If you are confronted with any sort of criminal attempt, do not resist, as a simple mugging can easily end up turning into murder.

The Guatemalan Tourist Institute (INGUAT) and National Police have set up a special police force, POLITUR, created to patrol tourist destinations and deal directly with tourists. You will hopefully see them present in most major tourist destinations, including Tikal and Flores. You can also call ASISTUR, a tourist assistance service of INGUAT, by dialing ✆ **1500** from any phone in the country.

Shameless Plug

If you're going on to Guatemala for any extended time or travel, you'll want to pick up a copy of *Frommer's Guatemala.*

any of the other major tourist destinations in Belize), depending on group size. Budget an additional BZ$100 to BZ$300 per person per day for multiday excursions. In Belize City, call **Discovery Expeditions** (✆ 223-0748; www.discoverybelize.com) or **S & L Travel and Tours** (✆ 227-7593; www.sltravelbelize.com). In San Ignacio, you can call **Pacz Tours** ★★ (✆ 824-2477 or 824-0536; www.pacztours.net) or **Yute Expeditions** ★★ (✆ 824-2076; www.inlandbelize.com).

GETTING AROUND

BY TAXI OR MINIVAN   Minivans and collective taxis leave throughout the day plying the route between Tikal and Santa Elena/Flores. Minivans and collective taxis charge between Q50 and Q60 per person each way. From Santa Elena, you can catch a bus back to the border. A private cab from Tikal to Santa Elena/Flores will run around Q350 to Q450 each way. Between Tikal and El Remate, the fare is about Q150 to Q200.

BY CAR   There are several local car-rental agencies at the airport. Of these, a good choice is **Tabarini Rent A Car** (✆ 502/7926-0253; www.tabarini.com). All rent small jeeps and SUVs. Do get a four-wheel-drive vehicle; even though you may never need the traction or off-road ability, the extra clearance will come in handy. Rates run from Q350 to Q450 per day.

ORIENTATION

There is no village or town inside Tikal National Park. After having paid your Q150 admission at the entrance booth 18km (11 miles) south of the ruins, you will eventually come to the large central parking area and visitor center. This is where you will find the three hotels and campsite reviewed in "Where to Stay," later in this chapter, as well as the two museums and a collection of simple restaurants. The ruins themselves are about a 15- to 20-minute walk through the forest from the trail entrance here.

You'll spot a post office and telegraph office on the left as you arrive at the parking area. You'll find a public phone in the Stelae Museum. There is no bank or ATM here in Tikal, and most of the little restaurants and gift stands accept only quetzales. Moreover, while some of the hotels here do accept credit cards, the phone connections are spotty, and they sometimes have problems getting the authorizations. It's best to bring quetzales to pay for your entire stay. Also, be sure to bring plenty of insect repellent with you—the bugs here are rapacious.

Tikal National Park is open daily from 6am to 6pm. If you'd like to stay in the park until 8pm (for sunset and nocturnal wildlife viewing), get your admission ticket stamped at the office behind the Stelae Museum. If you arrive after 3pm, your admission is good for the following day as well. If you are staying multiple days, you must pay the admission fee each day. The best times to visit the ruins are in early morning and late afternoon, which are the least crowded and coolest times of day.

FAST FACTS   There are no banks, medical facilities, laundromats, or other major services available at Tikal. All of these can be found in Flores and Santa Elena, some 64km (40 miles) away; see p. 274.

Exploring Tikal

Tikal, one of the largest Mayan cities ever uncovered and the most spectacular ruins in Guatemala, ranks with Mexico's Chichén Itzá in pre-Columbian splendor. However, unlike at Chichén Itzá, the ruins of Tikal are set in the middle of a vast jungle through which you must hike from temple to temple. The many miles of trails through the park provide numerous opportunities to spot interesting birds such as toucans and parrots and such wild animals as coati-mundi, spider monkeys, howler monkeys, and deer. Together, the ruins and the abundance of wildlife make a trip to Tikal an absolute must for anyone interested in Mayan history, birdwatching, or wildlife viewing.

Tikal was a massive ceremonial metropolis. So far, archaeologists have mapped about 3,000 constructions, 10,000 earlier foundations beneath surviving structures, 250 stone monuments (steles and altars), and thousands of art objects found in tombs and cached offerings. There is evidence of continuous construction at Tikal from 200 b.c. through the 9th century a.d., with some suggestion of occupation as early as 600 b.c. The Maya reached their zenith in art and architecture during the Classic Period, which began about a.d. 250 and ended abruptly about 900, when for some reason Tikal and all other major Mayan centers were abandoned. Most of the visible structures at Tikal date from the Late Classic Period, from 600 to 900.

No one's sure just what role Tikal played in the history of the Maya: Was it mostly a ceremonial center for priests, artisans, and the elite? Or was it a city of industry and commerce as well? In the 16 sq. km (6 sq. miles) of Tikal that have been mapped and excavated, only a few of the buildings were domestic structures; most were temples, palaces, ceremonial platforms, and shrines. Workers are excavating the innumerable mounds on the periphery of the mapped area and have been finding modest houses of stone and plaster with thatched roofs. Just how far these settlements extended beyond the ceremonial center and how many people lived within the domain of Tikal is still to be determined. At its height, Tikal may have covered as much as 65 sq. km (25 sq. miles).

MAKING THE MOST OF YOUR VISIT

Tikal is such an immense site that you really need several days to see it thoroughly. But you can visit many of the greatest temples and palaces in 1 day. To do it properly, as a first-time visitor, you should probably hire a guide. Guides are available at the visitor center and charge around Q80 to Q160 for a half-day tour of the ruins,

---

Money

The Guatemalan monetary unit is the quetzal. At press time, the exchange rate was 8 quetzales to the U.S. dollar, and 11.63 quetzales to the British pound. If you're coming from Belize, your best bets for changing dollars into quetzales are at the border or at the numerous banks in Santa Elena and Flores (see "Flores & Santa Elena," later in this chapter). Most of the hotels and restaurants in Tikal, in fact, will exchange dollars for quetzales, although they may give you a slightly less favorable rate than you would get at a bank.

A Familiar Site

Tikal provides such a stunning and unique landscape that it was chosen for an exterior shot in George Lucas's *Star Wars,* as well as the site of a famous series of Nike commercials.

depending on the size of your group. In addition, most hotels and all tour agencies in the region offer guided tours for a similar price.

A WALKING TOUR

To orient yourself, begin your tour of Tikal at the visitor center and neighboring Stelae Museum. Here you'll find some informative exhibits and relics, as well as an impressive relief map of the site. See "The Museums," below, for more information on the steles.

A full tour of Tikal will require an extensive amount of walking, as much as 9.7km (6 miles). The itinerary described here will take you to most of the major temples and plazas, and can be accomplished in about 3 to 4 hours. If your time is really limited, you should follow the signs and head straight to the Great Plaza. If you have a full day, consider this route:

Walking along the road that goes west from the museum toward the ruins, turn right at the first intersection to get to **twin complexes Q** and **R.** Seven of these twin complexes are known at Tikal, but their exact purpose is still a mystery. Each complex has two pyramids facing east and west; at the north is an unroofed enclosure entered by a vaulted doorway and containing a single stele and altar; at the south is a small palace-like structure. Of the two pyramids here, one has been restored and one has been left as it was found, and the latter will give you an idea of just how overgrown and ensconced in the jungle these structures had become.

At the end of the Twin Complexes is a wide road called the **Maler Causeway.** Turn right (north) onto this causeway to get to **Complex P,** another twin complex, a 15-minute walk away. Some restoration has been done at Complex P, but the most interesting points are the replicas of a stele (no. 20) and altar (no. 8) in the north enclosure. Look for the beautiful glyphs next to the carving of a warrior on the stele, all in very good condition. The altar shows a captive bound to a carved-stone altar, his hands tied behind his back—a common scene in carvings at Tikal. Both these monuments date from about A.D. 751.

From Complex P, head south on the **Maudslay Causeway** to **Complex N,** which is the site of **Temple IV, the Temple of the Two-Headed Serpent ★★★.** Finished around A.D. 740, Temple IV is the tallest structure in Tikal and is 65m (213 ft.) from the base of its platform to the top. The first glimpse you get of the temple from the Maudslay Causeway is awesome, for the temple has not been restored, and all but the temple proper (the enclosure) and its roof comb are covered in foliage. The stairway is occluded by earth and roots, but there is a system of steep stairways (actually rough-hewn wooden ladders set against the steep sides of the pyramid) to the top of the temple. The view of the setting and layout of Tikal—and all of the Great Plaza—is magnificent. From the platform of the temple, you can see in all directions and get an idea of the extent of the Petén jungle, an ocean of lush greenery. **Temple III (Temple of the Great Priest)** is in the foreground to the east; **temples I** and **II** are farther on at the Great Plaza. To the right of these are the **South Acropolis** and **Temple V.**

Temple IV, and all the other temples at Tikal, are built on this plan: A pyramid is built first, and on top of it is built a platform; the temple proper rests on this platform and is composed of one to three rooms, usually long and narrow and not for habitation but rather for priestly rites. Most temples had beautifully carved wooden lintels above the doorways. The one from Temple IV is now in the Völkerkunde Museum in Basel, Switzerland.

From Temple IV, walk east along the **Tozzer Causeway** to get to the **Great Plaza,** about a 10-minute walk. Along the way you'll pass the twin-pyramid Complex N, the **Bat Palace,** and Temple III. Take a look at the altar and stele in the complex's northern enclosure—two of the finest monuments at Tikal—and also the altar in front of Temple III, showing the head of a deity resting on a plate. By the way, the crisscross pattern shown here represents a woven mat, a symbol of authority to the Mayas.

THE GREAT PLAZA ★★★

Entering the Great Plaza from the Tozzer Causeway, you'll be struck by the towering stone structure that is Temple II, seen from the back. It measures 38m (125 ft.) tall now, although it is thought to have been 43m (140 ft.) high when the roof comb was intact. Also called the Temple of the Masks, from a large face carved in the roof comb, the temple dates from about A.D. 700. Walk around this temple to enter the plaza proper.

Beat the Crowds

Tikal fills up with tour buses most days, with the hours between 10am and 2pm being the busiest period. I prefer visiting the Great Plaza either before or after the main crowds have left. Feel free to reverse the order of this walking tour if it will help you avoid the masses.

Directly across from Temple II you'll see Temple I (Temple of the Great Jaguar), the most striking structure in Tikal. Standing 44m (145 ft.) tall, the temple proper has three narrow rooms with high corbeled vaults (the Mayan "arch") and carved wooden lintels made of zapote wood, which is rot resistant. One of the lintels has been removed for preservation in the Guatemala National Museum of Archaeology and Ethnology in Guatemala City. The whole structure is made of limestone, as are most others at Tikal. It was within this pyramid that one of the richest tombs in Tikal was discovered. Believed to be the tomb of Tikal ruler Hasaw Chan K'awil, when archaeologists uncovered it in 1962, they found the former ruler's skeleton surrounded by some 180 pieces of jade, 90 bone artifacts carved with hieroglyphic inscriptions, numerous pearls, and objects in alabaster and shell. **Note:** Tourists can no longer scale temples I or III. However, those in need of serious cardio workouts will get their fill climbing some of the other temples.

The **North Acropolis** (north side of the Great Plaza) is a maze of structures from various periods covering an area of 8.5 hectares (21 acres). Standing today 9m (30 ft.) above the limestone bedrock, it contains vestiges of more than a hundred different constructions dating from 200 B.C. to A.D. 800. At the front-center of the acropolis (at the top of the stairs up from the Great Plaza) is a temple numbered **5D-33.** Although much of the 8th-century temple was destroyed during the excavations to get to the Early Classic temple (A.D. 300) underneath, it's still a fascinating building. Toward the rear of it is a tunnel leading to the stairway of the **Early Classic** temple, embellished with two 3m-high (10-ft.) plaster polychrome masks of a god—don't miss these.

Directly across the plaza from the North Acropolis is the **Central Acropolis,** which covers about 1.6 hectares (4 acres). It's a maze of courtyards and palaces on several levels, all connected by an intricate system of passageways. Some of the palaces had five floors, connected by exterior stairways, and each floor had as many as nine rooms arranged like a maze.

Before you leave the Great Plaza, be sure to examine some of the 70 beautiful steles and altars right in the plaza. You can see the full development of Mayan art in them, for they date from the Early Classic Period right through to the Late Classic Period. There are three major stylistic groups: the steles with wraparound carving on the front and sides with text on the back; those with a figure carved on the front and text in glyphs on the back; and those with a simple carved figure on the front, text in hieroglyphs on the sides, and a plain back. The oldest stele is no. 29 (now in the Tikal Museum—see "The Museums," below), dating from A.D. 292; the most recent is no. 11 in the Great Plaza, dating from A.D. 869.

If you head south from Temple II, you will come to the area known as **El Mundo Perdido (The Lost World).** This plaza contains the **Great Pyramid,** which stands 35m (115 ft.) high and is the oldest excavated building in Tikal. This pyramid is one of the most popular spots for watching the sunset. If you've timed it right, you might be able to hang out here and watch the show; otherwise, make a mental note to get your bearings and come back later, if possible. Directly east of the Great Pyramid is the **Plaza of the Seven Temples,** which dates to the Late Classic Period. Bordering this plaza on the east side is an unexcavated pyramid, and behind this is Temple V. This entire area is known as the **South Acropolis.** You can climb Temple V, but be forewarned, the climb, both up and down a very steep and rather rickety wooden

---

 SUNRISE, sunset

Tikal is a magical and mystical place. Many claim that this magic and mystique is only heightened around sunrise and sunset. Sunsets are easier to catch and a more dependable show. Sunrises tend to be more a case of the sun eventually burning through the morning mist than of any impressive orb emerging. However, afternoons can often be clear, especially during the dry season, allowing for excellent sunset viewing from the tops of the main temples here. In either case, much of the attraction can be found all around you, as the bird and animal life of the jungle are much more active around sunrise and sunset. If you're staying right at the ruins, your chances are better of catching either or both of these occasions.

If you're not staying inside the national park, minivans and collective taxis leave Flores and El Remate early enough to get you to the Tikal entrance gate at 6am when it opens. This will generally enable you to get to the top of one of the main temples by 6:30am, which is usually still early enough to catch the sun burning through the mist just over the rainforest canopy.

If you plan on staying for sunset, be absolutely positive that your return transportation will wait for you. The park officially closes at 6pm. Depending on the season, the sun will set below the treetops anywhere between 5 and 6pm, allowing just enough time to watch the spectacle and get out of the park in time.

Tip: If you're planning on catching either the sunrise or the sunset, it's a very good idea to bring along a flashlight, just in case.

stairway, is somewhat harrowing. The view from above is beautiful. However, the steep pitch of the pyramid's original stairway is almost as scary as the climb.

If you cross through the South Acropolis to the east and then turn north in the general direction of the Great Plaza, you will come to the East Plaza. From here you can walk southeast on the Mendez Causeway to **Temple VI (Temple of the Inscriptions),** which contains a nearly illegible line of hieroglyphics that are the most extensive in Tikal. It's worth coming out this way just for the chance to spot some wild animals, which seem to be fairly common in this remote corner of the park.

THE MUSEUMS

The most formal museum here has been officially christened the **Sylvanus G. Morely Museum,** but is also known as the **Tikal** or **Ceramic Museum.** This museum contains a good collection of pottery, mosaic masks, incense burners, etched bone, and steles that are chronologically displayed—beginning with Pre-Classic objects on up to Late Classic pieces. Of note are the delicate 7.6 to 13cm (3- to 5-in.) mosaic masks made of jade, turquoise, shell, and stucco. There is a beautiful cylindrical jar from about A.D. 700 depicting a male and female seated in a typical Mayan pose. The drawing is of fine quality, and the slip colors are red, brown, and black. Also on exhibit are a number of jade pendants, beads, and earplugs, as well as the famous **stele no. 31,** which has all four sides carved. On the two sides are spear throwers, each wearing a large feathered headdress and carrying a shield in his left hand; on the front is a complicated carving of an individual carrying a head in his left arm and a chair in his right. It is considered one of the finest stele examples from the Early Classic period. Another fine attraction here is the reconstruction of the tomb of Hasaw Chan K'awil, who was also known as Ah Cacao, or "Lord Chocolate." The museum is located between the Jungle Lodge and the Jaguar Inn.

The second museum is known as the **Lithic** or **Stelae Museum** and is in the large visitor center, which is on your left as you arrive at the parking area coming from Flores. This spacious display area contains a superb collection of steles from around the ruins. Just outside the front door of the museum is the scaled relief map (mentioned above) that will give you an excellent perspective on the relationships among the different ruins here at Tikal. Both museums are open daily from 9am to 5pm. A Q80 admission will get you into both.

 seeing the forest FROM THE TREES

Just outside the entrance to Tikal National Park is the **Canopy Tour Tikal** (© **502/7926-4270;** www.canopytikal. com). A series of treetop platforms is connected by heavy wire cables, allowing more adventurous travelers to zip from platform to platform via a harness-and-pulley system. Canopy Tour Tikal actually has two separate zipline tours to choose from: a somewhat slower tour for wary souls and a faster system for adrenaline junkies. They also have a series of trails and hanging suspension bridges through the thick rain forest here. This attraction is open daily from 7am to 5pm, and the cost is Q240 per person, including shuttle transportation to or from Tikal or El Remate. For transport to and from Santa Elena or Flores, add on an extra Q40.

Tip: Visit the museums only if you have extra time or a very specific interest in either the steles or the ceramic works. The ruins themselves are by far a much more interesting attraction.

Where to Stay

There are only three hotels and a campground at the little Tikal village near the entrance to the ruins. Unless you have more than 2 days to spend exploring the region, I personally recommend staying near the ruins at least 1 night, as it allows you to enter early and stay late. It also allows you to avoid the Great Plaza and North Acropolis during the peak period of the day, when they are swarmed with day-trippers.

Although the ruins are officially open from 6am to 6pm, those staying at the site can usually finagle their way in even earlier. Better yet, those staying at the site can have their admission ticket stamped, allowing them to stay inside the park until 8pm. When the moon is full or close to full, that's enough time to catch both the sunset and the moonrise from the top of one of the temples here.

Note: Rooms are often difficult to get at the park, and making reservations is essential during the high season. However, communication with the hotels here is difficult and undependable, and many reserve all of their high-season bookings for groups and prepaid package tours. Overbooking on behalf of these hotels is also not uncommon. Demand is high, and rooms are very limited. If you're going for just a couple of nights, go with an organized tour to save yourself some hassle; if you plan to spend more time in the area or don't mind spending a night in Flores or Santa Elena if necessary, you can probably make your arrangements in Tikal.

Note: All of the hotels below get their electricity from generators, and some run these generators only for limited periods throughout the day. None has air-conditioning, and even though most have fans, these fans will do you little good on a hot night when the generator isn't running.

EXPENSIVE

Jungle Lodge   Also known as Posada de la Selva, this is the biggest and most upscale hotel right at the park. However, that's not saying much. At times there can be a cattle-car feel to the operation, and service can be lax. The majority of the rooms are housed in duplex bungalows, with high ceilings, white-tile floors, two double beds with mosquito netting, and a ceiling fan. Each has its own little porch with a couple of chairs, which are great places to sit and read a book or do some bird-watching. The bungalows are connected by stone paths through lush gardens. Two junior suites feature king-size beds, a large Jacuzzi-style tub (but without jets), and private patios in both the front and back of the room. There are also 12 older rooms with polished cement floors and shared bathroom facilities.

Tikal village, Petén. © **502/7861-0447** or 502/2476-8775. Fax 502/2476-0294. www.junglelodgetikal. com. 50 units (40 with private bathroom). Q1,200 bungalow; Q320 double with shared bathroom. MC, V. **Amenities:** Restaurant; bar; small outdoor pool. *In room:* No phone.

Tikal Inn   Set back amid the trees, the Tikal Inn is the farthest hotel from the entrance to the ruins as you walk down the old airstrip. The best rooms here are the individual bungalows, which feature high thatch roofs, tile floors, local furniture and textiles, and rustic wood trim. The smaller rooms in the main building have cement floors. All of the rooms are airy and cool, but feel pretty Spartan. As at the Jungle

Lodge, there's a refreshing pool here, and these folks even have a small Internet cafe. Meals are served family-style, and the food is a definite step up from the fare served at the *comedores* (restaurants) near the campground.

Tikal village, Petén. © **502/7861-2444** or ©/fax 502/7861-2445. www.tikalinn.com. 32 units. Q560-Q640 double. Rate includes breakfast. MC, V. **Amenities:** Restaurant; bar; small outdoor pool. *In room:* No phone.

INEXPENSIVE

Jaguar Inn 🍴   This is the most humble and economical of the hotels right at the park. Still, the rooms are all quite clean, spacious, and well-kept. Most come with two queen beds and a small veranda strung with a hammock. The best rooms are a couple of large second-floor affairs. However, I also like bungalow no. 10, with its king-size bed and private veranda. If you're on a tight budget, you can also camp here, or rent one of their hammocks with mosquito netting and a locker for Q40 per person. These folks offer electricity 24 hours per day.

Tikal village, Petén. © **502/7926-0002** reservations in Santa Elena, or 502/7783-3647 at the lodge. Fax 502/7926-2413. www.jaguartikal.com. 14 units. Q488 double. AE, MC, V (5% surcharge). **Amenities:** Restaurant; small outdoor pool; Wi-Fi. *In room:* No phone.

CAMPING

Just off the main parking lot at the site is a nice lawn with some trees for shade, marked and designated as the camping area. You can also set up your tent on some concrete pads, under an open-air thatch palapa roof. The camping area has simple shared shower and toilet facilities, and a communal cooking area. The campground (no phone) charges Q80 for the privilege of putting up a tent and using the facilities. You can also rent hammocks and pitch them under open-air palapas for an additional Q40.

Tip: If you plan on sleeping in a hammock, or even taking an afternoon siesta, you should really try to get a mosquito net that fits over the hammock. Most of the places that rent and sell hammocks in this area have these nets.

Where to Dine

Most folks who stay near the ruins take all their meals at their hotel. If you're looking for variety or staying at the campsite, there are several little *comedores* between the main camping area and parking lot and the gate at the beginning of the road to Flores. As you arrive at Tikal from Flores, you'll see them on the right side; **Comedor Imperio Maya, Comedor La Jungla,** and **Comedor Tikal** are the best of the bunch. All are rustic and pleasant, and all serve hefty plates of fairly tasty food at low prices. You can get a large serving of roast chicken with rice, beans, and fresh tortillas, along with a drink, for around Q40.

Within the area of the ruins, you'll find picnic tables beneath shelters and itinerant soft-drink peddlers, but no snack stands. If you want to spend all day at the ruins without having to walk back to the parking area for lunch, take sandwiches. Most of the hotels here and in Flores, as well as the *comedores,* will make you a bag lunch to take into the park.

Tikal After Dark

Aside from hanging around at your hotel bar or at one of the simple *comedores,* or swinging in a hammock at the campsite, the best nighttime activity here is to visit the ruins by moonlight. Those staying near the entrance to the ruins can have their admission ticket validated to allow them to roam the park until 8pm, and in some cases even later, depending on the disposition of the guards. If the moon is waxing, full, or just beyond full, you're in for a real treat. *Tip:* Before venturing into the park at night, be sure to ask around as to the current level of safety inside the park after dark.

EL REMATE ★★

32km (20 miles) E of Flores; 32km (20 miles) S of Tikal; 60km (37 miles) W of Melchor de Mencos

El Remate is a small village on the eastern shores of Lake Petén Itzá that is a popular spot in which to stay while visiting Tikal. It's located about midway between Flores and Tikal, which means that staying here cuts travel time between your hotel and the ruins. El Remate is much more tranquil and pristine than Flores or Santa Elena. Currently, a handful of budget lodgings can be found in the tiny village here, while more upscale options can be found on the shores of the lake heading north out of the village.

Essentials

GETTING THERE & DEPARTING

By Minivan Scheduled and independent minivans ply the route between Santa Elena/Flores and Tikal throughout the day. Any of these will drop you off in El Remate. For more information on these, see "Getting Around" on p. 38 and below. Fares from Flores to El Remate run around Q20 and Q40 per person each way.

By Car El Remate is located about 1.6km (1 mile) north of Ixlú (El Cruce). The road is paved and in good shape all the way from the Belize-Guatemala border 60km (37 miles) away.

GETTING AROUND

El Remate is a tiny village, and you can easily walk anywhere in town. Some of the hotels listed below are located 1.6km (1 mile) or so north of the village, on the road that circles Lake Petén Itzá. If you're in El Remate, you'll most likely want to go to Tikal, visit Santa Elena and Flores, or explore the region.

By Taxi Taxis charge between Q150 and Q200 for the one-way trip between El Remate and Tikal, and around Q100 to Q150 for the trip between El Remate and Santa Elena and Flores. The higher rates are for a minivan that can hold anywhere from six to eight passengers. A taxi is your best option if you decide to explore the area around the lake. There are often taxis hanging around the small village. If not, your hotel can call one for you. Be sure to have your hotel set a fair price, or be prepared to bargain, as the first price you are quoted is almost assuredly above the going rate and subject to some negotiation.

By Minivan If you don't have a car, the best way to get around is by minivan. Scheduled and unscheduled minivans ply the route between Flores and Tikal throughout the day. All of these pass through El Remate, dropping off and picking up passengers. You can get a minivan at almost any hotel in El Remate, or walk a few hundred yards out to the main road to Tikal and flag one down. The ride takes about a half-hour to either Tikal or Flores, and the one-way fare is from Q20 to Q40 per person.

What to See & Do

The village of El Remate itself is very small and provincial, with little of interest to tourists. Most people use El Remate as a base for explorations of the ruins at Tikal. However, as small lodges and isolated resorts start to pop up here, many tour and activity options will follow.

Just west of El Remate is the **Biotopo Cerro Cahuí,** a small nature reserve with some trails and good wildlife-viewing opportunities. More than 180 species of birds have been spotted here. A couple of loop trails climb uphill from the entrance and at various points offer excellent views of the lake. I recommend visiting this park with a guide, as a spate of robberies and attacks against tourists closed it for a period several years ago. The reserve is open daily from 8am to 4pm, and admission is Q40.

One of the most popular activities in El Remate is **renting a canoe or kayak** for paddling around on the lake. Most of the hotels in town either rent kayaks or canoes, or can arrange one for you. Rates run around Q35 per hour, or around Q120 per day.

Similarly, most of the hotels in town either rent or provide **mountain bikes** for their guests, or can arrange for their rental. The dirt road that circles Lake Petén Itzá is excellent for a mountain-bike ride. Rates are about Q60 per day.

Finally, the village of El Remate is gaining some local renown for its woodcarving. You'll see several roadside stands set up on the route between Ixlú and El Remate, and onward to Tikal. If you ask around El Remate, you might even be able to visit one or more of the artisans.

 Watch Out for Crocs

If you're out on the lake during the day-time, scan the shoreline northwest of El Remate and try to pick out the **"Sleeping Crocodile,"** a silhouette formed by the shape of the forested hills as they descend toward the lake. If you can't pick it out, ask a local for help.

Where to Stay & Dine

Most folks take their meals at their hotels. You'll find some simple *comedores* in the center of the village. The best of these is probably **El Muelle** (☏ **502/5514-9785;** www.elmuellehotel.com), which has a great view of the lake, as well as a swimming pool, which you can use if you eat here. If you're looking for something different, try the restaurant at the **Hotel Mon Ami** (☏ **502/7928-8413;** www.hotelmonami. com), which features a mix of Guatemalan, French, and Italian fare.

VERY EXPENSIVE

La Lancha Resort ★★   This is filmmaker Francis Ford Coppola's Guatemalan piece of his minihotel chain in the Mundo Maya. The main lodge has a commanding view of the lake and features a soaring, open-air, A-frame thatch roof oriented toward the view. Below the lodge is a kidney-shaped pool. A steep trail leads down to the shore of the lake, where you'll find a swimming area and some canoes and kayaks. The rooms are all duplex bungalows. The "lake view" units are quite spacious, while the "jungle view" rooms are more compact. All are tastefully and artistically decorated and very comfortable. All feature a shared wooden veranda, and you can probably figure out the view from the room names. Plans here include the addition of some independent suites with private plunge pools.

Lago Petén Itzá, Petén. © **800/746-3743** in the U.S., or ©/fax 502/7928-8331 in Guatemala. www. lalanchavillage.com. 10 units. Q1,680–Q2,240 double. Rates lower in the off season; higher during peak periods. AE, MC, V. **Amenities:** Restaurant; bar; bike rental; outdoor pool. *In room:* A/C, minifridge, no phone, free Wi-Fi.

MODERATE

Hotel Gringo Perdido Three kilometers (1¾ miles) north of El Remate, on the dirt road that circles Lake Petén Itzá, you'll find one of Guatemala's original jungle lodges. This little offbeat paradise is arranged along the lakeshore, with shady rustic hillside gardens, a little restaurant, a quiet camping area, and rooms ranging from a rustic dormitory to some almost plush private bungalows. The whole thing seems to blend into and get swallowed up by the rainforest. The Gringo Perdido, which means "the lost American," offers good swimming in the lake, 3.2km (2 miles) of nature trails, and tranquillity. This little lodge borders the Biotopo Cerro Cahuí.

3.2km (2 miles) west of El Remate, Petén. © **502/2334-2305** or 502/4899-4615. http://gringo-perdido. blogspot.com. 13 units (2 with shared bathroom). Q560 double with shared bathroom; Q720 double with private bathroom. Rates include breakfast and dinner. Q40 per person to camp, with meals extra. V only (with 8% surcharge). **Amenities:** Restaurant. *In room:* No phone.

INEXPENSIVE

In addition to the places listed below, a few very inexpensive options, catering to the backpacker crowd, are right in El Remate. I recommend simply walking around to see which one best suits your fancy and budget. One good option is **Hotel Mon Ami** (© **502/7928-8413;** www.hotelmonami.com).

La Casa de Don David Hotel 🗲 This hotel's rooms are located in a series of buildings arrayed around a large and lush garden area. All are clean and simple. There's an open-air octagonal hammock hut for reading and resting, and you can catch a glimpse of Lake Petén from here. Most of the rooms have air-conditioning, and you'll pay slightly more for these. My favorite room is no. 13, which is a corner unit with a private hammock on its front porch. The hotel offers bicycles free for guest use. David Kuhn and his wife, Rosita, have lived in this area for more than 30 years, and they are a wealth of information and advice. David was the original *gringo perdido* of the nearby nature lodge (see above), but left there to open this delightful little place.

El Remate, Petén. © **502/7928-8469** or 502/5306-2190. www.lacasadedondavid.com. 15 units. Q320–Q416 double. Rates include 1 meal (breakfast, lunch, or dinner). MC, V. **Amenities:** Restaurant. *In room:* No phone.

La Mansión del Pájaro Serpiente ★ 🗈 Set off the main road to Tikal, on a hillside overlooking the lake, this place has both standard and deluxe bungalows, beautiful gardens, and a friendly atmosphere. The bungalows feature beautiful stone and woodworking details, with local textile and crafts filling out the decor. The deluxe rooms feature televisions and air-conditioning. Several rooms are quite large and should be classified as junior suites, as they also have a separate sitting area just off the bedroom. The "honeymoon suite" comes with its own plunge pool and is high up the hill, with a great view. The midsize free-form pool is set amid lush gardens, and almost feels like a natural pond in the jungle. The open-air restaurant has a great view of the lake and specializes in local cuisine. The owners raise peacocks, and there are always several wandering around the grounds.

El Remate, Petén. ©/fax **502/7926-8498** or 502/5702-9434. 11 units. Q360 double; Q440 deluxe double. No credit cards. **Amenities:** Restaurant; outdoor pool. *In room:* No phone.

El Remate After Dark

El Remate is a quiet village. Most visitors head to the small bar at their hotel or hostel to chat with fellow travelers, or they take tours. One popular tour offered at night involves journeying to the lake to see crocodiles. This 2-hour tour involves a ride in a small motor launch with a high-powered flashlight or headlamp. The guide will scan the shore and inlets for the red reflection of the crocodiles' eyes. If you're lucky, they won't submerge as you slowly approach. All of the hotels in town can arrange this tour. The cost is between Q150 and Q240.

FLORES & SANTA ELENA ★

64km (40 miles) SW of Tikal; 135km (84 miles) NW of the Belizean border; 451km (280 miles) NE of Guatemala City

Since accommodations in Tikal are limited, most travelers either choose to (or must) overnight in the sister cities of Flores and Santa Elena. Still, this is not necessarily such a bad thing. Flores itself is a picturesque little town built on an island in the middle of Lake Petén Itzá. A narrow causeway connects Flores to Santa Elena. There's a lot more to do and see in Flores and Santa Elena than there is closer to Tikal, and a far wider range of hotels and restaurants to choose from.

Seen from the air, Flores appears almost perfectly round. This quiet town, with its colonial-style buildings and cobblestone streets, is one of the most fascinating in Guatemala. Though most people spend time here only en route to or from the Tikal ruins, Flores is well worth exploring for a day or two. A walk around the circumference of the island presents a sort of Venetian experience. Buildings come right down to the water's edge. In fact, since the lake's water level has risen over the years, some of the outlying streets and alleys are flooded. Dugout canoes, kayaks, and motor launches sit at makeshift docks all around the circumference of the island.

Santa Elena, Flores's mainland counterpart, on the other hand, is a ramshackle, modern boomtown with little at all to recommend it. However, Santa Elena is where you'll find the airport, the bus stations, a host of hotels, and a good view of Flores. Just to the west of Santa Elena is the town of San Benito, a rough-and-tumble area with little appeal to visitors. The name Flores is often used as a bucket term encompassing the island of Flores itself, along with Santa Elena and San Benito.

Flores is the unofficial capital of the Petén region of Guatemala. El Petén has always been a remote region, and it was here, on the banks of Lake Petén Itzá, that the Itzá people, descendents of the Mayas, resisted Spanish conquest until the end of the 17th century. Hernán Cortés had visited the Itzá city of Tayasal, which once stood on the far side of the lake, in 1525 but had not tried to conquer the Itzás, who had a reputation for being fierce warriors. However, in 1697, the Spanish finally conquered the Itzás, and Tayasal became the last Indian city to fall under Spanish rule. Two years after taking Tayasal, the Spanish moved to Flores, an island that could easily be defended. They renamed this island Nuestra Señora de los Remedios y San Pablo de los Itzaes and between 1700 and 1701 built a fort here. In 1831, the island was once again renamed, this time being given the name Flores in honor of a Guatemalan patriot.

Flores & Santa Elena

ACCOMMODATIONS ■
Hotel Casa Elena de las
  Flores **14**
Hotel Del Patio **15**
Hotel Petén **2**
Hotel Petén Espléndido **12**
Hotel Santana **1**
La Casona de la Isla **4**
La Casona del Lago **13**

DINING & NIGHTLIFE ◆
AAdictos **10**
Bar Raíces **11**
Café Arquelógico Yaxhá **7**
Capitán Tortuga **3**
Cool Beans **6**
La Luna **5**
Las Puertas **9**
Pizzería Picasso **8**

ATTRACTIONS ●
Aktun Kan **16**

Flores

Calle Fraternidad
Calle Unión
Av. La Libertad
Av. Flores
Parque Central
Calle 10 de Noviembre
Calle 30 de Junio
Av. Reforma
Av. Santa Ana
Calle 15 de Septiembre
Calle Central
Callejón El Crucero
Calle Centroamérica
Calle Sur

0   100 yds
0   100 m

See inset above

Isla Santa Barbara

FLORES

LAKE
PETÉN
ITZÁ

0   1/4 mi
0   0.25 km

SAN BENITO

1a Calle

SANTA ELENA

2a Calle
3a Calle
Parque Central
4a Calle (Calle Principal)
4a Av.
4a Calle A
5a Calle
5a Av.
6a Av.
7a Av.
8a Av.
3a Av.
Calzada Virgilio Rodríguez Macal

Airport

To Tikal &
El Remate

✝ Church
ⓘ Information
✉ Post office

Horsing Around

One of the most curious pieces of local history revolves around a sick horse that was left in Tayasal by Hernán Cortés when he passed through the area. The Itzás had never seen horses before, and as soon as Cortés left, they began worshiping it. When the horse died, a stone statue of it was made, and the worship continued until Spanish missionaries arrived in Tayasal 100 years later. The missionaries, appalled by this idolatry, proceeded to pitch the blasphemous statue into the lake. To this day the legendary horse statue has never been discovered, though searches continue to be launched from time to time.

Essentials
GETTING THERE & DEPARTING
BY PLANE   See "By Plane" under "Essentials" in "Tikal," earlier in this chapter.

BY CAR   To get here from Belize, see "By Car" under "Essentials" on p. 260, earlier in this chapter.

The road between Tikal and Flores is a good, paved road, and the trip takes around an hour by car. To get to either of the sister towns from Tikal, head south out of the ruins and turn right at Ixlú (El Cruce). Continue on past the airport. You will come to Santa Elena first. Stay on the main avenue into town and head toward the lake, where you will find the causeway over to Flores.

BY BUS   For information on getting to Flores and Santa Elena by bus from Belize, see "By Bus" under "Essentials" on p. 261, earlier in this chapter. See "Getting Around," below, for details on getting from Santa Elena and Flores to the ruins.

There are several companies operating first-class buses to and from Guatemala City. **ADN** (© 502/2251-0610 in Guatemala City, or 7924-8131 in Santa Elena; www.adnautobusesdelnorte.com) and **Línea Dorada** (© 502/2232-5506 in Guatemala City, or 7926-0070 in Santa Elena; www. lineadorada.info) both operate out of the main bus terminal in Santa Elena, located about 8 blocks south of downtown along 6a Avenida. The trip to Guatemala City takes about 8 to 10 hours, and first-class fares run around Q190 to Q280.

GETTING AROUND
If you're in Santa Elena or Flores, you'll most likely want to go to Tikal or explore the region around Lake Petén.

BY MINIVAN   If you don't have a car, the best way to get around this area is by minivan. Minivans from Flores and Santa Elena to Tikal leave roughly every hour between 5 and 10am, and less frequently thereafter. These minivans leave from Tikal for the return trip roughly every hour from noon to 6pm. Every hotel in Flores and Santa Elena can arrange a minivan pickup for you. The trip usually takes an hour and costs Q50 to Q60 per person each way. You can buy a round-trip fare at a slight savings; however, this commits you to a specific minivan company, and I've found I prefer paying a little extra to have more flexibility in grabbing my return ride when I'm ready to leave.

BY TAXI   Taxis charge between Q350 and Q450 for the one-way trip between Flores or Santa Elena and Tikal. Between Flores or Santa Elena and El Remate, the fare is around Q100 to Q150. The higher rate is for a minivan that can hold anywhere from six to eight passengers. A taxi is your best option if you decide to explore the area around the lake. Be sure to bargain, as the first price you are quoted is almost certainly above the going rate and subject to some negotiation.

BY CAR   If you have your own car, the road between Santa Elena and Flores and Tikal is paved, well-marked, and heavily traveled. It's about 32km (20 miles) from Flores to Ixlú (El Cruce), and another 32km on to the park and ruins of Tikal.

For information on renting a car, see "Getting Around" on p. 263, earlier in this chapter.

BY BUS   Very inexpensive local bus service connects Flores and Santa Elena to Tikal and several neighboring communities. However, this service is infrequent, slow, and often uncomfortably overcrowded. Línea Dorada (see above) has three daily buses from Santa Elena to Tikal leaving at 5 and 8:30am and at 3:30pm. The return buses leave Tikal at 2 and 5pm. Ask at your hotel or around town for current schedules, as they change periodically. The trip takes 2 hours; the one-way fare is Q50.

ORIENTATION

The town primarily known as Flores actually consists of three smaller towns that have merged. Flores proper sits on a small island out in Lake Petén Itzá, and is connected to the mainland by a long causeway. On the mainland are Santa Elena (nearest the airport) and San Benito (closer to the bus terminal and market). Whether you arrive by air or by bus from Guatemala City or Belize, you will come into town from the east. The road in from the airport leads straight through Santa Elena to the market and bus terminal, while the causeway to Flores is a turn to the right in the middle of Santa Elena. While there are a host of budget lodgings in San Benito, especially around the bus terminal, I strongly advise most travelers to stick to Santa Elena and Flores proper.

FAST FACTS   You'll find numerous banks in downtown Flores and Santa Elena. Most have ATMs, and many of these will work with your debit or credit card. Check with your home bank and the PLUS or Cirrus systems in advance to confirm. All will exchange money. Most of the hotels and restaurants in Flores and Santa Elena will also exchange dollars for quetzales, although they may give you a slightly less favorable rate than you would get at a bank.

The **Flores post office** is on the Avenida Barrios, 1 block south of the Parque Central, or Central Park, which is in front of the church. **Santa Elena's post office** is on Calle 4 and Avenida 7. Both are open Monday through Friday from 8am to 5pm. To contact the **local police,** dial ✆ **502/7926-1365.**

There is an information booth run by the Guatemalan Tourist Board, **Inguat** (✆ **502/7926-0533;** www.visitguatemala.com), at the Flores airport, and another one in downtown Flores (✆ **502/7867-5334**) on Avenida Flores, on the north side of the Central Park. Both can help provide basic maps to the region and ruins, as well as brochures for local hotels and tour agencies.

What to See & Do

Flores is a wonderful town to explore by walking. The whole island is only about 5 blocks wide in any direction. At the center is a small central park or plaza, anchored by the town's Catholic church. Be sure to take a peek inside to check out the beautiful stained-glass windows. After first exploring the island on foot, you should have a look at the island from the perspective of a boat.

One of the most popular things to do in Flores is take a **tour of the lake ★**. You will be inundated with offers for boat tours. Ask at your hotel or one of the local tour agencies, or talk to the numerous freelancers approaching you on the street. Be sure to inspect the craft beforehand, if possible, and make sure you feel comfortable with its lake-worthiness. Also, make sure your guide is bilingual. These tours last anywhere from 1 to 3 hours, and usually include stops at La Guitarra Island (Guitar Island), which features a picnic and swimming area, as well as at the mostly unexcavated ruins of Tayasal. Here, be sure to climb **El Mirador ★**, a lakeside pyramid that offers a fabulous view of Flores. Many of these tours also stop at the small **Petencito Zoo** and **ARCAS** (www.arcasguatemala.com), a conservation organization and animal rehabilitation center that has some interpretive trails and displays of rescued animals either in recuperation or unable to be released. These tours cost between Q80 and Q160 per person, depending on the length of the tour and the size of your group. Don't be afraid to bargain. Entrance to the zoo is an extra Q20.

You can also explore the lake on your own in a kayak or canoe. These are also rented all around Flores. Again, ask at your hotel or at one of the local tour agencies. Rates for kayaks and canoes run around Q20 per hour. Be careful paddling around the lake; when the winds pick up, especially in the afternoons, it can get quite choppy and challenging.

If you're a spelunker, you might want to explore **Aktun Kan (Cave of the Serpent),** a large cavern just outside of Santa Elena. The cave takes its name from a legend about a giant snake living there. But don't worry, it's only a legend. Yet another legend has it that this cave is connected to a cave beneath the church on Flores. To reach the cave, either walk south out of Santa Elena on the road that crosses the causeway from Flores, or ask a taxi to take you out there. The fare should be around Q15 round-trip. Although there are lights in the cave (admission Q15), be sure to bring a flashlight for a little extra illumination.

A host of local tour operators here can arrange any of the tours listed above, as well as guided tours to Tikal and the ruins listed below. The best of these are **Martsam Travel ★★** (© 866/832-2776 in the U.S. and Canada, or 502/7867-5093 in Guatemala; www.martsam.com) and **San Juan Travel** (© **502/5847-4738**).

YAXHA, EL CEIBAL & OTHER NEARBY RUINS

If your life's passion is Mayan ruins or you simply crave more adventure than you have had so far on your visit to El Petén, you should think about visiting some of the more remote ruins of this region. In addition to exploring seldom-visited Mayan ruins, you'll be traveling through uninhabited jungles where you'll likely encounter a great deal of wildlife, which might include coati-mundi, howler and spider monkeys, anteaters, tapirs, and possibly even jaguars.

Thanks to the publicity and infrastructure bestowed upon this site by the TV show *Survivor: Guatemala,* **Yaxhá ★★** is now one of the prime archaeological sites to visit in Guatemala. In fact, this is the third-largest Mayan ceremonial city in

Guatemala—behind Tikal and El Mirador. Be sure to climb **Temple 216 ★★★**, located in the East Acropolis. This is the tallest structure here, and provides excellent views of lakes Yaxhá and Sacnab, as well as the surrounding rainforests. The sunsets here rival those in Tikal. Yaxhá is one of the few Mayan cities to retain its traditional Mayan name, which translates as "green waters." You can combine a visit to Yaxhá with a trip to the ruins of **Topoxté,** which are located on a small island in Lake Yaxhá. This small yet intriguing site is thought to have been a residential city for local elites. However, it was also a fortified city where Mayan warriors put up a valiant defense against Spanish forces. ***Note:*** You'll probably be warned, and see the signs, but just in case, do not swim in Lake Yaxhá, as it is home to a robust population of crocodiles. Many organized tours here also include a stop at the nearby minor ruins of Nakum, which are currently being excavated. However, this makes for a long day. The turnoff for the 11km (7-mile) dirt road into the site is located about 32km (20 miles) east of Ixlú, or El Cruce. The Q80 admission grants you access to Yaxhá, Topoxté, and Nakum. If you want to stay at Yaxhá, camping is allowed at a well-tended campsite down by the lakeshore.

Another popular site is **El Ceibal ★**, which offers one of the most scenic routes along the way. To reach El Ceibal, you first head the 64km (40 miles) from Flores to Sayaxché, which is a good-size town for El Petén (it even has a few basic hotels). From Sayaxché, you must hire a boat to carry you 18km (11 miles) up the Río de la Pasión. El Ceibal is a Late Classic–era ruin known for having the only circular temple in all of El Petén. There are also several well-preserved steles arranged around one small temple structure on the central plaza, as well as a ball court. Many of the designs at El Ceibal indicate that the city had extensive contact with cities in the Yucatán, but whether this contact was due to trade or to warfare is unclear. Your best bet for visiting El Ceibal is to book the excursion with one of the tour agencies in Flores or Santa Elena. Full-day trips run around Q600 to Q800. Overnight trips can also be arranged, combining a visit to El Ceibal with even more obscure Mayan sites such as Aguateca and Petexbatún. If you get to Sayaxché on your own, look for **Viajes Don Pedro** (✆ **502/7928-6109**). These folks run regular boats to El Ceibal and charge around Q500 per person round-trip. However, if you have a group, be sure to try to negotiate a flat rate for the boat, which should carry anywhere from four to eight people. If you want to stay in this area, check out **Chiminos Island Lodge ★** (✆ **502/2335-3506;** www.chiminosisland.com), which has six rustic yet luxurious cabins in the rainforest on a small island in the waters of the Petexbatún Lagoon.

Uaxactún (pronounced "Wah-shahk-*toon*") is another Mayan ceremonial center located 24km (15 miles) north of Tikal. Though many of the pyramids and temples here have been uncovered, they have not been restored nearly as extensively as those at Tikal. One of the most interesting finds at Uaxactún is what is believed to be the oldest-known astrological observatory yet discovered in the Mayan world. In Group E, on the eastern side of these ruins, you can watch a sunrise from the observatory temple that lines up precisely with other temples on the equinoxes and solstices. Your best bet for visiting Uaxactún is to book the excursion with one of the tour agencies in Flores or Santa Elena. Full-day trips cost about Q600 to Q800 and can be combined with a stop at Tikal, although I think that's trying to cram too much into a single day. If you have your own four-wheel-drive vehicle, you can drive here yourself. The ruins at Uaxactún are open daily from 6am to 6pm, and no admission is charged. However, you must reach it by passing through Tikal National Park, and so you must pay the

Tikal entrance fee of Q150. Moreover, be forewarned that the dirt road between Tikal and Uaxactún is sometimes not passable during the rainy season. Be sure to ask locally about current conditions before heading off.

Finally, truly adventurous travelers can book a multiday jungle trek to **El Mirador ★★**, the largest Mayan ceremonial city in Guatemala. Barely excavated, El Mirador features the tallest pyramidal structure in the known Mayan world, La Danta, which reaches some 79m (260 ft.) in height. The trip here involves at least 5 days of hiking and jungle camping. **Martsam Travel ★★** (© **866/832-2776** in the U.S. and Canada, or 502/7867-5093 in Guatemala; www.martsam.com) is the best operator to contact for one of these trips.

STUDYING SPANISH

Eco Escuela de Español ★ (© **502/5940-1235;** www.ecoescuelaespanol.org) runs a community-based language school program in the small village of San Andrés, on the shore of Lake Petén Itzá. The program costs just Q1,200 per week, including lodging and three meals daily with a local family, as well as 4 hours of daily class time, usually one-on-one. The setting allows for intensive language instruction, as well as many chances to really interact with the local culture and natural surroundings.

If you want to stick closer to the action in town, check in with the **Dos Mundos Spanish Academy** (© **502/5830-2060;** www.flores-spanish.com), which offers a wide range of course and accommodations options.

Where to Stay

EXPENSIVE

Hotel Villa Maya ★   Hotel Villa Maya is located about 5 minutes from the airport, on the shores of Lake Petén Itzá, but away from the twin cities and toward Tikal. The setting and surrounding forests are lovely. Peace and quiet, if that's what you're looking for, are an added bonus, on top of the slightly reduced travel time to the ruins. However, if you want access to the restaurants and shops in Flores, you'll need either your own car or a taxi. Most of the rooms are found in a series of two-story buildings, set on the edge of the lake. Local hardwoods are used generously to trim detail and furnish the place. The rooms are simple, spacious, and clean, and each comes with a small triangular balcony overlooking the lake. The hotel also has a pool with a cascading waterfall, as well as a wonderful dock and deck area over the lake.

15 min. from Santa Elena Internacional Airport on Lake Petenchel, 4km (2½ miles) north of the well-marked turnoff on the road from Santa Elena to Tikal. © **502/2223-5000** reservations in Guatemala City, or 5410-1592 at the hotel. Fax 502/2334-8134. www.villasdeguatemala.com. 56 units. Q1,000 double. AE, MC, V. **Amenities:** Restaurant; bike rental; Jacuzzi; pool; room service; watersports equipment rental; free Wi-Fi. *In room:* A/C, minibar.

MODERATE

Hotel Del Patio   This hotel's central courtyard, with its tall fountain flowing into a cloverleaf pool, is classic colonial Guatemala. The rooms are simple, clean, and comfortable, although the decor is definitely dated, and you can find better deals around town. I'd opt for a second-floor unit, just so you can admire the courtyard from above as you enter and exit your room. A midsize kidney-shaped pool and tiny gym, as well as a good international restaurant, round out the amenities.

Calle 8 and Av. 2, Santa Elena, Petén. © **502/7926-0104** or 502/7926-1229. Fax 502/7926-3030. www.caminoreal.com.gt. 21 units. 488 double. AE, MC, V. **Amenities:** Restaurant; bar; small gym; pool; room service. *In room:* A/C, TV.

Hotel Petén Espléndido   This modern upscale hotel is located in Santa Elena just off the causeway on the shore of Lake Petén Itzá, with a great view of Flores. The rooms feature contemporary decor and more modern amenities than you'll find anywhere else in town. The bathrooms are even equipped with telephones, and four rooms are truly fitted out for travelers with disabilities. The best rooms are the second-floor rooms with balconies directly fronting the lake. If you don't get one of these, the hotel's waterfront restaurant has a great view and serves good international and local cuisine. There's a relaxing and refreshing pool area with a separate Jacuzzi. This place offers a free airport shuttle, as well as free paddle boats for use on the lake, and has a helpful tour desk and concierge.

1a Calle 5-01, Zona 1, Santa Elena, Flores, Petén. ☏ **502/2360-8140** reservations number in Guatemala City, or 502/7926-0880 at the hotel. Fax 502/7926-0866. www.petenesplendido.com. 62 units. Q720–Q1,200 double. AE, DC, MC, V. **Amenities:** Restaurant; bar; concierge; outdoor pool; room service. *In room:* A/C, TV, hair dryer, safe.

La Casona del Lago ★★   This is the most luxurious hotel of a group run by a small local chain, although it's also the only one not on the island of Flores proper. (Don't confuse this with La Casona de la Isla, which is part of the same chain and in Flores.) Still, this hotel is located right on the shores of the lake, with excellent views of its waters and picturesque island city. The three-story building is built in an L-shape, around a central pool and Jacuzzi area, and painted a bright primary blue, with sparkling white trim. Rooms are spacious, with two double beds, white-tile floors, a couple of sitting chairs, and a separate desk area, and they feature a host of modern amenities, including 21-inch televisions.

Calle Litoral, Zona 1, Santa Elena, Flores, Petén. ☏/fax **502/7952-8700.** www.hotelesdepeten.com. 32 units. Q704–Q784 double. Rates include full breakfast and taxes. AE, DC, MC, V. **Amenities:** Restaurant; outdoor Jacuzzi and pool; free Wi-Fi. *In room:* A/C, TV, hair dryer.

INEXPENSIVE

Hotel Casa Elena de las Flores ☺   This neat little hotel in downtown Santa Elena offers well-kept rooms at a fair price. Still, most of the rooms are on the small side, and their televisions are tiny. At the center of the hotel is a pretty little pool and lovely interior courtyard with shady palm trees. The pool even has a water slide, which is a hit with children. The hotel is kept immaculate, and there's a friendly air to the whole operation. You'll find a simple restaurant on the grounds, as well as an inviting second-floor bar. For a good view, head up to the unfinished rooftop terrace.

Av. 6 and Calle 2, Santa Elena, Petén. ☏ **502/7926-2235.** Fax 502/7926-0097. www.casaelenadelas flores.com. 28 units. Q360–Q416 double. AE, MC, V. **Amenities:** Restaurant; small outdoor pool; room service; free Wi-Fi. *In room:* A/C, TV.

Hotel Petén   From the street, this hotel looks very modest. Walk through the doorway, though, and you'll find an attractive small courtyard with tropical plants, a tiny semi-indoor pool, and a nice brick-and-stucco building of several floors. The rooms are all well-kept. The best rooms are those on the top two floors with private balconies and an excellent view of the lake. In fact, only five rooms here don't have a lake view, so when you reserve or check in, be sure you get one that does. There's a popular restaurant on the ground floor. These folks also have an in-house tour company, and are owned by the same company as a couple of other nearby hotels, in case this one is full.

Calle 30 de Junio, Flores, Petén. ☏/fax **502/7867-5203.** www.hotelesdepeten.com. 21 units. Q384–Q416 double. Rates include taxes. AE, DC, MC, V. **Amenities:** Restaurant; Jacuzzi; pool. *In room:* A/C, TV.

Hotel Santana ★ 🛥 This is a great choice if you're looking to snag a lakefront room with a balcony and a view, all at a very good price. Most of the rooms here fit the criteria I just mentioned, and those on the third and fourth floors have the best views—still, be sure you get a lakeview room, and not one of the less desirable interior affairs. The rooms here are all cool, clean, and fairly spacious, and a definite cut above the rest of the options on the island of Flores in this price range. The large open-air dining room is a delightful place to sit and enjoy the lakeside setting as well. There's a small kidney-shaped pool, with a built-in waterfall and swim-up bar, in a little courtyard to the side.

Calle 30 de Junio, Flores, Petén. ✆/fax **502/7867-5123** or 502/7867-5193. www.santanapeten.com. 35 units. Q320–Q480 double. AE, MC, V. **Amenities:** Restaurant; outdoor pool; free Wi-Fi. *In room:* A/C, TV.

La Casona de la Isla La Casona de la Isla shows the same attention to service as the other properties run by this local hotel group. The guest rooms here are all fairly small and lack much in the way of style, but they do have tile floors, ceiling fans, and air-conditioning—although some of these A/C units can be rather old and noisy. Most come with a private balcony, and almost all of these have good views of the lake. The hotel is built in an L-shape around a stone terrace with lush gardens and a small swimming pool featuring a sculpted stone waterfall and separate Jacuzzi. Its restaurant serves good Guatemalan and international fare in a small dining room off the lobby, and there's a back patio bar with an excellent view overlooking the lake.

Calle 30 de Junio, Flores, Petén. ✆ **502/7867-5163.** www.hotelesdepeten.com. 26 units. Q416–Q456 double. Rates include taxes. AE, DC, MC, V. **Amenities:** Restaurant; bar; outdoor Jacuzzi and pool; free Wi-Fi. *In room:* A/C, TV.

Where to Dine

There are tons of places to eat around Flores and Santa Elena. Most are simple affairs serving local and Mexican cuisine, and geared toward locals and the backpacker crowd. Most of the hotels listed above have restaurants, and most of these are quite dependable. **El Mirador Restaurant** at the Hotel Petén Espléndido (p. 281) serves good but far from spectacular international fare; however, the setting is certainly the most elegant you'll find in this neck of the woods.

In addition to the places listed below, **Pizzeria Picasso** (✆ **502/7867-5198;** Calle 15 de Setiembre, across from El Tucán) serves pretty good wood-oven pizza and a variety of pastas.

Café Arqueológico Yaxhá ★ 🍴 GUATEMALAN/MAYAN This is a relaxed and welcoming spot that serves excellent local fare, including dishes based on pre-Colombian recipes and ingredients. I recommend the Pollo Xni Pec, which is chicken in a spicy tomato sauce served with yucca. The German owner is an archaeologist, and photos of archaeological sites adorn the walls, books on the subject matter are available to browse, and talks, slide shows, and guided tours are often offered. This is also a good place to come for coffee drinks and fresh-fruit smoothies.

Calle 15 de Setiembre, across from El Tucán, Flores. ✆ **502/5830-2060.** www.cafeyaxha.com. Main courses Q30–Q90. AE, MC, V. Daily 7am–9pm.

Capitán Tortuga ★ INTERNATIONAL This popular restaurant has a long and wide-ranging menu. You can get everything from pizzas to barbecue ribs to vegetarian shish kebabs. They also have a wide range of coffee and espresso drinks, as well as ice creams and freshly baked desserts. The large main dining room sits under a high thatch roof. However, I prefer the tables on the small outdoor patio that fronts the lake, or those in the second-floor, open-air dining room reached from a stairway out back. Service can be slow at times, but if you're with a group or sharing a drink with fellow travelers, you might not mind.

Calle 30 de Junio, next to La Casona de la Isla, Flores. © **502/7867-5089.** Main courses Q32–Q120. AE, MC, V. Daily 11:30am–11pm.

La Luna ★★ INTERNATIONAL   This hip little restaurant is the most creative and refined option in Flores. The menu ranges from steak in pepper sauce to lobster tails, with a host of fish and chicken—and even some vegetarian—options in between. I recommend starting things off with some stuffed peppers or a falafel side. There are three separate dining areas, and all are artistically decorated. My favorite room features a faux ceiba tree in the center and a wild sculpture on one wall made of wood and mirrors.

Calle 30 de Junio, across from La Casona de la Isla, Flores. © **502/7867-5443.** Main courses Q40–Q130. MC, V. Mon–Sat noon–11pm.

Flores & Santa Elena After Dark

There are several bars along Calle Sur fronting the lake just over the bridge as you enter Flores. Of these, **AAdictos** (no phone) is one of the liveliest. For a view of the lake and a happening dance, DJ, and party scene, you can head to **Bar Raíces** (© **5521-1843**), at the far western end of Calle Sur. Another good option, near the center of the island, is **Las Puertas** ★ (© **7867-5242;** corner of Calle Centroamérica and Avenida Santa Ana), which is a popular bar/restaurant that has nightly DVD movie showings and occasionally live music. Finally, for a mellow scene, try **Cool Beans** ★ (© **5571-9240;** Calle 15 de Setiembre), a popular place for tourists and itinerant backpackers, with a convivial, laid-back vibe, free Wi-Fi, plenty of board games, and a view of the lake to boot.

FAST FACTS: BELIZE

FAST FACTS

American Express   American Express Travel Services is represented in Belize City by **Belize Global Travel Services Ltd.,** 41 Albert St. (© **227-7185**), which can issue traveler's checks and replacement cards, and provide other standard services. They are open Monday through Friday from 8am to noon and 1 to 5pm, and on Saturday from 8am to noon. To report a lost or stolen Amex credit card or traveler's checks within Belize, call the local number above, or call collect to © **336/393-1111** in the U.S.

Area Codes   There are no area codes in Belize. All local phone numbers are seven-digit numbers.

ATM Networks/Cashpoints   See "Money & Costs," p. 42.

Business Hours   Banks are generally open Monday through Friday from 8am to 4:30pm. However, in many small towns, villages, and tourist destinations, bank hours may be limited. In very few instances, banks have begun opening on Saturday. Belizean businesses tend to be open Monday through Friday from 8am to noon and from 1 to 5pm. Some businesses do not close for lunch, and some open on Saturday. Most bars are open until 1 or 2am, although some go later.

Car Rentals   See "Getting There & Getting Around" in chapter 3 and "Airline, Hotel & Rental Websites," below.

Drinking Laws   The legal drinking age in Belize is 18, although it is often not enforced. Beer, wine, and liquor are all sold in most supermarkets and small convenience stores Monday through Saturday. No liquor is sold on Good Friday or Easter Sunday. On Election Day, no liquor can be sold until 6pm.

Driving Rules   See "Getting There & Getting Around," p. 38.

Drugstores   There are a handful of pharmacies around Belize City and in most of the major towns and tourist destinations. Perhaps the best-stocked pharmacy in the country can be found at **Belize Medical Associates,** 5791 St. Thomas Kings Park, Belize City (© **223-0303;** www.belizemedical.com).

Electricity   Electricity is 110-volt AC, and most outlets are either two- or three-prong U.S.-style outlets.

If you wish to access the Internet with your own computer, bring a **connection kit** of the right power and phone adapters, a spare phone cord, and a spare Ethernet network cable—or find out whether your hotel supplies them to guests.

Embassies & Consulates   The **United States Embassy** is located in Belmopan on Floral Park Road (© **822-4011;** http://belize.usembassy.gov). The **British High Commission** is located in Belmopan at Embassy Square

(© **822-2981;** www.ukinbelize.fco.gov.uk). You can contact the **Canadian Honorary Consul** in Belize City at 80 Princess Margaret Dr. (© **223-1060**).

Emergencies   In case of an emergency, dial © **90** from anywhere in Belize. This will connect you to the police. In most cases, © **911** will also work. I've listed the various numbers for fire departments, ambulances, and hospitals in the "Fast Facts" sections throughout the book.

Gasoline (Petrol)   Gasoline is sold as "unleaded" and "super." Both are unleaded; super is just higher octane. Diesel is available at most gas stations as well. At press time, a gallon of super cost around BZ$10.

Holidays   For more information on holidays, see "Belize Calendar of Events" in chapter 3.

Hospitals   **Belize Medical Associates,** 5791 St. Thomas Kings Park, Belize City (© **223-0303;** www.belizemedical.com), is a modern, 24-hour private hospital, with emergency care and numerous private-practice physicians. The country's main public hospital, the **Karl Heusner Memorial Hospital,** Princess Margaret Drive, Belize City (© **223-1548**), is also open 24 hours and has a wide range of facilities and services.

Insurance   For information on traveler's insurance, trip-cancellation insurance, and medical insurance while traveling, please visit www.frommers.com/planning.

Internet Access   Cybercafes can be found at most major tourist destinations around Belize. Wi-Fi is also increasingly common, and many hotels are offering it free. Throughout the book, I list that hotels provide free, or for a fee, Wi-Fi and high-speed Ethernet access. For help locating cybercafes and other establishments where you can go for Internet access, please see the destination chapters throughout this book.

Language   English is the official language of Belize, and it is almost universally spoken. However, Belize is a very polyglot country, and you are likely to hear and come across Spanish, Creole, and Garífuna. For some help in communicating in Spanish and Creole, see chapter 13.

Laundromats   Most folks rely on their hotel's laundry and dry-cleaning services, although these can be expensive. Where they exist, I've listed laundromats and laundry options in the "Fast Facts" sections of the destination chapters.

Legal Aid   If you need legal help, your best bet is to first contact your local embassy or consulate. See "Embassies & Consulates," above, for contact details. Alternatively, ask at your hotel for an appropriate recommendation.

Lost & Found   Be sure to tell all of your credit card companies the minute you discover that your wallet has been lost or stolen, and file a report at the nearest police precinct. Your credit card company or insurer may require a police report number or record of the loss. Most credit card companies have an emergency toll-free number to call if your card is lost or stolen; they may be able to wire you a cash advance immediately or deliver an emergency credit card in a day or two. It's a good idea to write this number down and carry it someplace separate from your wallet or credit cards. **Visa**'s emergency number is © **800/847-2911** toll-free in the U.S., or call 410/581-9994 collect from Belize. **American Express** cardholders and traveler's check holders should call © **800/221-7282** toll-free in the U.S., or 336/393-1111 collect from Belize. **MasterCard** holders should call © **800/627-8372** toll-free in the U.S., or 636/722-7111 collect from Belize.

   If you need emergency cash over the weekend when all banks and American Express offices are closed, you can have money wired to you via **Western Union** (© **800/325-6000** in the U.S. and Canada, or **227-0014** in Belize; www.westernunion.com), although the service charges are substantial.

Mail   Most hotels will post a letter for you, and there are post offices in the major towns. It costs BZ$1 to send a letter to the United States, and BZ$1.20 to send a letter to Europe. Postcards to the same destinations cost BZ$.50 and BZ$.60, respectively.

If your postal needs are urgent, or you want to send anything of value, several international courier and express-mail services have offices in Belize City, including **DHL,** 41 Hydes Lane (✆ **223-4350;** www.dhl.com); **FedEx,** 1 Mapp St. (✆ **224-5221;** www.fedex.com); and **Trans Express,** 41 Albert St. (✆ **227-2332**). All can arrange pickup and delivery services to any hotel in town, and sometimes in the different outlying districts.

Measurements   American measurements are the norm in Belize, although the metric system is making slight inroads.

Newspapers & Magazines   Belize has no daily newspaper. There are four primary weeklies: *Amandala* (www.amandala.com.bz), the *Reporter* (www.reporter.bz), *Belize Times* (www.belizetimes.bz), and the *Guardian* (www.guardian.bz). Most come out on Friday, and all are relatively similar in terms of content, although with some differing and usually obvious political leanings. *Amandala* and the *Reporter* actually publish twice weekly and are my favorites.

Passports   See www.frommers.com/planning for information on how to obtain a passport.

For Residents of Australia   Contact the **Australian Passport Information Service** at ✆ **131-232,** or visit the government website at www.passports.gov.au.

For Residents of Canada   Contact the central **Passport Office,** Department of Foreign Affairs and International Trade, Ottawa, ON K1A 0G3 (✆ **800/567-6868;** www.ppt.gc.ca).

For Residents of Ireland   Contact the **Passport Office,** Setanta Centre, Molesworth Street, Dublin 2 (✆ **01/671-1633;** www.irlgov.ie/iveagh).

For Residents of New Zealand   Contact the **Passports Office** at ✆ **0800/225-050** in New Zealand or 04/474-8100, or log on to www.passports.govt.nz.

For Residents of the United Kingdom   Visit your nearest passport office, major post office, or travel agency or contact the **United Kingdom Passport Service** at ✆ **0870/521-0410** or search its website at www.ukpa.gov.uk.

For Residents of the United States   To find your regional passport office, either check the U.S. State Department website or call the **National Passport Information Center** toll-free number (✆ **877/487-2778**) for automated information.

Police   The police in Belize are generally rather helpful; there is a dedicated tourism police force in Belize City. Dial ✆ **90** or **911** in an emergency. You can also dial ✆ **227-2222.**

Smoking   Belize has yet to pass any no-smoking legislation, and aside from a handful of hotels that are entirely nonsmoking, few others have true nonsmoking rooms or floors. Similarly, many restaurants don't have a nonsmoking section. Luckily, so much dining in Belize is alfresco that this may not be a problem, especially if you can snag an upwind seat.

Taxes   There is a US$39 departure fee that must be paid in cash (in either U.S. or Belize dollars) at the international airport upon departure, although sometimes the fees are already included in your airline ticket; the land exit fee is US$19. There is a 9% hotel tax added to all hotel bills, and there is a 12.5% GST tax on all goods and services. A 10% service charge is sometimes added to restaurant bills. Take this into account when deciding how much to tip (if the service is really good, an extra 5%–10% is fine).

Telephones Belize has a standardized seven-digit phone numbering system. There are no city or area codes to dial from within Belize; use the country code, 501 (not to be confused with the area code for the state of Arkansas), only when dialing a Belizean number from outside Belize.

For directory assistance: Dial ✆ **113** if you're looking for a number inside Belize; for numbers to all other countries, dial ✆ **115** and (for a charge) an operator will connect you to an international directory assistance operator.

For operator assistance: If you need operator assistance in making a call, dial ✆ **115,** whether you're trying to make a local or an international call.

Toll-free numbers: Numbers beginning with 0800 and 800 within Belize country are toll-free, but calling a 1-800 number in the States from Belize is not toll-free. In fact, it costs the same as an overseas call.

See "Staying Connected," on p. 51, for tips on calling to and from Belize.

Time Belize is on Central Standard Time, 6 hours behind Greenwich Mean Time. Belize does not observe daylight saving time.

Tipping Most Belizeans don't tip. Many restaurants add a 10% service charge. However, if the service is particularly good, or if the service charge is not included, tipping is appropriate.

Toilets There are very few public toilets or restrooms in Belize. About the only ones I know of are located at the little cruise-ship tourist village on Fort Street in the Fort George section of Belize City. However, most hotels and restaurants will let tourists use their facilities.

Water The water in most major cities and tourist destinations in Belize is ostensibly safe to drink. However, many travelers react adversely to water in foreign countries, and it is probably best to drink bottled water throughout your visit to Belize.

AIRLINE, HOTEL & CAR-RENTAL WEBSITES

AIRLINES

Air France
www.airfrance.com

Air New Zealand
www.airnewzealand.com

Alitalia
www.alitalia.com

American Airlines
www.aa.com

British Airways
www.british-airways.com

Caribbean Airlines (formerly BWIA)
www.caribbean-airlines.com

Continental Airlines
www.continental.com

Cubana
www.cubana.cu

Delta Air Lines
www.delta.com

Iberia Airlines
www.iberia.com

Japan Airlines
www.jal.co.jp

Korean Air
www.koreanair.com

Lan Airlines
www.lanchile.com

Lufthansa
www.lufthansa.com

Philippine Airlines
www.philippineairlines.com

Qantas Airways
www.qantas.com

South African Airways
www.flysaa.com

Swiss Air
www.swiss.com

TACA
www.taca.com

United Airlines
www.united.com

US Airways
www.usairways.com

CAR-RENTAL AGENCIES

Avis
www.avis.com

Budget
www.budget.com

Hertz
www.hertz.com

Thrifty
www.thrifty.com

MAJOR HOTEL & MOTEL CHAINS

Best Western International
www.bestwestern.com

Radisson Hotels & Resorts
www.radisson.com

USEFUL TERMS & PHRASES

English is the official language of Belize, but the country is one of the most polyglot places on the planet. In addition to English, many Belizeans speak Spanish, and among some members of the population, this is the primary language. You will find Spanish prevalent in the northern and western regions, near the borders with Mexico and Guatemala, but given Belize's long history of immigration, Spanish speakers can be found throughout the country. In fact, conversations among Belizeans are often a mix of English and Spanish ("Spanglish"), with a fair amount of Creole thrown in for good measure.

Creole, or Kriol, is the local patois, a colorful, rhythmic, and often difficult-to-understand dialect. Although based primarily on English, it takes some getting used to before most Westerners can grasp the pronunciations and sentence structures that distinguish Belizean Kriol. While this was originally the language of former black slaves and their descendants, today most Belizeans understand and speak Kriol, and they will often use it among themselves in the presence of foreigners if they don't want to be understood.

In addition to English, Spanish, and Kriol, Belize's Garífuna (or Garinagu) people have their own distinct language, while the various Maya tribes still speak primarily their native languages.

CREOLE TERMS

Creole, or Kriol, is largely based on English, although it does incorporate words and syntax from various African languages as well. Once you get the hang of certain pronunciations and syntactical phrasings, however, it's actually quite easy to understand. Almost any Kriol speaker will understand you if you speak in English. However, they'll be really impressed if you start inserting various Kriol words and phrases into your conversations.

Basic Words

Agen Again
Aks To ask
An And
Bak Back
Bwai Boy
Chinchi A very small amount
Daata Daughter
Da At, on, in, to
Da Is, am, are

Da It is
Deh/di Am, is, are (located); for instance, "Ih deh pahn di boat" means "He/she is on the boat"
Dehn Them
Di The
Doe Door
Fi To
Fo For

Ih   He, she, it
Kunku   Small
Nize   Noise
Noh   Isn't it so?
Shudda   Should have
Tideh   Today
Uman   Woman

Unu   You all
Vex/bex   Angry
Waata   Water
Wudda   Would have
Yaiy   Eye
Yaiy waata   Tears, literally "eye water"
Yerriso   Gossip

Menu Items

Bail op   Traditional dish made with cassava, cocoa, sweet potatoes, plantains, boil cake, and fish or pig's tail
Bambam   Traditional dish made with cassava
Bami   Cassava bread
Chimoaleh   Traditional dish of blackened chicken soup and rice; *chimole* in Spanish
Dukunu   Dish of mashed and steamed corn, wrapped in a leaf, similar to a *tamal*
Eskabaycheh   Pickled onion soup with chicken or fish; derived from the Spanish word *escabeche* ("pickled")
Garnache   Fried tortilla topped with beans and rice

Janny kake   Traditional fried or baked bread, served at breakfast
Konks   Conch
Panades   Traditional dish of finely chopped fish wrapped in a tortilla
Recado   Red *achiote* paste
Reyeno   Soup made with chicken, pork, and boiled eggs
Rise and beanz   Rice and beans with coconut milk
Rompopo   Alcoholic drink similar to eggnog
Strech-mi-gots   Traditional taffy
Tablayta   Coconut candy

Wildlife

Bilam   Small river fish
Chaaly prise   Large rat
Gaalin   Heron
Gibnut   Paca
Gwaana   Iguana
Hooyu   Owl
Jankro   Vulture
Janny fidla   Fiddler crab
Kwash   Coati, coati-mundi

Taapong   Tarpon
Tuba   River fish
Waari   Wild pig or peccary
Waata daag   River otter
Weewi ants   Leaf-cutter ant
Wowla   Boa constrictor, also used to refer to a type of basket used for processing cassava for bread

Folklore & Traditional Terms

Anansi/Hanaasi   Popular character in local folklore, portrayed as the trickster and hero of local tales
Bram   A dance party held at Christmas; a type of dance at parties
Brokdong/Brukdown   Traditional folk music, from "break down"
Gombeh   Typical hand drum made with goatskin

Punta   Sensual and vigorous dance, also refers to its accompanying music
Sambai   Full-moon fertility dance
Tata Duhendeh   Mythical forest gnome, with no thumbs and backward feet
Wine op   A lively, hip-swinging dance

SPANISH TERMS

BASIC PHRASES

English	Spanish	Pronunciation
Good morning	Buenos días	*Bweh*-nohss dee-ahss
Good afternoon/evening	Buenas tardes	*Bweh*-nahss *tahr*-dehs
Good night	Buenas noches	*Bweh*-nahss *noh*-chehs
How are you?	¿Cómo está usted?	*Koh*-moh eh-*stah* oo-*stehd*
Very well	Muy bien	*Mwee byehn*
Thank you	Gracias	*Grah*-syahss
Good-bye	Adios	Ad-*dyohss*
Please	Por favor	Pohr fah-*vohr*
Yes	Sí	See
No	No	Noh
Excuse me (to get by someone)	Perdóneme	Pehr-*doh*-neh-meh
Excuse me (to begin a question)	Disculpe	Dee-*skool*-peh
Give me	Deme	*Deh*-meh
Where is . . . ?	¿Dónde está . . . ?	*Dohn*-deh eh-*stah*
the station	la estación	la eh-*stah*-syohn
the bus stop	la parada	la pah-*rah*-dah
a hotel	un hotel	oon oh-*tehl*
a restaurant	un restaurante	oon reh-stow-*rahn*-teh
the toilet	el servicio	el ser-*bee*-syoh
To the right	A la derecha	Ah lah deh-*reh*-chah
To the left	A la izquierda	Ah lah ee-*skyehr*-dah
Straight ahead	Adelante	Ah-deh-*lahn*-teh
I would like . . .	Quiero . . .	*Kyeh*-roh
to eat	comer	ko-*mehr*
a room	una habitación	oo-nah ah-bee-tah-*syohn*
How much is it?	¿Cuánto?	*Kwahn*-toh
The check	La cuenta	La *kwen*-tah
When?	¿Cuándo?	*Kwahn*-doh
What?	¿Qué?	Keh
What time is it?	¿Qué hora es?	Keh *oh*-rah ehss
Yesterday	Ayer	Ah-*yehr*
Today	Hoy	Oy
Tomorrow	Mañana	Mah-*nyah*-nah
Breakfast	Desayuno	Deh-sah-*yoo*-noh
Lunch	Almuerzo	Ahl-*mwehr*-soh
Dinner	Cena	*Ceh*-nah

English	Spanish	Pronunciation
Do you speak English?	¿Habla usted inglés?	*Ah*-blah oo-*stehd* een-*glehss*
Is there anyone here who speaks English?	¿Hay alguien aquí que hable inglés?	Eye *ahl*-gyehn ah-*kee* keh *ah*-bleh een-*glehss*
I speak a little Spanish.	Hablo un poco de español.	*Ah*-bloh oon *poh*-koh deh eh-spah-*nyohl*
I don't understand Spanish very well.	No (lo) entiendo muy bien el español.	Noh (loh) ehn-*tyehn*-doh mwee byehn el eh-spah-*nyohl*

NUMBERS

English	Spanish	Pronunciation
one	uno	(*oo*-noh)
two	dos	(dohss)
three	tres	(trehss)
four	cuatro	(*kwah*-troh)
five	cinco	(*seen*-koh)
six	seis	(sayss)
seven	siete	(*syeh*-teh)
eight	ocho	(*oh*-choh)
nine	nueve	(*nweh*-beh)
ten	diez	(dyehss)
eleven	once	(*ohn*-seh)
twelve	doce	(*doh*-seh)
thirteen	trece	(*treh*-seh)
fourteen	catorce	(kah-*tohr*-seh)
fifteen	quince	(*keen*-seh)
sixteen	dieciséis	(dyeh-see-*sayss*)
seventeen	diecisiete	(dyeh-see-*syeh*-teh)
eighteen	dieciocho	(dyeh-*syoh*-choh)
nineteen	diecinueve	(dyeh-see-*nweh*-beh)
twenty	veinte	(*bayn*-teh)
thirty	treinta	(*trayn*-tah)
forty	cuarenta	(kwah-*rehn*-tah)
fifty	cincuenta	(seen-*kwehn*-tah)
sixty	sesenta	(seh-*sehn*-tah)
seventy	setenta	(seh-*tehn*-tah)
eighty	ochenta	(oh-*chehn*-tah)
ninety	noventa	(noh-*behn*-tah)
one hundred	cien	(syehn)
one thousand	mil	(meel)

DAYS OF THE WEEK

English	Spanish	Pronunciation
Monday	lunes	(*loo*-nehss)
Tuesday	martes	(*mahr*-tehss)
Wednesday	miércoles	(*myehr*-koh-lehs)
Thursday	jueves	(*wheh*-behss)
Friday	viernes	(*byehr*-nehss)
Saturday	sábado	(*sah*-bah-doh)
Sunday	domingo	(doh-*meen*-goh)

BELIZEAN WILDLIFE

with assistance from E. Z. Weaver

For such a tiny country, Belize is incredibly rich in biodiversity. Whether you come to Belize to check a hundred or so species off your lifetime list, or just to check out of the rat race for a week or so, you'll be surrounded by a rich and varied collection of flora and fauna. The information below is meant to be a selective introduction.

In many instances, the prime viewing recommendations should be taken with a firm dose of reality. Most casual visitors and even many dedicated naturalists will never see a jaguar or kinkajou in the wild. However, anyone working with a good guide should be able to see a broad selection of Belize's impressive flora and fauna.

See "The Lay of the Land" in chapter 2 for more information, as well as "Tips on Health, Safety & Etiquette in the Wilderness" in chapter 5 for additional tips on enjoying Belize's flora and fauna.

FAUNA

Mammals

Belize has some 150 identified species of mammals, ranging from the majestic jaguar to the rowdy howler monkey. Note that the dolphin and manatee have been included in the "Sea Life" section, later in this chapter.

Jaguar

Jaguar　*(Panthera onca)*　This cat measures from 1.1 to 1.8m (3½–6 ft.) plus tail, and is distinguished by its tan/yellowish fur with black spots. As jaguars are protected by Belize's hunting ordinances, the country maintains one of the healthiest populations in Central America. **Prime Viewing:** Although they exist throughout mainland Belize, jaguars are extremely hard to see in the wild. The best places to spot them are in the Cockscomb Basin Wildlife Sanctuary and Río Bravo Conservation Area.

Puma

Puma *(Puma concolor)*   Nearly 1.5m (5 ft.) long when fully grown, these feline predators are the largest unspotted cats in the region. Also known as a mountain lion, the puma is brownish, reddish-brown, or tawny in color with a white throat. **Prime Viewing:** Southeastern, western, and southern Belize in the lowland forests and semiopen areas.

Jaguarundi

Jaguarundi   *(Herpailurus yaguarondi)*   This smallish to midsize cat, with a solid black, brown, or reddish coat, can occasionally be spotted in a clearing or climbing trees. **Prime Viewing:** Wet and dry forests throughout Belize.

Ocelot

Ocelot   *(Leopardus pardalis)*   The tail of the tiger cat (as it's called in Belize) is longer than its rear leg, which makes for easy identification. Ocelots are mostly nocturnal, and during the daytime they sleep in trees. **Prime Viewing:** Dense forests in all regions of Belize.

Margay

Margay *(Leopardus wiedii)* An endangered species, it's one of the smaller wildcats of the region and (like its cousin, the ocelot) is often found in trees. **Prime Viewing:** Forests in all regions of Belize.

Gibnut

Gibnut *(Agouti paca)* This nocturnal rodent (also called a paca) inhabits the forest floor, feeding on fallen fruit, leaves, and some tubers dug from the ground. **Prime Viewing:** Most often found near water throughout many habitats of Belize, from river valleys to swamps to dense tropical forest. However, you're almost as likely to see gibnut on a restaurant menu as in the wild.

Neotropical Otter

Neotropical Otter *(Lutra longicaudis)* The neotropical otter goes by many nicknames in Belize, including *perro de agua* (water dog) and *lobito de río* (little river wolf). **Prime Viewing:** In rivers and streams throughout the country.

Baird's Tapir

Baird's Tapir *(Tapirus bairdii)* Known as the "mountain cow" in Belize, the tapir is active mostly at night, foraging along riverbanks, streams, and forest clearings. **Prime Viewing:** The Stann Creek and Toledo districts of southern Belize and the Cayo District of western Belize.

Coati-mundi

Coati-mundi *(Nasua narica)* This raccoon-like mammal is one of few with the ability to adapt to habitat disturbances. During the night, they tend to hunt along open trails; during the day, they stay hidden within the deeper bush. **Prime Viewing:** Found in a variety of habitats in Belize, from dry scrub to dense forests, on the mainland as well as some coastal islands.

Collared Peccary

Collared Peccary *(Tayassu tajacu)* These black or brown piglike animals travel in small groups (larger where populations are still numerous) and have a strong musk odor. **Prime Viewing:** Throughout dry and moist forests in most of Belize.

Anteater

Anteater   *(Cyclopes didactylus)*   Also known as the pygmy anteater, this nocturnal creature grows up to 18cm (7 in.), not counting its thick tail (which is as long as or longer than its body). **Prime Viewing:** Wet forests in all regions of Belize.

Armadillo

Armadillo   *(Dasypus novemcinctus)*   Also known as the dilly in Belize, these prehistoric-looking animals are nocturnal and terrestrial. **Prime Viewing:** All regions.

Northern Tamandua

Northern Tamandua   *(Tamandua Mexicana)*   Also known as the collared anteater, the northern Tamandua grows up to 77cm (30 in.) long, not counting its thick tail, which can be as long its body. It is active diurnally and nocturnally. **Prime Viewing:** Low- and middle-elevation forests in most of Belize.

Three-Toed Sloth

Three-Toed Sloth *(Bradypus variegates)* The three-toed sloth has long, coarse, brown-to-gray fur and a distinctive eye-band. There are three long, sharp claws on each foreleg. Except for brief periods to defecate, these slow-moving creatures are entirely arboreal. **Prime Viewing:** Low- and middle-elevation forests in most of Belize. While sloths can be found in a wide variety of trees, they are most commonly spotted in the relatively sparsely leaved Cecropia (see later in this chapter).

Kinkajou

Kinkajou *(Potos flavus)* The nocturnal, tree-dwelling kinkajou is appropriately nicknamed "nightwalker" in Belize. **Prime Viewing:** Strictly nocturnal and extremely hard to see, the kinkajou nevertheless is found in forests throughout Belize.

Spider Monkey

Spider Monkey *(Ateles geoffroyi)* A large monkey (64cm/25 in.) with brown or silvery fur, this creature is often hunted for its meat and is listed as endangered in some countries. **Prime Viewing:** The Orange Walk (northwestern), Cayo (western), and Toledo (southern) districts of Belize.

Howler Monkey

Howler Monkey *(Alouatta pigra)*   Known locally as a baboon, this highly social creature grows to 56cm (22 in.) in size. Because the species travels only from tree to tree (limiting their presence to dense jungle canopy), a community-based conservation organization protects the land along the Belize River for the howler monkey, ensuring that their food trees are not destroyed to make way for pasture. **Prime Viewing:** In the lowland forests that encompass Belize's mainland. Sightings are pretty much guaranteed at the Community Baboon Sanctuary (see "What to See & Do" in chapter 6).

Red Brocket Deer

Red Brocket Deer *(Mazama americana)*   Also known as the antelope in Belize, these small animals measure 1 to 1.4m (3¼–4½ ft.). Small, straight antlers distinguish the male. **Prime Viewing:** Southern and southeastern Belize and some coastal islands.

Hairy-Legged Bat

Hairy-Legged Bat *(Myotis keaysi)*   The hairy-legged bat grows to a whopping 5.1cm (2 in.) in length, not including the length of its tail. **Prime Viewing:** All regions of Belize, in forests, rock crevices, gardens, and buildings.

Birds

Belize has at least 618 identified species of resident and migrant birds. The variety of habitats and compact nature of the country make this a major bird-watching destination.

Jabiru Stork

Jabiru Stork (*Jabiru mycteria*) One of the largest birds in the world and an endangered species, the jabiru stands 1.5m (5 ft.) tall, with a wingspan of 2.4m (8 ft.) and a .3m-long (1-ft.) bill. The birds arrive in Belize from Mexico in November and fly north with the first rains in June or July. **Prime Viewing:** The Crooked Tree Wildlife Sanctuary, located 53km (33 miles) north of Belize City, has the largest population in the country. (See "En Route North: Crooked Tree Wildlife Sanctuary" in chapter 9.)

Keel-Billed Toucan

Keel-Billed Toucan (*Ramphastos solfurantus*) The canoe-shape bill and brightly colored feathers make the national bird of Belize almost instantly recognizable. The toucan is about 51cm (20 in.) in length. **Prime Viewing:** Throughout the country's lowland forests, nesting in the holes of tree trunks.

Scarlet Macaw

Scarlet Macaw (*Ara macao*) Over most of its range, the scarlet macaw is endangered. However, in 1996, a new population of more than 100 birds was "discovered"

301

south of the Cockscomb Basin Wildlife Sanctuary. **Prime Viewing:** The wet lowland forests of the Toledo District in southern Belize.

Ocellated Turkey

Ocellated Turkey *(Agriocharis ocellata)* This colorful bird has a thin, light-blue head and neck with orange-yellow knoblike wattles on the top that it will proudly display. The wings and tail are rounded with shimmering metallic bronze primaries and metallic emerald-green shoulders; the feathers are a dark, shiny brown, barred with a metallic shimmering green that looks black in poor light. **Prime Viewing:** Northern and western Belize.

Frigate Bird

Frigate Bird *(Fregata magnificens)* The frigate bird is a naturally agile flier and swoops (unlike other birds, it doesn't dive or swim) to pluck food from the water's surface—or more commonly, it steals catch from the mouths of other birds. **Prime Viewing:** All coastal regions of Belize. Man-O-War Caye is a protected nesting site for this bird (see "Dangriga" in chapter 8).

Red-Footed Booby

Red-Footed Booby *(Sula sula rubripes)* This unique bird experiences many color changes during its life. Adult boobies have a blue-gray bill and eye ring, and pink skin about the bill base. The head and neck are washed with yellow, and the white body holds black primary and secondary feathers. The feet and legs of the aptly named species are all red. **Prime Viewing:** Half Moon Caye National Monument, Belize's first national park, is now the protected home for more than 4,000 red-footed boobies (see "The Outer Atolls" in chapter 7), but these birds can be found in all coastal regions of Belize.

Montezuma's Oropendola

Montezuma's Oropendola *(Pasrocolius montezuma)* Also called "yellowtails" in Belize, these birds have a black head and chest, a yellow-edged tail, a large black bill with an orange tip, and a blue patch under the eye. **Prime Viewing:** Throughout Belize.

Osprey

Osprey *(Pandion haliatus)* These large (.6m/2 ft., with a 1.8m/6-ft. wingspan) brownish birds with white heads are also known as "fishing eagles." In flight, the osprey's wings "bend" backward. **Prime Viewing:** Throughout Belize, although predominantly near the coasts, or out on the cayes, flying or perched in trees near water.

Roseate Spoonbill

Roseate Spoonbill *(Ajaia ajaja)* This large water bird is pink or light red in color, with a large spoon-shape bill. They were almost made extinct in the United States because their pink wings were sought for feather fans. **Prime Viewing:** Along the coast and in the wetlands of northern Belize.

Cattle Egret

Cattle Egret *(Bubulcus ibis)* The cattle egret changes color during breeding: A yellowish buff color appears on the head, chest, and back, and a reddish hue emerges on the bill and legs. They are often seen following behind tractors, because these stir up insects. **Prime Viewing:** Throughout the country. As the name implies, almost always found accompanying livestock.

Pygmy Owl

Pygmy Owl *(Glaucidium brasilianum)* This small (about 38cm/15-in.) grayish brown or reddish brown owl is also known as the *lechucita listada* ("little striped screech owl"). Unlike most owls, they are most active during the day. **Prime Viewing:** Throughout Belize.

Boat-Billed Heron

Boat-Billed Heron *(Cochlearius cochlearius)* This midsize heron (about 51cm/20 in.) has a large black head, a large broad bill, and a rusty brown color. **Prime Viewing:** Throughout the country, near marshes, swamps, rivers, and mangroves.

Laughing Falcon

Laughing Falcon *(Herpetotheres cachinnans)* This largish (56cm/22-in.) bird of prey is also known as the *vaquero* (cowboy) in Belize. The laughing falcon's wingspan reaches an impressive 94cm (37 in.). **Prime Viewing:** Throughout the country.

Mealy Parrot

Mealy Parrot *(Amazona farinose)* This large, vocal parrot is common in lowland tropical rainforests throughout Central and South America. Almost entirely green, it has a touch of blue on the top of its head and small red and blue accents on its wings. It has a short, squared-off tail. **Prime Viewing:** Lowland humid and rain forests nationwide.

Scarlet Rumped Tanager

Scarlet Rumped Tanager *(Ramphocelus costaricensis)* With a striking scarlet red patch on its backside, this is one of the most commonly sighted tanagers in Belize. **Prime Viewing:** Throughout the country, in lowland and mid-elevation areas.

Invertebrates

Creepy-crawlies, biting bugs, spiders, and the like give most folks chills. But this group, which includes moths, butterflies, ants, beetles, bees, and even crabs, sponges, mollusks, and lobster, includes some of the most abundant, fascinating, and easily viewed fauna in Belize. See "Sea Life" for marine invertebrates.

Blue Morpho

Blue Morpho   *(Morpho peleides)*   The large blue morpho butterfly, with a wing-span of up to 15cm (6 in.), has brilliantly iridescent blue wings when opened. Fast and erratic fliers, they are often glimpsed flitting across your peripheral vision in dense forest. **Prime Viewing:** Countrywide, particularly in moist environments.

Leafcutter Ants

Leafcutter Ants   *(Atta cephalotes)*   You can't miss the miniature rainforest high-ways formed by these industrious red ants carrying their freshly cut payload. The ants do not actually eat the leaves, but instead feed off a fungus that grows on the decomposing leaves in their massive underground nests. **Prime Viewing:** Can be found in most forests countrywide.

Golden Silk Spider

Golden Silk Spider   (Nephila clavipes)   The common Neotropical golden silk spider weaves meticulous webs that can be as much as .5m (2 ft.) across. The adult female of this species can reach 7.6cm (3 in.) in length, including the legs, although the males are tiny. The silk of this spider is extremely strong and is being studied for industrial purposes. **Prime Viewing:** Lowland forests countrywide.

Mexican Red Rump Tarantula

Mexican Red Rump Tarantula   (Brachypelma vagans)   This misnamed spider actually features a distinctively red abdomen, not rump. Also known as the Mexican Black Velvet spider, it is the most common tarantula in Belize. This is a terrestrial spider that digs a large burrow. **Prime Viewing:** Forests and lowlands nationwide.

Brown Bark Scorpion

Brown Bark Scorpion   (Centruroides gracilis)   The most common scorpion found in Belize, this fearsome critter packs a mean sting, but is not considered life threatening or very dangerous. Averages around 7.5 to 10cm (3–4 in.) in length. **Prime Viewing:** Under rocks and litter in forests from sea level to middle elevations nationwide.

Leaf Mantis

Leaf Mantis   (Choeradodis strumaria)   A member of the praying mantis family, this leaf-mimic insect has a distinct camouflage, thanks to a very enlarged thorax. **Prime Viewing:** Moist forests countrywide.

Sea Life

Boasting the longest continuous barrier reef in the Americas, Belize has a rich diversity of underwater flora and fauna. Any visitor to Belize's beach or island resorts should take some time to peek at the various undersea wonders of the ocean and barrier reef, whether it be by snorkeling, scuba diving, or riding in a glass-bottom boat.

West Indian Manatee

West Indian Manatee *(Trichechus manatus)* Manatees in Belize are Antillean manatees, a subspecies of the West Indian manatee. Belize is home to the largest known concentration of Antillean manatees in the wider Caribbean. These "sea cows" can reach lengths of 3 to 4m (10–13 ft.) and weigh 499 to 1,588kg (1,100–3,500 lb.). **Prime Viewing:** Coastal mangroves, particularly in the Southern Lagoon off of Gales Point (p. 157) and Swallow Caye Manatee Reserve (p. 138).

Manta Ray

Manta Ray *(Manta birostris)* Manta rays are the largest type of rays, with a wingspan that can reach 6m (20 ft.) and a body weight known to exceed 1,361kg (3,000 lb.). Despite their daunting appearance, manta rays are quite gentle. If you are snorkeling or diving, watch for one of these extraordinary and graceful creatures. **Prime Viewing:** All along the barrier reef, particularly in deeper water, or alongside steep walls and drop-offs.

Stingray

Stingray *(Dasyatis americana)* True to their name, these rays can give you a painful shock if you touch the venomous spine at the base of their tails. Be careful when wading in sandy areas, where they prefer to bury themselves. **Prime Viewing:**

All along the coast and barrier reef, especially in shallow sand or grassy areas. Pretty much guaranteed on the Shark-Ray Alley (p. 117) excursion.

Whale Shark

Whale Shark *(Rhincodon typus)* Although the whale shark grows to lengths of 14m (46 ft.) or more, its gentle nature makes swimming with them a special treat for divers and snorkelers. Although 3 or 4 days before and after the full and new moons in April and May are the best times to interact with the sharks, they are often sighted in the summer months as well. **Prime Viewing:** Gladden Spit, off Placencia (see "Placencia" in chapter 8).

Nurse Shark

Nurse Shark *(Ginglymostoma cirratum)* The most frequently spotted shark in Belizean waters, this species spends most of its time resting on the ocean floor. Nurse sharks reach lengths of 4.3m (14 ft.), their heads are larger than those of most sharks, and they appear to be missing the bottom half of their tail. **Prime Viewing:** All along the coast and barrier reef. Pretty much guaranteed on the Shark-Ray Alley (p. 117) excursion.

Leatherback Sea Turtle

Leatherback Sea Turtle *(Dermochelys coriacea)* The world's largest sea turtle (reaching nearly 2.4m/8 ft. in length and weighing more than 544kg/1,200 lb.) is now an endangered species. **Prime Viewing:** Sightings are exceedingly rare, so it's highly unlikely that you'll spot them nesting on the coast of Belize, but you might get lucky and spot them in the sea.

Hawksbill Sea Turtle

Hawksbill Sea Turtle *(Eretmochelys imbricata)* The hawksbill turtle is a shy, tropical, reef-dwelling species that feeds primarily on sponges. Although they're registered on the endangered species list, commercial exploitation exacerbates the species' continued decline. **Prime Viewing:** All along the coast and barrier reef.

Moray Eel

Moray Eel *(Gymnothorax moringa)* Distinguished by a swaying serpent-head and teeth-filled jaw that continually opens and closes, the moray eel is most commonly seen with only its head appearing from behind rocks. At night, however, it leaves its home along the reef to hunt for small fish, crustaceans, shrimp, and octopus. **Prime Viewing:** All along the coast and barrier reef.

Barracuda

Barracuda *(Sphyraena barracuda)* The barracuda is a slender fish with two dorsal fins and a large mouth. Juvenile barracudas often swim near the shore, so exercise caution, as attacks on humans occasionally occur. **Prime Viewing:** All along the coast and barrier reef.

Bottle-Nosed Dolphin

Bottle-Nosed Dolphin *(Tursiops truncates)* Their wide back fin, dark-gray back, and light-gray sides identify bottle-nosed dolphins. Dolphins grow to lengths of 3.6m (12 ft.) and weigh up to 635kg (1,400 lb.). **Prime Viewing:** Along the coast and barrier reef.

14

Fauna

BELIZEAN WILDLIFE

Loggerhead Sponge

Loggerhead Sponge *(Spheciospongia vesparia)* This barrel sponge is a large, stubby, purplish creature. Its large, central depression often plays host to small fish; shrimp and other sea life dwell in its canals. **Prime Viewing:** All along the barrier reef.

Elkhorn Coral

Elkhorn Coral *(Acropora palmata)* Elkhorn coral was formerly the dominant species in shallow water throughout the Caribbean, forming extensive thickets in areas of heavy surf. Since 1980, populations have collapsed from disease outbreaks, with losses compounded locally by hurricanes, increased predation, and bleaching. **Prime Viewing:** Along the barrier reef.

Brain Coral

Brain Coral *(Diploria strigosa)* Named for its striking physical similarity to a human brain, brain coral has been growing continuously in the waters off Belize for at least a century, though it's vulnerable to hurricanes. **Prime Viewing:** All along the barrier reef.

Porous Coral

Porous Coral *(Porites)*   The branches of this pink coral have a fuzzy appearance during the day, when its polyps are extended. **Prime Viewing:** All along the barrier reef.

Moon Jelly

Moon Jelly *(Aurelia aurita)*   Like most jellies, the moon jelly is almost transparent. That four-leaf-clover–like area on its top is its reproductive organs. **Prime Viewing:** All along the coast and barrier reef.

Sally Lightfoot Crab

Sally Lightfoot Crab   (Grapsus grapsus)   This is a midsize crab with a colorful carapace that can range from dark brown to deep red to bright yellow, with a wide variation in striations and spotting. **Prime Viewing:** On rocky outcroppings near the water's edge on the cayes and coasts nationwide.

Spiny Lobster

Spiny Lobster (Panulirus argus) Lacking the large claws found on the Maine lobster, this is, nonetheless, the main commercial lobster harvested throughout the Caribbean and an important piece of the Belizean economy. Primarily nocturnal, the spiny lobster can reach some 60cm (24 in.) in length, but is more typically around 20cm (8 in.). **Prime Viewing:** Tucked into crevasses in coral and under rocks all along the barrier reef.

Amphibians

Frogs, toads, and salamanders are actually some of the most beguiling, beautiful, and easy-to-spot residents of tropical forests.

Rufescent Salamander

Rufescent Salamander *(Bolitoglossa rufescens)* This very small (3.8cm/1½-in.) brown amphibian is also known as the "northern banana salamander," which is fitting since it can often be found in banana leaves. **Prime Viewing:** Forest floors and creek beds, particularly in the Stann Creek, Toledo, and Cayo districts.

Red-Eyed Tree Frog

Red-Eyed Tree Frog *(Agalychnis callidryas)* This colorful 7.6cm (3-in.) frog usually has a pale or dark green back, sometimes with white or yellow spots; blue-purple patches and vertical bars on the body; orange hands and feet; and deep red eyes. **Prime Viewing:** This nocturnal frog can be found in forests throughout Belize. It is often best to look on the undersides of broad-leafed plants.

Maya Rain Frog

Maya Rain Frog *(Eleutherodactyulus chac)* This small, skinny frog is usually brown or yellowish, with webbed toes and red eyes. **Prime Viewing:** Forests in southeastern, southern, and western Belize.

Marine Toad

Marine Toad *(Bufo marinus)* This 20cm (8-in.), wart-covered toad is also known as *sapo grande,* or "giant toad." The females are mottled in color, while the males are uniformly brown. **Prime Viewing:** This terrestrial frog can be found in forests throughout Belize.

Mexican Burrowing Toad *(Rhinophrynus dorsalis)* This bloblike, 7.6cm (3-in.) toad will inflate like a blowfish when frightened. It often has a single red, orange, or yellow line down the center of its brown or black back. **Prime Viewing:** This terrestrial frog can be found throughout Belize.

Reptiles

Belize's reptile species range from the frightening and justly feared fer-de-lance pit viper and American crocodile to a wide variety of turtles and lizards. (Note that the sea turtle is included in the "Sea Life" section, earlier.)

Snapping Turtle

Snapping Turtle *(Chelydra serpentina)* This turtle's back is brown, olive, or black and marked with three ridges of sharp bumps—which might explain why it's also known as *tortuga lagarto* ("alligator turtle") in Belize. **Prime Viewing:** In ponds and streams throughout Belize.

Boa Constrictor

Boa Constrictor *(Boa constrictor)* Adult boa constrictors average about 1.8 to 3m (6–10 ft.) in length and weigh more than 27kg (60 lb.). Their coloration camouflages them, but look for varying patterns of cream, brown, tan, gray, and black with ovals and diamonds. **Prime Viewing:** In forests and mangroves countrywide, including on some of the offshore cayes.

Fer-de-Lance

Fer-de-Lance *(Bothrops asper)* Also known as a tommygoff in Belize, this venomous and aggressive snake can grow to 2.4m (8 ft.) in length. Beige, brown, or black triangles flank either side of the snake's head, while the area under the head is a vivid yellow. **Prime Viewing:** All regions. This snake is arboreal as a youngster and becomes terrestrial as it grows larger and older.

Mussurana

Mussurana *(Clelia clelia)* This bluish-black, brown, or grayish snake grows to 2.4m (8 ft.) in length. While slightly venomous, this snake is a rear-fanged snake and of little danger to humans. In fact, it is prized and protected by locals, since its primary prey happens to be much more venomous pit vipers, such as the fer-de-lance. **Prime Viewing:** Forests in central, southeastern, and western Belize.

Rattlesnake

Rattlesnake *(Crotalus durissus)* Look out for its triangular head, 1.8m (6-ft.) length, the ridge running along the middle of its back, and (of course) its rattling tail. **Prime Viewing:** Throughout the country.

Shiny Skink

Shiny Skink *(Mabuya brachypoda)* This midsize (7.6cm/3-in.) brown lizard with a narrow head and short legs is also known as "snake waiting boy." **Prime Viewing:** Throughout the country.

Silky Anole

Silky Anole *(Anolis sericeus)* This small (5.1cm/2-in.) gray lizard can be hard to spot, as it often aligns itself on a blade of grass when startled. **Prime Viewing:** On the ground and forest floors throughout the country.

Leaf-Toed Gecko

Leaf-Toed Gecko *(Phyllodactylus tuberculosus)* You'll have no problem spotting this 6.4cm (2½-in.) gecko on rocks and on the ground—it loves to be around buildings and other areas of human activity. **Prime Viewing:** Central, southeastern, and western Belize.

Smooth Gecko

Smooth Gecko *(Thecadactylus rapicaudus)* This gecko's autonomous tail detaches from its body and acts as a diversion to a potential predator; it grows back later in a lighter shade. **Prime Viewing:** In northwestern, western, and southern Belize, especially where humans can be found.

Green Iguana

Green Iguana *(Iguana iguana)* Green iguanas, not surprisingly, are green in color, but vary in shades ranging from bright green to a dull grayish-green. The iguana will often perch on a branch overhanging a river and plunge into the water when threatened. **Prime Viewing:** All regions of the country, living along the rivers and streams. Often seen sunning on exposed rocks or tree limbs.

Basilisk

Basilisk *(Basiliscus vittatus)* The basilisk can run across the surface of water for short distances by using its hind legs and holding its body almost upright; thus, the reptile is also known as "the Jesus Christ lizard." **Prime Viewing:** In trees, rocks, and forest floors, especially near water in tropical rainforests.

Morelet's Crocodile

Morelet's Crocodile *(Crocodylus moreleti)* This reptile can grow to a length of 4m (13 ft.), although the average specimen measures less than 2.4m (8 ft.). Adults are brown or blackish in color, while young Morelet's crocodiles are olive or yellowish, with dark bands on their bodies and tails. **Prime Viewing:** Northern and central coastal Belize, in most of the freshwater lowland interior rivers, lagoons, and ponds.

American Crocodile

American Crocodile *(Crocodylus acutus)* This endangered species is distinguished from the Morelet's crocodile by their generally larger size and narrower snout. While they can reach lengths of 6.4m (21 ft.), the majority are much smaller, usually less than 4m (13 ft.). **Prime Viewing:** Near swamps, mangrove swamps, estuaries, large rivers, coastal lowlands, and islands.

FLORA

Trees

Despite the cliché to the contrary, it's often a good thing to be able to identify specific trees within a forest. We've included illustrations of the leaves, flowers, seeds, or fruits to get you started.

Ceiba

Ceiba *(Ceiba pentandra)* Also known as the kapok tree, ceiba trees are typically emergent (their large umbrella-shaped canopies emerge above the forest canopy), making the species among the tallest trees in the tropical forest. Reaching as high as 61m (200 ft.), their thick columnar trunks often have large buttresses. Ceiba trees may flower as little as once every 5 years, especially in wetter forests. **Prime Viewing:** Countrywide.

Guanacaste

Guanacaste *(Enterolobium cyclocarpum)* The guanacaste, or tubroos, tree is one of the largest trees found in Central America. It can reach a total elevation of more than 40m (130 ft.), its straight trunk comprising 9.1 to 12m (30–40 ft.) of the height (the trunk's diameter measures more than 1.8m/6 ft.). **Prime Viewing:** Countrywide. A particularly impressive specimen gives its name to Guanacaste National Park (see "Belmopan" in chapter 10).

Gumbo-Limbo

Gumbo-Limbo *(Bursera simaruba)* The bark of the gumbo limbo is perhaps its most distinguishing feature: A paper-thin outer layer is red when peeled off the tree, revealing a bright green bark underneath. The bark is reportedly used as a remedy for gum disease, and gumbo-limbo bark tea allegedly alleviates high blood pressure. Another remarkable property of this tree is its ability to root from its cut branches. When a branch is cut and planted right end up, roots will develop and leaves will sprout, forming a new tree within a few years' time. **Prime Viewing:** Primary and secondary forests, countrywide.

Strangler Fig

Strangler Fig *(Ficus aurea)* This parasitic tree gets its name from the fact that it envelops and eventually strangles its host tree. The strangler fig actually begins as an epiphyte, whose seeds are deposited high in a tree's canopy by bats, birds, or monkeys. The young strangler then sends long roots down to the earth. The sap of the strangler fig is used to relieve burns. **Prime Viewing:** Primary and secondary forests, countrywide.

Caribbean Pine

Caribbean Pine *(Pinus caribaea)* This fast-growing pine species is the defining tree of the Mountain Pine Ridge area of western Belize. The tree is actually fire resistant, and benefits from controlled burns. The resin is used as an adhesive and insect repellent. **Prime Viewing:** Mountain Pine Ridge Forest Reserve (see chapter 10).

Mahogany

Mahogany *(Swietenia macrophylla)* The national tree of Belize, the mahogany tree can grow to heights of more than 30m (100 ft.). Mahogany wood is heavy and strong, and resists rot and termites. From its wood, artisans and carpenters craft the world's finest furniture. **Prime Viewing:** Primary and secondary rainforests, countrywide.

Craboo

Craboo *(Byrsonima crassifolia)* The craboo's flowers are beautiful orange and yellow racemes about 15cm (6 in.) long. The tree also bears a small orange-yellow berry, whose flavor varies from bland to sweet, acidic, or even cheeselike. The flowers usually bloom around April, with fruits gathered around June. Hurricane Iris destroyed many Belizean craboo trees in 2001. **Prime Viewing:** Countrywide.

Red Torch Ginger

Red Torch Ginger (Nicolaia elatior)   The tall red torch ginger plant has an impressive bulbous red bract, often mistaken for the flower. The numerous, small white flowers actually emerge out of this bract. Originally a native to Indonesia, it is now quite common in Belize. **Prime Viewing:** Countrywide, particularly in moist environments and gardens.

Flowers

Belize has more than 4,000 species of flowering plants, including some 250 orchid species.

Black Orchid

Black Orchid (*Encyclia cochleatum*)   The black orchid is the national flower of Belize. The plant's most distinguishing feature is its lip, which resembles the shape of a clamshell valve. The flower is a deep blackish color with purple veins, and its leaves are a greenish-yellow with purple spots. The black orchid is sometimes likened to an octopus because of its straggling "tentacles" and its ability to thrive in a damp environment. **Prime Viewing:** Countrywide, particularly in moist environments.

Heliconia

Heliconia   *(Heliconia collinsiana)*   There are more than 250 species of tropical heliconia. The flowers of this species are darkish pink in color, and the underside of the plants' large leaves are coated in white wax. **Prime Viewing:** In the Toledo and Stann Creek districts.

Hot Lips

Hot Lips   *(Psychotria poeppigiana)*   Also called "devil's ear" in Belize, its small white flowers (inside the red "lips") attract a variety of butterflies and hummingbirds. **Prime Viewing:** In the undergrowth of dense forests, countrywide.

Index

See also Accommodations and
Restaurant indexes, below.

General Index

A